RELIGIOUS DIVERSITY AND HUMAN RIGHTS

RELIGIOUS DIVERSITY AND HUMAN RIGHTS

Edited by Irene Bloom, J. Paul Martin, and Wayne L. Proudfoot

Columbia University Press NEW YORK

Columbia University Press
Publishers Since 1893
New York   Chichester, West Sussex

Copyright © 1996   Columbia University Press

Library of Congress Cataloging-in-Publication Data
Religious diversity and human rights / edited by Irene Bloom, J. Paul
    Martin, and Wayne L. Proudfoot.
        p.   cm.
    Includes bibliographical references and index.
    ISBN 0–231–10416–2 (cl). — ISBN 0–231–10417–0 (pa)
    1. Human rights—Religious aspects.   2. Religions.   I. Bloom,
Irene.   II. Martin, J. Paul.   III. Proudfoot, Wayne L., 1939–   .
BL65.H78R45   1996
291.1'77—dc20   96–18261
                                                                    CIP

FOR LOUIS HENKIN

Contents

Acknowledgments

This book has been a long time in gestation. The project to consider broadly the various roles of religion and religious communities in the evolving tradition of human rights was initiated more than ten years ago at a conference sponsored by the Jacob Blaustein Institute for the Advancement of Human Rights in collaboration with Columbia University's Center for the Study of Human Rights and University Committee on Asia and the Middle East. The editors are grateful to the Blaustein Institute, and to its knowledgeable, dedicated, and unfailingly kind director, Sidney Liskofsky. We are indebted also to Richard Maass of the Administrative Council of the Blaustein Institute and to David Sidorsky, also a member of that Council and of Columbia's Department of Philosophy; both have served as reliable supporters in the course of planning for the conference and for the book.

We have benefited greatly from the guidance and help of Ainslie T. Embree of the Department of History and the Society of Senior Scholars at Columbia, who generously read and perceptively commented on each of the essays in this volume as well as its total shape and focus. His help and suggestions have been invaluable. Wm. Theodore de Bary, John Mitchell Mason Professor Emeritus, Special Service Professor, and Director of the Society of Senior Scholars at Columbia University, offered generous support throughout the process. So did our friend Paul Valliere, part of the original planning group at Columbia who left us in the course of the project for Butler University's Department of Religion but remained with his former colleagues throughout, both in spirit and in ongoing effort.

Martin Amster, doctoral candidate in the Department of East Asian Languages and Cultures at Columbia and administrative assistant to the University Committee on Asia and the Middle East, provided not only competent and intelligent technical and editorial help but also unfailing encouragement. We appreciate too the constant goodwill and friendly assistance of Mariana Stiles.

Always present to us as a source of support and guidance has been Louis Henkin, the guiding spirit and strong anchor of human rights studies at Columbia and member of the Society of Senior Scholars. It is to him that this book is dedicated, with profound gratitude and deep affection.

—The Editors

RELIGIOUS DIVERSITY AND HUMAN RIGHTS

RELIGIOUS DIVERSITY AND HUMAN RIGHTS

An Introduction

⁓

IRENE BLOOM

To many observers of contemporary world politics, the relation between religion and human rights appears to be fundamentally antagonistic. As challenges to religious tolerance have persisted and religious tensions have increased in the world in recent years, it has become harder for any but the most idealistic to sustain without significant qualifications an alternative vision of religion as primarily an ethical inspiration and an energizing force in human rights thinking and practice. That vision, frequently evoked in the decades following the adoption of the Universal Declaration of Human Rights, was based on an underlying confidence that, despite cultural differences and ethnic and religious tensions, there might be found in the world's religions some common denominator of respect for human dignity and a shared commitment to the wellbeing of all human beings. While such a confidence has not altogether disappeared from recent discussions, it has come to be jostled, and all but crowded out, by a variety of views, spanning the political spectrum, that emphasize the potency of cultural differences over common values and the prevalence of conflict over consensus.

One of the stronger statements of what might be called the "conflict model" is found in Samuel P. Huntington's provocative essay, "The Clash of Civilizations?" published in the Summer 1993 issue of *Foreign Affairs*. Huntington argues powerfully that in the coming century, "The clash of civilizations will dominate global politics" and that the prime mover behind the controversy, contention, and, ultimately, the clashes, is—and will continue to be—religion:

> Civilizations are differentiated from each other by history, language, culture, tradition and, most important, religion. The people of different civilizations have different views on the relation between God and man, the individual and the group, the citizen and the state, parents and children, husband and wife, as well as differing views of the relative importance of rights and responsibilities, liberty and authority, equality and hierarchy. These differences are the product of centuries. They will not soon disappear. They are far more fundamental than differences among political ideologies and political regimes.[1]

Huntington regards these fundamental differences as "cultural fault lines" among civilizations, believing not only that they represent the world's future crisis points, but that the deepest rifts derive from the heart of religion.

Huntington's view has evoked considerable controversy, one of the most telling criticisms being directed at his insistence that global conflict derives primarily from the nature of civilizations themselves rather than from the policies of states.[2] However, even those who do not share Huntington's perspective are obliged to confront the same dismal evidence that he is grappling with: the growing prevalence and intensity of ethnic and religious conflict in the world and the complex—indeed, seemingly paradoxical—relation between religion and human rights.

Guardian of tradition and matrix of traditionalism, religion fosters and treasures up differences and divisions even as it devotes itself to universal ideals. Even, or perhaps especially, in the case of those religions with universalistic concerns and world-wide followings—in those religions commonly recognized as "world religions"—religious authorities typically interpret central beliefs and core values in terms of time-honored models, and religious communities identify their members according to centuries-old criteria about who is to be included within the fold. Even in the case of religions with claims to universalism there seems be an unmistakable particularism involved not only in the ways religious doctrines are preserved and transmitted but in the ways religious communities are defined and organized.

Human rights thinking, on the other hand, is commonly presented as conceptually unencumbered, being modern and Western in its origins, secularistic in its persuasions, and, above all, universalistic in its claims. It is relatively unburdened by the weight of tradition or by beliefs that are divisive rather than inclusive. More important, its fundamental category is *the human* in the sense that the major human rights documents are concerned with what belongs to all human beings by virtue of their humanity rather than with what defines them as members of a particular culture, civilization, or religious community.

But this view of the person obviously involves a kind of deliberate abstraction, and the abstraction has inevitably invited questions. What modern belief or practice is wholly, or even largely, unembedded in tradition? Can it be true that human rights thinking, while couched in secular language, is really unrelated to older traditions, especially at the existential level, in summoning forth the idealism and energy of its adherents? If the provenance of human rights thinking is, in fact, the modern West, in what sense can its claims be taken as universal? Or can they *not* be taken as universal? To this familiar list, the authors of the essays in this volume add several more questions, questions that give this book its special character and purpose. Does a "conflict model" of religions and civilizations adequately describe the world in terms of both actuality and potentiality? Should religion in the contemporary world be seen as a source not only of differences and division but of common values and shared energies? If so, how are those shared values actually expressed and those energies exerted? How does the diversity of religious belief and practice in the world relate, both actually and potentially, to the moral universalism implied by human rights?

In an effort to provide a fresh perspective on these questions, we have tried in these essays to explore: 1) the applicability or pertinence of the language of human rights, including such terms as "individualism" and "collectivism," in non-Western contexts; 2) the bearing of traditional concepts of the person on modern human rights thinking; 3) the sources of and limitations on the idea and practice of religious tolerance; and 4) the role of religious ideas and institutions in influencing human rights situations in several of the most troubled and contentious areas of the contemporary world: the Islamic world, India, Latin America, and the former Soviet Union. This is not to say, of course, that these are the only areas of the world where pressing human rights problems pertain; clearly, they exist all over the world. But these we take to be both significant and illustrative.

PART 1: NEW PERSPECTIVES ON MAJOR RELIGIOUS TRADITIONS

The six essays in part 1 are devoted to considering the ways in which the relations between individuals and collectivities have been understood over time in the perspective of several of the world's major religious traditions. Deferring consideration of human rights issues per se, the authors of these essays endeavor to address what we consider to be prior questions having to do with the ways the individual is conceptualized in different cultural contexts and the ways the interests and potentialities of individuals have been understood in relation to those of communities. The religions surveyed are Judaism, Christianity, Islam, Hinduism, Buddhism, and Confucianism, each of them either a world religion or a tradition that has, over the course of centuries, played a part in shaping the lives of a very large segment of humanity. Each may be said to have made "a contribution to an ever-living discussion, taken up in diverse terms by different generations," as Lenn Goodman puts it in the opening essay on Judaism. Each has had a varied career in more than one cultural context, helping to shape as well as being shaped by those distinct contexts.

One of the central contentions of this book is that, while the conventional wisdom has been that these religious traditions are essentially "collectivist" in their orientation, insisting on the interests of the community over those of the individual, this now appears to be far too unnuanced a characterization. We find views of the relation between individual and community to be dynamic within particular traditions and actual religious practices to be diverse in the societies in which these traditions have evolved. Our finding is that, in the conceptual realm, even where there is no allowance or sanction for an *adversarial* relation between the individual and the community or the state, space is generally made for or claimed by the individual within a holistic order; in the realm of religious practice, individual determinations and choices often abound. Frequently there is a certain tension between ideal and reality, but almost invariably this space for the individual finds a certain protection. We suggest that individuality, rather than being a given, is a construction which many of the great religious traditions tend to foster over time, in different ways, given their different insights into the phases of a human lifetime and their projections of an ultimate human destiny. Another common theme found in these essays is that there is a profound and complex connection between the metaphysical ideas that are central to given traditions—whether these have to do with the idea of God, the cosmic process, or the metaphysical structure of reality—and their particular conceptions of the individual and individual dignity.

In discussing the conception of the individual in classical Judaism, Lenn Goodman observes that:

> The biblical Law, in addressing all ages, defines no normative type. Rather it opens up the space for human individuality to construct itself. In opening up rather than defining that space, it uses the same method of silence and negativity that it employs to allow our minds to construct the idea of God: man is created in God's image, and God is to be assigned no delimiting shape . . . No stereotypic role is to delimit human scope.

Goodman sees the biblical model of the family as providing a matrix for the emergence of individuality and the commandment to "love thy neighbor as thyself" as both resting on and fostering individuality in that it is addressed to an individual moral agent and seeks the good of individuals. He suggests that, in their time, the Hebrew prophets:

> elicit more explicitly from the Mosaic repertoire of themes the underlying premise that there is more to man than that which lives and works and dies—not an afterlife, necessarily, but a dimension of our being that is not exhausted by our overt acts but lives on a level of the unseen, the level of prayer and intention, social act and omission as well as social presence in the Temple throng or fighting force.

Again, "The Rabbis discovered value in the very fact of uniqueness: If man is created in the image of God, that is in part because every human being, like God, will be unique."

Writing about Hinduism, Joseph Elder draws attention to the highly individual nature of Hinduism's ancient texts and lawbooks, in contrast with the highly collective nature of Hinduism's practicing social groups. He suggests that a fundamental feature of the Vedic literature and the Precepts of Manu, as ancient repositories of cultural ideals, is that "they were not trying to describe the world that actually existed but the world as they believed it *should* exist if one accepted certain cosmological 'givens.' " These "givens," which included the "right" of each individual to ultimate cosmic justice through the "law" of *karma,* implied the participation of the individual *qua* individual in an ultimately orderly cosmic process. The freedom or liberation of the individual through participation in this cosmic process was also among the tradition's highest ideals. Elder observes that, despite their antiquity and a certain remoteness, historically, from actual social practice, these ideals have continued to inspire and impel India's most influential reformers, including Mohandas Gandhi. He looks to the possibility that resort to these ideals may one day figure in the evolution of a larger spirituality with implications for the world as a whole.

Robert Thurman, in reflecting on the Buddhist tradition, finds the metaphysics of the person found in Mahayana Buddhism to be conducive to the most fully realized individuality. In Thurman's view,

> The question of human rights is never merely an ethical question; it is equally a metaphysical question, bound up with a culture's fundamental view of what sort of thing is a 'human being.' And that rests on the determination of what is matter, what is mind, what is reality.

What might initially be seen as a paradox—namely, that the Buddhist meta-physical teaching of selflessness (*anatma*) should have been ethically conducive to the emergence of spiritual individualism—is, for Thurman, *not* actually paradoxical but both metaphysically and psychologically *necessary*. In his view,

> A central thesis bears repeating, i.e., that selflessness is the logical and social seal of the "autonomy" and unique value of the individual over and above his/her collec-tivity because a metaphysically given fixed "self" would be incompatible with any living, changing individual, and a socially constructed role-ascriptive "self" would be inevitably a stereotypical, traditional pattern of personality imposed upon the unique, novel, particular person.

As in Thurman's view the Buddhist theme of no-self is to be understood not as a denial but as an assertion of the ultimate value of the individual human personality, so in Irene Bloom's discussion of Confucianism that tra-dition is seen as one in which the individual is understood to be not only socially but also biologically and cosmically contextualized and yet at the same time recognized and fulfilled rather than submerged in the larger whole. Bloom presents Confucianism as a worldly spirituality that takes as its high-est ideal the psychological as well as moral fulfillment of the individual within the context of the family, the community, and the larger home that is the uni-verse and that recognizes the development of individual personality to have ultimate significance.

John Langan, in reflecting on Christian views of the relation of individual and the collectivity, discusses similar issues and introduces several other themes of immense importance for this volume, including the continuing, if sometimes unacknowledged, influence of religious traditions on contempo-rary "secular" moral philosophy in the West. Langan observes that one of the functions of human rights norms is "to regulate the ways in which people who come from different traditions, ideologies, and cultures may deal with each other." This task involves "preventing our violation of persons from outside our culture" and "setting up mutually or universally recognized norms for the protection of all, including ourselves." Langan argues that, out of the major religious traditions there has issued a fundamental and still lively and effective concern for the value of individual human lives. As he puts it, "The basic con-tribution to the shaping of our norms for the treatment of others comes from our religious traditions" and "this has continuing strength and validity even after truth-claims have been dismissed."

In considering the role of the individual in the Islamic tradition, Richard Bulliet draws attention to yet another of our major themes, the great diversity of currents and possibilities offered by a major world religion in the course of its evolution in a remarkable *variety* of cultural contexts. Bulliet points out that, in the case of Islam, this has meant that, rather than being confronted with a monolithic religious orthodoxy, individual Muslims have almost always had choices that they could make—choices of a religious teacher, for example, and choices in the translation of religious teaching into a way of life. While focusing on Islam, Bulliet's discussion reminds us that each of the major traditions is both highly complex at any given point in its history and extremely dynamic in its evolution over time. To acknowledge that "religious diversity" is to be found *within* the traditions themselves hardly less than *among* them detracts nothing from a recognition of the constants and commonalities that sustain and inspire adherents of human rights.

PART 2: ON RELIGION, SECULARITY, AND RELIGIOUS TOLERATION

One of the most significant issues involved in discussions of the relation of religion and human rights is whether the idea of human rights should be considered a distinctively *secular* development, involving a break from an older, religious worldview. Richard Ashcraft adopts an historical approach to understanding the origins of human rights thinking in the early modern West. Ashcraft focuses on John Locke, demonstrating that Locke's own deep religious beliefs and motives figured crucially in his political thought and calling into question the prevalent view of Locke as one who turned away from an older religious worldview and toward a "modern, secular" perspective. Locke's views on natural law, the social contract, and religious tolerance may be considered among the most important sources of inspiration for the later development of Western concepts of human rights. Locke's ideas certainly marked a movement toward modernity; yet, in light of Ashcraft's work, the familiar trope "modern, secular" comes to seem problematical as a characterization of Locke's thought. Emphasizing the particularity, specificity, and the dynamism of the historical process, Ashcraft considers a carefully developed historical perspective as essential not only to an understanding of Locke himself but, equally, to an understanding of human rights as an ongoing historical movement. As he puts it, an historical framework "reinforces our consciousness that . . . rights are impermanent, that they are the products of political struggle, and that organized human action is necessary to guarantee their preservation."

Sharing a similar appreciation for a richness of historical texture in the study of religious ideas, David Little, Abdulaziz Sachedina, and John Kelsay examine attitudes toward religious liberty and freedom of conscience both in Western Christianity and in Islam and discover "deep and surprising parallels between the Western and Islamic traditions." Parallel to the ideas of natural law and personal conscience in Western Christianity, these three historians of religion find within Islam an idea of personal conscience based on the belief in universal guidance by Allah. This idea of an inviolable personal conscience is, at least, one of the strands within the fabric of Islam and as such, figures among the rich variety of resources and possibilities that the tradition offers to its adherents.

PART 3: RELIGION AND RIGHTS IN THE CONTEMPORARY WORLD

The four essays in part 3 explore the role of religious ideas and institutions in influencing human rights situations in several areas of the contemporary world. The areas deserving of exploration are virtually limitless; for present purposes we have chosen to focus on the recent evolution of Hindu nationalism in India, on the role of the Roman Catholic Church in Latin America since the 1960s, on the history of Russian Orthodoxy and the human rights movement in the part of the world known for most of the twentieth century as the Soviet Union and more recently as the Commonwealth of Independent States, and on a variety of perspectives on human rights that have emerged in recent decades in the Islamic world.

While the religious systems and institutions involved are different, and the societies and cultures both various and complex, some common threads that emerge in the four essays are: the problems and challenges posed by involvement of the traditions in rapidly changing and often difficult political environments; the remarkable dynamism of the traditions; and the felt need, in many parts of the world, to interpret human rights ideas and standards in terms of the indigenous religious beliefs and values that have shaped people's lives for so many centuries. In some parts of the world, including India and much of the Islamic world, human rights ideas have been understood by many as a challenge to traditional values on the part of Western observers whose appreciation of indigenous cultural dispositions and religious beliefs or of social and economic realities may be found wanting. In other parts of the world, including Latin America and much of Eastern Europe, the problems have had to do less with the perceived "foreignness" of human rights norms than with the confrontation between religious institutions and authoritarian political regimes or, more recently, with conflicts among ethnic and religious groups who perceive their interests to be at odds. Different as these circumstances are, a common response within the religious traditions has been to turn within as well as without and to probe the depths of the tradition to discover the resources it offers for responding to the powerful challenges of the modern world. In almost every case it appears that new meaning and fresh possibilities are found in those depths of tradition.

Mark Juergensmeyer, in discussing "Hindu Nationalism and Human Rights" in contemporary India, touches on several of these themes. He notes that the ideological polarization that has emerged in recent decades between Hindu nationalists and secularists (or "antifundamentalists," as he calls them) reflects the complex challenges for human rights and civil society in India. "There is no question that Hindu nationalists hold the potential of threatening human rights," he observes; "alas, secular antifundamentalists have that potential as well." Juergensmeyer views with interest and a certain qualified optimism the attempts of contemporary scholars associated with the Hindutva movement to rediscover "an authentic, inclusive Indian cultural tradition" which would allow for both cultural integrity and the tolerance necessary for the continued evolution of a civil society in the world's largest democracy.

In "Catholicism and Human Rights in Latin America" Margaret Crahan surveys the involvement of the Roman Catholic Church in the cause of human rights in Latin America since 1960. She draws attention to the importance, since Vatican II in the early 1960s and the Conference of Latin American Bishops in Medellín in 1968, of a growing acceptance within the Catholic church of political, economic and religious pluralism in the world and an increasing tendency of the Church as an institution and of Catholics as individuals to participate in the struggle for change and in debates over strategies to accomplish it. Crahan acknowledges that divisions remain concerning morally acceptable political and economic strategies to achieve greater respect for human rights, attributing these divisions to the complexities of Latin American societies as well as to the diversity of positions represented within the Church. She acknowledges as well that the Church has attempted to promote change at the same time that it has committed itself to community solidarity and reconciliation within societies—no doubt a complex agenda. As she puts it, "The difficulties involved make the accomplishment of its stated objectives—peace, justice, and human rights—as difficult as it is transcendental." Yet she can also affirm that a strong commitment to human rights among church people in the face of repressive governments, terrorist movements, and increasing societal violence, has tended *over time* to increase consensus on the basic rationale for such work.

In reflecting on "Russian Orthodoxy and Human Rights," Paul Valliere explains that Orthodox views of the relation of the individual to the community, expressed in the idea of *sobornost'* (or wholeness) and *lichnost'* (or personality), are not such as to encourage individualism. Yet, as he observes,

> Like all great faith traditions, Orthodoxy comprises concepts of human dignity which can at least support, if they do not necessarily generate, the idea of human rights. Furthermore, under the pressure of historic challenges people often find new meaning in traditional ideals. Thus, while some of the most important ideals of Orthodoxy tend to discourage individuals from viewing themselves as rights-bearers over against the community, and discouraged the community from viewing itself as distinct from the state, these ideals did not prevent a lively Orthodox rights movement from developing in the very untraditional circumstances of the Soviet Union.

Not only did members of the Russian Orthodox community find new meaning in traditional ideals, but, as Valliere shows, its clerical and lay leaders also developed a new legal consciousness, with attention to law becoming a distinguishing characteristic of both the Orthodox and Soviet human rights movements.

The book concludes with the observations of Miriam Cooke and Bruce Lawrence on the position of "Muslim Women between Human Rights and Islamic Norms," a discussion that widens into a larger reflection on the nature of human rights discourse in the world at large in the latter half of the twentieth century. While recognizing the continuing importance of Qur'ānic ideals in discussions of social morality throughout the Islamic world, Cooke and Lawrence also emphasize the importance of the particular social and economic circumstances of the diverse societies that form part of that world as well as the diversity of motives among Muslim respondents to Western ideas of human rights. This particularity and this diversity, they suggest, are as much a part of the story of the struggle for human rights in the world today as debates over the significance, relevance, and applicability of the values set forth in the Universal Declaration of Human Rights.

Valliere's story of a remarkable struggle on the part of members of the Orthodox rights movement and the observations of Cooke and Lawrence about ongoing struggles in the Islamic world may well direct us back to a perception of Richard Ashcraft in his essay in part 2 of this book. "In the end," Ashcraft writes, "it is perhaps most salutary to grasp the meaning of human rights in terms of a cumulative political struggle composed of many concrete victories, each of which needs to be understood in terms of its historical, sociological, and political dimensions." Here we find an unmistakable truth emerging from the complex reality of religion and human rights: despite the universalism implied in its premises and affirmed in its achievements, the human rights movement itself entails struggles that must be carried on in many parts of the world in response to particular problems and conditions, with the energy and courage for such struggles coming from individuals who, while ultimately sharing some common goals and aspirations, often draw on religious resources that remain richly and irreducibly diverse. By accepting the importance of this "cumulative political struggle" for human rights throughout the world, we in turn may be forced to acknowledge our acceptance of a kind of "conflict model," but in this case, the conflict will be understood to involve not clashes along civilizational "fault lines" but local struggles in support of a larger cause.

NOTES

1. Samuel P. Huntington, "The Clash of Civilizations?" *Foreign Affairs* 72, no. 3 (Summer 1993): 2–26.

2. See the responses to Huntington, especially that of Fouad Ajami, in *Foreign Affairs* 72, no. 4 (September/October 1993): 2–26.

PART ONE

New Perspectives on
Major Religious Traditions

I

THE INDIVIDUAL AND THE COMMUNITY IN THE NORMATIVE TRADITIONS OF JUDAISM

LENN E. GOODMAN

In 1980 the Knesset of Israel severed the last formal ties between Israeli and British law and instructed judges who found no grounds for a decision in statute, case law, or analogy to form their decisions "in the light of the principles of freedom, justice, equity and peace of Israel's heritage." A large body of British precedent and principle had been taken up as statute during the years 1922–1980, when British Mandatory law provided the requisite backdrop. In taking the historic step of severing the link to the colonial past and setting a more ancient heritage in its place, the Knesset was careful to specify that recourse to the traditional canon was for its humanity.[1] No parochial traditionalism was to be erected on the basis of this law. But the formal judicial process was reopened to a source of inspiration too long held at arm's length. The hope: to reenliven the universal human values of Jewish law. What are those values, and how can their timeless principles be disentangled from the particularities of specific epochs?

The question has been asked repeatedly in Jewish history, a fact that aids us in addressing it. For religions based on revealed scriptures characteristically regard their sacred texts not as fixed archaeological records but as timeless touchstones of inspiration, whose very ambiguities open up new and always relevant meanings. Fundamentalisms, whether minimalist or maximalist, movements of revival, renaissance, and reform, typify monotheistic cultures precisely because the mere positivity of a text or practice will never seem fully adequate to the deepest meanings and highest demands of the core documents. These, like any sacred symbols, will point beyond their historicity toward their Source, and new efforts will constantly be made to reopen their true intensions. Fictively these intensions are recovered from the past, but their practical locus is normative and present, creatively constructed for this moment, no matter how atavistically their prescriptive force may be sought in the recent past or remote antiquity. Radical departures in pursuit of narrow themes will generate heresy, militancy, sects, or cults. Closely reasoned steps of argument and subtle shifts of emphasis, informed by sensitivity to the continuity and inner logic of broader themes, will yield evolution, enlarging and refining the potentials of the past. But whether inspired or misguided, such elaboration is always selective and interpretive.

Judaism conserves a rich variety of form and content in the historically variegated efforts to articulate its fundamental norms. But three basic idioms emerge—Mosaic, Prophetic, and Rabbinic. It is not my aim to analyze their differences sweepingly, as though the underlying values were exhausted once their syntax was parsed and the terms of reference in which they are couched accurately labeled—"Wisdom Literature," "Priestly Document," "Elohist Tract." Such analysis can be valuable, but as a means to an end, not an end in itself. When the end product is sheer fragmentation, snipping a text into tiny slips of paper or parchment whose scattered array belies thematic unities long evident to the authors and recipients of shared traditions, it may be useful to complement archeological stratigraphy with something of the synchronic method of the Biblical and Rabbinic authors themselves—not as a denial of historicity but as a means of trying to catch a glimpse of what lies beyond the excavation's rim.

For the Torah, as Maimonides explains (*Guide* 1:2), is not a work of history or poetry (although it uses their techniques) but a book of laws. To be critically appropriated as a possession for all times, it cannot be read purely as an expression of one time, a repository of the language and limitations of its original audience, whose understanding it accommodates. It must be read as well as a contribution to an ever-living discussion, taken up in diverse terms in each generation, but always pursuing the same goals and resting its case on the same ultimate idea of what is absolute and, accordingly, what is compromisable. If we really believe that the Torah is inspired by the Eternal, and that it is a heritage (Exodus 15:17), we will not suppose that its normative message is spent in a single generation. My purpose here, then, is to look past the shifts of language and scene to uncover the perennial norms that give unity to the Jewish project of defining what the God of Abraham expects of us. Such a task is always and necessarily creative, inductive, active, and collaborative, rather than sheerly receptive, analytic, passive, or dogmatic. The aim is not to reach a point where we no longer sense whether we are reading Hebrew or Aramaic, Arabic or English, but to raise our own consciousness, through what we elicit from the old texts, to the level of their appropriable principles.

The theme we shall trace through its variegated expressions is the relationship of the individual to the community. For the normative traditions of Judaism, unlike many familiar views, do not see that relationship as the focal point of social struggle. In every period, the Jewish sources, like other traditional normative systems, reject the cliché of a zero-sum game between communal and individual interests. Rather than the competition that the Sophists envision, the Torah and the works that elaborate and explicate its themes set forth a complementarity of interests. Autonomy is not the antithesis but the aim of communal norms; individual fulfillment is both the means and the end of the Law's implementation. For this to be true, of course, such fulfillment cannot be defined arbitrarily, reductively, or subjectively. It must comprehend within itself the moral and the spiritual dimensions of our being.

THE MOSAIC FOUNDATION

The people of Israel, who are the cultural bearers of the Jewish religion and law, an ethnicity forged by their linkage to that law, originate as a people in a crisis. Israel's experience as an identified minority, persecuted and enslaved in Egypt,[2] precipitates the Judaic idea of the individual and of individual dignity. The marks of that experience are visible in the norms of the Mosaic law and even in its cosmological, historical, and protohistorical preambles. Characteristically: "Thou shalt not pervert the justice due to the stranger, or to the orphan, nor take the widow's garment in pawn. Remember that a slave is what thou wert in Egypt, and the Lord thy God redeemed thee thence. That is why I command thee to do this" (Deuteronomy 24:17–18).

The values that form Israel inform the West as well. They give normative content to Israel's identity but also underlie Christian claims to the testament of Israel, and Muslim claims to the parentage of Abraham and heritage of the prophets. They underwrite modern secular revisions too, whether the debt is openly acknowledged or concealed by recasting and restructuring—in Locke, the Deists, Republicans, and Philosophes, Spinoza, Freud, Marx, Weber, Durkheim, Lévi-Strauss.[3] Even where specifics are sublimated or sublated, the original thematic remains crucial to the elaboration of the tradition.

What then is the legacy of Egypt? There is to be no permanent slavery among Israelites, except at the express demand of the slave.[4] The system of debt slavery that Joseph exploited in Egypt (Genesis 47:20) is abolished. Accordingly, there is no permanent alienation of land. What is sold is in effect a lease of no more than 49 years (Leviticus 25:8–18, 23–25). So there is to be no permanently dispossessed class or caste. Priests and Levites may own no land but must depend on the dues reserved for them. They will not become a wealthy landed class like the priests of Egypt (Numbers 18:20–24; cf. 34–35, Genesis 47:22).[5] No interest may be taken on loans from fellow Israelites (Deuteronomy 23:20–21; Exodus 22:24), and their debts must be remitted in the seventh year, when the land enjoys its "sabbath" and lies fallow (Deuteronomy 15:1–10; Leviticus 25:1–7). After the seventh such sabbath, the land reverts to its ancestral owners (Leviticus 25:8–55). So Israelites may always return to their familial estates. The cycle of debt slavery and dispossession, with its correlative amassing of lands in the priesthood is permanently broken.[6] From the Book of Ruth we learn that the system did not function perfectly. But the ideas it enunciates became a permanent heritage.

The Torah holds forth its laws of land tenure, debt release and redemption with a view to ending destitution (Deuteronomy 15:4–5). Yet it allows for the persistence of need even as it pursues its elimination (Deuteronomy 15:11). The appeal behind the provision of surplus "gleanings" and the produce of the corner of the field as the patrimony of the poor (Leviticus 19:9–10; 23:22, Deuteronomy 24:19–22) is the same as that underlying the prohibition of injustice to the stranger, forbidding retention of a day worker's wages overnight, taking a widow's clothing in pawn, or keeping a poor man's cloak beyond sundown (Exodus 22:25–27), or any person's millstone—the same as that which prohibits selling kidnapped brethren or entering a debtor's house to claim collateral: "remember that you were a slave in the land of Egypt" (Deuteronomy 24:6–7, 10–15, 17–22). Unlike Francis Galton or Garrett Hardin, the Torah does not seek the elimination of need by elimination of the needy. Galton, the founder of eugenics, hoped for a humane end to human misery through state aid to the advantaged and socioeconomic suppression of the destitute, to breed out the "inferior" and promote the "superior," gradually but inexorably. Hardin advocates a new ethic for "spaceship earth," triage of entire races and peoples, by withholding food aid from the starving to reduce their numbers and prevent their "swamping the lifeboat" or laying waste "the commons."[7]

The Torah, arising in a far less prosperous age, does not read the human condition as requiring or even permitting such desperate and self-defeating measures. It expresses confidence that life will flourish if creatures are fruitful and multiply and fill the earth (Genesis 1:28).[8] It seeks to ensure, through the active collaboration of all Israelites, that the poor not be allowed to die out and vanish from the land: to preserve their lives, restore them to their property and see them established is a blessing for the nation (Deuteronomy 15:7–11; cf. Leviticus 25:35). Guiding the scheme is the precious value of human self-sufficiency—each man under his own vine or fig tree (1 Kings 4:25, 2 Kings 18:31, Zechariah 3:10; cf. Proverbs 27:18).[9] Thus, even when the remission of debts is overturned by a legal fiction, in the interest of commerce,[10] or when the growth of the idea of freedom leads to the abolition of slavery, the ideal of the economically autonomous individual remains, a fountain of concrete legal obligations: The poor can sue at law for their just maintenance,[11] and the highest charity is defined not as self-sacrifice or condescension but as imparting to another the means of self-sufficiency.[12]

Central among the Mosaic institutions that echo the Egyptian experience is the Sabbath. The petition for a break (the literal sense of *shabbat*) was the original demand Moses brought before Pharaoh (Exodus 5:1). The request was rejected: "Why, Moses and Aaron, do you sunder the people from their work? Go back to your toils" (Exodus 5:4). Pharaoh refuses to differentiate the slaves from their labors, just as he refuses to distinguish Moses and Aaron from the slaves. The Sabbath becomes a symbol of the existential autonomy of the individual, the irreducibility of person to task, and God Himself is envisioned ceasing from His work (Genesis 2:2–3): Even He is not confined to His task; and man, created in God's image, is freed by the Law, commanded to rest and thus to know himself apart from his uses. Even animals may not be worked on the Sabbath, lest servants be excluded from full enjoyment of the Sabbath rest (Deuteronomy 5:14–15)—and lest we imagine that beasts are mere tools.

The Sabbath is called a sign ('*ot*) of God's act of creation (Exodus 31:17). But it reenacts the cessation, not the work; and when the Torah says that God stopped and rested (*shavat va-yinnafash*—Exodus 31:17) the Midrashic poets can almost hear God's restful sigh, even now breathing into us the sacred soul (*nefesh*) imparted to humanity through rest, playfully taking the intensive/causal form of the verb (*yinnafash*) to suggest that God did not rest (Psalms 121:3–4), but gave rest, and with it, spirit. Israel's liberation is thus linked with God's creation. The Sabbath is a memorial of both (*zekher le-ma'aseh bereshit; zekher yitzi'at Mitzraim*). For God too does not act by constraint—not automatically. Freedom is the condition of existence, and creativity is the mark of freedom.

Again from the experience in Egypt, we have the commandment against looking down on the Egyptian (Deuteronomy 23:8; cf. Isaiah 19:25). The stated reason: that we were strangers in Egypt. The sufferings of our stay are not held against the nation, and the ethos of vindictiveness is inverted, giving the lie to Nietzsche's claim that the workshops of morals are fueled by the spirit of vengeance (*Genealogy of Morals* 1:7). For ethics here takes its rise dialectically in moral rejection of a merely reactive response, as the Torah expands and generalizes the commandment not to scorn the Egyptian: There are commandments not to hate one's brother in one's heart (Leviticus 19:17), not to oppress a stranger (Exodus 23:9—"for you know the heart of a stranger"), to love the stranger (Deuteronomy 10:19, Leviticus 19:34), to love one's fellow as oneself (Leviticus 19:18, 19:34). Even the idea of one law for the stranger and the homeborn alike (Leviticus 18:26; cf. 16:29, 24:22, Numbers 15:30) is a dialectical counterpart of the ethical response to Egypt. The process is still going on when Jesus admonishes: "Love thine enemies, bless them that curse thee, do good to them that hate thee, and pray for them that despitefully use and persecute thee" (Matthew 5:44). The Torah does not issue that command, which might ring paradoxical when enemies could not be accorded a figurative or literal *clementia* from the heights of spiritual or temporal power. But it does command us to aid our enemy in righting and reloading his fallen ass (Exodus 23:4–5). For even enemies are human beings. And, as Maimonides explains, it is an object of the Law to cement the bonds that link us and to improve our character, through actions that will soften the pumice of irascibility in the soul. Spinoza follows and extends this reading when he offers a psychologistic model for the power of love in dissolving hatred.[13]

A crucial corollary of the injunction to love the stranger and to love our fellows as ourselves is the idea of equality, a conception formative of the idea of law and of that of humanity. Human equality rests on and gives substance to the existential dignity which the law and the community exist to serve and promote—not in place of God's service but as the chief means by which God desires and intends to be served.[14] Before the giving of the Law, every man did what was right in his own eyes (Deuteronomy 12:8, 13:19; cf. Judges 17:6, 21:25). But in God's eyes, and so in the Law's eyes, all persons are of equal existential worth. Thus judges may not favor wealth and stature, or even poverty or merit (Exodus 23:2–3, Leviticus 19:15). The prooftext: Exodus 23:6: "Thou shalt not pervert the judgment of thy poor in his cause." Maimonides glosses: "even if he is poor in piety, do not pervert his judgment."[15]

The Torah freely reports that the idea of deciding cases by uniform rules came to Moses from a foreign source, his Midianite father-in-law, Jethro (Exodus 18). But uniformity alone is not equality. For persons might be treated uniformly according to their station. In Hammurabi's Code the death penalty for theft was commuted to thirtyfold restitution if the theft was from a royal estate, tenfold if from a gentleman, fivefold if from a commoner. A blow is punished by sixty stripes of an oxhide scourge—if it was directed at a superior.[16] The idea that social dominance or prominence is profoundly irrelevant to the crucial issues of justice rests on the recognition that human deserts are at some level existential, and positive. That idea is alien to Hammurabi. Yet any broad uniformity militates in the direction of categorical deserts, and recognition of such deserts at some level is a moral necessity in any legal system: Minimally, for example, there is a uniform desert of access to the laws.[17] The very idea of the rule of law presses for equal treatment of equal cases (Exodus 12:49, Leviticus 24:22, Numbers 15:16, 29). Thus the provisions for a permanent, public, written law (Exodus 24:7, Deuteronomy 17:11; 27:3, 8; 31:11–12, 24–26) press toward constitutionality, as evident in God's command that each king of Israel closely study and follow the Law:

> When he sitteth on his royal throne, he shall write himself a copy of this Torah, from the book in the charge of the Levitical priests. And he shall keep it by him and read from it all the days of his life, so that he learn to revere the Lord his God by keeping all the provisions of this Law and performing all these statutes, and his heart not grow haughty toward his brethren, and that he not diverge to the left or the right from its command, so that his reign and that of his offspring in the midst of Israel may long endure (Deuteronomy 17:18–20).[18]

When fused with the idea of the inviolable worth or dignity of the individual as a creature of God, the invariance of rules becomes humanity's most powerful ethical and legislative tool. It meant, to begin with, that recompense for deaths or injuries must be proportioned only to the injury and not the stature or grandeur of the party offended against (Exodus 21:23–26, Leviticus 24:17–22, Numbers 35:29–34). The dignity of all human beings is alike for free or slave, man or woman, young or old.

It is the work of centuries—and a task by no means completed—to single out those dimensions of human dignity that are truly existential from the claims of ego or custom that are mere encrustations of our universal desire for dignity—at our own or others' expense. But an immediate requirement, when the equality of human dignities was first enunciated in a vengeance culture, was the distinction between murder, manslaughter and accident. The Cities of Refuge are the Torah's response, protecting from blood vengeance homicides who are not premeditated murderers (Exodus 21:13, 18–19, Numbers 35:9–29). Correspondingly, there is capital punishment (not vengeance) and a rejection of blood payment or corporate accountability for murder (Numbers 35:31, Exodus 21:12, 14).

The Torah's insistence on individual accountability for offenses (Deuteronomy 24:16) articulates the identity of the moral person and singles out the moral agent as the actor on whose choices and omissions, virtues and weaknesses, the fate of the community will depend (Leviticus 26:3–33). Hammurabi's Code rules that the *children* of a negligent builder shall die (230), that a creditor's son is killed if the distrained son of a debtor dies on his account (116); an assailant's daughter dies if he causes the death by miscarriage of another man's daughter (209–14).[19] In the ancient codes, and not a few modern ones, property crimes can be capital. The Torah, as Moshe Greenberg explains, sharply divides crimes against persons from crimes against property: the latter are never capital. Thus adultery is a crime by a couple against God (Genesis 20:6, 39:8, Leviticus 20:10), not simply by a wife against her husband. So there is "no question of permitting the husband to mitigate or cancel the punishment" (Leviticus 20:10, Deuteronomy 22:22–23), just as there is no royal pardon for murderers.[20] God Himself oversees the uniformity of the Law, and God's character came clearly into the light when Abraham argued and haggled with Him for the Cities of the Plain: better to spare the wicked majority than let the wicked and the righteous fare alike.

The procedural guarantees[21]—presumption of innocence, protection against self-incrimination, strict rules of evidence and testimony—that are the glory of Western law—reflect the Torah's valuation of the individual. Thus the demand for two witnesses in a capital case—"no one shall die by the testimony of a single witness" (Numbers 35:30, Deuteronomy 19:15). Even habeas corpus and the right to a jury trial, which are not Biblical institutions, take on the absoluteness and sanctity of biblical rights, which God Himself should honor. Job, in the midst of his sufferings can expect a trial.[22] And the visions of apocalypse called forth by thoughts of God's universal justice take on a juridical, procedurally safeguarded form, down to the inclusion of adversarial advocates for the prosecution and the defense. God Himself formalizes His covenant with Israel by calling heaven and earth to witness (Deuteronomy 4:26; cf. 31:28; 32:1, 40); no default will be determined on a single party's say so. The earthly counterparts to these cosmic guarantees safeguard personal liberty, life—and property, to be sure—but, crucially, they protect human dignity, defined to engulf and transcend all of these.

The family, as biblically construed, is the matrix for the emergence of individuality (Genesis 2:24). Personal identity is preserved and nurtured by the protection of sexual privacy. It is not submerged in the identities of parents but matures and emerges sound and independent, capable of entering a mature relationship with another autonomous person and adequate to the construction of a new household. This cycle affords the Torah's rationale for the prohibition of incest,[23] and for all social institutions. As Albert Einstein writes:

> The highest principles for our aspirations and judgments are given to us in the Jewish-Christian religious tradition. It is a very high goal which, with our weak powers, we can reach only very inadequately, but which gives a sure foundation to our aspirations and valuations. If one were to take that goal out of its religious form and look merely at its purely human side, one might state it perhaps thus: free and responsible development of the individual, so that he may place his powers freely and gladly in the service of all mankind. There is no room in this for the divinization of a nation, of a class, let alone of an individual. . . It is only to the individual

that a soul is given. And the high destiny of the individual is to serve rather than to rule, or to impose himself in any other way.[24]

The paradigmatic marriage is dyadic: a man leaves his father's and his mother's house and cleaves unto his wife. Despite the long tolerance of polygamy, the paradigm persists: the way of a man with a maid (Proverbs 30:19), thy neighbor's wife (Exodus 20:14)—or Job's.[25] Marital exclusivity even models God's intimacy with Israel (Exodus 20:5, 34:14, Deuteronomy 4:24, 5:9, 6:15, 1 Kings 19:10, 14; Joel 2:18, Zechariah 1:14, 8:2). Ultimately, polygamy will be spat out—not simply in response to "cultural influences" (for one must always ask why one cultural pattern is appropriated and another rejected)—but by the powerful idea of monogamy itself. The same process can be seen in modern times among thoughtful leaders of Islam. For scriptural ideals can in time make intolerable what has long been tolerated, through their dialectic with social standards, cultural experiences, and intellectual judgments. Core values are reaffirmed, and what proves incompatible with them—anthropomorphism, slavery, polygamy—is ejected.

Biblical legislation, often explicated in the biblical narrative, does much to form the ideal of individuality as we know it. But in Mosaic and patriarchal times the state is not the principal threat to personhood. The modern sovereign state, which both fosters and threatens individuality, the totalitarian state, which seeks to exploit and submerge the individual, even the omnicompetent welfare state, with all its techniques of empowerment and inducements to dependency, do not yet exist. The institutions that are created biblically are deemed ancillary, not antithetical, to individual interests, which in turn are not sharply set apart from communal goals. Traditional norms often presume the harmony of individual and group interests. Whether out of naïveté or wisdom, license is not mistaken for freedom and communal potentials for abuse are not seen as powers. The individual is not radically isolated from the social body to whose interests his own are linked.

The fundamental social commandment of the Mosaic corpus, "Love thy neighbor as thyself" (Leviticus 19:18), typifies the Mosaic method of legislation and its goals in integrating the individual in the community. It both rests upon and fosters individuality. It addresses the individual and urges those whom it addresses to seek the good of others, by fostering fellowship and fellow feeling (*re'ut*, community)—a sense of common interests and shared concerns, making another's good one's own. That ideal is not left an isolated abstraction but interpreted in concrete actions that give it operational meaning—from the immediate ban on vengeance and grudges (vv. 17–18) to the prohibition of talebearing on the one hand and diffidence on the other (v. 16). Indeed, the commandments biblically linked with the Golden Rule form a tight nexus arising from the primal commandment to pattern ourselves on God's ways, and expressing itself, for example, in a delicately balanced pair of obligations to reprove our fellows when they do wrong, but not to shame them.[26]

The bond of the individual to the community is a familiar feature of ancient and traditional societies. Even a rather alienated figure like Socrates will not accept life beyond the polis that he knows, and where (however partially and unfairly) he is known (*Crito* 53D–54B; *Apology* 30–31). His alienation gives him the distance he needs to see and perhaps to state that fact, but not to alter it. Plato, who spent years away from Athens and was ready to assume a leading role in the life of some other polis, will address the question of justice only by dealing pari passu with the private politics of the soul and the public foundations of state legitimacy. Aristotle, a *metic* at Athens, finally forced to leave it on the death of Alexander, argues that a person who would live alone is either above or below humanity—a beast or a god; for man is by nature a creature of the polis (*zoon politikon*). But in each case, the linkage of person to polis serves the person and is justified by the worth of individual humanity, even (and especially) when individuals are called on to make sacrifices for the group.

Somewhat provincially, even chauvinistically, Aristotle argues that the fully human life, the humane life, is possible only for a free man in a (Greek) polis: slaves do not enjoy humanely fulfilled lives. Greek women rarely had the access to intellectual or public engagement that would have made them fully free. And non-Greeks seemed to Aristotle too submerged in stultifying autocracies, without the agora, palaestra, baths, theaters, schools, and walks that fostered the articulation of personhood in a public setting. It was in such institutions as these that Greek individuality came to be. Greek literature, science, mathematics, philosophy, and art are its testimonies, unique and irreplaceable.

The Torah, with its own institutions of law, universal and objective history, and the unique, historically rooted monotheism articulated in biblical cosmology, mysticism, ritual, and morals, is a comparable and complementary gift, capable of synthesis with the best the Greeks can offer. Just as one story may absorb another as its subplot, Israel's ideas of universal history, objective truth and justice, subsume what they find valid in all cultures and spew out or transform what does not meet their overarching vision. It was not for nothing that God chose a stiffnecked nation inured to the practice of criticism. For, whether the fruits of Israelite criticism are intellectual or social, its roots are moral.[27]

Surveying the biblical canon, Maimonides, a philosopher imbued with the teaching of Aristotle as well as the wisdom of the Torah, finds that its institutions always seek the individual's perfection. He defines the generic purpose of laws not just Platonically, as the integration of disparate human interests, but also with a view to the value of individual differences, thus assigning laws the rather subtler project of integrating otherwise disparate characters: human laws seek only to regulate our material interactions—to adjudicate our conflicts, restrain aggression and overreaching, promote our material welfare, impartially allocate the goods and ills that the human condition lays before us. But a divine law pursues two higher goals: the improvement of our character (Plato's "education," Aristotle's moral development) and provision for our intellectual and spiritual fulfillment (Plato's vision of the sun, Aristotle's intellectual life).[28] These higher goals are approached by way of symbols, not merely by the familiar legal means of prescription and sanction. Paradigmatic actions draw us, through habit, to standards of reasonableness whose abstract description may be quite beyond us. But speech is not the aim here. What matters is our moral appropriation of dispositions toward thoughtful choice making. Once these are facets of our character, virtuous actions will be spontaneous and reliable. Thoughtful and appropriate choices will be, as Aristotle put it, second nature.[29]

Intellectual and spiritual perfection are not imposed but invited, through mythic symbolisms, the Torah's oblique discourse about God.[30] The problematics of that discourse, in which prophets boldly speak of the Creator in terms proper to His creation, awaken us to God's transcendence of all description and direct us toward the idea of God's absolute perfection, whose glory is His creation of each thing for its own sake—its perfection, an emblem of His goodness. No biblical injunction escapes these three headings: cooperation (civil and penal integration in pursuit of the common good), moral improvement (the establishment of kindness, generosity, and dignity in our ethos),[31] and intellectual perfection (the invitation to holiness, critical apprehension of God's transcendence, and the concomitant ability to interpret His Law to others, allowing them, too, to become morally autonomous and, insofar as humanly possible, intellectually self-sufficient).[32]

Just as Aristotle grounded his understanding of politics on empirical study of some 158 constitutions, Maimonides did not draw his Mosaic jurisprudence from the air but founded it on his own catalogue of the Torah's 613 commandments, on his explication of the Mishnaic code, and on his codification of the halakhic corpus in the fourteen-volume *Mishneh Torah*.[33] No law was found whose purpose is subordination of the interests of the individual to the group. Although Maimonides did hold that the community is more important than the individual,[34] he grounded its importance biblically in the dignity and worth of its members. Laws, he acknowledged, in their generality, can disaccommodate individuals (*Guide* 3:34). But even that is in the interest of those individuals, which animal shortsightedness (appetite and passion) might lead them to misperceive. For the individual is not always or necessarily the best judge of his own interests; and only lawlessness results when each person simply judges his own case.[35]

Maimonides did not expect each individual to work out his own destiny alone; he shared the biblical idea that the destiny of individuals is wrapped up in that of their fellows, forebears, and descendants—that Abraham finds fulfillment not in his personal wealth, nor even solely in his personal discovery of God, but in the knowledge that through his descendants all the peoples of the world will be blessed; Moses finds fulfillment not in his personal fortunes, nor even in his personal experience of God, but in his responsibility for the people—seeking to know God's ways for the sake of learning how to govern (Exodus 33:13), wishing to God that every Israelite were a prophet (Numbers 11:29), and praying to God (Exodus 32:32) to be blotted from His book if the people must be destroyed for their lapse. Moses will not accept life apart from the nation (and will accept no substitute nation) any more than Socrates will accept life apart from Athens.

THE PROPHETIC RECENSION

In the writings from the times of the Judges, Kings, and Prophets of Israel the biblical ideals are reconstituted and the Mosaic ideal of individuality reformulated and reenlivened. Human individuality had been central to the Mosaic nisus. Yet no "definition" of the human person emerges in the Pentateuch. For the Mosaic idiom is not abstract but concrete. So, even when its work is reflective, no expression like *zoon politikon* will emerge. Besides, to speak of individuality is to speak of freedom; to define it is to limit freedom. The Torah bears enough prescriptive weight without setting boundaries to the normative personality. In later ages this was done, reading the roles of ascetic saints and rabbinic sages into the lives of the Patriarchs or even of David, Boaz, Shem, and Eber. But the Mosaic Law, addressing all ages, defines no normative type but opens the space for human personhood to construct itself, trusting the same method of silence it used in allowing our minds to find the idea of God. For man is created in God's image, and God, too, is assigned no delimiting shape. Every title of perfection belongs to Him, and all imperfections must be denied of Him—even those implicit in our positive predications. The same, in moral terms, holds true for man: No vice must restrain him. The very word for sin is "stumble." No wrong is in our interest. Human fulfillment springs from righteousness, as God's rule is founded in righteousness (Proverbs 10:2, 11:4–5, 19; 13:6, 14:34, 15:9, 16:12, 25:5). But no stereotypic role hobbles our steps. The character we are taught by practice and example finds its feet in any human context. For kindness, thoughtfulness, self-respect, purity, and holiness are always relevant. The intelligence that symbol and indirection invite us to develop at the growing core of our identity is an openness to understanding, cramped by no catechism but drawn toward God, who is infinite, and toward love and understanding of His creation, whose wonders, subtleties and complexities are illimitable.[36]

The egoist is absent from the Mosaic canon except in passages of self-betrayal like Lamech's boast or Cain's "Am I my brother's keeper?" (Genesis 4:9). No heroic ego centers the Pentateuch, for the same reason that there is no portrait of the lineaments, ancestry, or deepest motives of the Creator: the Torah is not a saga but a law, filled out not with battle scenes or love triangles but with cosmology, history, ethical tableaux. God is absolute. Man is not; but his dignity, hence his freedom, is a kind of finite absolute. Like God, man is in a way inscrutable. But he too is an end in himself—so that all the prescriptions made to him can rest on two: the love of God and the love of self— the latter not a sin but an axiom, without which the commandment to love one's fellow as oneself becomes an empty formalism. Yet the Torah's love of self is not self-exaltation but a pursuit of self-perfection, including moral and spiritual self-perfection, as we express it. In the biblical idiom: "Circumcise, then, thy heart!" (Deuteronomy 10:16, with Deuteronomy 30:6, Leviticus 26:41). Paganism is the ethos of Lamech made cult. The epic, we have suggested, celebrates human vices and virtues by making them reflections of divine counterparts—themselves projected from the vividness of the human drama. The epic hero is the human boaster projected to the heavens, with a bard's help, then reflected down again, now magnified to superhuman scale, and still bearing the aura of divinity. There will be heroism but no epic heroes in the Torah.

As the history progresses whose meanings the Torah defines, and as the people whose mission it elaborates moves onto the stage of history, individuals do emerge: a David, whose lyric spirituality articulates a unique identity, a Jephtha whose desperate isolation bespeaks his hunger for social integration, an Amos or Hosea, voicing the interiority of prophetic experience. It might be imagined that notions of individuality and personality do not emerge from the communal matrix until, say, the Renaissance or the Enlightenment—with the new literary form of the familiar essay, one colleague says. But this is an illusion, spun from the romantic anthropology of the type canonized by Lévy-Bruhl and others who suppose that in traditional societies culture is somehow undifferentiated from nature, categories unreflective and undifferentiably compact—so that individuals *cannot* differentiate themselves from the mass, from one another, from the group and its norms, from natural objects and natural kinds fixed in the iconography of totem and taboo. Such anthropological views have long been discredited by the work of Lévi-Strauss, Mary

Douglas, and Malinowski before them. The ideas persist through their romantic appeal and the projective uses made of their invidious characterizations of the "other," who is located elsewhere than we locate ourselves in the nature-culture polarity.[37]

As for the literary expression of personality—the essay, in which one personality addresses the less clearly delineated but still individuated persona of a single listener in intimate and less formal tones than those of the public harangue or treatise—it is not Montaigne's invention but emerges from the ancient epistolary art modeled in the letters of Seneca. It is well developed in the medieval Arabic *risāla*, which guards the intimacy of tone by preserving the epistolary fiction that a single close friend or confidant is addressed.[38] This is the form and tone of address adopted by the Ikhwān al-afa' or Sincere Brethren of Basra, by Ibn Tufayl, and by Maimonides in the *Guide to the Perplexed*. But epistolary prose and essays are not the only avenues to the intimacy expressive of individuality. The same poet-warrior who danced naked before the ark of the Lord and created that spiritual intimacy by which *we* bless our Creator—David, the shepherd slingsman who sang his troubled king to sleep, who married that king's daughter and was loved by that king's son, even as he displaced him—is also the founding figure of an intimate genre, not of prose but of poetry. The genre of the Psalms is not the work of a single pair of hands, any more than the Psalms themselves are. But it is the vehicle of a personality whose failings we know (with the aid of prophet critics close to the court) as intimately and deeply as we know the spiritual and material heights of his ambitions. It is no accident that David is the figure, despite his weaknesses, so often chosen as a namesake. For his personality does emerge as few do from antiquity. He steps forward as a hero and epitome of many of the Torah's humanistic values, although—and in part because—his individuality is never wholly predictable.

Sexuality is present everywhere in David's personality—in his beauty, his appeal to the maidens as a warrior, his flawed relations with Michal, his betrayal of Uriah, even in the last flickerings of bodily warmth in his deathbed—or its structural mirror image, the story of his Moabite ancestry told in the Book of Ruth. Biblical personhood finds its core in sexuality, the primal focus of adult individuality in us all. It is because we all have sexual aspirations, vulnerabilities, and deserts that the Torah legislates as it does, seeking not "to regulate every aspect of life," but to define and protect the libidinal core in which our individuality is invested. Even the modern (and ultimately incoherent) notion that some areas are too intimate for law to enter is a reflex of the privacy and dignity the Torah seeks to demarcate and defend.

Against rape the Mosaic canon addresses both a civil and a penal remedy. The offense is never a mere larceny against paternity. The heart of the crime is pinioned as the humbling of the victim—a degrading of her dignity. The Mosaic remedies clearly seek to mitigate the savageries of the ancient honor-shame culture we glimpse in the story of the rape of Dinah and the excess of her brothers' vengeance (Genesis 34). But the remedies proposed—death for the rape of a betrothed or married woman, or marriage without divorce for the (statutory) rape of a single woman (Deuteronomy 22:22–28), demand a civil society in which criminal penalties will be exacted, and in which communal relations make marriage thinkable between a woman and her seducer.[39] The law here seeks only to enforce earnestness. The idea of pre-marital intimacy without courtship is no part of this model, and rape as a weapon rather than a concupiscent excess is not here addressed. Shechem's were the passions of an over-ardent suitor (Genesis 34:2–4, 6, 8–12). But the decline of civil standards brought excesses of a type only dimly presaged in Dinah's story (Judges 19–21).

With no central government to define and enforce due proportion, the atrocities of anarchy return, bringing back the exemplary vengeance condemned by Jacob in his sons (Genesis 34:30, 49:5–7) and the collective blood liability vigorously combated by the later Prophets (Ezekiel 18:4). It was against the backdrop of such lawlessness that the prophet and judge Deborah emerged, responding to the needs that would create the biblical monarchy. Her song gives voice to her people's sense of triumphant liberation from terrorized vassalage to a brigand state whose pillage had cleared the roads of travelers (Judges 5:6). Deborah pictures the mother of the robber general Sisera at a latticed window awaiting his return, her well-protected ladies answering her doubts with images of the booty that has delayed the chariots: "a cunt, two cunts for every man-head." The women, whose fantasies egg on their sons' search for aggrandizement, picture the delicate finery of the female captives: embroidered cloth in many colors about every neck as spoil (Judges 5:28–30). The day is not Sisera's, however, but Deborah's and Jael's. The song of triumph, fuller than Miriam's at the sea, is the work of an individual who proudly differentiates herself from the nation and its leaders, on their white asses: the precincts of Israel were vacant, the people could not draw water without the whirr of arrows—"until I arose, Deborah, until I arose, a mother in Israel." No words spoken for or about or against women since—not the long tradition of petulant misogyny or timid fastidiousness, nor even the sticky-sweet uxorites that seek to circumscribe a woman's "place" with platitudinous praise—could rob all women afterwards of the sense of pride and vindicated right that accrues from Deborah's triumphant singing in the first person—not arrogant or spiteful but rejoicing in the restoration of civility: "And the land had peace for forty years" (Judges 5:31).

The tradition of misogyny that grows from Hellenistic world-weariness and betrays itself in the obiter dicta of many later authorities is well entrenched in medieval Judaism. Woman in the abstract here often becomes the repository of projected ambivalences toward the emotions, the senses, and the body; and institutions are deflected from imparting dignity, to the assignment of disadvantaged or disparaging postures to women. Yet the accretion never wholly obscures the normative themes: Moses could learn from God Himself that Zelophehad's daughters rightly claimed their father's inheritance (Numbers 27:7; cf. 36:10), in keeping with the Law's concern for the survival of every Israelite house. The ruling did not establish the equal inheritance of daughters with sons in rabbinic law. Rather, daughters and their descendants took second place to surviving sons and their descendants. But daughters came ahead of any other claimants, including fathers, brothers, sisters, grandfathers, and other kin of the deceased. And male heirs were obligated to support their unmarried sisters, even if it reduced the men to beggary. Commenting on the biblical provision, *Sifre* (133 to Numbers 27:7) remarks, "Man prefers men to women, but the Creator shows equal regard for all." Drawing on this theme, Falk writes,

> Just as the Torah uses human language to express divine ideas, it also uses the world of ideas of a patriarchal society to express universal truths. It therefore still requires feminist analysis and critique in order to create a more general and universal interpretation. The story concerning the daughters of Zelophehad, who brought about a correction of the law of inheritance, should be used as the model for this process, which is an ongoing responsibility of each generation and a special challenge of ours.[40]

Our ideas of equality may differ from those of Moses or the Rabbis. Such alterations are inevitable with the change of social and economic circumstances. Where we look for recognitions of autonomy, earlier sources may seek equality in the provision of maintenance. Not every age or situation makes possible the strong woman celebrated in Proverbs 31, who invests in foreign trade and agricultural real estate while carrying on a flourishing textile and garment industry under her own roof. Such a woman is a fitting exemplar of the biblical ideal of economic self-sufficiency and is textually acknowledged as the fitting recipient not only of her children's praises but of the profits of her enterprise. Her activities are not found in every epoch and social circumstance. But what is constant is the ideal of dignity that emerges from her portrayal even more clearly than the tableaux of the economic enterprises on which her realization of that dignity depends. Thus Edith Hamilton writes:

> The Bible . . . looks at women as human beings, no better and no worse than men.
> . . . The Old Testament writers, writing of a general's great victory, Barak's over

"Sisera with his chariots and his multitude," would set down how he cried out to a woman when she bade him go fight, "If thou wilt go with me, then will I go: but if thou wilt not go with me, then will I not go." And Deborah answered, "I will surely go with thee. [But the glory will not be thine; for the Lord will deliver Sisera into the hands of a woman]" (Judges 5:8–9). Bad women and faulty women are plainly dealt with . . . "A continual dropping on a very rainy day and a contentious woman are alike" (Proverbs 27:15), but the criticisms are always reasonable and well founded. So too is the praise. After a long acquaintance with the remarkable ladies of the romancers and poets of other lands, it is refreshing to stand on firm ground with the author of the last chapter of *Proverbs*, whose mother, we are told, had taught him, and who had never an idea that woman was the lesser man or some bright angelic visitant.[41]

The Mosaic themes are not discarded by the Prophets but are taken up and reinterpreted: where Leviticus offered ritual means of purging unexpiated guilt, the prophets demand spiritual cleanliness and moral purity, eliciting more explicitly the underlying Mosaic premise that there is more to man than what lives and works and dies—not an afterlife, to be sure, but an aspect of our being not exhausted by our overt acts, a spiritual reality that lives and acts in prayer and intent, inwardly, not just as a presence in the Temple throng or fighting force. The idea is implicit in the Law—in the ritual concern with unaccounted blood (Deuteronomy 21:7), in the institution of the Sabbath, even in the splendid dramatic irony of Cain's words to God, "Am I my brother's keeper?" But, as prophecy unfolds, the Mosaic theme of an unseen dimension becomes an open thesis—"man doth not live by bread alone, but by everything that issueth from the mouth of the Lord doth man live" (Deuteronomy 8:3; cf. 1 Samuel 15:22–23). Now working on an explicit level, the theme is an organizing, structuring principle. The risk and worth of moral agency rise above price (Psalms 49:8).

The prophetic recasting of the Mosaic message modifies and simplifies but does not strike down any pillar of the Law. For all remain present and accessible in the Torah. But the core principles are underscored, the themes synthesized. Thus, Amos (2:8) reenlivens the outrage that first informed the ordinance against keeping garments in pledge (Exodus 22:25) and makes it emblematic of the full range of social neglect. Castigating luxury, he calls the Temple cult itself an obscenity, when it is tainted by the hypocrisy of those who would make of it a surrogate for moral purity (5:12–27; cf. Malachi 1:7–8).

"Hear God's word, ye Lords of Sodom"—so Isaiah addresses the elite of Judah and Jerusalem, fearless of the kings whose names preface his message, including Menassah, who will be his death: "Give ear to the Torah of our God, you people of Gomorrah: "What need have I of your many sacrifices?" saith the Lord, "I am surfeited with burnt offerings of rams . . . When you come before me, who sought this of you, to tramp through My courts? Bring Me no more false oblations. Incense is loathsome . . . I shall not bear iniquity in assembly . . . When you pray at length, I do not hear; your hands are full of blood. Wash and cleanse, shed the evil of your doings . . . Seek justice, aid the oppressed, defend the fatherless and take the part of the widow. Come now, let us reason together," saith the Lord, "though your sins be red as scarlet, they shall be as wool . . . " (Isaiah 1:11–18; cf. Amos 7:14–17).

A prophet, as R. H. Charles put it, paraphrasing Marcus Jastrow, is a "forthteller" not a "foreteller."[42] Muḥammad, who aspired to prophecy, well understood that a prophet was not merely a poet or a soothsayer; he deeply resented the notion that he was either (Qur'ān 52:29, 69:40–43). Rather, he was an admonisher, like those before him, bearing a message of accountability (Qur'ān 53:35–56). Saadiah analyzes religious scriptures in general in the same terms:[43] Prophets convey a moral message, and their warnings have the force not of mere predictions but of indictments. Surveying the indictments found in Amos, Micah, Isaiah, and Jeremiah, Richard Bergren finds that every charge cites specific "apodictic" commandments of the Torah, those in which God's categorical demands are voiced not as mere regulations of civil or religious life but as vital constituents in the very meaning of the covenant. All of the warnings of disaster address moral offenses or outright disloyalty—perversion of justice, acceptance of bribes, use of false weights and measures, usury, taking garments in pledge, usurping property, withholding wages, mistreating widows, orphans, and strangers, dishonoring parents. The prophets indict lying, talebearing, perjury, theft, and the shedding of innocent blood. But the only charges in matters of cult are apostasy, sorcery, idolatry, and child sacrifice.[44] The crimes call for prophetic indictment and divine retribution, because they are secret—or so public that even the agencies that should control them are implicated in them.[45] The offenses threaten the very ethos that is the locus of God's covenant. They are the work of individuals, but they corrupt and imperil the nation, and the conscience of individuals must join with the responsibility of leaders to stem the tide.

When Micah (6:8) sums up the Torah's demands: "It hath been told thee, O man, what is good and what the Lord expecteth of thee—only this: the practice of justice, the love of kindness, and modesty in walking with thy God," the reduction is a synthesis, not a winnowing.[46] Thus we read: "Moses was given six hundred thirteen commandments. David summed these up in eleven (Psalm 15), Isaiah in six (33:16–17), Micah in three (6:8), Isaiah again in two (56:1), and finally Habakkuk founded them all in one principle, fidelity" (*Makkot* 23b–24a). Like the words of Hillel (*Shabbat* 31a), which it anticipates, Micah's summation could well bear the rider, "The rest is commentary. Go forth and learn it." For the entire Torah can be construed as interpretive commentary, giving concrete definition to the ideals of justice, kindness and humility. The prophets, for their part, do not merely comment on the Mosaic norms. They voice the principles on which those norms and the accompanying narratives are commentary. They synthesize analytically, joining together the thematic threads to reweave the fabric: the individual who grapples with a Micah or Isaiah will not complacently presume that the world was made for his amusement or his family's prosperity. The acid cynicism of Ecclesiastes dissolves shallow worldliness, just as Israel's mordant irony at the exodus ("weren't there any graves in Egypt?") dissolves all complacent afterworldliness.

Universal human brotherhood and the consent of the governed are corollaries (not foundations) of the biblical ideas of human existential equality and dignity before God. In Mosaic terms the relationship between God and creation is construed contractually, as a covenant entered freely: Israel has a covenant with God, publicly and unanimously accepted, acknowledging the misfortunes that will follow failure to keep its terms (Exodus 24:7, Deuteronomy 27, 1 Kings 1:36, 1 Chronicles 16:36, Nehemiah 5:13, 8:6). The consent of the governed is a consent to be governed. It means assumption of duties, communally, for all time, not individually or contingently but existentially. When Israelites accept God's laws—agree to keep the Sabbath as an eternal sign between themselves and God, to tell their children of the exodus from Egypt—they make a commitment not only to the preservation of their peoplehood but to the preservation of its meaning. They bring to bear the full force of culture and familial tradition to ensure that the core values that locate and lock that meaning in place will not be lost. The duties and dignities that the tradition embodies will be sacred to the community, which itself becomes an object of special concern because it bears these values and ideas. But the community as such will not become sacred. Even the idea of a king or ruler other than God, ultimately even the idea of a personal messiah, will become morally, and so intellectually, problematic. The individual must not "break away" from the community (Avot 2.4); but neither is he or she its creature. For the community exists to foster the growth of the individual, whose adequate development fosters the advancement of the community.

The Torah figures God's covenant with Israel as a marriage or a parent-child relationship, since these involve no mere exchange of goods but a giving of one's being. God, the prophets say, reflecting on the vicissitudes of history, may chastise His people, but will not forsake them. God calls it unthinkable to abandon His children or the wife He has espoused (Isaiah 50:1, 54, Jeremiah 2:2, 31:20; Hosea esp 11:1–11, 13:8; Ezekiel 23). Or, with God in the maternal role,[47] God will give suck to Her children at Jerusalem and not forsake them

(Isaiah 66:11–13, cf. 42:14, 49:15, Deuteronomy 32:11, Job 38:28–29). Committing themselves to God and His Law for all their generations, the people recognize an existential bond with one another. Beyond any literal contract, this covenant touches our identities as individuals who share a common history, face a common danger and a common joy, and pursue a common destiny, as fellow Israelites, sharers in a transpersonal, intergenerational encounter with the one God.

Every nation's history, in its depth and complexity, progressively determines a unique path—in literature, art, law, plastic design. Unique, not fixed, for cultures change, grow, and differentiate, as individual decisions demarcate and explore the finer scale of our personal odysseys. Israel's historic commitment of its culture to interpreting the commands of the Transcendent forever sets the terms of reference of Jewish norms: truth and goodness here will always be inseparable. Since the values are universal, the principle, at this level of generality, may sound vacuous or commonplace. But even at so high a level of abstraction, subtle determinations have been made—truth, not relativity or emptiness; goodness, not power or cunning. Exclusivity is not the theme, for the values enunciated invite emulation. But, as history unfolds, the distinctiveness becomes pronounced.

In any culture commitments are made to symbolic modes that may seem arbitrary if viewed externally to their own logic. In Israel, these commitments are moral and intellectual. That is not unique. But perhaps what is distinctive is the moral reading given to the intellectual, and the intellectual, critical reading given to the moral: Israel shall have no other God; and, while the God of the Universe cannot be conceived to have no other people,[48] He will know no other people quite as He has known Israel, through the *mitzvot*, setting Israel apart as a nation of priests, a light and a blessing to the nations of the world. The blessing, that those who observe the lives of individual Israelites should be moved to say: Blessed is the man whose God is that man's God.

In the Temple of Jerusalem, the Rabbis record, sacrifice was offered for the atonement of all nations' sins (*Sukkah* 55b). The Prophets in their way too pursue Abraham's idea of God's universality as Creator, Ruler, and universal Judge: all nations worship God, wittingly or unwittingly (Malachi 1:11; cf. Psalms 113:3–4). All will enjoy the universal peace that knowledge of the Lord will bring as it wells up over humanity "as water covers the sea" (Isaiah 11:9), counterpart of the ancient Flood provoked by human lawlessness, when water did not keep its place. None will be excluded from the prosperity and joy, when men beat their swords into ploughshares and spears into pruning hooks, nation ceases to wage war against nation, and they no longer study warfare.[49] The most powerful yearning for freedom and national rebirth renounces all desire for worldly domination: The nations whom hardship or custom have rendered wolfish or lionish in their ethos will lie peacefully with their more pastoral fellow peoples, once the ideas of the Law have in the fullest sense gone forth from Jerusalem. Israel shall be the little child that leads them, not by force or threat of violence, but by example. Living by her laws, Israel will demonstrate the strength and wealth of human goodness; and other nations, whether peaceable or turbulent in their histories, will gladly build on her example.[50]

The prophet's is the moral voice of the social critic, visionary of the virtualities of defeat or triumph latent in every human choice, demystifier of God's intent. Boldness, as the rabbis tell us, is a sine qua non of prophecy,[51] and Maimonides argues that prophecy will not be restored to Israel until she has regained autonomy in her land. In exile and subjection, the spiritual and insightful, who have the philosophic and poetic gifts of prophets, lack the confidence to proclaim their visions—or even to see them clearly.[52] When a Moses confronts Pharaoh, or a Nathan, armed with no more than a parable, traps the passionate King David into passing sentence on his own act (2 Samuel 12), or an Elijah (1 Kings 18:18) answers an Ahab: "It is not I who have troubled Israel, but thou and thy father's house, by abandoning the commandments of the Lord"—intellectual courage transmutes alienation into action. Prophecy is not an eremitic wailing but a vivid analysis of the source and remedy of grievance, a historical and political as well as moral vision, that refuses to sink into mere chronicling of national shames or royal glories. Here spiritual consciousness rises above mystic ascesis or sacerdotal sycophancy. As Amos says (3:8), voicing the compelling urgency that singles out a prophet: "The lion hath roared, who will not fear? The Lord God hath spoken, who can but prophesy?" The power of moral truth is never lost to the successors and heirs of the prophets. It grounds the right to free thought and free expression (cf. Job 4:2, 7:11) and retains a broader base in the imperative to truth and the need to impart it. Maimonides describes this inner urgency in the language of emanation (*Guide* II 11, 12). But he reads emanation itself by reference to the highest form of charity, which makes the recipient self-sufficient, modeling God's creative act, like a teacher's imparting of insight. As Plotinus said, a candle is not extinguished when it lights another; when an idea is shared, the gift does not diminish the giver.

Perhaps we catch sight of what is most universal in the Prophets when we see (despite romantic notions of orality) that they were a literate band, not mere isolated eccentrics ranting in the city gates or at the thrones of kings. They taught and wrote, trained up disciples and preserved the visions and words God had given them, as a heritage to endure beyond its moment. The desire to explain, to write books, to make others capable in thought, was itself an *imitatio Dei*. For God does not withhold but imparts truth, as He imparts being, to make His creatures, as it were, self-sufficient, allowing them to sustain their being, take charge of their lives, and pursue adequacy in their understanding—much as He is Self-sufficient in being, free in action, absolute in understanding, and rather proud of His own book.

THE WORK OF THE RABBIS

The Rabbis again recast and reconstruct, but still on the ancient Mosaic floor. The new idiom is studious, dialectical, respectful of sources, deferential to precedents, punctilious with distinctions. Superficially, the Rabbis seem to treat biblical precepts more as oracular springboards of homily and pegs of doctrine than as fixed legal dicta. Yet, beneath the apparent manhandling of language, they are profoundly sensitive to the moral and spiritual thematics as well as the jots and tittles of text.[53] They save the vital biblical norms in an alien, hostile, even overwhelming milieu, in part by intellectualizing the life of Torah, shifting praxis into realms of symbolic virtuality, or into the realm of conscience.[54] The Temple cult is not practiced but studied; prayer replaces sacrifice as a vehicle of spiritual expression, and repentance replaces sacrifice as a medium of atonement.[55] Civil and criminal laws that once regulated a society now become intellectual delights. Talmudic *haverim*, fellows of the Rabbinic collegiality, adopt the laws of Levitical purity, reenacting the old priestly role and laying claim to a spiritualized and intellectualized successorship to the Priests. As the laws of purity are extended to all Israel, every family table becomes a surrogate of the altar of the lost Temple in Jerusalem.[56]

The first task of the Sages who laid down the case law that grounds the Mishnah was to apply biblical legislation in concrete cases. In this sense these jurists (like American Supreme Court justices) were interpreters, not legislators. None of them was a Moses, or even a Hosea. Yet their concerns were profoundly practical. Safrai remarks of the Tannaim, the bearers of the traditions of practice codified in the Mishnah, that even their aggadah "is not like folklore, and does not contain spirits and fabulous creatures."[57] But as the discussions of Tannaitic decisions eddied and swirled to form the corpus that enlarges the Mishnaic code with the extensive and digressive commentary, the Gemara, much was swept into the discourse, of common sense, allegory, ritual fastidiousness, legend, logic, homily, rhetoric, hyperbole, superstition, wordplay, philosophy, anecdote, science, and lore. The engulfed material was of all degrees of relevance and all levels of sophistication. Narrowness and cosmopolitanism, cynicism and skepticism came together alongside their dialectical bedfellows, optimism, idealism, hope, credulity, and critical analysis.

Looking back on the priestly heritage, the Rabbis could sincerely mourn the loss of the Temple cult, with its clear-cut therapy of atonement "for all your sins," yet strike a melancholy ironic note, allowing for the case that the High Priest in the rites of atonement might well be an illiterate. Not the sons but the disciples of Aaron were the ideal.[58] The Temple cult and its world were gone. But the tragic loss was also an opening into which the Rabbis would build a way of life as far from the ways of the Priests as the Prophets were from the Patriarchs. All the while, the great moral and intellectual themes held steady; and, even as they innovated, the Rabbis could warrant new practice as "a reminiscence of the Sanctuary of Hillel's day."[59]

In the miniature history of Mishnah *Avot*, as Safrai points out, "The first saying, of the Men of the Great Assembly, sets down the requirement that the administration of justice be humanized"—this, he explains, is the meaning of "be cautious (*metunim*) in judgment," as the Rabbis' analysis, and ours, of the bias of biblical law clearly shows—"that a Sage raise many disciples, and that a 'fence' be made around the Tora."[60] The Torah itself mandates safeguarding the law (Deuteronomy 4:2). But it is the Rabbis who achieve this, by reapplying—broadening and narrowing—the Torah's themes, gleaned from the hints of its language. Thus even the "fence" or *seyag*, often thought of as a margin of rigor, is in fact a margin of safety, guarding the humane values of the Law. For, as we have seen, one cannot expand the requirements of any law without fathoming and framing its intentions.

Safrai sees more yet, as he lists the formative maxims of the rabbinic method: "The next saying states that the world is established on three pillars: Tora study, worship, and the doing of good deeds." The third voices the dictum of Antigonos urging service without view to a reward. "None of these views and conceptions are found in the Bible"—although they thematize its central concerns. All "are innovations of the Sages. Thus the programmatic opening of the tractate *Avot*, which states that it was from Moses and the Prophets that the Tora derives, in content testifies to the measure of creative innovation embodied in the oral Tora of the Sages."[61] As Novak remarks, "the Law itself requires judicial authority to be operative," but the very verse (Deuteronomy 17:11) that ordained strict adherence to juridical rulings "was used by the Rabbis to justify rabbinic innovation, that is, the rabbinic creation of positive law." Just as Abraham had to take his stand, morally speaking, so did the Rabbis: "the covenant seems to call forth not only a human response" but "human initiative," even "the limitation of revelation to make room for this essentially human contribution to the covenant."[62] Indeed, the Rabbis modeled revelation itself not on a tug-of-war, but on the more familiar dialectic of instruction, as a matter of co-creation. Thus, catching a hint of paradox in the words that cap the biblical account of Moses' receipt of the Decalogue, "when He finished speaking to him" (Exodus 31:18), they ask, "How could Moses have learned the whole of the Torah, whose measure is called 'greater than the earth' (Job 11:19)? Surely Moses was taught the principles"—and elaborated the rest on that basis.[63]

The very idea of an oral Torah was the vehicle of rabbinic creativity and of the humanization that was its goal. As Safrai explains:

> Even where many details are given in the Written Tora, Oral Tora may not only explain and further specify, but also introduce substantial innovations. Deut. 26:1–11 gives a detailed description of the commandment of first fruits or *bikkurim*, a subject which is further elaborated in the Mishnah tractate *Bikkurim*. In fact, however, there is much new material, such as detailed halakhot stating that *bikkurim* are not to be brought from fields which are under suspicion of having been stolen . . . It is also stated that proselytes may bring but do not recite [the festive declaration] because of the formulation "which God swore to our fathers to give to us" (Deut. 26:3). But one Tanna teaches: "A proselyte . . . may bring and declare. Why? —'And thou [Abraham] shalt be the father of a multitude of nations' (Gen. 17:5)."
>
> Although the roots of these sayings and halakhot can be pointed out in the Tora and the Prophets, it is evident that they imply a substantial further development. Indeed, in a historical perspective, it appears that Second Temple Judaism, and especially the Pharisees and their predecessors, did humanize the court system, attract a great number of students, make "fences" around the Tora, etc. Rather than just a commentary on the Written Tora, Oral Tora in this perspective represents a new creative development which sprang from deep religious sources. It represents the will to fulfil the commission imposed on man, spelled out in ritual or inter-human commandments in religious and ethical teachings.[64]

The fixity that was a bastion of stability and fairness in the written Law challenged the ingenuity of the jurists. The idea of a parallel oral law gave them the flexibility to create without seeming radically to innovate, and without departing from the framework of the written Torah. Thus the insistence that the oral law (as long as it was evolving) remain oral. This is not nostalgia for a preliterate age; the Mosaic Torah itself mandates that its Law be written. But orality gave room to creativity. As Rabbi Yannai put it

> Had the Torah been given cut and dry, no one could stand on his feet. Why? "And the Lord said unto Moses . . ." —Said Moses unto Him: Lord of the universe, tell me, just how is the halakha? He said unto him "Turn aside after the majority" (Exodus 23:2); if the majority exonerate, the accused is exonerated, but if they convict, he is convicted. Therefore, the Tora must be studied both according to the forty-nine ways to declare impure and according to the forty-nine ways to declare pure.[65]

The Written Torah itself requires that judges exercise discretion. So they must study each issue and point of law dialectically. The Oral Torah is the stage on which they do so, and when it is written it becomes the record of their deliberations. As Falk remarks, "Study allows the sage not only to identify himself with the Torah, but to become a Master of the Torah, a title which should actually be reserved to God alone."[66]

Attuned to the idioms and institutions of a traditional society, Aristotle understood the position well. Facing Plato's ambivalence between the rule of law and that of men, he found a middle ground in custom and custodianship:

> even if it be better for certain individuals to govern, they should be made only guardians and ministers of the law. For magistrates there must be [cf. Deuteronomy 16:18]. . . . There may indeed be cases which the law seems unable to determine, but such cases a man could not determine either. But the law trains officers for just this purpose and appoints them to determine matters left undecided by it to the best of their judgment. Further, it permits them to make any amendment of the existing laws which experience suggests. So he who bids the law rule may be deemed to bid God and reason alone rule, but he who bids man rule adds an element of the beast; for desire is a wild beast, and passion perverts the minds of rulers, even when they are the best of men.   (*Politics* 3:16, 1287a 21–31)

Rabbinic creativity is never radical or arbitrary, nor even adversarial, although it is dialectical. The innovation it values does not uproot but brings to fruition the themes of the written Torah. But innovation it is. Thus, reflecting on their own creative role, the Rabbis remark that the laws of release from vows, "hover in the air without support"; the detailed legislation of the Sabbath, the Festival Offerings, and sacrilege "are like mountains hanging by a hair, for Scripture here is sparse and the laws many" (Mishnah *Hagigah* 1.8). Juridical practice often established halakhah, and popular usage could void it. Thus the Sages' ban on gentile oil was overturned, since the ruling was not accepted in practice. The fanciful, often tenuous Midrashic links of Halakhah to Scripture, are frequently forged long after the legislative fact;[67] their verbal elan is emblematic of the equally subtle legislative creativity that they underwrite. Such creativity was both self-conscious and normative. Rabbi Joshua, revealingly, asks two disciples what innovation (*iddush*) they have learned in the House of Study; when they demur with traditionalist cant, "We are your disciples and it is of your water that we drink," he admonishes them: "The House of Study cannot exist without innovation." The new idea they go on to report is a gloss of Rabbi Elazar ben Azariah's, which ends: "Just as a plant bears fruit and multiplies, so do the words of the Torah bear fruit and multiply."[68]

Some of what unfolds as a rabbinic way of life and thought will prove stultifying, narrow. or superstitious. The sifting of sense from nonsense in the rabbinic corpus is not yet completed. Indeed, it has barely begun. Yet for the critical and watchful, these veins yield gold. Commenting on a particularly astute affirmation by the Sages of divine transcendence, Maimonides remarks, "Would that all their words were like it!" (*Guide* 1:59). The miasma of some rabbinic passages renders all the more brilliant and beaconlike their core thematic insights. Many are pertinent to our theme: rabbinic bookishness bespeaks an intellectualism that is no unworthy reflex of the spiritual purity and earnestness of the prophetic books and that blossoms as a reverence for the intrinsic value of learning; Torah for its own sake becomes its motto.[69] Study of Torah, of the rabbinic apprehensions of God's Law, becomes a value tantamount to the entire prescriptive content of the Law itself.[70] Such study is an open-ended quest, but that fact creates no sense of the defeat that prior generations felt at the thought of unending exploration.[71]

The subject active in such study is the individual, abetted by a catena of study partners who link, mind-to-mind, with the lively community of fellow scholars in all lands and ages. The goal is individual understanding. Paradoxically, but perhaps predictably, the maturation of Talmudic study as a way of life led to a hardening and narrowing of independent explorations for those who worked within the set tradition. Yet it called forth, even demanded, the most independent explorations for those who ventured forth from it, in or even near its penumbra, to test its categories, claims, and values in the larger world which was their proper sphere.

Practical fulfillment of the Torah is not discarded by the Rabbis; but it undergoes a sea change in their hands. The Tannaim (first century B.C. to second century C.E.) and Amoraim (second century and after) made it their task to concretize the biblical norms, define their boundaries, marshal them into system. Some brittleness in the new complex was perhaps inevitable. But limits were consciously set to the growth of rigorism and the overgrowth of legalism. The biblical commandments and the rabbinic ordinances that interpreted them (e.g., the daily putting on of phylacteries for prayer to fulfill the commandment to keep God's imperatives constantly before one's eyes and "bind them for a sign upon thy hand"—Deuteronomy 11:18) were to be performed, as we have seen, not slavishly but "for the sake of heaven" (*Avot* 2.12, cf. 1.3, 2.4)—as intrinsic goods. Since the *mitzvot* were the will of God, their performance made them acts of worship and spiritual expression, quite apart from their proximate or specific functions. Thus each moment was to be infused with awareness of God's presence, imparting holiness to all creaturely acts, an aim not unworthy of the prophetic spirit or out of keeping with the Mosaic goal of making all Israel, as the bold metaphor had put it, a nation of priests. Even when exile and persecution had robbed the Torah of its full robustness as a political, military, economic, and social code, the surviving community, the providential remnant foreseen by the prophets (e.g., Zephaniah 3:13), could still infuse communal and personal life with the mission of holiness (cf. *Avot* 2.19) and could keep it alive in practice—in marriage and family law, commercial dealings among Israelites, communal affairs, intellectual and devotional exercises, the dietary laws, Sabbath observances, and the calendar of festivals and fasts.

The ultimate subject, in all these dimensions of what came to be called Jewish life, was again the individual, articulated in the community and given a role and a goal by its norms, but still a freely choosing subject, whose life could be made an act of worship, by the inclination of the will. The perfection of individual life remained the aim. True, the notion that observance was an end in itself fed upon rabbinic legalism to generate a kind of legal positivism.[72] But the same rabbinic idea, of the intrinsic value of the *mitzvot* as God's commandments, allowed the moral, spiritual, and intellectual values that underlie the commandments to percolate through them to every aspect of life, throughout each workday, Sabbath, or festival, imparting the intensionalities of holiness to each act or gesture and forging a diction of piety that gave meaning even to what might seem the most trivial of human choices. Again the task of sifting legalism (and the obscurantism, authoritarianism, dogmatism, patriarchalism that were parasitic upon it) from authentic devotion (and its accompanying adventure of the mind and spirit) rested on the individual, the same who was the subject and the victim or beneficiary of the system at large. As Elijah, the Gaon of Wilna, remarked (the tradition in my family is that both of my mother's parents were descendants of his): Torah, like rain, nourishes both beneficial plants and noxious weeds (ad. Proverbs 24:31, 25:4). Individual human choices, modulating the tasks of human living, determine whether beautiful or ugly characters emerge from engagement with the Law. For, as Spinoza shows (*Ethics* 4, Prop. 4, Cor.), the difference between piety or humanity and self-serving pride is wholly a matter of intention.

Both Bible and Talmud are the products of many hands and many centuries. If we include within the literature of rabbinic discourse the Responsa, Codes, Midrashic elaborations of the legal (halakhic) and narrative (aggadic) phases of the tradition, we can see rabbinic literature continuing down to the present day. The Torah, by contrast, speaks in so commanding a voice that only commentaries remain possible: imitations reek of parody; and even commentaries typically fall prey to their material, submerged in the authority of the text, gasping free of it in clever or irrelevant homilies, or embedded in it, free only to trace its themes and stories, expatiate on its words, elaborate on its laws, compare readings of its sense, dissociate or reassociate its strands and elements, or otherwise catch hold of its beauties or grow lost in its forests. Some of us today may strive to recast a way of life or thought congruent with the scriptural themes; but few rise to a synthetic grasp of Torah's values and ideas. The Talmud is a help in this. For it can open a window on the scriptural world—but only when Scripture itself is not submerged, reduced to the hand-maid of rabbinics.

Talmudic discourse, with its Aramaic jargon and technical shorthand, has its great strength in its dialectical character. Glossing God's "Let us make . . ." in Genesis (1:26), the Rabbis remark that even God commences nothing with-out consultation.[73] With rare exceptions (like the sustained forensic dialogue of the Book of Job, or the inner psychological dialogue of Ecclesiastes or the dream dialogue of the Song of Songs) the biblical voice is not dialogic. Prophecy speaks with the authority of God Himself. Rarely does it expect an answer. Rabbinically there is constant conversation and cross talk, voices rais-ing and addressing problems about the Torah or one another's proposals and their implications—sometimes in a dialectic that extends across centuries. No possibly relevant corner of experience, science, or lore is irrelevant. That any-thing more than noise should be heard in this welter of voices is a tribute to the coherence of the rabbinic problematic and the discipline of the redactors. The exposition is anything but thematic. Yet, to scholars intimate with the written and "oral" canon, a remark in any sector can instantly illuminate any other, with never a fear that the insight will be less than germane. It is dialogue in this community of discourse that hones rabbinic thought and renders it self-critical, much as moral tact and cosmic wonder give the critical edge to prophetic discourse.

Reading carefully in the Torah, the Rabbis note that it is only after the creation of humanity that the world is described as "*very* good" (Genesis 1:31). Rabbinic humanism is the fairest fruit of the two thousand years of rabbinic reflection on biblical themes. The full rigor of the legalism and pro-ceduralism they derive from the Torah mitigates the severities and asperities of the Torah itself. Thus the laws of evidence and testimony are forged into a powerful obstacle to capital punishment: Not only must two witnesses concur independently and in circumstantial detail before the presumption of innocence gives way in capital cases, but there must also have been explicit and immediate warning to the criminal for an offense to count as capital.[74] Self-incriminating testimony is not admissible. For, it is argued, a person may have a desire to die.[75] Duress is out of the question. Ancient sur-vivals like the "bitter waters" are thickly hedged with restrictions (Numbers 5:12–29), rendering them legally moot and inoperative.[76] Simeon ben Shetah (ca. 80–50 B.C.), a militant judicial activist of the days of Alexander Yannai, avowed,

May I [never] see consolation[77] if I did not see one man chase another into a ruin; I ran after him, and saw a sword in his hand, the blood dripping, and the slain still twitching. I said: "Villain! Who killed this man? Either you or I, but what am I to do? Your blood is not given into my hands. For the Torah said: 'By testimony of two witnesses . . . shall he who is to die be put to death' (Deuteronomy 17:6)." May He who knows men's thoughts undo the man who slew his comrade.

(*Sanhedrin* 37b)[78]

Simeon had few compunctions about capital punishment.[79] But the Law made such punishment rare. In time, a court that issued one death sentence in seven years would be called a bloody Sanhedrin (Mishnah *Makkot* 1.10). Similarly, as Safrai remarks, "the laws of the 'rebellious son' which are laid down in Deuteronomy 21:18–21 are so radically limited by Tannaic halakha, that Tannaic tradition itself drew the conclusion: 'The rebellious son never was and never shall be' " (Sanhedrin 71a).[80]

The humanism that fosters strong presumptions in favor of the accused pervades rabbinic jurisprudence. Breaching any commandment—save those against idolatry, sexual license, and murder—is permitted, indeed required, to save a human life (*Sanhedrin* 74a). The prooftext: "You shall observe My institutions and My ordinances, which a man shall perform and live by. I am the Lord" (Leviticus 18:5). The idea of a law of life is taken here in a strong sense, making preservation and enhancement of life cardinal principles of the Law:[81] One may break the Sabbath to save a human life or even to relieve pain.[82] Cattle must be milked on the Sabbath, to prevent "the suffering of living beings." A pregnant woman's cravings permit her to eat on the Day of Atonement—since they might be signals of vital needs. And ravenous hungers must be fed—if need be, even by breaking the dietary laws.[83]

Rabbinic humanism is typified in the Mishnaic agricultural laws: seeking definition of the corners of the field biblically to be left unharvested for the poor, the Rabbis discover that their size, like the measure of good deeds in general, has no upper limit (Mishnah *Peah* 1.1). They specify a minimum but leave the maximum open and praise a community that harvests with a rope (presumably to save labor) and so augments the portion of the poor. They also extend the laws of the corner to a wide variety of crops (*Peah* 1.4). Understanding the nisus of the law, they can act confidently to expand its coverage without concern that they might unwittingly undermine some unfathomable hidden purpose.

Taking it as an axiom that the Torah's laws exist to promote and enhance human lives, the Rabbis lay down rules to regulate wages, hours, commerce, prices and profits (*Bava Batra* 8b). Their mandate, the spirit of the laws that forbid retaining a day worker's wages overnight or taking a millstone in pledge (Exodus 22:25–26, Deuteronomy 24:6, 10–12). Similarly, they find a mandate in the Torah for free universal education.[84] Even the "natural law" of self-preservation is bent to the demands of moral principle. To kill a would-be murderer is to prevent his sin, not merely "self-defense" (Mishnah *Sanhedrin* 8.6–7).[85] Only a presumption of deadly intent, not the protection of property, allows the use of deadly force against a burglar (Exodus 22:1); and one must not commit a murder even to save one's own life. If ordered to murder another or die, one must rather die, the Talmud ordains, resting on the presumption of existential equality we have noted: "Who knows that your blood is redder than his. Perhaps his blood is redder than yours" (*Pesaim* 25b, *Sanhedrin* 74a). Even to save a group one may not single out one member for death or defilement—"Better to let all be defiled than to betray a single soul of Israel."[86]

The Rabbis took seriously their task of interpreting the Law at its point of application. They freely used their authority, Sinaitic in their understanding, even to reverse the plain sense of biblical *mitzvot*, if it seemed to counter the Torah's larger thrust. They treated their boldest departures as self-evident, appealing to the canon at large to inform their inferences (*asmakhta*)[87] and proudly pictured Moses as unable to follow their technical debates. Even signs from Heaven could not overrule their majority vote. For was it not written that the Torah is no longer in heaven but on earth? The responsibility to interpret it is ours, not God's.[88] Reading the biblical accounts of actions that seemed lawless by their standards, the Rabbis embroidered their own legalism and proceduralism over complete episodes. Their amazing synchronicity ironed flat entire epochs of history but opened the whole body of scripture as a living florilegium of exempla. From the biblical injunction against destroying fruit trees in time of siege (Deuteronomy 20:19–20) they drew the categorical *mitzvah* they saw as the underlying premise: "Thou shalt not wantonly destroy" (*bal tashit*).[89] The method typifies their approach: The laws separating meat from dairy foods and utensils elaborate upon the repeated biblical injunction against seething a kid in its mother's milk;[90] the laws of slaughter (*shehittah*) again elaborate on biblical requirements, reaching an optimum, Maimonides argues, in balancing the concerns of humaneness and household economy.[91]

To elaborate a law one must grasp the values it seeks to serve. Otherwise, one could as easily forbid joining the *names* of milk and meat or the purchase of leather from improperly slaughtered animals. With an understanding of the relation of the dietary laws to the ideals of purity and peace, the Mosaic nisus grows clear, and modalities of elaboration can be debated. Hillel could confidently claim that in going to the baths he was fulfilling a *mitzvah*. His argument: if the Romans wash and scour the statues of their emperor set up in the theaters and circuses, and think this a worthy task and an honorable occupation, how much more should we, created in God's image, respect the human body and its form. But behind the midrashic argument stands the clear biblical thematic, here directly cited: "The pious man looks after himself" (Proverbs 11:17).

Guiding the entire progress of rabbinic elaboration is the delicately balanced assumption that perfection of human life is the Law's concern and that no human being lives a fulfilled life in isolation. Our condition is one of interdependence, and the very possibility of human dignity depends on mutual recognition, generosity of thought and action.[92]

If we draw together and sum up the values we encounter in the Mosaic, prophetic, and rabbinic norms about the individual and the community we find economic autonomy as the root and fruit of freedom. Immense value is placed on creative thought and productive work.[93] But the individual is not reducible to social or economic functions. We are valued for what we are, not just for being "useful" or "productive" members of society. These two facts are linked: Economic autonomy underwrites spiritual dignity and intellectual independence; these in turn are not simply ends in themselves. For the mind and heart belong to the ethical and intellectual subject. And it is the perfection of the human subject that the Law pursues. Supporting the dignity of that subject, we find a strict legalism and proceduralism, in the service not just of social order but of individual rights, conceived in terms of positive human deserts of well being and of privacy. Personal interest here includes the moral, social, and spiritual dimensions of our identity. Distinctive institutions— laws, myths, and rituals—serve to enhance our moral development and to evoke spiritual discovery. Dialogue, criticism, and comparison strike off the rough edges of tradition, burnishing and polishing the values at the core. Crowning the system are the commitments of rabbinic humanism. In the values it articulates and in subtly shifting the angle of a judge's seat from that of arbiter to that of arbitrator, this tradition still has much to offer the global culture in which it arises.

The life the Law was given to preserve and perfect is the life of the individual. The Rabbis underscore the value of that life when they write homiletically that to slay a single human being is like destroying the world; and to save a single life, like saving the world. The thought is not just of the progeny who might have descended from one couple, but of human uniqueness: ordinary mortal craftsmen, they argue, form things in a mold, and every casting is alike. But when the Holy One, blessed be He, creates human beings, no two are identical.[94] Each holds an irreplaceable world of possibilities; each is sacred. Shmuel Sambursky, the Israeli physicist and historian of cosmology, used to compare this rabbinic teaching with the vexations of Greek philosophers over the idea of uniqueness: from Plato, who placed value, truth, being, and even unity at the plane of the universal, to Aristotle, who argued that there is no science of the individual and that what individuates particulars is accidental to their true being, down to the late Neoplatonists, who struggled with the notion of a universal yet personal "guardian spirit," and Averroes, who held that you and I are the same individual but for the matter that divides us, all of the thinkers who followed the gnomic counsel of Heraclitus, "Look to the common," were bemused by individuality and tended to equate uniqueness with idiosyncrasy and hence irrationality.

Following their biblically mediated intuitions, the Rabbis find uniqueness precious: each human being, like God, is unique. Each is like a species, exploring and pressing the boundaries of its nature, seeking to transcend its world of possibilities. The value of community is attendant on this prior value. Aristotle showed the value of the community by arguing that man by nature is a social animal. It is because of our social nature that our virtues and vices are culturally mediated and socially defined—affability, niggardliness, magnificence, magnanimity. The Torah, founding not only a system of law but a way of life, addresses the same fact, our social nature, in its own language: mythic where Aristotle is speculative, historic and particular where Aristotle is scientific and universal, intimate and normative where Aristotle is clinical and descriptive. It records (Genesis 2:18): "And the Lord God said, 'It is not good for the man to be alone.' "

NOTES

1. *Sefer Ha-ukkim* (The Statutes of Israel) 1980, 163, officially translated as *Laws of the State of Israel* (*L.S.I.*). The 1980 principle was founded on Israel's Declaration of Independence, 1948 (1 *L.S.I.* 3): "The State of Israel . . . will foster the development of the country for the benefit of all its inhabitants; it will be based on freedom, justice, and peace as envisaged by the prophets of Israel." The Supreme Court of Israel ruled that the Declaration did not have constitutional or legal force but did express "the vision of the people and its credo" and contain "the guiding principles for the interpretation of statutes." Zeev *v.* Acting District Officer of Tel Aviv, *H.C.* 10/48, in *Selected Judgments of the Supreme Court of Israel* 68, and Shtreit *v.* the Chief Rabbi of Israel, *H.C.* 301/63, 18 *P.D.* 11/598.

2. "And there they became a nation," Deuteronomy 26:5; Passover *Hagaddah*.

3. See C. L. Becker, *The Heavenly City of the Eighteenth-Century Philosophers* (New Haven: Yale University Press, 1968; 1932); J. M. Cuddihy, *The Ordeal of Civility* (New York: Oxford University Press, 1974); Peter Gay, *Freud, Jews, and Other Germans* (New York: Oxford University Press, 1978; Eugene Kamenka, *The Ethical Foundations of Marxism* (London: Routledge, 1972; 1962).

This chapter was written for the present book at the request of Irene Bloom and revised for inclusion in my book *God of Abraham*, published by Oxford University Press in 1995. It appears here by permission.

4. Exodus 21:1–6, Deuteronomy 15:12–18. Some modern commentators think that the law banning return of fugitive slaves (Deuteronomy 23:16) could never have been enforced, since its effect would have been to abolish involuntary servitude. That, I believe, was the intent.

5. "In contrast to temples in other cultures, the Jerusalem Temple did not possess land . . . a man would be disgraced for selling the 'field of possession,' even as a man would be glorified for redeeming his meadow and thus reclaiming it. . . . The great influence of this ruling can be seen from the fact that for generations after the destruction of the Temple most of the land in Palestine remained in the possession of small farmers. Even the *colonatus* laws of the later Roman administration were only introduced in Palestine toward the end of the fourth century, considerably later than was normal in the Roman Empire." Shmuel Safrai, *The Literature of the Sages First Part: Oral Tora, Halakha, Mishna, Tosefta, Talmud, External Tractates* (Assen and Philadelphia: Van Gorcum and Fortress Press, 1987), p. 132.

6. See Neal Soss, "Old Testament Law and Economic Society," *JHI* 34 (1973): 323–44; cf. Henry George's appreciation of Moses.

7. See Francis Galton, *Hereditary Genius* (London: Macmillan, 1925; 1869), pp. 33–40, 343–45; Garrett Hardin, "Living on a Lifeboat," *Bioscience* 24 (1974): 561–68.

8. Cf. Isaiah 45:18; Mishnah *Yevamot* 6.6, *Gittin* 4.5: procreation is a good and central to God's purpose in creating the universe.

9. For the rabbinic ideal of economic self-sufficiency, see *Avot de Rabbi Nathan* 31, ed. A. Cohen, *Minor Tractates of the Talmud* (London: Soncino, 1984), p. 29a.

10. Hillel established the device known as the *prosbul* (lit. "for the Court"), fictively transmuting private debts into public obligations, to mitigate the effects of biblical remission (*shemittah*), by preserving credit even in the face of the Sabbatical year. His authority was Deuteronomy 15:9; see Mishnah *Shevi'it* 10.3, in *The Mishnah*, tr. Herbert Danby (Oxford: Oxford University Press, 1933; reprinted, 1977), p. 51. See Ze'ev W. Falk's discussion of the evolution of the norm, from a moral suasion to a formal institution, *Religious Law and Ethics: Studies in Biblical and Rabbinical Theonomy* (Jerusalem: Mesharim, 1991), pp. 101–2.

11. Deuteronomy 15:7–8; *Sifre* Re'eh 116, ad loc., ed. S. Zuckerman and S. Luria (Wilna: Fine and Rosenkrantz, 1866); Deuteronomy 27:19; Isaiah 10:1, 3:14–15, 1:16–17; Proverbs 3:27; Ben Sirah 4:3 and 34:21, ed. E. J. Goodspeed (Chicago: University of Chicago Press, 1965; 1938); Josephus, *Antiquities* xx 9.7, LCL 9:505; *Against Apion* ii 27. "A community that has no synagogue and no shelter for the poor must first provide for the poor," Judah ben Samuel he-Hasid (d. 1217), *Sefer Hasidim*, ed. J. Wistinetzki, (Frankfurt: Wahrmann, 1924), pp. 374–75; cf. *Tosefta* Peah 4.9: Refusal to give charity is tantamount to idolatry. *Shabbat* 104a: charity must "run after the poor," not passively await them. For the institutions that realize these ideals, see J. Bergmann, *Ha-Tzedakah be-Yisrael* (Jerusalem: Sifre Tarshish, 1944; repr. 1975).

12. Maimonides, *Code* VII 2, Gifts to the Poor 10.7, tr. Isaac Klein (New Haven: Yale University Press, 1979), p. 91: "The highest rank, which is unsurpassed, is that of one who upholds the hand of an Israelite reduced to poverty by giving him a grant or loan, entering into partnership with him, or finding him work, to strengthen his hand, so that he need not beg. Of this Scripture says, 'Thou shalt sustain him; as a client and a resident shall he live with thee' (Leviticus 25:35)." I translate according to Maimonides' sense and Saadiah's understanding of the *ger* as a client, which the Rambam here adopts. Cf. Isaac Napaha ad

Isaiah 58:8 ff. in Bava Batra 9b; Louis Jacobs, *Religion and the Individual: A Jewish Perspective* (Cambridge: Cambridge University Press, 1992), pp. 25–27.

13. Spinoza, *Ethics* 3 Prop. 43; 4 Prop. 46.

14. Deuteronomy 4:1, 5:30, 8:1, 16:20, 30:6, 16, 19; Leviticus 18:5; *Avot* 4.24.

15. Maimonides, *Code* XIV, I Sanhedrin 20.4–5, tr. A. M. Hershman (New Haven: Yale University Press, 1967; 1949), pp. 60–61. Sarna glosses "thy poor" as "Those who depend on you for justice." *Jewish Publication Society Torah Commentary: Exodus.*

16. See G. R. Driver and John C. Miles, tr., *The Babylonian Laws* (Oxford: Clarendon Press, 1955), 1:17, 2:500.

17. Cicero abused legality in claiming that Catiline's conspiracy denied him access to the machinery of justice.

18. I translate in accordance with the traditional reading adopted in the codes. The Jewish Publication Society translation parses verse 18 to make the Levitical priest the actual scribe, but the constitutional theme is unaffected.

19. Driver and Miles, tr. *The Babylonian Laws*, 2:83, 47, 79.

20. Moshe Greenberg, "Some Postulates of Biblical Criminal Law," in J. Goldin, ed., *The Jewish Expression* (New Haven: Yale University Press, 1976), pp. 18–37.

21. The concept is biblical. In the *Jewish Publication Society Torah Commentary: Numbers*, Jacob Milgrom explains that the word *mishpat* in the seemingly odd phrase *ukkat mishpat* (Numbers 35:29) means procedure. Thus: "Such shall be your law of procedure"—your judicial or procedural rule, the law that regulates the administration of justice.

22. See Job 10:2, 15; 13:15, 18; 14:17; cf. Shevu'ot 31a; and see my commentary on Saadiah's *Book of Theodicy*, Introduction, p. 35, n. 8.

23. See *God of Abraham*, ch. 7.

24. Albert Einstein, September 15, 1933, *Out of My Later Years* (New York: Philosophical Library, 1950), p. 23; cf. Henri Bergson, *Two Sources of Morality and Religion*, tr. R. A. Audra and C. Brereton, p. 95. See Midrash *Tanhuma* Nitzavim, 25a; Philo, *De Decalogo* X 36–43, LCL 7:23–29; with *De Confus. Ling.*, XXXVII 183–198, 4:111–19; Louis Brandeis, *The Jewish Problem and How to Solve It* (New York: Zionist Essays Publication Committee, 1915), p. 5; Yehiel Michael of Zlotchov ap. Martin Buber, *The Way of Man According to the Teachings of Hasidism* (London: Routledge, 1950), p. 17; Zusya in M. Buber, *Tales of the Hasidim*, tr. Olga Marx (New York: Schocken, 1947–1948), 1:251; Buber's *Between Man and Man*, tr. R. G. Smith (New York: Macmillan, 1947), p. 200.

25. For Job's monogamy, see Ginzberg, *Legends of the Jews*, tr. Szold, 2:241.

26. See Maimonides, "Eight Chapters," 4; cf. *Code* 1: The Book of Knowledge; 2: Ethical Laws 6. 8, ed. Hyamson, 55b.

27. Cf. H. A. Alexander, "The Critical Temper in Judaism," separatum (Los Angeles: University of Judaism, 1985).

28. *Guide* 3:26–28, 2;40, ed. Munk, 3:57–62, 2:85–87.

29. *Nicomachaean Ethics* 2; cf. Plato, *Laws* 719E-720; *Guide* 3:33, Munk 3:73–74.

30. *Guide* 3:28, Munk, 3:60b-62; cf. Ibn Tufayl, *Hayy Ibn Yaqzan*, Goodman, 156, 161–65.

31. *Guide* 3:35, Munk, 3:75–77.

32. *Guide* 2:6, 12, 36–38, 3:17; 5:18; Munk 2:16–18, 24b-26b, 77b-83b, 3:34b, 37b-39.

33. Maimonides, *Book of the Commandments*, tr. Chavel. The Mishnah Commentary, written in Arabic, is the *Kitab al-Siraj* or *Perush ha-Mishnah*, tr. Fred Rosner (New York:

Feldheim, 1975). The Code is the *Mishneh Torah*, called the *Yad Hazakah*; the YJS English translation is nearing completion.

34. Maimonides, *Guide* 3:12, ed. Munk, 3:18–22.

35. Maimonides, *Guide* 3:34, 2:40, 3:26–28, 32, 1:2, ed. Munk, 3:74b-75, 2:85–87, 3.57–62, 3:69–73, 1.13–14b.

36. Cf. David Bohm, *Causality and Chance in Modern Physics* (London: Routledge, 1957), pp. 130–46.

37. See my "Mythic Discourse" in *Myths and Fictions*, ed. B. Scharfstein and S. Biderman (Leiden: Brill, 1993). pp. 51–112.

38. For the origins of the *risālah* form, see my "The Greek Impact on Arabic Literature," in *The Cambridge History of Arabic Literature: Arabic Literature to the End of the Umayyad Period* (Cambridge: Cambridge University Press, 1984), pp. 460–82; cited here, page 476.

39. I speak of statutory rape, since the verb *yifateh* entails seduction. But Dinah was not seduced but "humbled" by Shechem (*va-ye'aneha*—Genesis 34:2).

40. Falk, *Religious Law and Ethics*, p. 54; cf. p. 119.

41. Edith Hamilton, *Spokesmen for God: The Great Teachers of the Old Testament* (New York: Norton, 1949), pp. 99–100.

42. M. Jastrow, "*Ro'eh* and *ozeh* in the Old Testament," *Journal of Biblical Literature* 28 (1909): 56: a prophet's "main purpose is to speak out in the name of a Deity, to speak forth rather than foretell"; R. H. Charles, *A Critical and Exegetical Commentary on the Book of Daniel* (Oxford: Oxford University Press, 1929). As Harry Orlinsky writes, "it is sad that scholars continue to refuse to distinguish between the diviner-seer (foreteller) and the prophet (forthteller), i.e., between the likes of an Eli, Samuel, the unnamed 'men of God,' Nathan, Ahijah, and Elisha (from the eleventh to the ninth centuries)—all of whom were diviners and attached to shrines or to diviner guilds or orders, and constitute a phenomenon common to the ancient Near East—and those like Hosea, Amos, Isaiah, and Micah, who make their appearance after about 800 b.c.e. and are a uniquely Israelite phenomenon," in Baron, Wise, and Goodman, *Violence and Defense* (Philadelphia: Jewish Publication Society, 1977), p. 57; cf. Orlinsky's *Essays in Biblical Culture*, pp. 39–65.

43. Saadiah, *ED* 3:6, Kafih, p. 130; Saadiah Gaon, *The Book of Beliefs and Opinions*, tr. Samuel Rosenblatt (New Haven: Yale University Press, 1948; reprinted 1967), p. 155; see *God of Abraham*, ch. 6..

44. Richard Bergren, *The Prophets and the Law* (Cincinnati: HUC, 1974), esp. pp. 182–83; cf. Numbers Rabbah 11.7. Zedekiah's rescinded emancipation proclamation on the lifting of Nebuchadnezzar's siege (Jeremiah 34) provokes a "prophetic judgment speech," although the offense seems to violate a non-"apodictic" law, the sabbatical release of slaves (Deuteronomy 15:12–15). But the real offense, Bergren argues (pp. 68–79), was against a covenant with God, since besieged Jerusalem had sworn to free the slaves. This cuts matters very fine. For Jeremiah stresses that real penitence was demanded—concretely, restoration of the Torah's remission of slavery. The people had broken their bond, but in doing so had reverted to ignoring God's law.

45. Falk lists "the duty to restore lost objects (Deuteronomy 22:1–3), the exemption of the mill from seizure in distress (Deuteronomy 24:6), the duty to restore a pledge at dawn (Deuteronomy 24:10–11), as well as the provisions in favor of employees (Deuteronomy 24:14–15) and of disadvantaged persons (Deuteronomy 24:17–22)" as paradigm cases of

moral rules. He adds that the prohibition of false weights and measures (Deuteronomy 25:13–16) appeals to conscience rather than to public sanctions. Falk, *Religious Law and Ethics*, p. 71.

46. Cf. 2 Samuel 15, Hosea 6:3; Jeremiah 22:16, 31:34.

47. See Phyllis Trible, "Depatriarchalizing Biblical Interpretation," *Journal of the American Academy of Religion* 41 (1973): 30–48, repr. in Elizabeth Koltun, ed., *The Jewish Woman: New Perspectives* (New York: Schocken, 1976), pp. 217–41: "Israel repudiated the idea of sexuality in God . . . the nature of God in Israel defies sexism"; cf. Trible's *God and the Rhetoric of Sexuality* (Philadelphia: Fortress Press, 1978); Virginia Ramey Mollenkott, *The Divine Feminine: The Biblical Imagery of God as Female* (New York: Crossroad, 1983).

48. See Amos 9:7; Israel is not alone in being saved from slavery: The Syrians, Cushites, and Philistines too have been redeemed by God.

49. See Malachi 1:11. God judges all nations. Damascus, Philistia, Tyre, Edom, Moab are not immune (Amos 1–2). For universal peace, Isaiah 11:6–9, 2:4; Micah 4:3, mimicking and reversing Joel 3:10.

50. Isaiah 2:3, 11:6; Maimonides, *Code*, Book of Judges: Kings and Wars, 11–12, tr. A. Hershman (New Haven: Yale University Press, 1963; 1949), pp. 238–42.

51. Genesis Rabbah 27; Maimonides, *Guide* 1:46, 2: 38, ed. Munk, 1:49b-53, 2:82–83b.

52. *Shabbat* 92a, *Nedarim* 38a; *Guide* 2:36; 3:18; ed. Munk, 2:80, 3:38–39.

53. For the Rabbis' technique of making biblical themes explicit, see Max Kaddushin, *The Rabbinic Mind* (New York: JTS, 1952); *A Conceptual Approach to the Mekhilta* (New York: JTS, 1969).

54. "Halakhah in general could function as a legal system only by authority of the state. Lacking recognition, Halakhah became a system of morality and entirely lost its legal character. Take, for example, the abolition of Jewish criminal jurisdiction by the Roman administration, even before the destruction of the Temple. As a result, most of the rules of tractate Sanhedrin became social conventions of the rabbis and their followers, and were no longer law. This was a decisive step in the privatization of Halakhah." Falk, *Religious Law and Ethics*, p. 100, cf. p. 115.

55. "How did they order the matter in the days of fasting? They used to bring out the Ark into the open space in the town and put wood ashes on the Ark and on the heads of the President and the Head of the Court; and each one took ashes and put them on his head. The eldest of them then uttered these words of admonition: 'Brethren, it is not written of the men of Nineveh (Jonah 3:10) that God saw their sack cloth and their fasting,' but that 'God saw their deeds, that they turned away from their evil way,' and in the Prophets, 'Rend your heart, not your garments' (Joel 2:13)." (Mishnah *Ta'anit* 2.1). Safrai remarks: "The essence of repentance is to leave the path of sin and to decide not to return to it. . . . fasting is considered only a means of awakening man to repentance." Safrai, *Literature of the Sages*, p. 118.

56. See Jacob Neusner, *Judaism: The Evidence of the Mishnah* (Chicago: University of Chicago Press, 1981); *Avot* 2.13; Safrai, pp. 126, 129.

57. Safrai, p. 84.

58. See Mishnah *Yoma* 1.6; cf. the advisory role of the *parhedrin* (palhedrin) toward the High Priest, *Yoma* 1.1, a projection of the rabbinic role. For the disciples of Aaron, see *Yoma* 91b; Mishnah *Avot* 1.12; E. E. Urbach in Baron, Wise, and Goodman, *Violence and Defense*, pp. 89–90; Safrai, p. 103.

59. See Safrai, pp. 11, 15. Hillel died ca. 10 C.E.

60. Safrai, p. 50; cf. S. T. Lachs, *Humanism in Talmud and Midrash* (Rutherford, N.J.: Fairleigh Dickinson University Press, 1993).

61. Safrai, p. 50.

62. David Novak, *Jewish Social Ethics* (New York: Oxford University Press, 1992), p. 37.

63. Tanhuma, Ki Tissa 16; cf. Falk, p. 132.

64. Safrai, p. 51; cf. *Avot* 2.11–12; as Safrai explains, the "flowing spring" is a metaphor of creativity.

65. Y. *Sanhedrin* 4, 22a; Safrai, p. 49.

66. Falk, *Religious Law and Ethics*, p. 118, citing *Avodah Zarah* 19a.

67. See Safrai, pp. 146–68; cf. p. 124: even in the "well grounded" laws of purity, immense legislative structures were cantilevered well beyond the Scriptural givens.

68. Cf. *Shabbat* 135a, *Bava Batra* 110b, *Hagigah* 1, 75d, *Sota* 3a, Y. *Sota* 3, 18d. Safrai (p. 51) explains Hillel's comment, "He who increases Torah increases life" (*Avot* 2.7; cf. 1.13, 5.22) as an encomium of creativity.

69. *Avot* 1.3, 4.5, 6.1, *Avot de Rabbi Nathan* 28ab, *Sifre* to Deuteronomy 41, 48.

70. Mishnah *Peah* 1.1, tr. Danby, *Mishnah*, p. 10; *Avot*, 6.1, 2.9; but cf. 1.17, 2.2.

71. Ecclesiastes 1:17–18; 6:8, 12; cf. 2:15–23; with *Avot* 2.21.

72. See I. Heinemann, *Ta'amei Ha-Mitzvot* (Jerusalem: Histadrut, 1949), vol. 1; Solomon Ibn Adret of Barcelona (1235–1310), the Rashba, Responsum no. 94; Louis Jacobs, *Theology in the Responsa* (London: Routledge, 1975), p. 64. But the Rashba's positivism, targeting a rationalism he feared was reductionistic, did not exclude spiritual or mystical rationales of the intrinsic value of the *mitzvot*.

73. *Genesis Rabbah* 8.8–9; 1.1; 13; cf. *Berakhot* 55a; Philo, *De Opificio Mundi* 4, 15–16, LCL 1.15; Maimonides, *Guide* 2:6, ed. Munk, 2:16–18. The imagery is reversed but the theme held constant in *Avot* 4.10: only God can judge alone.

74. *Sanhedrin* 33b–34a, 81b, 84b. For the procedural protections in capital cases, Mishnah *Sanhedrin* 4.1 (which also bans reversal of acquittals in capital cases); for the ban on hearsay, 4.5; Danby, *Mishnah*, p. 387. For the exclusion of circumstantial evidence, *Tosefta* to *Sanhedrin* 8.3; cf. *Baba Kamma* 73a: "Evidence voided in part is voided altogether." Cf. Urbach in Baron, Wise, and Goodman, *Violence and Defense*, pp. 104–8.

75. Raba in *Sanhedrin* 96; cf. Mishnah *Ketubot* 2.9, Danby, 247; Maimonides, *Code* XIV, *H. Sanhedrin* 18.6, YJS 14.52–53: "Perhaps he was one of those who are in misery, bitter in soul, who long for death . . . The principle that no man is to be declared guilty on his own admission is a divine decree." Yet, as Urbach notes (Baron, Wise, and Goodman, p. 107), "in a civil case the admission of fault or liability had the power of one hundred witnesses."

76. The Rabbis demand warning by the husband before two witnesses, naming the suspected third party, overt ignoring of the warning, again certified by two witnesses other than the husband, and consent by the wife to the ordeal. Her refusal made her subject to divorce without return of the marriage settlement. But insufficient warning or inadequate testimony left divorce the only remedy, *with* return to the wife of her marriage settlement. Cases under this law could come only before the full Sanhedrin of 71 high court judges in Jerusalem. Renewed sexual relations of the married couple between the warning and the ordeal voided the procedure and required their divorce with return of the settlement. So did the husband's relenting in his demand for the ordeal. Any premarital or extramarital

affairs on his part nullified his demand; so did any significant physical handicap in either party; Mishnah *Sotah* 1–5, Danby, pp. 293–98; Maimonides, *Code* IV, *Sotah*, ed. I. Klein, YJS, 341–64; Abraham Chill, *The Mitzvot* (Jerusalem: Keter, 1974), pp. 322–24. The requirement of consent ensured that the ordeal would be little practiced. It was magical from the outset—the only commandment, Nahmanides remarks, that depended on a miracle—and the Mishnah treats its practice as legendary: the ordeal was expected to produce identical effects on the lover as on the woman who drank the waters. Maimonides is rather casual about the composition of the waters themselves: "some bitter ingredient such as wormwood or the like" (p. 356); he implies (p. 358) that the ordeal's efficacy rested on popular belief. In Second Temple times, following a hint in Hosea (4:14), the Sanhedrin abolished the ordeal completely, arguing that adultery was too widespread to allow the required presumption of a husband's innocence.

77. The oath is expressed euphemistically, suppressing the word "never."

78. The same Talmudic passage pictures a judge instructing a witness in a case like Shimeon's: "If that is what you saw, you saw nothing." Shimeon saw enough to call the aggressor "villain," but cannot charge him with murder. He invokes God's punishment on the murderer, not verbally presuming the guilt of the man before him. The Muslim jurist Ibn Khallikan (1211–82) reports several similar stories in his *Biographical Dictionary*, tr. B. Mac Guckin de Slane (Paris and London, 1842; repr. Beirut: Librairie du Liban, 1970) 4.276.

79. See Urbach, in Baron, Wise, and Goodman, p. 109.

80. Safrai, p. 131. The Talmud is not reporting that the Torah legislates for a null class but voicing the Rabbis' determination that no case will ever meet the Torah's standard for capital punishment in this matter: The statute will be of regulative value only, as penal laws today are sometimes used to make possible therapeutic and social interventions. As Falk renders the dictum of R. Simon: "Why should he be executed for having eaten a quantity of meat and drunk a measure of wine? This case should therefore not be understood as an actual ruling; it never happened in the past nor will it happen in the future, but was meant as a theoretical paradigm." Simon, *Religious Law and Ethics*, p. 119.

81. Cf. Deuteronomy 5:30, 6:3, 18, 4:40, 5:26. If quality of life is understood to include preservation of communal and sacred values, then preservation and enhancement of life may be called *the* cardinal principles.

82. Mishnah *Yoma* 8.6, Danby, p. 172, and *Yoma* 84a, 85ab; cf. Mishnah *Shabbat* 2.5, Danby, p. 102, and *Shabbat* 30, 32a, *Kiddushin* 39b. Babes are delivered normally on the sabbath and boys are circumcised even if the day of circumcision falls on the sabbath; a sick child is not circumcised until recovered, Mishnah *Shabbat* 18.3, 19.5.

83. Mishnah *Yoma* 8.5–6, Danby, p. 172, and Gemara ad loc.

84. *Pesahim* 72b, *Ketuboth* 105a; see Ben Zion Bokser in M. Konvitz, ed., *Judaism and Human Rights* (New York: Viking, 1972), pp. 151–52.

85. As George Fletcher notes, Jewish law generalizes the defense of human life from one's own to that of others, and stiffens it from an option to an obligation, pegged to the rule "Neither shalt thou stand idly by the blood of thy neighbor" (Leviticus 19:16); "Talmudic Reflections on Self-Defense," in Robert Gordis, ed., *Crime, Punishment, and Deterrence: An American Jewish Exploration* (Los Angeles: Wilstein Institute, 1989), p. 71. He writes: "However challenging it might be to think of self-defense in the talmudic mode as a duty of concern for others, this way of thinking strains the capacity for solidarity in

modern society. It is surely possible to adapt the talmudic communitarian mode of thinking to contemporary problems, but one should not be surprised that the influential thinkers in Western law (e.g. Kant, Hegel, and Blackstone) found it necessary to focus not on rescue but on the aggressor's threat to the legal order" (p. 72).

86. Mishnah *Terumot* 8.12, Danby, *Mishnah*, p. 62; Israel Lipschutz (1782–1860), *Tif'eret Israel* quoted by Danby.

87. Pesahim 168a, 173b, Bava Metzia 48b, Sanhedrin 24b; Safrai, *Literature of the Sages*, 83.

88. *Bava Metzia* 59b, citing Deuteronomy 30:12. God, they said, rejoiced at this citation: "My children have triumphed over Me." Medieval anti-Jewish polemicists made this dictum a scandal; see Marc Saperstein, *Decoding the Rabbis* (Cambridge: Harvard University Press, 1980), p. 4.

89. See S. R. Hirsch's meditation "Do Not Destroy!" tr. I. Grunfeld, *Judaism and Human Rights*, ed. Milton Konvitz (New York: Viking Press, 1972), pp. 259–64; David Novak, *Jewish Social Ethics*, ch. 6.

90. Exodus 23:19, 34:26, Deuteronomy 14:21; Mishnah *Hullin* 8, Danby, 524–25.

91. Mishnah *Hullin* 1, Danby, pp. 513–15; Maimonides, *Guide* 3:26, ed. Munk, 3:58.

92. *Yevamot* 62b-63a ad Genesis 5:2; Midrash *Tanhuma* 12.

93. E.g., Mishnah, *Sanhedrin* 3.3, *Avot* 1.10.

94. *Sanhedrin* 4.5, Danby, pp. 387–88.

2

HINDU PERSPECTIVES ON THE INDIVIDUAL AND THE COLLECTIVITY

JOSEPH W. ELDER

In this paper I shall base much of my discussion of the Hindu view of the nature of the individual and the nature of the collectivity on what is generally termed the "Vedic" literature. This includes the four large groupings of Vedas (Ṛg Veda, Yajur Veda, Sāma Veda, and Atharva Veda) and their "descendent" śākhās (branches), saṃhitās (compilations), Brāhmaṇas, Āraṇyakas, and Upaniṣads. Within Hinduism, these texts are seen as especially sacred; in fact, they are referred to as the *Śruti* (what is heard, revealed, implying a supra-human origin). From this literature I shall draw especially on the *Chāndogya Upaniṣad* ("descended" from the Sāma Veda and dated somewhere between the seventh and the fifth centuries B.C.E.) that presents in particularly lucid fashion the doctrines of transmigration and of the unity of the *Brahman* (World Spirit) and *Ātman* (the unconditioned Self). Scholars differ in their estimated dates for this "Vedic" literature. However, there is general agreement that the four large groupings of the Vedas (the Ṛg, Yajur, Sāma, and Artharva Vedas), were composed between 1500 and 500 B.C.E. and flourished as oral recitations for centuries before they were finally written down in their present form around the eighth or ninth centuries C.E. There is also general agreement that most of the Upaniṣads were composed between 600 and 300 B.C.E.

I shall base much of my subsequent discussion of "duties" and "correct action" on what is considered to be somewhat later (post-Vedic) literature, the

Smṛti (what is remembered, what is tradition, implying a merely human origin). From *this* literature I shall draw especially on the *Manava Dharma Śāstra* (the Precepts of Manu, sometimes referred to and translated by Bühler as the *Laws of Manu*, dated somewhere between 200 B.C.E. and 200 C.E.), that is considered to be ultimately "descended" from the Black Yajur Veda. Over the years the *Manava Dharma Śāstra* has acquired a particularly prominent place within Hinduism. In fact, in the days of the British raj, certain court decisions rendered by British judges made reference to principles enunciated in the Precepts of Manu in the mistaken notion that these "precepts" had once upon a time actually been enforceable "laws," and hence could be used as precedents on which to adjudicate current disputes.

It may be worth noting that the Hindu literature describing the "ultimate" nature of the individual and the collective is considered especially sacred and historically earlier—what is "revealed," what does not have a human origin. The Hindu literature describing "duties" and "correct action" is considered less sacred and historically later—what is "remembered," what has a human origin, and what is therefore less authoritative and less undisputed. This in itself may have certain implications for any later discussions of Hinduism and human rights.

The Individual in Vedic Literature
The Nature of the Individual

One of the classical Hindu statements of the nature of the individual is found in the *Chāndogya Upaniṣad*. The great sage, Uddālaka, is instructing his son, Śvetaketu, regarding the nature of ultimate truth. In the process, he presents some dramatic imagery.

> "As the bees, my son, make honey by collecting the juices of distant trees, and reduce the juice into one form.
> "And as these juices have no discrimination, so that they might say, I am the juice of this tree or that, in the same manner, my son, all these creatures, when they have become merged in the True (either in deep sleep or in death), know not that they are merged in the
> True . . .
> "Now that which is that subtile essence, in it all that exists has its self. It is the True. It is the Self, and thou, O Svetaketu, art it."
>
> *(Chāndogya Upaniṣad* 6:9.1–4)[1]

"Place this salt in water, and then wait on me in the morning."

The son did as he was commanded.

The father said to him:

'Bring me the salt, which you placed in the water last night.'

The son having looked for it, found it not, for, of course, it was melted.

The father said: "Taste it from the surface of the water. How is it?" The son replied: "It is salt."

"Taste it from the middle. How is it?"

The son replied: "It is salt."

"Taste it from the bottom: How is it?"

The son replied: "It is salt."

The father said: 'Throw it away and then wait on me.'

He did so; but salt exists for ever.

Then the father said:

"Here also, in this body, forsooth, you do not perceive the True (Sat), my son; but there indeed it is.

"That which is the subtle essence, in it all that exists has its self. It is the True. It is the Self, and thou, O Śvetaketu, art it."   (Ibid., 6:13, 1–3).

These passages illustrate the classical Hindu doctrine of the unity of the *Brahman* (World Spirit, Supreme Principle, First Principle) and *Ātman* (the unconditioned Self, Individuality). According to the classical doctrine, *Brahman* fills all time and space. From *Brahman* all things have emerged—all forms and phenomena, all gods and all humans. *Brahman* resides in all things, including the human Soul. In fact, *Brahman* and the human Soul are one.

This perception does not, as such, uniquely elevate human beings. For all other apparently individual phenomena also share, with human beings, their oneness with *Brahman*. All perceptual distinctions, distinctions between plants and animals, colors, matter, things visible and things invisible, and also between individual human beings, are *māyā* (illusion, unreality, ignorance). Behind everything, infusing everything, being everything is *Brahman*.

According to the Upaniṣads, it is not enough for a person to recognize the existence of *Brahman* in order to obtain release (*mokṣa*) from the chains of existence. For one to obtain release (*mokṣa*), one must also recognize that one's own *Ātman* (unconditioned Self) IS *Brahman*, and *Brahman* IS one's own *Ātman*. In the words of the great sage, Uddālaka: "It is the Self, and thou, O Śvetaketu, art it."

Related to this classical Hindu view of the unity of *Brahman* and *Ātman* is the classical Hindu view of the perfectibility of the individual. For the individual seriously committed to the religious path, the goal in life is the ultimate dissolution of the distinctions between one's own *Ātman* and the ultimate

Brahman. This ultimate dissolution of distinctions, this ultimate attaining of freedom/release, is referred to by Hindus as *mokṣa* (freedom, release), and by Buddhists and Jains as *nirvāna*. On this point the three religions are united: the ultimate purpose of an individual's life is attaining freedom/release (*mokṣa, nirvāna*). Attaining this freedom/release is difficult—but not impossible. The very fact that freedom/release is considered possible through human perfection sets the classical Hindu, Buddhist, or Jain view of the individual apart from the classical Greco-Roman and Judaeo-Christian positions of human imperfection and of ultimately limited human capacities. A corollary of these views is that, according to the Hindu, Buddhist, or Jain views, no divine intervention is required for an individual to attain freedom/release. However, according to Judaeo-Christian views, divine intervention (in the form of forgiveness, mercy, grace, etc.) is required to make up for individuals' imperfections, so that they may attain release (i.e., salvation). According to such views, imperfect humans can never be fit for heaven on their own merits. If they are ever to enter heaven, they will do so only according to Divine will. Not until the later periods of devotional (*bhakti*) Hinduism (from the sixth century C.E. in south India and from the eighth century C.E. in north India) does one find systematic Hindu references to the relationships between Divine will and individuals' own efforts to attain freedom/release (*mokṣa*). The Divine will may be so all-powerful that one can do nothing toward attaining one's own release (*mokṣa*) from the cycle of reincarnation. Everything depends on Divine will, as in the following:

> O Lord . . . if You take the initiative [to save], wherefore my exertions? And if You do not take the initiative, of what use even then are my efforts?
>
> (Vedānta Deshika's fourteenth-century C.E. Aṣṭabhujāṣṭaka)[2]

Or Divine will is powerful, but it can be swayed by the intensity of one's love and devotion (*bhakti*), as in the following:

> I am false. My heart is false, my love is false; but I, this sinner, can win Thee if I weep before Thee, O Lord, Thou who art sweet like honey, nectar, and the juice of sugarcane! Please bless me so that I might reach Thee.
>
> (Mānikkavāchakar's eighth-century C.E. *Tiruccatakam*)

While Hinduism, Buddhism, and Jainism share their perceptions of the perfectibility of the individual and of the individual's potential for attaining freedom/release (*mokṣa, nirvāna*) unaided, they differ in their suggested approaches for attaining that freedom/release. The classical Jain view requires destroying inert matter (*ajīva*) and annihilating *karma* (*nirjarā*) to free the unbound living-matter (*jīva*). The classical Buddhist view requires recognizing the twelve preconditions of dependent co-arising, perceiving the Four Noble Truths: suffering, the source of suffering (i.e., desire. craving), the cessation of suffering, and the path leading to the cessation of suffering (i.e., the Eightfold Path of right views, right intention, right speech, right action, right livelihood, right effort, right mindfulness, and right concentration), and possessing faith in the Three Jewels (the Buddha, the precepts, and the monastic order). Within Hinduism, different schools of philosophy, and numerous religious teachers, have suggested a variety of pathways to freedom/release. Underlying all of these different Hindu pathways is the concept of nonattachment—indifference to whatever gain or loss might result from one's efforts. The centrality of nonattachment in Hinduism is spelled out in the *Bhagavad Gītā*, when on the eve of the great *Mahābhārata* battle, Kṛṣṇa, disguised as Arjuna's charioteer, instructs Arjuna on the nature of the universe.

> In action alone be thy interest,
> Never on its fruits;
> Let not the fruits of action be thy motive,
> Nor be thy attachment to inaction.
>
> Abiding in discipline, perform actions,
> Abandoning attachment, Dhanaṃjaya,
> Being indifferent to success or failure;
> Discipline is defined as indifference.[3]

Nonattachment and indifference do not mean inaction and resignation. To the contrary, an individual who wishes to obtain freedom (*mokṣa, nirvāna*) must actively undertake a discipline/path (*yoga*). "Abiding in discipline [*yoga*] perform actions" says Lord Kṛṣṇa. The individual bent on freedom/release can choose from among several disciplines/paths (yogas). The path of knowledge (*jñānayoga*) holds that constant hearing, thinking about, and meditating upon the sacred scriptures enable one to move forward toward freedom/release. The path of activity (*karmayoga*) holds that performing certain kinds of acts (including sacrificial rites, daily and seasonal rituals, and acts of self-denial and renunciation) enables one to advance toward freedom/release. And the path of devotion to the Divine (*bhaktiyoga*) holds that expressing one's intense love of God in any worshipful manner enables one to progress along the path to freedom/release. Each discipline/path focuses the freedom-seeker's attention on some point that does not arouse desires. Each discipline/path identifies some set of activities that may, for seekers, in time become virtually spontaneous, transcending the apparent paradox of needing to undergo nonfreedom or discipline in order to achieve freedom/release.

Within the classical Hindu framework it is expected that an individual's active search for freedom may well span scores, if not hundreds, or thousands, of transmigrations (*samsāra*) of the soul (*Ātman*). During each transmigration the soul carries with it whatever uncompensated spiritual merit or demerit it has accumulated during previous lives. As the Precepts of Manu states:

> . . . in the next world neither father, nor mother, nor wife, nor sons, nor relations stay to be his companions; spiritual merit alone remains (with him). Single is each being born; single it dies; single it enjoys (the reward of its) virtue; single (it suffers the punishment of its) sin. Leaving the dead body on the ground like a log of wood, or a clod of earth, the relatives depart with averted faces; but spiritual merit follows the (soul).[4]

According to the classical Hindu view. the characteristics of each individual's rebirth are shaped by the individual's past habits and acts/deeds (*karma*). The "law" of *karma*, as it is sometimes called, is that every meritorious act an individual performs will be rewarded—in some subsequent life if not in this life. Similarly, every sinful act an individual performs will be punished—in some subsequent life if not in this life. The form one receives at each rebirth is at least in part a consequence of the uncompensated sins and merits of one's previous lives—sins and merits of acts, statements, or thoughts. As the Precepts of Manu explains:

In consequence of (many) sinful acts committed with his body, a man becomes (in the next birth) something inanimate, in consequence (of sins) committed by speech, a bird, or a beast, and in consequence of mental (sins he is reborn in) a low [rank]. (12:9)

According to the classical Hindu view, even those persons who are reborn into a low rank, if they are sufficiently meritorious in their observances of the correct behavior (*dharma*) for low-rank people, may be reborn in their next incarnation into the rank of the brāhmaṇs (the highest of the four mythical ranks of humans, to whom were assigned the tasks of studying and teaching the Vedas, performing sacrifices, giving and accepting alms, etc.). Once people have achieved the rank of brāhmaṇs, they may point their actions in one of two directions—either toward happiness in a future rebirth, or toward the cessation of all future rebirths through freedom (*mokṣa*) from the cycle of reincarnation and the union of their Ātman with the supreme *Brahman*. Again, as Manu says:

> The acts prescribed by the Veda are of two kinds, such as procure an increase of happiness and cause a continuation (of mundane existence), and such as ensure

> supreme bliss and cause a cessation (of mundane existence). . . He who sedulously
> performs acts leading to future births becomes equal to the gods; but he who is
> intent on the performance of those causing the cessation (of existence) indeed,
> passes beyond (the reach of) the five elements.   (12:88–90)

The classical Hindu view of the individual actively submitting to a disci-
pline/path (*yoga*) in order to obtain a happy rebirth, or even to attain freedom
(*mokṣa*) from the cycle of reincarnation, parallels the popular Hindu view of
the individual actively undergoing austerities (*tapas*) in order to obtain a boon
(*varadāna*) from one or more of the deities. Hindu epics and legends are filled
with accounts of such individuals: the King Manu, after practicing abundant
austerities (*tapas*), received the boon from Brahma that would make Manu the
protector of all creatures at the time of the world's dissolution.[5] The seer
Bhagīratha performed austerities (*tapas*) for ten thousand years, and, as a
boon, Śiva released the Ganges River from his own twisted hair (ibid. 322–23).

Viṣṇu stood on his big toe an entire millennium and obtained as a boon
from Śiva the famous discus with which Viṣṇu slew the mighty demon
Śrīdāman (ibid. 91). The beautiful Pārvatī performed many months of austerities (*tapas*) in a lonely place, with matted hair and clothes of tree bark, in
order to obtain the boon that Lord Śiva would be her husband (ibid.
161–64). The semidivine Harikeśa performed such lengthy austerities (*tapas*)
that he was overgrown by a hill of ants who ate away his flesh, leaving only
his bones. In return Śiva granted him the boon that he would be free from
birth, death, and all disease and would be the giver of food and bounty to
people (ibid. 331–34).

According to the epics and legends, even demons and wicked persons who
performed austerities (*tapas*) could obtain boons from the gods. Thus the
demon Dāruka, through performing austerities (*tapas*), received the boon that
he could be killed only by a woman (ibid. 200–201). Similarly, the demon
Hiraṇyakaṣipu performed austerities with his arms raised, his eyes staring at
the sky, and only his big toe touching the ground. In return, Hiraṇyakaṣipu
received a 96,000-year boon during which he could not be killed by god,
demon, man, or beast, nor could he be killed in daytime or at night, nor could
he be killed indoors or outdoors (ibid. 76–79). In a similar fashion, the demon
Maya and two companion demons performed austerities (*tapas*) including
starving themselves to emaciation, sitting in cold water in winter, subjecting
themselves to the sun's heat augmented by the heat of four fires during the hot
season, and remaining in the open during the monsoon rains so that their
bark clothing became caked with mud, weeds, and slime. In return, the
demon Maya and his two companion demons received the boon that the
fortress they would build would be invulnerable to the weapons of all crea-

tures—even the gods except for a single arrow that would have to be shot by Śiva (ibid. 189–98).

According to the generally held view, austerities (*tapas*) performed in one life could bring a boon in the next. Thus, Vikshavati, daughter of Vikshavasa, performed austerities for twelve months, eating only that food that came to her readily—without cooking or begging. At the end of the twelve months the Godess Mīnākṣī appeared before her in the form of a three-year-old girl asking her what boon she wished. When Vikshavati replied that she wanted the three-year-old goddess to sit in her lap, the Goddess Mīnākṣī replied that she would, indeed. come and sit in Vikshavati's lap—but in Vikshavati's next life, when Vikshavati would be Queen of the Pandiyas. Sure enough, in Vikshavati's next life, when she was Queen of the Pandiyas, and she and her husband were performing a fire ceremony to obtain a child, out of the fire-pit stepped a three-year-old girl, who climbed onto the Queen's lap. This girl was none other than the Goddess Mīnākṣī who—in the guise of a small child—had entered the world and fulfilled the boon she had promised to Vikshavati in Vikshavati's previous incarnation.[6]

Any discussion of the individual in Vedic literature would be incomplete without looking at least briefly at the metaphysical assumptions underlying the nature of the individual. In addition to the general perception of the unity of the *Brahman* (World Spirit) and the many Ātmans (unconditioned selves) was the view that every individual was composed of two elements: *puruṣa* (often equated with the self, the Ātman, the soul, the real) and *prakṛti* (often equated with nature, the nonsoul, the material, the illusory).

The *puruṣa* or Ātman, on the one hand, transmigrates from one body to another, carrying with it the moral merits and demerits from its previous lives according to the law of *karma*. *Puruṣa* is changeless and eternal. It can, under appropriate circumstances, fuse with the eternal World Spirit, the *Brahman*.

The *prakṛti* (the original or natural form, the primal substance), on the other hand, does nothing of itself. It evolves and is shaped by the *puruṣa*. It can itself be subdivided in turn into constituent parts. The *Bhagavad Gītā* (7:4) lists eight such component parts: earth, water, fire, air, space (*ākāśa*), mind (*manas*), intellect-will (*buddhi*), and the I-sayer or ego (*ahaṃkāra*). The human body is made up of component parts of *prakṛti*, as is every other material object in the universe. And the component parts of a body are themselves undergoing constant change.[7] The human soul (*puruṣa*), however, is eternal and unchanging.

Various schools of Hindu and Buddhist philosophy differed in their explanations of how the soul (*puruṣa*) is released from its bondage to the body (*prakṛti*). For example, the fourth-century C.E. Sāṃkhya school of philosophy maintained that *puruṣa* breaks its bondage to *prakṛti* through perceiving the essential difference between itself and *prakṛti*. The eleventh-century C.E. Vaiṣnavite philosopher Rāmānuja concluded that God created *prakṛti* in the spontaneous spirit of play (*līlā*); therefore the soul (*puruṣa*) could free itself from *prakṛti* only through resigning itself to God's will (*prapatti*). Virtually all philosophical schools (except the Materialists, or Cārvākas) maintained that any individual should try to free his or her soul (*puruṣa*) from bondage to matter (*prakṛti*).[8]

The Duties of the Individual

According to the earliest *Ṛg Veda* hymns, there were two categories of Āryas (the term by which the second millennium B.C.E. inhabitants of the Indian subcontinent referred to themselves): nobility (kṣatra) and ordinary people (viś). The earliest hymns sometimes added a third category of Ārya: poet-priest (brāhmaṇ). The later, famous *Ṛg Veda* "Hymn of the Primeval Man" (*Puruṣasūkta, Ṛg Veda*, 10:90) describes the origins of four different categories of persons, each category emerging from a different body part of the sacrificed Primeval Man (*Puruṣa*): the brāhmaṇ (poet-priests) from his mouth, the rājanya (warriors) from his arms, the vaiśya (ordinary people) from his thighs, and the śūdra (servants) from his feet. In the *Ṛg Veda* the term varṇa (classification, color, category) distinguishes only between the Āryas ('noble') and the Dāsas (non-Āryas).

In the later Brāhmaṇa literature (around 900 B.C.E.), the term varṇa begins to be applied to the four categories of Āryas (brāhmaṇ, kṣatriya, vaiśya, and śūdra). This usage continues in the later scriptures. The Brāhmaṇa literature begins to distinguish between the śūdras and the other varṇas; for example, the śūdras are considered unfit to sponsor brāhmaṇ-performed sacrifices; furthermore, they are barred from being present at the sacrifices of others.

By the time of the Precepts of Manu (between 200 B.C.E. and 200 C.E.), a clear separation had been established between the śūdra varṇa (now called ekajāti: once-born) and the brāhmaṇ, kṣatriya, and vaiśya varṇas (now called dvijāti: twice-born). śūdras cannot undergo the twice-born initiation (*upanayana*) ceremony that marks the beginning of Vedic studies; hence, by default, śūdras are barred from knowing the path to the idealized stages of life. Śūdras cannot marry according to the four highest forms of marriage; they must marry only other śūdras (3:13). And they cannot give their cooked food to brāhmaṇs (4:223).

The Precepts of Manu identifies several categories of persons lower even than the śūdras. These include: 1) the "base-born" (*apadasa*)—usually the off-

spring of higher-*varna* women and lower-*varna* men; 2) outcastes (*vrātya*)—
Āryans and their offspring who ignore their Vedic duties and who, as a consequence, are ritually cast out by their duty-performing relatives, i.e., barred
from joint eating, drinking, smoking, marriage-arranging, worshiping, or
(sometimes) even talking; and 3) Dāsas or persons speaking a barbarian (*mlec-cha*) language.

Although the Precepts of Manu states that there is no fifth *varna* (10:4),
over time the scriptures come to make a distinction between two categories of
śūdras: the "not-excluded" śūdras (*aniravasita*) and the "excluded" śūdras
(*niravasita*); with the 'excluded' śūdras considered to be polluting. And in the
later scriptures, reference is made to a fifth class (*pañcama*) below the other
four *varnas*.

The importance of these distinctions between categories of persons is
reflected in the classical Hindu concept of duty or correct action (*dharma*).
According to the Precepts of Manu, relatively few duties apply to all categories
of persons. Even in the following passage, the prescribed duties apply only to
the members of the four *varnas*:

> Abstention from injuring (creatures), veracity, abstention from unlawfully appro-
> priating (the goods of others), purity, and control of the organs, Manu has declared
> to be the summary of the law for the four [varnas].   (10:63)

Far more duties apply to a person on the basis of that person's rank (*varna*),
that person's current historical age (*yuga*), that person's stage of life (*āśrama*),
and that person's gender.

1. The Individual's Duties According to Rank (*Varna*)

a. Performing Correct Occupations: As far as an individual's occupational
duties according to rank (*varna*) are concerned, the Precepts of Manu states
the following:

> But in order to protect this universe He, the most resplendent one, assigned sepa-
> rate (duties and) occupations to those who sprang from his mouth, arms, thighs,
> and feet. To brāhmans he assigned teaching and studying (the Veda), sacrificing for
> their own benefit and for others, giving and accepting (of alms). The kṣatriya he
> commanded to protect the people, to bestow gifts, to offer sacrifices, to study (the
> Veda), and to abstain from attaching himself to sensual pleasures. The vaiśya to tend
> cattle, to bestow gifts, to offer sacrifices, to study (the Veda), to trade, to lend
> money, and to cultivate land. One occupation only the lord prescribed to the śūdra,
> to serve meekly even these (other) three [varnas].   (1:87–91)

To stress the importance of each individual performing the duties assigned to the rank (*varṇa*) into which that person is born, the Precepts of Manu states:

> It is better (to discharge) one's own (appointed) duty incompletely than to perform completely that of another; for he who lives according to the law of another [*varṇa*] is instantly excluded from his own. (10:97)

b. Consummating Correct Marriages; Occupational duty (*dharma*) is only one aspect of duty according to one's *varṇa*. Another aspect is the duty (*dharma*) of correct marriage according to one's *varṇa*. The Precepts of Manu contains numerous passages dealing with the principles of correct marriage. These principles are complex and sometimes even apparently contradictory.[9] However, the generally endorsed principle is that members of the twice-born *varṇa* should marry twice-born spouses of an equal *varṇa*:

> a twice-born man shall marry a wife of equal [*varṇa*] who is endowed with auspicious (bodily) marks. A (damsel) who is neither a *Sapiṇḍa* on the mother's side, nor belongs to the same family on the father's side, is recommended to twice-born men for wedlock and conjugal union. (3:4, 5)

The only consistent modification of this principle concerns second wives and other subsequent wives. According to the Precepts of Manu, twice-born men can take second wives and subsequent wives from *varṇas* lower than their own. However, the first wife should always be of the same *varṇa*. Concern over the mixture of the *varṇas* (*varṇa saṃkara*) runs like a theme through the Vedic and post-Vedic literature. Thus, in the *Bhagavad Gītā*, when Arjuna is lamenting his duty to slay his kinsmen and thereby destroy their families, he says:

> Upon the destruction of the family, perish
> The immemorial holy laws of the family;
> When the laws have perished, the whole family
> Lawlessness overwhelms also.
>
> Because of the prevalence of lawlessness, Kṛṣṇa,
> The women of the family are corrupted;
> When the women are corrupted, o Vṛṣṇi clansman,
> Mixture [of *varṇas*] ensues.
>
> Mixture [of *varṇas*] leads to naught but hell
> For the destroyers of the family and for the family. (1:40, 41, 42)

c. Behaving with Correct Virtue. In addition to occupational duty and correct marriage, there is a third aspect of duty according to one's *dharma* and that is the principle that the higher one's *varna* is the more virtuous should be one's behavior. As an illustration of this principle, for example, the Precepts of Manu says:

> In (a case of) theft the guilt of a śūdra shall be eightfold, that of a vaiśya sixteenfold, that of a kṣatriya two-and-thirtyfold, that of a brāhman sixty-fourfold, or quite a hundredfold, or (even) twice four-and-sixtyfold; (each of them) knowing the nature of the offense.   (8:337, 338)

Śūdras, being morally inferior, are expected to be more criminal. Thus, when śūdras steal, their guilt is light. Brāhmans, being morally superior, are not expected to be criminal. Therefore, when brāhmans steal, their guilt is heavy.

2. The Individual's Duties According to the Current Historical Era (*Yuga*)

The Precepts of Manu accepts the premise that the universe is continually being created and destroyed—each creation and destruction comprising a "great age" (*mahāyuga*). Each "great age," in turn, is divided into four ages (*yugas*), beginning with the perfect age (*kṛta yuga*) and deteriorating by quarters into the successively less perfect (*tretā, dvāpara,* and *kali*) ages:

> In the *kṛta* age *Dharma* is four-footed and entire, and (so is) Truth; nor does any gain accrue to men by unrighteousness. In the other (three ages), by reason of (unjust) gains . . . *Dharma* is deprived successively of one foot, and through (the prevalence of) theft, falsehood, and fraud the merit (gained by men) is diminished by one fourth (in each).   (1:81, 82)

Life is one-quarter shorter in each successive age; virtue is one-quarter less rewarded; and people achieve the ends for which they sacrifice one quarter fewer times. The Precepts of Manu contends that within these shifting historical ages individuals' duties (*dharmas*) also differ.

> One set of duties (is prescribed) for men in the *kṛta* age, different ones in the *tretā* and in the *dvāpara,* and (again) another (set) in the *kali,* in proportion as (those) ages decrease in length.   (1:85)

Even the chief virtue shifts from age to age:

> In the *kṛta* age the chief (virtue) is declared to be (the performance of) austerities, in the *tretā* (divine) knowledge, in the *dvāpara* (the performance of) sacrifices, in the *kali* liberality alone.   (1:86)

Times of distress are more common in the *kali* age than in the three earlier ages. The Precepts of Manu acknowledges that in times of distress brāhmans may be unable to teach the Vedas, kṣatriyas may be unable to protect the people, etc. The Precepts of Manu further acknowledges that in such times of distress individuals of all *varṇas* may be permitted to pursue alternative occupations:

> Learning, mechanical arts, work for wages, service, rearing cattle, traffic, agriculture, contentment (with little), alms, and receiving interest on money, are the ten modes of subsistence (permitted to all men in times of distress).   (10:116)

Even though the Precepts of Manu permits individuals in times of distress to pursue occupations other than their ideal *varṇa* ones, the Precepts of Manu—even in times of distress—prohibits individuals from abandoning certain *varṇa* rules of marriage. Thus, regardless of how severe the times of distress are, men of the two highest *varṇas* are *not* permitted to take as first wives women of the śūdra *varṇa*:

> A śūdra woman is not mentioned even in any (ancient) story as the (first) wife of a brāhman or of a kṣatriya, though they lived in the (greatest) distress.   (3:14)

Similarly, adultery in all instances is forbidden:

> For by (adultery) is caused a mixture of the . . . (*varṇa*) among men; thence (follows) sin, which cuts up even the roots and causes the destruction of everything.   (8:353)

3. The Individual's Duties According to Stage in Life (*Āśrama*)

The Precepts of Manu declares that all brāhman, kṣatriya, and vaiśya youths should undergo an initiation (*upanayana*) ceremony in which they receive the sacred thread marking their second birth. The age of initiation varies with the rank (*varṇa*) of the youth. Brāhmans, as the highest of the twice-born *varṇas*, are ready earliest. Vaiśyas, as the lowest of the twice-born *varṇas*, are ready last.

> In the eighth year after conception. one should perform the initiation (*upanayana*) of a brāhman, in the eleventh after conception (that) of a kṣatriya, but in the twelfth that of a vaiśya.   (2:36)

Once initiated, a youth is ready to begin repaying the three obligations (*ṛṇa*) imposed on him by his births: his obligations to the seers (*ṛṣi*), to his forefathers (*pitr*), and to the gods (*deva*). During the first (student/*brahmacārin*) stage, the individual is to remain celibate and to study the Vedas. During this stage he repays his debt to the seers (*ṛṣi*) by learning the Vedas, serving his guru, and preserving his guru's hermitage. During the second (house-holder/*gṛhastha*) stage, the individual is to marry, follow an occupation according to his *varṇa*, acquire control over economic and political resources, and dispense these resources for the maintenance of brāhmaṇs, hermitages, and places of Vedic learning, According to the Precepts of Manu:

> As all living creatures subsist by receiving support from air, even so (the members of) all orders subsist by receiving support from the householder . . . therefore (the order of) householders is the most excellent order.   (3:77, 78)

The way in which an individual repays his debt to his forefathers (*pitr*) is to procreate sons. Sons in turn can procreate grandsons who, in turn, can pro-create great-grandsons. And sons, grandsons, and great-grandsons are indispensable for the performance of the sacred *śrāddha* ceremonies in which balls of cooked rice, meal, etc. (*piṇḍa*) are fed to the spirits of the forefathers. This feeding of the forefathers' spirits by successive generations of descendants brings comfort to those spirits and allows those spirits to progress in generational stages until they finally merge into the realm of the demigods (*manus*), and need no longer be fed by their descendants.

When a householder "sees his (skin) wrinkled, and (his hair) white, and the sons of his sons" (Precepts of Manu, 6:2), he is to end his householder stage and enter the third (forest hermit/*vānaprastha*) stage. Abandoning his belongings, turning over his household affairs to his sons, committing his wife to the care of his sons or taking her with him, the individual is to enter the forest and concentrate his attention on practicing austerities and per-forming various fire sacrifices. Through these fire sacrifices, he repays his debts to the gods (*deva*).

After an individual has repaid his three debts (to the seers, his forefathers, and the gods), and has abandoned all attachment to worldly objects, he is free to enter the fourth (wandering ascetic/*sannyāsin*)—and final—stage of life. As the Precepts of Manu says:

> When he has paid the three debts, let him apply his mind to (the attainment of) final liberation; he who seeks it without having paid (his debts) sinks downwards.   (6:35)

The ascetic in the fourth stage is always to wander alone, possessing neither fire nor dwelling, depending on alms, desiring neither to live nor to die, con-stantly reciting the Vedas and reflecting on "the departure of the individual soul from this body and its new birth in (another) womb, and on its wanderings through ten thousand millions of existences. In this way:

> A twice-born man who becomes an ascetic, after the successive performance of the above-mentioned acts, shakes off sin here below and reaches the highest *Brahman* [the Absolute]. (6:85)

For purposes of this essay, perhaps the most significant fact regarding the stages (*āśramas*) of life is that the same individual is called on to perform manifestly different duties at different stages of his life. At certain times of life he is to be celibate; at other times he is to marry and procreate children. At certain times of his life he must amass wealth and power; at other times he must abandon all worldly possessions. At certain times of life he must live in his guru's house, at other times in his own home, at other times he must have no shelter at all. What is sometimes demanded, at other times is prohibited—depending entirely on the life stage (āśrama) in which the individual happens to be.

4. The Individual's Duties According to Gender

The Precepts of Manu draws a distinction between men and women—not only regarding their status relative to each other, but also regarding their duties. At times women are dealt with as a category apart—almost as though they belong to their own *varna*. For example, the Precepts of Manu says that when witnessing in a lawsuit:

> Women should give evidence for women, and for twice-born men twice-born men (of the) same kind, virtuous śūdras for śūdras, and men of the lowest [varna] for the lowest. (8:68)

At other times, the Precepts of Manu likens the status of women to that of śūdras, and the lower twice-born:

> Let him who desires bodily purity first sip water three times, and then twice wipe his mouth; but a woman and a śūdra (shall perform each act) once (only). (5:139)

> . . . slaying women, śūdras, vaiśyas, or kṣatriyas, and atheism (are all) minor offences causing loss of caste. (11:67)

At still other times the Precepts of Manu deals with women as though they have no moral significance or moral autonomy:

Let no wise man swear an oath falsely, even in a trifling matter; for he who swears an oath falsely is lost in this (world) and after death. No crime, causing loss of caste, is committed by swearing (falsely) to women.   (8:111, 112)

In childhood a female must be subject to her father, in youth to her husband, when her lord is dead to her sons; a woman must never be independent.   (5:148)

And at still other times the Precepts of Manu sees women as generic instigators of sin:

It is the nature of women to seduce men in this (world).   (2:213)

Given these views of women, it is not surprising that the Precepts of Manu does not insist that women undergo the same initiation (*upanayana*) ceremony, and observe the same four stages of life that men do. Instead, women are prescribed a lesser version of the initiation ceremony and the four stages of life, with their husbands replacing the gurus and gods. According to the Precepts of Manu:

The nuptial ceremony is stated to be the Vedic sacrament for women (and to be equal to the initiation), serving the husband (equivalent to) the residence in (the house of the) teacher, and the household duties (the same) as the (daily) worship of the sacred fire.   (2:67)

Similarly, the Precepts of Manu makes it clear that a woman's first duty is to revere her husband as her god, regardless of his personal unworthiness:

Though destitute of virtue, or seeking pleasure (elsewhere), or devoid of good qualities, (yet) a husband must be constantly worshipped as a god by a faithful wife.
(5:154)

A faithful wife, who desires to dwell (after death) with her husband, must never do anything that might displease him who took her hand, whether he be alive or dead.
(5:156)

As far as men are concerned, the Precepts of Manu declares that they have a duty to avoid those situations where women might seduce them.

. . . the wise are never unguarded in (the company of) females. For women are able to lead astray in (this) world not only a fool, but even a learned man, and (to make) him a slave of desire and anger. One should not sit in a lonely place with one's mother, sister, or daughter; for the senses are powerful, and master even a learned man. (2:213–15)

The Precepts of Manu also advises men to honor the women of their households—even if only for pragmatic reasons:

> Where the female relations live in grief, the family soon wholly perishes; but that family where they are not unhappy ever prospers . . . Hence men who seek (their own) welfare, should always honour women on holidays and festivals with (gifts of) ornaments, clothes, and (dainty) food. In that family, where the husband is pleased with his wife and the wife with her husband, happiness will assuredly be lasting.
>
> (3:57–60)

The Rights of the Individual

As far as individual "rights" (i.e., an individual's justified claims or entitlements) are concerned, classical Hinduism provides several instances of "rights," none of which correspond to a concept of "human rights," i.e., justified claims to which all individuals—*as human beings*—are entitled (without having to do, or say, or believe anything). One such instance concerns the "rights" of someone who has performed austerities (*tapas*) to receive a boon (*varadāna*) from the gods. The term for boon, i.e., *varadāna*, can be translated literally as: "the granting of a boon that is asked for." This means the individual must ask for the boon—and usually the individual must also have performed considerable austerities in order to be entitled to ask for, and receive, such a boon.

The Hindu epics and legends repeatedly illustrate the fact that, once an individual has performed enough austerities, the gods cannot refuse to grant a boon to that individual—even if the gods know that the individual claiming the boon will use it for evil purposes. Thus, the gods knew that such demons as Maya (the creator of havoc) and Hiranyakaśipu (a king of the demons) would use their boons for evil purposes; nonetheless, once those demons had performed sufficient austerities, the gods could not deny some boon to them. The stories also make it clear that the gods can negotiate the exact nature of the boon. For example, the demon Maya, after performing severe austerities, asked Lord Brahma for a boon to enable him to build a fort that would be impregnable to the gods. Brahma replied that this was too much to ask. He and the demon Maya finally settled on a boon enabling Maya to build a fort that would be impregnable to everything but a single arrow shot by Śiva. Similarly, the demon Hiranyakaśipu requested eternal freedom from the threat of death. Lord Brahma limited his boon to 96,000 years. From the point of an individual's rights, however, the gods cannot grant *no* boon to one who has performed sufficient austerities. The performer of austerities has a justified claim to *some* boon from the gods—a boon that *must* be granted, in some later life if not in this life.

An even more broadly extended instance of an individual's justified claims (i.e., "rights") within Hinduism concerns the concept of *karma* and the belief that a cosmic "law" of *karma* operates throughout the universe. According to the "law" of *karma*, once an individual has performed a meritorious deed, that individual is entitled to be rewarded for it. In fact, that individual *shall* be rewarded for it—in some later life if not in this one. This is the intrinsic nature of the universe. Similarly, once an individual has performed a sinful deed, that individual is sure to be punished for it—in some later life if not in this one:

> For whatever purpose (a man) bestows any gift, for that same purpose he receives (in his next birth) with due honour its (reward).   (4:234)

> . . . an iniquity (once) committed, never fails to produce fruit to him who wrought it. He prospers for a while through unrighteousness . . . but (at last) he perishes (branch and) root.   (4:173, 174)

One of the later purāṇas elaborates on this principle that every good deed an individual performs is (ultimately) rewarded and every evil deed is (ultimately) punished.[11] According to this purāṇa, an adulterer in the last human life will be forced to embrace a burning metal image in this human life; a person guilty of incest in the last human life will be impotent in this one; a woman-killer or performer of abortions will be reborn a sickly member of an uncivilized tribe; a virgin-killer will be reborn an untouchable with leprosy; a brāhman-killer an untouchable with tuberculosis; a cow-killer a midget among untouchables. According to this same purāṇa, an individual who meticulously performed his or her correct duties (*dharmas*) and regularly worshiped God in the last human life will be reborn into the home of a learned and gentle brāhman in this life, with the opportunity to attain freedom/release (*mokṣa*) at this life's end. The cosmic order is—and must be — just. How can it be otherwise? For the cosmic order is only a manifestation of *Brahman*, the Absolute, the Supreme Principle, the Ultimately True.

A related instance of an individual's justified claims (i.e.. "rights") within Hinduism may concern the "right" of a member of the twice-born ranks (*varṇa*) to advance within the classical four stages (*āśramas*) of life. However, this "right" differs from the two "rights" just discussed.

The "right" to receive boons, and the "right" to receive rewards and punishments according to the "law" of karma are accessible to everyone regardless of gender or rank (*varṇa*). To the extent the Vedic literature identifies "human rights," they are these two: the "right" to compensation from the gods (if one performs sufficient austerities). ant the "right" to ultimate cosmic justice (through the "law" of *karma*). No person, regardless of how foolish or despicable, can be deprived of these two "rights."

The "right" to advance within the classical four stages of life is *not* available to everyone. It is reserved for male members of the twice-born ranks. To this extent such "rights" might be considered "privileges" rather than "rights," since they are entitlements reserved for a limited segment of the population. Being born a male member of the twice-born ranks in itself, however, does not entitle a person to pass through the classical four stages of life. Only after a male member of the twice-born ranks has engaged in certain acts does he have the "right" to move to the next stage of life.

As mentioned earlier, an individual at birth owes three debts, i.e., to the seers (*ṛṣis*), the forefathers (*pitṛs*), and the gods (*devas*). One must earn the "right" to pay off each of these three debts by appropriate actions. Thus, a male member of the twice-born ranks earns the "right" to enter the student stage and to repay his debts to the seers by undergoing the initiation (*upanayana*) ceremony. Having entered the student stage and having repaid one's debts to the seers by serving one's guru, one earns the "right" to enter the householder stage by completing the student stage, giving a gift of a cow to one's guru, and performing the returning-home (*samāvartana*) ceremony. Having entered the householder stage and having repaid one's debts to one's forefathers through begetting sons and raising them till *they* beget sons, performing the ancestor-feeding ceremonies, and carrying out other householder obligations, one earns the "right" to become a forest hermit. And having entered the forest-hermit stage and having repaid one's debts to the gods by performing fire sacrifices, one earns the "right" to enter the final, wandering-ascetic stage.

If an individual enters one of these stages without having earned the "right," that individual may generate cosmic repercussions. The *Mahābhārata* (Adi Parva, Astika Parva) tells the story of the sage Jaratkaru, who had bypassed the householder stage and had directly entered the wandering-ascetic stage. One day in his wanderings Jaratkaru saw (but did not recognize) his ancestors hanging upside down in a great hole, suspended by a grass rope that was being gnawed by a rat. When Jaratkaru inquired of these ancestors why they were suffering such miseries, his ancestors informed him that one of their descendants named Jaratkaru had doomed them by refusing to marry and have sons who would continue the lineage. Jaratkaru was appalled when he recognized that he was to blame. He forthwith renounced his vows of celibacy, married, and procreated sons to continue the lineage.[12]

One point worth noting in this discussion of the classical Hindu concept of individual "rights" is the fact that all the individual "rights" described so far pertain to the spiritual world. They are "rights" that the gods or the cosmic order are expected to maintain. The existence of such spiritual or ethical "rights" is borne out repeatedly in the sacred texts of classical Hinduism. However, within classical Hinduism there is little evidence of what might be called individual "secular rights"—"rights" that the secular order must guarantee or protect.

This does not mean that in classical Hinduism a king or ruler controlling the secular order can behave any way he pleases. The duties (*dharmas*) of a king are spelled out in considerable detail in the Precepts of Manu, the *Artha Sāstra*,[13] and various texts on statecraft and the art of ruling. According to these texts, the major task of the king is to protect the world and preserve its divinely ordained order. Thus, for example, the Precepts of Manu states:

The king has been created (to be) the protector of the . . . (*varṇa*) and orders, who all according to their rank, discharge their several duties. (7:35)

> (The king) should carefully compel vaiśyas and śūdras to perform the work (prescribed) for them; for if these two [varṇas] swerved from their duties, they would throw this (whole) world into confusion. (8:418)

The king's main method for preserving order is through punishment:

> Punishment alone governs all created beings, punishment alone protects them, punishment watches over them while they sleep; the wise declare punishment (to be identical with) the law . . . All . . . (*varṇa*) would be corrupted (by intermixture), all barriers would be broken through, and all men would rage (against each other) in consequence of mistakes with respect to punishment. (7:18–24)

The righteous king must punish with absolute impartiality:

> Neither a father, nor a teacher, nor a friend, nor a mother, nor a wife, nor a son, nor a domestic priest must be left unpunished by a king, if they do not keep within their duty. (8:335)

This means that the king must spare no effort in determining the facts of any judicial case that comes before him:

> As a hunter traces the lair of a (wounded) deer by the drops of blood, even so the king shall discover on which side the right lies, by inferences (from the facts). When engaged in judicial proceedings he must pay full attention to the truth.
>
> (8:44, 45)

For if the king inflicts punishment wrongly, the "law" of *karma* guarantees the king's own destruction:

> A king who properly inflicts (punishment), prospers with respect to [virtue, plea-
> sure, and wealth]; but he who is voluptuous, partial, and deceitful will be destroyed,
> even through the (unjust) punishment (which he inflicts).   (7:27)

Thus, the king, according to classical Hindu doctrine, is supposed to dispense justice, punish wrongdoers, and maintain the cosmically ordained order within his realm. He does these because they are his duty (*dharma*). The classical scriptures also note that the king will personally benefit—spiritually as well as materially—if he fulfills his duty; likewise the king will personally suffer if he fails to fulfill his duty:

> Whatever meritorious acts (such a brāhmaṇ) performs under the full protection of
> the king, thereby the king's length of life, wealth, and kingdom increase.   (7:136)

> A king who (duly) protects (his subjects) receives from each and all the sixth part of
> their spiritual merit; if he does not protect them, the sixth part of their demerit also
> (will fall on him).   (8:304)

In none of the classical Hindu descriptions of the king's duties does one find the notion that the subjects of a king are "entitled" to justice. Even when the subjects feel the king has dispensed punishment wrongly, their charge is that the king has failed in his duty—not that the subjects have failed to receive some kind of justice to which they were "entitled."

In the Tamil epic, *Cilappatikaram* (The Lay of the Anklet, estimated date: second or third century C.E.), the faithful wife of Kōvalan discovers that Kōvalan has been executed by the King's men on the false accusation that Kōvalan had stolen the Queen's anklet—an anklet filled with pearls. The enraged wife stands before the King's throne and announces that she is the widow of the executed man. The King replies: "there is no injustice in putting a robber to death. Do you not know that that is the duty of a king?" Kōvalan's widow responds: "King of Korkai, you went astray from the path of duty." When the King breaks open the ostensibly stolen anklet and sees gems rather than pearls, he recognizes that he has, indeed, gone astray from the path of duty. The anklet in question is not the Queen's; it belongs to Kōvalan's widow! Had the King inspected the anklet as he should have while Kōvalan was still alive, Kōvalan would never have been executed! Recognizing his blame, the King cries out:

"For the first time I have failed in my duty as protector of the southern kingdom. No way is left open to me save to give up my life."

So saying, the King collapses in a fatal swoon. Standing above the dying King, Kōvalan's widow announces:

"Today we have seen evidence of the sage's warning. *The Divine Law appears in the form of death before the man who fails in his duty.*"[14]

No mention is made of the fact that Kōvalan was "entitled" to a fair trial, or that he had the "right" to be considered innocent until proved beyond any reasonable doubt to be guilty. Instead, the King is declared to be guilty for having failed in the correct performance of his duty. The King must be—and is—punished through the cosmic processes of *karma*. He brought his punishment upon himself.

Nowhere in classical Hindu scriptures does one find any suggestion that subjects dissatisfied with their king's performance of his duty (*dharma*) should revolt against him. To the contrary, the king is defined as surpassing all created beings in luster. Those who hate him or transgress his decrees will be punished and destroyed.

> For, when these creatures, being without a king, through fear dispersed in all directions, the Lord created a king for the protection of this whole (creation), Taking (for that purpose) eternal particles of Indra, of the Wind, of Yama, of the Sun, of Fire, of Varuṇa, of the Moon, and of the Lord of wealth (Kubera). Because a king has been formed of particles of those lords of the gods, he therefore surpasses all created beings in lustre. . . . The (man) who in his exceeding folly hates him, will doubtlessly perish; for the king quickly makes up his mind to destroy such (a man). Let no (man), therefore, transgress that law which the king decrees with respect to his favourites, nor (his orders) which inflict pain on those in disfavour.   (7:3–13)

In the idealized society of classical Hinduism, each individual performs his/her duty (*dharma*) and thereby contributes to overall societal order/harmony. This vision of societal order/harmony is praised in the later Vedic literature, as well as in the epics and purāṇas.

Inasmuch as the societal *objectives* to be achieved by each person performing her/his duties (*dharma*) are not stressed, virtue lies simply in each person performing her/his duties. If, in actuality, the final outcome proves to be less than a perfectly harmonious society—if, indeed, it proves to be a society filled with apparent injustice—that may be because of illusion (*māyā*), or that may be because any one human's perspective on justice is bounded by that person's current lifetime (whereas cosmic justice works itself out over many lifetimes), or that may be because we are today living in the *kali yuga*—the fourth, and most degenerate historical age, an age cosmically characterized by shortcomings and disharmonies.

THE COLLECTIVITY IN VEDIC LITERATURE

The Nature of the Collectivity

One of the striking features of classical Hinduism is its almost total absence of reference to collectivities as *entities*. The Precepts of Manu contains sections describing the "duties of women," the "duties of kings," the "eternal laws for a husband and his wife who keep the path of duty," the "ordinances of studentship," "(the law concerning) the behavior of vaiśyas and śūdras," and "the law for all [*varṇa*] in times of distress," etc. But in none of these does one discover that collectivities—as collectivities —are being assigned collective tasks, responsibilities, obligations, etc. *Individuals* occupying positions (for example, positions within the varṇa hierarchy) are instructed to behave in certain ways. And whichever *individual* occupies the position of king is supposed to see to it that punishment is meted out to offenders and that individuals fulfill the roles of their *varṇas*. But nowhere does the Precepts of Manu suggest that individuals in a common category (e.g., vaiśya) should organize themselves into a collective entity that—as a collective entity—was (or even should be) accountable for certain ritual or secular performances.

However, one does find in the Precepts of Manu reference to existing collectivities such as castes (*jāti*), guilds (*śreṇi*), families, and groups inhabiting specific regions or districts (*deśa*) who had their own collective structures And even their own laws.

> (A king) who knows the sacred law, must inquire into the laws of castes (*jāti*), of districts, of guilds,[15] and of families, and (thus) settle the peculiar law of each.   (8:41)

Similarly, the Precepts of Manu instructs a king that, in matters of dispute between abstract legal principles and actual lineage and caste practices, established group practices should take precedence over abstract legal principles:

> What may have been practised by the virtuous, by such twice-born men as are devoted to the law, that [the king] shall establish as law, if it be not opposed to the (customs of) countries, families, and castes (*jāti*).   (8:46)

Unfortunately for later scholars, virtually nothing in the Śāstras or purāṇas provides details—even for illustrative purposes—regarding those customs of "countries, families, and castes (*jāti*)" that were seen to take precedence over the practices of the "virtuous" when those practices of the "virtuous" opposed such customs.

Evidence of the gap between the idealized world of the Hindu precept-enunciators and the actual world of many different groups living side by side and observing their varied customs is captured in a description of Indian society written by the Chinese monk Hsüan-tsang, who visited India in the seventh century C.E.:

> With respect to the division of families, there are four classifications. The first is called the Brāhmaṇ (*Po-lo-men*), men of pure conduct. . . . The second is called Kshattriya (*T'sa-ti-li*), the royal [class]. . . . The third is called Vaiśyas (*Fei-she-li*), the merchant class. . . . The fourth is called Śūdra (*Shu-t'o-lo*), the agricultural class. . . . In these four classes purity or impurity of [class] assigns to every one his place. When they marry they rise or fall in position according to their new relationship. . . . Besides these there are other classes of many kinds that intermarry according to their several callings. It would be difficult to speak of these in detail.[16]

One might guess that in the first portion of Hsüan-tsang's description he was reporting the "official" four-*varṇa* version of Indian society as described to him by brāhmaṇs. And one might guess that in the second portion of his description he was reporting what he himself actually observed—a society containing many classes that intermarried "according to their several callings" about whom it would be difficult to speak in detail.

The Duties of the Collectivity

The contrast between the highly individual nature of Hinduism's ancient tests and lawbooks and the highly collective nature of Hinduism's practicing social groups continues in the realm of the duties of the collectivity. The Śāstras instruct individual brāhmaṇs, kṣatriyas, vaiśyas, and śūdras to behave in certain ways. They go so far as to suggest that if everyone behaves appropriately, there will be worldly—and perhaps even cosmic—order. In fact, the Śāstras indicate that, in the beginning of time, this was the original intention behind the creation of the four ranks (*varṇas*):

> . . . in order to protect this universe He, the most resplendent one, assigned separate (duties and) occupations to those who sprang from his mouth, arms, thighs, and feet. (1:87)

In fact, it was purportedly to try to preserve this original order that the Precepts of Manu were composed:

In order to clearly settle [the brāhmaṇs'] duties and those of the other [*varṇas*] according to their order, wise Manu sprung from the Self-existent, composed these Institutes (of the sacred law). (1:102)

As mentioned earlier, the Precepts of Manu recognizes that, through a constant process of falling away, this world deteriorates from the age of perfect order (*kṛta yuga*) to the age of one-quarter order (*kali yuga*):

[In the *kṛta* age] (Men are) free from disease, accomplish all their aims, and live four hundred years . . . but in the *Treta* and (in each of) the succeeding (ages) their life is lessened by one quarter. The life of mortals, mentioned in the Veda, the desired results of sacrificial rites and the (supernatural) power of embodied (spirits) are fruits proportioned among men according to (the character of) the age. (1:83, 84)

It is the view of many in India that Hindus today are living in the *kali* age—the age of one-quarter order. This both accounts for—and is manifested in—the current low level of public morality, the nonconformity to the rules of *varṇa*, the lack of deference to brāhmaṇs, the decline of Vedic studies, the absence of respect by the young for the old, dissension within families, and the general breakdown of law and order. The fact that this is the *kali* age also explains why no one can restore order to the current chaos—no king (regardless of how hard he might try), no learned brāhmaṇs, no gurus, no laws, and no courts. No one can restore order . . . because this is the age of disorder.

The highly individual perspective presented in the classical Hindu texts is modified in only a very few instances. In one such instance, as mentioned earlier, the Precepts of Manu states that the general morality of a king's subjects contributes to the king's own personal merit or demerit (8:304). In another instance, the Precepts of Manu suggests that a wife's virtues contribute to her husband's and her husband's ancestors' heavenly bliss:

Offspring, (the due performance of) religious rites, faithful service, highest conjugal happiness, and heavenly bliss for the ancestors and oneself, depend on one's wife alone. (9:28)

In several other instances, the Precepts of Manu indicates that one's ancestors' spiritual states depend on one's own proper performance of the ancestral rites (3:146). And in at least one instance, the Precepts of Manu suggests that the punishment for a father's sins may fall on his sons and grandsons:

If (the punishment falls) not on (the offender) himself, (it falls) on his sons, if not on the sons, (at least) on his grandsons. (4:173)

Aside from these rather exceptional statements of one individual or group of individuals enhancing or diminishing the merit of another individual, the Precepts of Manu says little about transferable or collective merit and demerit. And it says virtually nothing about the duties of collectivities.

The Rights of the Collectivity

Just as the classical Hindu texts make little reference to collectivities as *entities* having prescribed duties; so the classical Hindu texts make little reference to collectivities as *entities* having established rights. To be sure, individuals occupying certain positions are seen to be entitled to identifiable privileges. Note, for example, the following passage from the Precepts of Manu:

> Know that a brāhmaṇ of ten years and kṣatriya of a hundred years stand to each other in the relation of father and son; but between those two the brāhmaṇ is the father. Wealth, kindred, age, (the due performance of) rites, and, fifthly, sacred learning are titles to respect; but each later-named (cause) is more weighty (than the preceding ones). Whatever man of the three (highest) [*varṇa*] possesses most of those five, both in number and degree, that man is worthy of honour among them; and (so is) also a śūdra who has entered the tenth (decade of his life).   (2:135–137)

Even a cursory examination of the above passage reveals that the collectivities being referred to (i.e., those people with sacred learning, the performers of rites, the aged, one's relatives, and the wealthy) are not viewed as corporate entities acting and reacting as coordinated groups. Instead, the collectivities being referred to above are actually categories of individuals characterized by certain similar qualities. The Precepts of Manu does not call for some large public ceremonies honoring all those people with sacred learning, or all those people who have performed rites, or all those people who have achieved a ripe old age. etc. (or their corporate representatives). Instead, the Precepts of Manu calls on individuals to show respect to *other* individuals who have acquired sacred learning, performed rites, achieved a ripe old age. etc. In the final analysis, even the collective rights described in the Precepts of Manu are directed ultimately toward interindividual—not intergroup—behavior.

At this point we come to a fundamental feature of the Vedic literature in general and the Precepts of Manu in particular. When the authors of this literature were making their pronouncements regarding society or social behavior, they were not trying to describe the world that actually existed. They were trying to describe the world as they believed it *should* exist if one accepted certain cosmological "givens." These "givens" included: the original creation of the four human *varṇas*; the assignment of different ranks, vocations, and duties (*dharmas*) to each of the *varṇas*; an original harmonious social order in which each *varṇa* performed its assigned duties (*dharmas*); the cycle of reincarnation; the "law" of *karma*, etc.

The authors of the Śāstras accepted these "givens." Within the context of these "givens," they then addressed such questions as: what *should* be the contemporary duties of brāhmaṇs? of kṣatriyas? of women? of students? To answer these questions, the authors engaged primarily in speculative deduction having little to do with the "real world." To the extent they did deal with the "real world," they tried to explain why the "real world" diverged so sharply from the "cosmologically given world." Why did so few people today follow the occupations and other duties (*dharmas*) they were originally assigned to follow? Why was there now so much disharmony in the world when originally there had been so much harmony?

The explanations the authors provided for these discrepancies were typically formulaic. The reason for the existence of so many intra-marrying groups today was because of the mixing of the *varṇas* (*varṇa saṃkara*). This occurred when men and women of different *varṇas*, through disapproved sexual unions with each other, produced mixed-*varṇa* children who, in time, married similar mixed-*varṇa* mates and thereby initiated new mixed-*varṇas* intramarrying groups. The reason why so few people followed the occupations to which they were originally assigned, or why so much disharmony existed in this world was because originally humans lived in a perfect age (the *kṛta yuga*); whereas today humans lived in the most imperfect age (the *kali yuga*). The fact that the authors of the Precepts of Manu provided a tautology ('things are imperfect in this age because this is an imperfect age') as an explanation suggests how self-enclosed and deductive their moral pronouncements were.

THE COLLECTIVITY IN HISTORIC PRACTICE

The Vedic and post-Vedic literatures described above are not the only available sources of information about society in India from 1000 B.C.E. to 1000 C.E. Folk tales, poems, dramas, and travelers' reports all provide glimpses into what may actually have been happening in India during this period. And what was happening appears to have differed considerably from the formulaic society of the Vedic literature. Non-Vedic "tribal" groups occupied significant portions of the land. The customs of designated people living in different regions of the subcontinent (e.g., Draviḍas in the south and Likkhivis in the north) differed noticeably from the recommended Vedic behaviors. Occupational guilds (hardly mentioned in Vedic literature) controlled markets and contributed surplus funds to build some of India's most magnificent monuments. Floods and famines forced people to migrate from one region of India to another.

Large and small Buddhist and Jain monasteries maintained their own complex financial and ritual relationships with the citizens in their surrounding countryside. Foreigners (*mlecchas*) with their own deities and rituals inhabited enclaves in India's seaports and cities. Rulers supporting Buddhism or Jainism (or Śaivism or Vaiṣṇavism) overthrew other rulers who supported one of the other groups, causing one set of priests to be replaced by another set of priests and requiring old temples and monasteries to be cleansed and rededicated and new temples and monasteries to be built. What the actual "rights" of individuals or collectivities were during this period must have varied from region to region, decade to decade, and enforcer to enforcer. It seems very unlikely, however, that the Precepts of Manu was the actual law of the land in any part of India for any length of time.

In the most recent millennium, with the arrival of Muslim rulers from Afghanistan, Central Asia, Iran, and Turkey, and European rulers from Portugal, Holland, France, and Britain, new systems of law came into effect defining individual and collective "rights" differently from anything articulated in the Precepts of Manu. In virtually all instances, these "rights" were indeed "justified claims or entitlements," but they were in almost all instances reserved for certain individuals or segments of the population, and hence might more appropriately be called "privileges." They were certainly not "human rights," i.e., justified claims to which all individuals—*as human beings*—are entitled (without having to do, or say, or believe anything).

The terms used for these newly instituted "rights" or "privileges" came from a variety of different languages and reflected a wide range of legal and political traditions. From Perso-Arabic roots came such terms as *darkhast, dastak, ḥaqq, mamul, nazr,* and *nazrana*—each of which referred to rights to such things as property, titles, harvest portions, freedom of movement, tax immunities, and liabilities, the use of symbolic objects (e.g., particular robes, slippers, turbans, umbrellas, emblems, etc.), positions in processions and seating orders, access to inner rooms, etc. In some areas of India the Arabic-origin word *ḥaqq* (entitlement) was linked to the Sanskrit-origin word *janm* (birth) to connote something like "birth-right." Established Sanskrit words such as *sampradāya* and *svāmibhogam* were applied to specific legal entitlements.

Following the East India Company's ascendancy and its efforts to define land "ownership" in order to collect taxes, an entire lexicon of terms came into use in India identifying "rights" of usage, "rights" to receive certain portions of the harvest, "rights" not to pay certain taxes, "rights" to collect taxes from certain villages, roads, etc. "rights" to give gifts/bribes, and "rights" to be in a position to receive gifts/bribes. Some of these "rights" were granted temporarily, others were granted "till death," others were granted "in perpetuity." Some "rights" were granted to individuals, others to lineages, or to entire villages, and others to castes (*jātis*).[17]

If one turns away from the classical Hindu texts and examines how Hindu society has actually functioned historically and in the recent past, one is struck by the elaborate rights and responsibilities of Hindu *collectivities*, particularly of Hindu castes (*jātis*). The North Indian *jajmāni* system described in such detail by William Wiser and by Thomas Beidelman[18] consists almost entirely of service/compensation exchange systems between caste lineages. Thus, in a *jajmāni*-dominated village, someone from the barbers' caste regularly shaves and cuts the hair of the men in the landowning caste. And someone from the carpenters' caste regularly repairs the landowners' plows, doorframes, and cart wheels. But *which* member of the barbers' caste cuts the hair, or *which* member of the carpenters' caste repairs the wooden equipment is not particularly relevant. At the end of each harvest, the landowners' caste gives a negotiated number of bags of grain to the barbers' caste and the carpenters' caste. The agreement to exchange haircutting or carpentering for grain is between caste (*jāti*) lineages—not between individuals. The precise amounts of these exchanges are not immutable. Over time, caste lineages lose or gain members, experience rises or declines in their political power, and discover their economic positions becoming stronger or weaker. As the needs and strategic positions of lineages change, so do their "rights." And representatives of their lineages reassess and renegotiate those "rights."

The word used throughout much of North India for these collective jajmāni rights is *ḥaqq*—a term of Arabic origin that can also be used to refer to individual rights. It is the barber lineage's *ḥaqq* and the carpenter lineage's *ḥaqq* to cut the hair or repair the wooden implements of the particular landowners' lineage and to obtain from that lineage bags of grain as collective compensation. Similarly, it is the landowner lineage's *ḥaqq* to have its hair cut by the barber lineage, or to have its wooden implements repaired by the carpenter lineage, and to provide those lineages with compensating bags of grain.

Despite the limited statements about collectivities in Hinduism's Vedic literature, one of the major features of Hinduism as it exists today is the caste system with its thousands of collectivities. For hundreds of years castes have collectively fulfilled their roles within the village exchange of services. They have collectively monitored the conduct of their own members. They have collectively settled disputes within and between castes. They have collectively paid fines and taxes. And they have collectively struggled to enhance their caste's status through a variety of measures including changing their names, upgrading their ritual behavior, hiring brāhmaṇs to perform services for them, renovating old temples and building new ones, establishing high schools and colleges, setting up scholarships and charitable trusts, and giving donations to public causes.

By way of conclusion, one can ask: what might be the reasons for—and what might be the consequences of—the marked discrepancies between the nature of Hindu individuals and collectivities in the Vedic literature and the nature of Hindu individuals and collectivities in actual historical practice?

Definitive answers to these questions—if indeed there are any—would require more time and space than are available here. But a few limited observations may be in order.

What might be the reasons for the marked discrepancies? One of the reasons might be found in the social positions of the authors of the Vedic literature. The men who composed such texts as the Precepts of Manu were probably themselves elite brāhman ritual specialists, trained in the Sanskrit language (with its focus on disciplines such as grammar), supported financially by their teaching activities as well as by their performance of sacred sacrifices and life-cycle rituals, isolated from nonelite groups and nonelite languages, with the time and inclination to engage in a kind of moral geometric exercise. They were not required to make pronouncements that could (or should) be enacted as "laws" and enforced by secular sanctions. Nor were they required to make observations regarding the ways people actually behaved. Their task (possibly self-appointed) was to proceed from a set of cosmological "givens" (e.g., the original four *varnas* with their designated occupational roles, an original society with cosmic order and harmony, etc.) and to trace out their ultimate implications, following principles of logic and deduction rather than principles of evidence and inference, or problems of practical application.

Historically, parallel exercises might be seen in the evolution of pronouncements by rabbis tracing the implications of passages in the Torah, and the evolution of pronouncements by muftis and qadis tracing the implications of passages in the Qur'ān. However, in the instance of the brāhman authors of the Precepts of Manu, as far as we can tell, there existed neither specific target-audiences nor enforcement mechanisms. They could develop the implications exclusively within a closed intellectual sphere. In the instances of the rabbis and the qadis, however, the implications they traced *did* have relevance for specific Jewish congregations and Muslim communities and *did* face problems of compliance and enforcement. Therefore the reasoning could not be carried out exclusively within a closed intellectual sphere. It seems reasonable to assume that this had *some* influence on the final pronouncements of the rabbis, muftis, and qadis.

What might be the consequences of the marked discrepancies between the nature of Hindu individuals and collectivities in the Vedic literature and the nature of Hindu individuals and collectivities in actual historical practice? The very fact that the Precepts of Manu was not designed for any specific target-audience or enforcement mechanism lends it a kind of historical disconnectedness that may have contributed to its survival—and even to its relevance for contemporary Hindus. Not that anyone refers to the Precepts of Manu today for anything other than intellectual exercise. But the Precepts of Manu presents a model that reflects what Hindu intellectuals at one point in time felt they could extrapolate from Hindu cosmological premises that applied to individuals and collectivities. If such extrapolations could be made at one point in time, why could they not be made at another—with as much or as little legitimacy, and as much or as little applicability?

Today, in India, more recent efforts have been made by Hindu intellectuals to extrapolate from the Hindu cosmological premises and to apply these extrapolations to the contemporary scene—efforts by such varied figures as Dr. Sarvepalli Radhakrishnan (the renowned philosopher), Mohandas Gandhi (leader in India's struggle for independence from the British), and Swami Karpatri (organizer of the post-Independence Rām Rājya Parishad political party). Beginning from the same Hindu cosmological premises, each of them has deduced his way to a different set of "Hindu" conclusions regarding individuals and collectivities in the present-day world. As with the Precepts of Manu, none of their conclusions are backed by the secular authority of the state or the official approval of a religious hierarchy. But that is not necessary for their statements to be taken seriously—and even to have a certain legitimacy—much as the Precepts of Manu has enjoyed a certain legitimacy.

When the Precepts of Manu was composed, it was self-consciously confined to a narrow circle of Sanskrit-knowing brāhman and twice-born elite. Today, by contrast, the extrapolations of such Hindu thinkers as Dr. Radhakrishnan, Gandhi, and Swami Karpatri (plus the extrapolations of many other people) are available for widespread public consideration and public discussion not only in India but also elsewhere in the world. One does not need to be a Sanskrit-knowing member of the twice-born *varṇas*. Anybody can enter the debate about many issues including the applicability (or inapplicability) of the Precepts of Manu and other classical Hindu texts to the contemporary world. The debate is, and is likely to continue to be, a long and lively one. It may never reach any clear "conclusions." Along the way new issues may be added to the debate. One of those new issues might be: what bases does Hinduism provide for the concepts of individual or collective "human rights" (i.e., justified claims to which all individuals— *as human beings*—are entitled without having to do, or say, or believe anything)? Out of the subsequent interchanges may emerge some new and creative Hindu perspectives on the "rights" of individuals and collectivities not only to spiritual justice (as articulated in the Precepts of Manu) but also to secular justice.

NOTES

1. Upaniṣads, English: *The Upaniṣads*, trans. Friedrich Max Müller (New York: Dover paperback reprint, vol. 1, 1962; Sacred Books of the East, vol. 1, 1879).

2. Wm. Theodore de Bary, ed., *Sources of Indian Tradition* (New York: Columbia University Press, 1958), p. 349.

3. *Bhagavad Gītā* 2:47, 48, trans. Franklin Edgerton, Harvard Oriental Series, vol. 38 (Cambridge: Harvard University Press, 1952).

4. Manu, *The Laws of Manu*, trans. Georg Bühler, Sacred Books of the East, vol. 25 (Oxford: Clarendon Press, 1886), 4:239–41. Although quoting the Bühler translation throughout, I prefer to render the title as the Precepts of Manu.

5. Cornelia Dimmit and J. A. B. van Buitenen, eds. and trs., *Classical Hindu Mythology: A Reader in the Sanskrit Purāṇas* (Philadelphia: Temple University Press, 1978), p. 71. Subsequent citations are in the text.

6. John Loud, *Sports of Śiva (Madurai): Transcreation of a Tiruvilaiyadal Puranam, Madurai Kandam* (Madurai: John A. Loud, 1982) pp. 16–18.

7. McKim Marriott, an anthropologist at the University of Chicago, has developed a thesis regarding the permeability of a person's boundaries and the transmission of pollution through those boundaries thereby affecting the person's bodily substance, ritual purity, and relative social status. His thesis fits comfortably within the concept of *prakṛti*. For details of this thesis, see his co-authored article (with Ronald B. Inden): "Caste Systems," in *New Encyclopedia Britannica*, 1974, vol. 14, pp. 982–91, and his chapter: "Toward an Ethnosociology of South Asian Caste Systems," in Kenneth David, ed., *The New Wind: Changing Identities in South Asia* (The Hague: Mouton, 1977), pp. 227–38 .

8. For a further discussion of the nature of the individual and various approaches to the *puruṣa / Prakṛti* distinctions, see Karl H. Potter, *Presuppositions of India's Philosophies* (Englewood Cliffs, N.J.: Prentice Hall, 1986), especially ch. 9.

9. For example, the principle that brāhmaṇ men should have legitimate access to the maximum number of women and śūdra men should have legitimate access to the minimum number of women collides with the principle that śūdra women possess qualities that pollute brāhmaṇ men. Compare this passage:

. . . a śūdra woman alone (can be) the wife of a śūdra, she and one of his own [*varṇa*] (the wives) of a vaiśya, those two and one of his own [*varṇa*] (the wives) of a kṣatriya, those three and one of his own [*varṇa*] (the wives) of a brāhmaṇ. (3:13)

with the following passage:

A brāhmaṇ who takes a śūdra wife to his bed will (after death) sink into hell; if he begets a child by her, he will lose the rank of a brāhmaṇ. (3:17)

10. *Sapiṇḍa* refers to all those relatives having the right to offer sacrificial balls of cooked rice, meal, etc. (*piṇḍa*) to the same ancestors, therefore those relatives with rather close blood relationships.

11. Purāṇaṣ Garuḍapuṛāna. English: *The Garuḍa-purāṇam*, trans. Manmatha Nath Dutt Shastri (Varanasi: Chowkhamba Sanskrit Series Office, 2d ed., 1968).

12. One of the principal criticisms against the sage Śaṅkarā (c. 788–820 c.e.), founder of the *dasanami* ascetic order and the *Advaita Vedanta* school of philosophy, was the fact that he permitted individuals to enter his ascetic order directly after the student stage. Hindus critical of Śaṅkarā maintain that such individuals have not earned the "right" to enter the wandering ascetic stage, since they have not yet repaid their debts to their forefathers.

13. Kautalya, *Kautilya's Arthasastra*, trans. Rudrapatna Shamasastry (Mysore: Mysore Printing and Publishing House. 6th ed., 1960).

14. Ilankovatikal, *Shilappadikaram (The Ankle Bracelet) by Prince Ilango Adigal*, trans. A. Danielou (New York: New Directions paperback, 1965), pp. 128–29.

15. Guilds (*śreni*) were apparently a form of industrial and/or mercantile organization that combined individual workers or workers' cooperatives into a single corporate body. Guilds could fix rules of work and work compensation, determine prices of commodities and services, regulate the training of apprentices, establish standards of quality, etc. Guilds could enforce their rules by fines and other punishments. Guilds could even expel recalcitrant members. The Pali scriptures describe guilds as having hereditary chiefs and councils of elders, as well as ceremonial banners and emblems that they could carry in local processions. Guilds sometimes made collective donations for religious purposes or for religious or public buildings. Occasionally they served as banks or insurance companies for their members or their members' widows and orphans. Guilds acted much as corporate entities, occasionally dominating market processes and at times loaning money to, and counseling, the king.

16. Hsüan-tsang, *Si-yu-ki: Buddhist Records of the Western World; Chinese Accounts of India*, translated from the Chinese of Hiuen Tsiang by Samuel Beal (Calcutta: Susil Gupta reprint, 1957–1958), vol. 2, p. 138.

17. For extensive illustrations of legal terms used by the East India Company, see Horace H. Wilson, *A Glossary of Judicial and Revenue Terms and of Useful Words Occurring in Official Documents Relating to the Administration of the Government of British India*, published under the authority of the East India Company (Calcutta: Eastern Law House, 1940; 1st ed. 1855). This compendium includes legal terms from Arabic, Bengali, Gujarati, Hindi, Hindustani, Kanarese, Malayalam, Marathi, Oriya, Persian, Tamil, Telugu, and Sanskrit.

18. William H. Wiser, *The Hindu Jajmani System; a Socio-economic System Interrelating Members of a Hindu Village Community in Services* (Lucknow: Lucknow Publishing House, 1958); Thomas O. Beidelman. *A Comparative Analysis of the Jajmani System*, Monographs of the Association for Asian Studies, VIII (Locust Valley. N.J.: J. J. Augustin. 1959).

3

HUMAN RIGHTS AND HUMAN RESPONSIBILITIES: BUDDHIST VIEWS ON INDIVIDUALISM AND ALTRUISM

ROBERT A. F. THURMAN

Addressing questions of human rights and responsibilities today, one first inevitably thinks of the context of such concerns and feels the need to establish the relevance of Buddhist views in particular. There are few Buddhists left in the world, our lifetimes having seen its role as a majority world religion diminished drastically under a tidal wave of Marxism and other forms of "modernity." Nevertheless, as His Holiness the Fourteenth Dalai Lama is fond of saying, "from Siberia up to the Thai border, more than a quarter of humanity . . . lives in cultures permeated with Buddhist patterns of thought, language, and behavior." There are vast differences in the ways cultures and individuals incorporate these patterns, so much so that the umbrella concept "Buddhism" tends to dissolve under analysis. But we may find certain basic views, habits, and values entrenched in the mentality of this mass of people, which we must reckon with in our attempt to evolve a globally viable conception and practice of human rights. Further, since something's disappearance does not necessarily signify its lack of importance or benefit, we may find Buddhist theoretical contributions to human rights thinking extremely helpful to our concerns. Particularly, the experience of the various Buddhisms as basically nontheistic ideologies in the midst of various theistic cultures is instructive to us today, since one of the major problems in modern ethical thought on human rights has to do with the conflict between traditional theistic systems and contemporary nontheistic (liberal humanist) or atheistic (Marxist) systems.

It can be seen immediately that there is little profit in mounting either a critique or an apology for a supposed "Buddhist view," as most previous work in this area has done. Non-Buddhists in the past have usually confused Buddhism with either Hinduism or Confucianism/Taoism, considered it a type of "traditional" world view, and have then come up with the idea that Buddhism lacks individualism, hence true compassion, and is apathetic about the world and society. Buddhists in the past have employed the highly sophisticated arguments developed in confrontation with the religious ideologies of their host cultures in Asia and have argued that the Buddhist view of a particular matter is the only sensible one for all possible situations. My approach will be somewhat different, trying in the spirit of the Buddhist liberative tradition to be self-critical as well as critical of certain dogmas of the contemporary tradition. The task is to explore the plurality of Buddhistic views, each within its own social and historical context, and then extrapolate what might be of value in the various contexts we find today.

It is helpful first to acknowledge my own bias and outline the conclusions I will reach. I consider the Buddhist philosophical approach immensely valuable, both for its uncompromising adherence to critical reason conceived as essential to, not preclusive of, spiritual, or enlightening experience, and for its vast philosophical literature, the legacy of millennia of some of the finest minds in the history of thought. I do not think, however, that Buddhist thought has ever developed all the answers for all time, as its ideals have only been imperfectly realized during the historical experiences of its thinkers in various social settings—and I include even Śākyamuni Buddha in axial age India. I therefore think it a most valuable exercise for modern thinkers to study and reflect upon the Buddhist philosophies, even to experiment with their various worldviews, empathetically as it were. Indeed, I consider it an indispensable part of a modern person's education, which should round out schooling in the thought of Plato, Aristotle, et al., with Śākyamuni, Nāgārjuna, Candrakīrti, Fa-tsang, Kūkai, Tsong Khapa, et al. But I also think that all of the existing forms of Buddhist ethics, always closely appropriate to their cultural settings (including those that consider themselves "trans-cultural," such as Zen or Vajrayāna), have flaws, are inherently open to modification, and require evolutionary effort based on their own rational and pragmatic principles. In sum, I think Buddhist thought has a real contribution to make to what we might call the "emergent global ethic," both in reflection and perhaps eventually in legislation. But I also think that both contemporary thought, especially the scientific humanist tradition, and contemporary global reality have a real contribution to make to Buddhist thought and institutions.

My procedure in this paper will follow these stages: 1) I will clarify certain methodological questions that prevent the dialogue from getting beyond the dismissive critique and the rigid apologetic; 2) I will present the main thrust of Buddhist ethics, here focusing on the crucial individualism-altruism tension; 3) I will inventory some main forms of Buddhism, showing how they stand in regard to fundamental principles and tracing the influence of their respective sociocultural settings; 4) I will then turn to where Buddhist thought can contribute constructive criticism of certain central dilemmas in current ethical thought and practice and provide a positive ethical perspective.

METHODOLOGY IN "HUMAN RIGHTS" DIALOGUE

Jack Donnelly, in his "Human Rights and Human Dignity [Analytic Critique of Non-Western Conceptions of Human Rights]," argues that no non-Western culture has the basic conception of "human rights," defined by him as "rights one has because one is a human being."[1] These are rights which "derive from the inherent dignity of the human person,"[2] or which are "naturally inhering in the human person" (ibid. 305). He finds that this concept of "natural human rights" goes back at least as far as Locke, with his famous guarantees of life, liberty, and property, to which Paine added education and social security. Donnelly finds the claims of non-Western writers that their own "social contracts" provided for such basic rights spurious, in that they confuse talk of "rights" with talk of duty, obligation, and privilege. He further finds it significant that one fails to find even the language of "rights" in the ancient texts adduced by his protagonists. In short, he makes the classic "Western" or "modern" case for the lack of real individualism in either "non-Western," or "pre-modern" cultures.

Having courageously staked the claim for the origin of true "human rights" in the modern west, he then decries the attempt on the part of some in the third world to denounce that concept as excessively individualistic. He concludes by saying that the "human dignity," which he allows was a concern of the traditional societies, can be better protected by the modern "human rights" concept than without it. By clarifying the difference between them, he feels he has preserved the "human rights approach as a distinctive option" (ibid. 315). And he warns that "if we lose the concept, we stand in greater danger of losing the practice as well" (ibid.).

In a basic way, Professor Donnelly's points are well taken. He should be congratulated for having the courage and clarity not simply to accept the claims of the cited "third world" writers on the grounds that they too, having been human beings all along, *must have had* some concept of human rights. There does seem to be a definite watershed in the seventeenth century in the history of human societies, ushered in by the collapse of the traditional, theocentric, geocentric worldview, the monarchical, hierarchical *ancien régime*, and the preindustrial economy. Toynbee refers to this time as the time of the birth of the religions of modernity, of belief in reason, in mechanistic materialism, in progress. It is well known that Locke himself was attempting to formulate laws of society based on atomistic individuals in imitation of Newton's formulations of the laws of matter and mechanistic forces. It would be foolish to claim that *such a form* of individualism ever existed *on a mass scale* prior to that time.

But Professor Donnelly, and the many other writers who perceive the uniqueness of modernity, may have missed the point of this newness, especially as regards the issue of human rights, not only its basic conception, but also its practice. The revolutionary positing of the "rights of man," however hallowed it may seem to us as members of our culture, in which it is dogma, may not be a new discovery of something indispensable for human dignity. It may rather be a somewhat desperate, perhaps ultimately ineffective BAND-AID that modern Western man tried to plaster over the mortal wound to human dignity inflicted by metaphysical materialism, psychological reductionism, and nihilistic ethical relativism. It is highly questionable as to whether the European industrial culture with the rights of man on its lips, guaranteeing all humans the right to life, liberty, and property, actually respected those guarantees during its world-conquering expansion and its exploitative colonialism.

Even now that the "rights" have been enshrined in the Universal Declaration of Human Rights, modernization holds the dooms of nuclear holocaust, pollution, and resource exhaustion over the heads of the peoples of the planet. We tend to think of ourselves as champions of liberty against the communists, and so we may be jolted by the Swedish view, or by the nonwhite view, which sees us and the major communist powers as partners in coercion, exploitation, and terrorization of everyone else, like giants locked together in a life or death struggle, heedless of the countless tiny creatures they trample as they thrash about. Or, even closer to home, while we deplore the Gulag Archipelago and feel thankful for our liberties and proud of our respect for human rights, we avoid reading *Bury My Heart at Wounded Knee*, and our federal and state agencies are still pursuing genocidal policies against the red human beings of this land. Ask any Amerindian. Then there is the whole slum and prison system full of blacks and the widespread revival of the Ku Klux Klan. Professor Donnelly speaks as a white intellectual when he thinks the practice of respect for human beings is a necessary concomitant of the concept of human rights. The issue is much more complicated.

The question of "human rights" is never merely an ethical question; it is equally a metaphysical question. It is inextricably tied in with a culture's fundamental view of what sort of a thing is a "human being." And that rests on the determination of what is matter, what is mind, what is reality. For example, in a strong theistic system, according to which a human being is a creation of an all-powerful God, who also therefore logically controls the being's destiny utterly, that being's ultimate concerns all have to do with his relationship to that God. Though there may be talk of "free will" on a relative level, and there may be certain "rights" and "obligations" within the social or natural sphere, there cannot finally be any question of "inalienable rights" because that being has no "rights" vis-à-vis his creator. All power is in the hands of the God; the individual is ultimately powerless. The God may or may not decree that beings should have certain rights over other beings or other things, and He or She may also decree that the beings have certain duties toward one another and toward Himself or Herself. (In a sense, it is in this type of traditional theistic system—Eastern and Western—that Professor Donnelly finds a fundamental lack of the modern concept of human rights.) In metaphysical terms, God is the only ultimate reality, the world and humans have only contingent reality, entirely dependent on their creator.

On the other extreme, there are various materialistic systems, ultimately nihilistic spiritually—e.g., the Lokayata system of ancient India, the Epicurean system, or the modern mechanistic worldview of physical science after Newton. In these systems, sense phenomena alone are reals. Beings are temporary accidents adventitiously enjoying sense experience. Spiritual subjectivity is illusory, automatically becoming nothingness at death. Hence temporary sense pleasure is the supreme value. In a sense, the modern concept of human rights is closely linked to this latter metaphysical picture, from which also emerges its lack of compellingness. That is, in this worldview, all beings are equal in that all have a right to maximal pleasure or happiness. For this they need their lives, their liberty, and their property. All are equally sensitive, in principle, during their accidental lives, and all are equally nothing after death. They have a relative responsibility to one another, not to infringe on each other's happiness, on the relative, accidental, social plane, but all have no ultimate responsibility to one another, because the worst that can happen to anyone is the anesthesia of annihilation by death.

Thus while it can be argued that each has inalienable rights, the immediate natural independent power to enjoy his adventitious existence, natural rights that cannot be suspended by any fundamental outside power, such as a creator, these rights are ultimately weak in that the possessor of these rights is ultimately nothing, and the violator of these rights suffers no worse than ultimate anesthesia.

Thus, while during times of peace and plenty, modern societies have seemed to derive from their human rights concept a remarkable concern for human rights and human potential, in times of war and scarcity they have shown an equally remarkable ability to engage in mass slaughter, oppression, and deprivation, in spite of a ringing concept of human rights.

It is useful to set up these extreme positions, in that the resultant parameters can anchor a set of coordinates that help us locate any particular world view or life ethos. I use a diagram here as a preliminary schematization of the extreme positions (diagram 1).

	Spiritualism (theistic/atheistic)	*Materialism* (theistic/atheistic)
Individualism rights	submerged in ultimate salvation/liberation	hedonistic, relative one-life, self-realization
Collectivism responsibilities	hierarchical web of duties—ordained for the mundane relative ("traditionality")	ultimate nothing unifying all in anesthetic state duties; temporary, pragmatic ("modernity")

As we can see from this scheme, Donnelly's "human rights concept" relates to the upper right box, and his perception of the "traditional" to the lower left, which categories he tends to relate to "Western" and "Eastern" types of societies, respectively. As a product of an upper-right society, he overlooks the lower-right, the final destiny of all "moderns," wherein all is appeased in the anesthesia of materialistic death. He also overlooks the upper-left, wherein the individualists of the traditional societies find a final release either in bliss or in the anesthesia of salvation or liberation.

Either of the two can be theistic. The spiritualistic theism is usually an all-pervasive form, spilling down into the social realm in the form of commandments and revelations. The materialistic form is usually a remote de-mythologized version wherein the creator is acknowledged as a primal engineer, but one divorced from any effective role in the immediate reality. Salvation here may be posited, but its cognitive credibility and hence motive power are almost completely eroded by the dominant, "rational," scientific materialism of secular culture, which reduces the spirit to electrical energies in the brain. The weakness of truly compelling rights in the spiritualist type and of truly compelling responsibilities in the materialist type probably account for their easily being overlooked, and provide much food for thought. We can create a more complex scheme to locate various human rights traditions, by introducing new variables into the picture (diagram 2).

The octagonal shape of this figure allows us to involve more variables and to introduce four basic polarities to express schematically ideal types of metaphysical/ethical worlds. One can play with this scheme extensively, taking

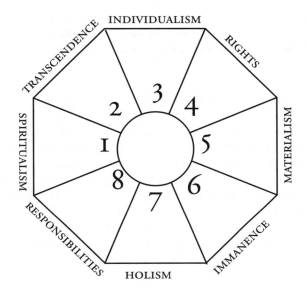

halves of the octagon to represent various ideal social types. Thus, the half
1–8–7–6 stands for traditional, monistic holism, or tribalism (type A);
2–1–8–7 for the type of traditional society Donnelly seems to have in mind
(type B); 1–2–3–4 for the world/ethos of traditional monasticism, which managed to maintain a kernel of "modernity" within most traditional societies
(type C); 2–3–4–5 for the world-ethos of industrial capitalism in its purest
inner-worldly ascetic form, as described by Weber (type D); 3–4–5–6 for the
type of modern society Donnelly credits with the "discovery" of the "human
rights concept" (type E); 5–6–7–8 for the world-ethos of industrial social-
ism/communism (type F); while 8–1–2–3 and 4–5–6–7 stand in an uncanny
way for two impossible forms which are yet presented as lies or dreams under
the banners of anarchism and totalitarianism, respectively. Undoubtedly there
has never been any real society in real history that would not be located in the
open center of such a typological scheme, off-center each in its own particular way. I only introduce such a diagram to illustrate how very much more
complex is the reality of the metaphysical/ethical mix of any society, Western
or Eastern, traditional or modern, than it may seem to one who is trying to
reduce that complexity to manageable categories fit to support sweeping generalizations. As for a sweeping generalization of my own, it would seem obvious that an ideal global worldview/ethic, the holy grail of contemporary
human rights thought, should come as close as possible to the true center of a
diagram such as this, at the precise balance-point of these four, and no doubt

other, polarities. It is clear that in the human rights context, rights need to be contemplated in juxtaposition with human responsibilities, as the two polar modes of relationship between self and other, other and self.

THE PRINCIPLES OF BUDDHIST ETHICS

In an essay on Buddhist ethics, "Buddhist Ethics: The Emptiness that Is Compassion,"[3] I refuted the misapprehension that Buddhist selflessness was either an ascetic self-abnegation or a mystic self-immersion in a formless absolute, and established that the central impact of the teaching of selflessness (*anātma*) was, metaphysically, the emergence of a spiritual individualism and, socially, an institutional facilitation of social individualism. A central thesis bears repeating, i.e., that selflessness is the logical and social seal of the "autonomy and unique value of the individual over and above his/her collectivity, because a metaphysically given fixed "self" would be incompatible with any living, changing individual, and a socially constructed, role-ascriptive "self" would be inevitably a stereotypical, traditional, general pattern of personality imposed upon the unique, novel, particular person" (ibid.).

A second major purpose of that essay was to show that there is a variety of ethical systems in Buddhist teachings, based on the differentiation of persons into various categories, based on their level of development away from egocentrism and egotism toward wisdom and altruism. For the least developed there is a basic deontological pattern of commandments, based on scriptural authority of the recorded pronouncements of the Buddha. For the more developed there is a complex set of teleological injunctions, based on pragmatic, developmental guidelines appealing to the reason and inner motivation of the practitioners. And for the most developed there is a third pattern of teachings, which, following Niebuhr's term developed in the Christian ethical context, I call "dialogical,"[4] which encourages the internalized rational judgment, or wisdom, and expanded sensitivity, or compassion, of the individual practitioners (ibid.).

In another essay, "The Politics of Enlightenment," I examined Aśoka's edicts and isolated four main principles, which I call 1) transcendentalism or individualism; 2) pacifism; 3) educational universalism;, and 4) compassionate socialism.[5] In a third essay, "Guidelines for Buddhist Social Activism," I traced the further elaboration of these principles set forth in a work written approximately four centuries later, the *Jewel Garland of Nāgārjuna*.[6] In those essays, I countered the mistaken notion of the "other-worldliness" of the Buddhist tradition and its conflation with the mystical traditions that abound in India, and I elucidated the workings of the underlying liberative thrust of the Buddhist Dharma. Here, I want to get away from the normative, textual, ideal principles to look at their impact on social reality more closely, to find the compromises and the failures to implement the ideals fully on any mass scale. A good beginning is to look at the biography of Śākyamuni Buddha himself.

The Buddha has been described by historians, following Karl Jaspers, as an outstanding "axial age"[7] figure, a charismatic, philosophically rationalistic ethical reformer who elucidated sensible principles for the newly emerging urbanizing societies of the mid-first millennium Eurasian *oikumene*. He discovered and taught the principles I mentioned above, answering the crises of the age—tribalism, militarism, elitism, materialism, etc.—with rational individualism, pacifism, universalism, and altruism. The famous four seals (*uddāna*) of his teaching: impermanence (*anitya*), agony (*duhkha*), selflessness (*anātma*), and liberation (*nirvāna*) may even today be viewed as a very realistic description of the facts of personal existence, if we credit the sociological analysis of Peter Berger et al., who have described the syndrome of the modern personality structure as afflicted by, hence having to come to grips with, a "peculiar openness" of identity, "anxious reflectiveness" from uncertainty about the self, differentiatedness of identity (i.e., no stable self), and individuatedness (i.e., ultimate isolation of the individual).[8]

Buddha's insight into the predicament of human beings in emerging mass society was remarkably successful. Further, his success as a teacher was also comparatively great. He was not persecuted or martyred, and he founded the unique and revolutionary institution of monasticism. This institution sheltered and nurtured individuals who sought to develop within themselves qualities, abilities, and liberties that the larger society was not at all ready to accept *en masse*. And the powers and principalities of the day not only accepted this institution, so radically threatening to their mundane concerns of control, exploitation, and mobilization, they even supported it handsomely.

The Buddha was born in the royal or warrior class and had a solid experience of materialistic power and pleasure in his early life, which undoubtedly gave him a clear view of the power structure of his society, its deep entrenchment in the psyches of the people, and its limitations. He then spent six years in the extreme disciplines of spiritual asceticism, seeking the heights of individualistic, other-worldly freedom. He tasted its transic ecstasies and also discovered its limitations. He then moved to a central spot between materialism and spiritualism and attained his unexcelled enlightenment by transcending the egocentric predicament altogether and gaining a realistic insight into the nature of life and death, self and society. He then spent the rest of his life in altruistic activity as a teacher, trying as best he could to assist his contemporaries and successors to unfold their own enlightenments, according to their own abilities and opportunities.

In walking out on his father and on his duty as a husband, father, and king, he announced in radical terms his right to liberty as a human individual. In abandoning his ascetic trances, including the deathlike transic state of suspended animation in the formless realms of nothingness and neither-consciousness-nor-unconsciousness, he announced to the world-escapists his right to life. In braving total psychic disintegration by opening up his self to incorporate the vast terrors of the subconscious instincts, as symbolized by the battle with Māra under the tree of life, he affirmed his right to enlightenment. He is asked by Māra in a final challenge, "By what right do you pretend to Buddhahood?" His famous earth-touching gesture is the symbol of his calling the goddess of earth to witness his long evolutionary struggle to become a human being through lifetimes of self-discipline, self-sacrifice, self-transcendence, and service to others and, among human beings, to realize his full human potential in supreme enlightenment.

Finally, by institutionalizing the monastic *Sangha* community, as a world of liberation within the world of bondage, he asserted the right to property. The silent act of holding out the mendicant's bowl to receive from the householder the daily meal with no offer of payment or even a word of thanks is a clear expression of a human being's right to have that necessary to sustain life, just because he or she is a human being, without being expected to fulfill any obligation or make any compensation. This is more starkly realized when we remember that, because of his shattering of all caste or class identities upon entering the monastic order, a Brāhman monk could receive from an untouchable, an untouchable from a Brāhman, and so forth. During his teaching ministry, he naturally asserted his right to free speech and freedom of religion, in a time of strong elite monopoly of learning and Brāhman orthodoxy of religion. Finally, by not using his attested yogic power to prolong his life beyond comfort for the benefit of his disciples, he asserted the right to die, choosing his time and attaining his well-earned rest in *Parinirvāna*.

In terms of responsibility, he exemplified the responsibility not to harm others and to prevent their harming each other and to heal those harmed. He manifested the responsibility to help others materially, intellectually, and spiritually. Most importantly, in a holistic society where the individual tended to be submerged in the social need, where *dharma* had previously meant mainly "duty," he exemplified and taught that the highest responsibility of the individual was to attain his or her own enlightenment, to attain that realization of selflessness, which is the fountainhead of a genuine ability to be responsive to others.

Now, where did he have to compromise his ideal vision, because of time and place and historical circumstance? The fundamental compromise is reflected in the public teaching and institution. In creating the separate world of the monastery, he left intact the social world of the times. He did not return to his throne to legislate a program of human rights, to dispense social justice, to implement universal education, to disband all armies, to abolish castes and classes, to engage in works of social welfare. In terms of teaching, his emphasis on the Individual Vehicle (*Hīnayāna*) teaching of the four holy truths, stressing the path of individual liberation from the egocentrist life cycle, the achievement of wisdom and *nirvāṇa*, and muting the world-transforming impact of great compassion (*mahākaruṇa*)—this choice of main teaching indicates his inability to proclaim publicly his complete idea for his society. He is said to have predicted that it would be at least four centuries before India would be ready for the widespread teaching of his Universal Vehicle (*Mahāyāna*).

In regard to women, he was unable to challenge the patriarchal customs of the times directly, and he is even said to have refused several times to create a women's monastic order, giving in finally to pressure from his foster mother and his disciple Ānanda. This women's order (*bhikṣuṇīsaṅgha*) eventually did become the first refuge for women to escape from the bondage of the tight family structure. There are many accounts of the early nuns, singing the praises of the Buddha and expressing relief at getting away from endless chores, oppressive mothers-in-law, and dreary husbands.

In recruitment for the order, he was more aggressive at first in laying down the revolutionary principle of everyone's right to freedom from the social matrix, inviting members of all castes and even reforming criminals, conscientious objectors, and so forth. But as time went by, in the interests of retaining the support of the kings, he compromised this wide-open stance and instituted rules that barred debtors, those in the armies, those accused of crimes, those whose parents refused them permission to renounce the world; acceptance would have created hostility against the order. Thus, while he never compromised his challenge against the caste system, the rules that began to accumulate naturally made entry to the order more difficult for those in the more lowly strata of society.

In sum, while his life exemplified all the basic human rights, and his teaching and institutional innovation created a social space for numerous persons to lay claim to their intrinsic right to "make meaningful" their "jewel-like evolutionary achievement of human embodiment endowed with freedom and opportunity,"[9] he was unable to impose these principles directly upon the whole society, so contrary was it to their traditional ideologies.

In terms of the typologies schematized in diagram 2, in a basically tribalistic society, of the type A (1–8–7–6, with a little bit of 2 and 5 beginning in the wildernesses and cities), he created an alternative world of type C (1–2–3–4) into which a person could enter if so inclined, but only at the price of renouncing or "dying to" the traditional world order. Thus, while it can be considered the planting of an important seed of a more liberty-oriented society, it was still very far from a full implementation of his own vision of a fully evolved human society—one devoted to nurturing each individual's full human potential, at peace, centered on education for all, and committed to full social and economic justice.

Finally, I should mention another powerful seed the Buddha planted in the popular imagination, wherein he communicated his vision for the world through stories set in a mythical past, the famous Former Life (*Jātaka*) stories. In this way, without directly demanding that the kings and elites of his day conform to his revolutionary principles, he could set them examples of what the ideal rulers of brighter past ages did by way of self-sacrifice, self-restraint, generosity, morality, tolerance, and compassion. Thus, his "demythologizing" critique of the Brāhman lore was complemented by a re-mythologizing through an exemplary popular literature that made his view of the purpose of human evolution available to the popular imagination. In this move, he reminds us of the remythologizing strategy of his colleague Confucius over in the Central Country of East Asia.

INVENTORY OF HISTORICAL BUDDHISMS

The development of Buddhism within India can be divided into three phases. Each new phase did not supplant the previous one, but incorporated it within the new form. By the end of Indian Buddhist civilization, around the end of the first millennium, all three coexisted in a loose integration. The first phase is that of the Individual, or Monastic Vehicle (*Hīnayāna*), which I have already described. The second is that of the Universal Vehicle (*Mahāyāna*), wherein the impact of compassion was openly and fully elaborated on all levels. The third is the Vajra Vehicle (*Vajrayāna*), wherein the previously esoteric meditative tradition was more widely spread popularly and more technically refined academically. These phases can be very roughly dated as from 500 B.C.E. to 0, from 0 to 500 C.E., and from 500 C.E. to 1000 C.E., respectively. During each of these periods there was a large-scale though nonviolent missionization of other parts of Asia. These other specific areas tended to receive the form of Buddhism dominant in India at the time, hence those missionarized earlier tended to resist the new forms evolved later in the Holy Land (*Āryavarta*), as they still do.

In regard to the first phase of the Individual Vehicle, I need not describe it again, except to repeat that for our purposes we may consider its main function to have been to provide an alternative social world wherein the fundamental, intrinsic human rights to enlightenment, life, liberty, and happiness, etc., became accessible to those who sought to claim them. The rights of the individual members of the traditional society were not asserted in any activist way, although the presence of the alternative community definitely exerted a tremendous impact, nor were the fundamental responsibilities of generosity, morality, and tolerance aggressively asserted except through example, story, and admonition. The monastic community provided a liberative educational vehicle for those who entered it and exercised a restraining, civilizing influence on the larger society as best it could.

This civilizing process came out in the open during the reign of the Emperor Aśoka (ca. 270–230 B.C.E.), who eventually converted to Buddhism personally and then actively promoted the Buddhist principles throughout the recently formed empire. In keeping with those principles, he showed tolerance for the plurality of religions, supporting all those who practiced what they preached, whether Buddhist or not.

For the time of Aśoka's reign, the alternative world of the *Saṅgha* became something like an establishment, seeking to transform society more actively through education and through encouragement of the emperor's legislative edicts. It is clear, however, that Aśoka in a sense overstepped the pace of development of the society, pushing the people too quickly toward nonviolence, including vegetarianism, self-cultivation, charity, and tolerance. Symbolically, one might say that he challenged too radically the traditional gods, suspending their sacrificial cults by transforming blood-sacrifice into charitable offerings.

Soon after his death, the dynasty fell, and his successors led a reaction marked by a revival of Brāhmaṇic fundamentalism. In spite of this overacceleration and subsequent retrenchment, the alternative order continued to exercise its influence, as well as to expand Buddhism beyond India. Śri Laṅkā was missionized by Aśoka's grandson (according to the traditional accounts) and the Theravāda form of the Individual Vehicle took root there to last until modern times. From Śri Laṅkā it eventually spread into Burma and Thailand. Aśoka also sent missions into Afghanistan and Iran, and perhaps even further westward, according to his own account.

Aśoka was a highly autocratic emperor and, in human rights terms, he set the example of a kind of Asian "monarchical socialism" that is very difficult for Westerners, with their experience of Magna Carta and revolutionary democracies, to understand. However, it is clear that in the Indian case, as often in the Chinese, it was the emperor who was the guarantor of the rights of the individual, forcing the pace of social change and protecting the individual from the oppressions of various intermediate elites. Thus a strong emperor could control the violence of local warlords by superior force, the economic oppression exerted by powerful mercantile interests by maintaining state granaries to prevent hoarding and by taxing private fortunes to finance public works, and the social oppression of caste elites by funding democratic educational institutions such as the Buddhist and Jain monastic schools. Naturally a weak emperor not only failed to check the abuses of regional, traditional powers, he also added to the people's burdens, and thus dynasties would fall. The latter cases have caused our perception of "Oriental despotism," and it takes our "modern" minds some effort to see the former's social benefit, usually the basis of the original formation of empires.

Toward the end of the first phase, the Buddhist order gradually became more activist in pressing for social change, less and less content to remain the anchor of an alternative social world, and more and more aggressive in transforming activity. This process culminated in a "new" form of Buddhism, the Universal Vehicle (*Mahāyāna*), whose foundation was a metaphysical insight into the absolute emptiness and universal relativity (*śūnyatā/pratītyasamutpāda*) of all things, including any personal *nirvāṇa*, and a corresponding ethical impulse toward universal compassion (*mahākaruṇa*), the drive to assist all beings to achieve their own fulfilling happiness in liberation and enlightenment.

Philosophically, this new movement, ushered in by the great Nāgārjuna, was critical of the excessive individualism of the Individual Vehicle monks who sought their own fulfillment in the alternative reality of their hypothetical "remainderless *nirvāṇa*." And institutionally, it was critical of the excessive aloofness of the monastic establishment, considering itself a place apart from and superior to the ordinary social world. Monasticism was still considered essential as the anchor of individualism against the tides of collectivism in the traditional society, but just as the individual saint was not considered perfect just through personal transcendence but had to strive beyond that, motivated by great compassion, to make liberation available to all, so also the monastic institution was to move beyond its anchoring function and actively promote the welfare and especially the education of all citizens. And just as the dualism of *saṃsāra* and *nirvāṇa* was challenged by the Mahāyāna's insight into ultimate nonduality, so the social dualism between monk and layperson was challenged by the drive of great compassion. Hence, the monasteries slowly developed into great educational centers, famous examples being the great universities of Takṣaśilā, Valabhī, Nālandā, Śrī Parvata, and Kāñcī.

The Universal Vehicle emerged in a social atmosphere of a refined, urban civilization of great wealth and sophistication. Some of the great figures of its scriptures are laymen, such as Vimalakīrti, and laywomen, such as Śrīmālā. The cold, analytical wisdom (*prañā*) of the Individual Vehicle whereby the personal release from the egocentric complex was achieved became the warm, intuitive transcendent wisdom (*prajñāpāramitā*), a goddess, the Mother of All Victors (*sarvajinamāta*). Human rights, now more taken for granted in a civilized, pluralistic society with large educated classes, and a powerful bourgeoisie (*vaiśyasie!*), were still anchored in the now pervasively accepted tenfold prohibitions/injunctions (not to take life/to save life, etc.). The focus in the Universal Vehicle, therefore, was on the positive injunctions to transcendent virtues, the "ultra-obligations" of transcendent generosity, morality, and tolerance. What had been ideal exemplary virtues in the *Jātakas* now took hold as positive precepts to be enacted by monastic and layperson alike. People of all walks of life, all occupations, and both sexes should now become enlightened, educated, and then actively responsible in society, as it were, with no need necessarily first to abandon the ordinary realm to enter the liberated realm of the order, although that option could still be helpful to some.

Of course, the social realm, with its ups and downs, its good rulers and its bad, could not realistically be expected to become so rapidly transformed. Therefore the messianic drive of compassion found its ideals realized in a variety of heavenly social realms, the famous "pure lands" or "Buddha-fields" of the Universal Vehicle Scriptures. These lands became imaginative icons for the populace wherein Buddhahood and social kingship fused in visions of unimaginable splendor. Emanating from this Beatific Realm (*sambhogakāya*), numerous divinized forms of Buddhas, "Buddhesses," and male and female bodhisattvas, appeared to succor the individual in his or her struggle to live up to the high ideals of the teachings. And mundane kings had a hard act to follow to come anywhere near the majesty and power of the celestial Dharma-king Amitābha, who caused even the splendor of Indra to pale. (As was noted in writings by Confucian scholars, Buddhism would cause the masses to lose reverence for the Central Country and its traditions!)[10]

During the ascendancy of the Universal Vehicle, its message of profound wisdom and loving solidarity with all life and its rich iconography enabled it to missionize much of Asia. Early on it spread through Central Asia to China, and its large-scale adoption in China after the fall of the Han up to its height in the T'ang and Sung is one of the wonders of history. From China it spread to Korea, Japan, and Vietnam, although the latter had another current coming from India and Śrī Lankā as well. It also spread as a further strand into the Śrī Lankā, Burman, and Thai traditions, though it never became too firmly entrenched wherever the Theravāda had become strict orthodoxy.

Now, the countries where the Theravāda Individual Vehicle prevailed accepted the original alternate social reality represented by the institutional presence of monastic Buddhism and preserved it in a pattern reminiscent of the one I described above in the account of early Buddhism in India. From a human rights perspective, adherents of the Theravāda tradition anchored individual rights, but in an alternative realm, and only gradually exerted pressure on the ordinary traditional societies. Without normatively accepting Universal Vehicle doctrine on any large scale, the latent Universal Vehicle in the *Jātakas* and in the basic Buddhist ethical principles gradually emerged and transformed the ordinary institutions of kingship, attempting with more or less success in various countries and periods to establish an Aśokan pattern of kingship by accepting a righteous king as the chief layperson, supporter of the order, and defender of the orthodox faith. Unfortunately, too often unscrupulous kings used the metaphysical/ethical dualism of the Individual Vehicle to give themselves room to act quite ruthlessly in the secular sphere, justifying it later by lavish support of the monastics with the other hand. There thus developed a pattern of despotic behavior vis-à-vis lay subjects, coupled with generosity and tolerance vis-à-vis the monastic order.

In the Mahāyāna countries, on the other hand, there arose the opposite problem. That is, the monastic establishment never did become strongly established culturally, independent of the political authority, at least, not for very long. Monastic communities enjoyed periods of patronage, quite lavish at times, but then succeeding regimes would strip them down again to recover lands and taxes and to reincorporate subjects back into the ordinary social realm. Therefore, when the Universal Vehicle entered with its focus on altruistic responsibilities, the fundamental individualistic rights anchored in the Individual Vehicle could not be taken for granted. And while the Universal Vehicle was highly popular, with its profound philosophy, its sophisticated meditative techniques for the intellectuals, its magnificent ideal of compassion, and its visionary profusion of religious devotionalisms for the populace, its leaders and institutions were all too often inclined or forced to compromise with secular imperial authority, unable effectively to exercise ethically critical leverage over the social power structure.

Thus, the universities of the East Asian countries never fused with the monastic establishment, which had been the creators of the first universities in India, but continued to be based on a classical Confucian model, turning out a secular (from the Buddhist perspective) elite. With the Neo-Confucian resurgence in the Sung, the traditional elite began to appropriate in their own terms some of the transcendentalist strategies of the Universal Vehicle, while the Ch'an houses revitalized the uncompromising pursuit of individual enlightenment associated with the Individual Vehicle. A very creative period ensued, but the Mongol invasion confused the picture, and we cannot trace where its evolution might otherwise have gone. An interesting point is that, to be really effective in causing liberative social evolution, the Buddhist ethical ideal seems to require the combined activity of the Individual Vehicle, with its anchoring of rights even in an alternative realm, and the Universal Vehicle, with its expansive promotion of altruistic responsibilities. Only in this way is it possible for Buddhism not to be subsumed into a static traditional holistic society.

When we come to the third phase in India, that of the Vajra Vehicle, we should expect to see the fullest flowering of over a thousand years of social evolution under the combined impetus of both the Individual Vehicle and the Universal Vehicles to further both individualistic rights and universalistic responsibilities. At first glance, to judge from secondary sources, it seems a dismal failure. We find even modern Buddhist writers labeling this period that of the "degeneracy" of Buddhism in India, with a previously sound monastic institution degenerating into Tantric popularistic ritualism, with the philosophical tradition of a long line of creative thinkers petering out and being swallowed up in a resurgent Neo-Hinduism, with waves of conquerors finally destroying effete dynasties, and Buddhism apparently disappearing altogether from the "land of its birth." The greatest figures of this period, the Great Adepts (*mahāsiddha*), seem to be frightful and unsavory characters, dabbling in the most scandalous sexual and aggressive magic.

To temper this discouraging picture, we should realize that most of the Western writers who have dealt with this period are products of a culture that has only a mere century of exposure to depth psychology, that most of the Buddhist writers on it come from cultures wherein either Individual Vehicle or Universal Vehicle is doctrinally normative, and hence the synthesis of either one into a new integration might look like a "degeneration." Likewise, if we recall the basic principles we have discussed at the heart of the Buddhist metaphysical/ethical tradition, Buddhism's institutional "disappearance" could be considered its success as well as its failure. Buddha created an alternative reality as a device to transform the ordinary social reality slowly and indirectly, at first for individuals through their enlightenments, eventually for society, which is merely all individuals. The goal is by no means a permanent dualism, and we can clearly see in the imagery of the Pure Land, for example, the "withering away" of the monastery as a sign of evolutionary success.

In fact, I do not consider the work to have been completed in the India of 1000 C.E., although perhaps a great deal more may have been accomplished than has been recognized. The actual reason for the institutional disappearance, however, is equally complimentary to Buddhism. The new invading rulers of the second millennium clearly took note of the Buddhist establishment as the immovable anchor of an ideal and habit of freedom, i.e., in their eyes, insubordination. Therefore they systematically set out to erase its every physical trace, razing monasteries, burning books and monks, and smashing devotional sites. Fortunately, by that time the impetus for social evolution no longer depended that heavily on buildings, books, and professionals, and it went on subterraneously, set back, of course, by having to deal with the level of culture of the conquering peoples.

With the above as prolegomenon, we can begin to look at the third phase itself. It began in the post-Gupta period in the north, and reached full flowering by the eighth century, especially under the Pala rulers of Bengal and Orissa. The Great Adepts, far from being simple-minded *sādhus* who could not manage the monastic discipline and could not embrace the bodhisattva responsibility, were graduates and masters of both traditions. They went beyond the monastic and academic and began a movement of outreach into every sphere of Indian life.

Take the example of Nāropa (ca. tenth–eleventh centuries C.E.), an outstanding monk, universally respected for his purity and insight. He was an abbot of Nālandā, a renowned scholar and teacher. Yet he felt that, while impeccably orthodox in both Individual and Universal Vehicles, he was still not fully enlightened in his heart, and he was not really taking up the ultra-responsibility of the bodhisattva. He abandoned his identities as monk and professor and went forth into nature, seeking the innermost core of the Dharma through Tantric Unexcelled Yoga (*anuttarayoga*) practice under his *guru*, Tilopa. He became, after incredible ordeals reminiscent of the Buddha's own period of ascetic tribulations, perfectly enlightened. He went on to teach thousands of disciples from all walks of life and even from all religions of the time, not just Buddhists, though his greatest disciple and heir was a Tibetan Buddhist named Marpa.

Nāropa's story illustrates how the Vajra Vehicle was not in any way a degeneracy of Buddhism, but rather the natural, creative evolution of Individual and Universal Vehicles in continuation of their civilizing missions. It does also, of course, indicate that the establishment of the day had become somewhat prey to formalism and hence no longer effective in carrying out its purpose without further development. It is reminiscent of Bodhidharma, or Hui-neng, or Dōgen, who renewed Buddhist practice in their eras by going to the heart of the matter and not staying with institutional strategies that, by themselves, were no longer adequate to the social moment.

Let us remember that the Individualist monasticism answered a need to create a space for individualism and the individual's rights to liberty and enlightenment within an excessively holistic society. Universalist messianism had answered a need to intensify the drive for social transformation through love, compassion, and altruistic ultra-responsibility by rousing the laity and expanding the educational activity of the monastics to include all those so inclined among the large urban educated classes. By the time of the third period, urban India was flourishing with unprecedented wealth; tolerance and individualistic pluralism were assured; there was little internal war; class boundaries were relaxed; and the educated were well taken care of by the establishment. But there was still the vast range of village India, and the untouched masses of tribal India, not to speak of the wild border countries such as Nepal, Tibet, Assam, and even far-flung islands such as the Isle of Gold (Java-Suvarṇadvīpa), and Japan. New ways of expressing enlightenment had to be manifested by these masters who were carrying on the civilizing program of the Dharma. They had to enter the realm of the "shamanic." They had to develop the ability to wrestle with the tribal deities of these new peoples within and without India, as indeed Śākyamuni had wrestled with Māra and Indra and Brahma to start the movement. Having over centuries greatly refined their civilizing techniques, they could integrate individualism and universalism in the immediate, apocalyptic approach of Vajrayāna.

In regard to the missionizing aspect of the third phase, the Great Adepts spread this integrated form of Buddhism to the hinterlands of India, to the villagers and the tribals, to the borderlands of Tibet and Nepal, and to the southeastern islands. Bodhidharma spread this new wave in a manner appropriate to China: his lineage of the Dharma saved the day during the late T'ang persecutions when official urban Buddhism suffered mightily, his heirs such as Pai-chang moving far away into the mountains. He cultivated the skill to deal with the uneducated and the provincial, and carried on teaching and practice free of the old formalisms. Kūkai spread the formally Tantric strand of this third period to Japan, where it served as a foundation of Japanese Buddhism, and the Zen masters of the Kamakura period continued that effort with the formless strand.

While these masters drew disciples from, and never condemned, the Individualist and Universalist institutions, they never depended on them either. On the contrary, the adepts who sustained the vitality of monasteries and schools throughout the second millennium with its tremendous political problems embodied and taught the fullest individualism; they were the most active universalists as well. And they never compromised one iota with the social power structures, at times being the only critical force against their excesses. In the case of the Tibetan representatives of this third-phase line of transmissions, they were the only tradition actually to take responsibility for government. Eventually, it fell to their lot to undertake the taming of the Mongol nations, which task they carried out quite successfully from the thirteenth to the seventeenth centuries.

None of these strategies ever did succeed in creating for long or on a mass scale a fully ethical society, which we could put right in the center of our chart above, where human rights were fully respected and human altruistic responsibilities were wholeheartedly accepted. But no other tradition anywhere, especially the modern one, has had such a success either. Careful examination of the historical record confirms that there were periods of great humanistic flowering in various civilizations. But we never get to see the full conclusion of these glorious moments, because of the magnetic effect they have on neighboring barbarians. Individualism, pacifism, universalism, and social harmony tend to produce fine arts, great wealth, liberated people, and military weakness, all of which invite conquest by cruder, poorer, highly conditioned, and militarily powerful peoples. Whether or not these people are ultimately conquered culturally by their victims' high civilization, they certainly interrupt the social experiments. So far we must conclude that there has been no perfect system.

Buddhist Contributions to Current Thought on Human Rights and Responsibilities

I mentioned earlier that a human rights concept cannot be compelling unless the basic concept of a "human" is clearly supportive of it. It is humans who claim their rights, and those who must respect them are also humans. What they think they are, and what they think the others are obviously control their treatment of themselves and others.

For example, if a basic human right is the right to life, a choice to override that right by another is only possible when based on a specific notion of what happens to the victim after death. Spiritualistic, religious killing is thus based on the theory that a God gave the victim his right to life, and thus that God can alienate that right by pronouncing such and such a person deserving of death. God will also take care of that person afterwards, either punishing or saving; it is God's problem not the problem of the righteous killer. Materialistic, scientific killing is based on the theory that humans have no soul, vital essence, spirit, or mental continuation, and that, while the victim has a right to life as a useful member of society, if he becomes useless or harmful, he can be reduced to the nothingness that is the ground reality.

There is no concern about salvation or damnation, and the rational killer need not worry about his own destiny being ultimately affected, as he too will soon join the victim in nothingness. As I mentioned above, the spiritualist devalues the relative reality, and the materialist devalues the ultimate reality. Thus, the strength of a claim of human rights depends on whether the claimant is believed to be a spiritual or a material being, or, as is more often the case, a kind of combination of the two.

To approach this from another perspective, the modern notion of human rights seems rather muddled. First, rights are said to be "natural," "inherent" in being human. Second, they are said to be "entitlements of persons," which implies that title has been granted by something else, God or society. They are said to be "inalienable," except in exceptional cases, yet they are also said to be "held primarily in relation to society." These statements contain clear contradictions, if they have any meaning at all without clarification of the metaphysical questions, "what is 'nature'?" "in what is the inherence?" "who or what has entitled?"

Now there are a variety of Buddhist metaphysical positions on the nature of reality. There are realistic systems, idealistic systems, and the most philosophically developed, the Central Way (Mādhyamika) is correctly called a relativistic system, with the understanding that here "relativism" does not mean "nihilism," but rather a position in the center between the extremes of absolutism and nihilism. This system holds that the absolute or ultimate reality of things is universal voidness of any form of intrinsic reality. This voidness, conceived as a thing apart, is itself also devoid of intrinsic reality. Therefore this voidness is the condition for the relative, empirical, and conventional relativity of all things. Thus, all things are ultimately void and no analysis or explanation can capture their reality; and all things are relatively conventional in that concepts and conventions make them what they are in experience and practice. Therefore a God has no intrinsic, static self, a human has no intrinsic self. All descriptions of relative reality are therefore hypothetical or conventional, and our subscribing to any one world or person picture is directly responsible for making it that way. This does not mean that reality is relatively random, in that world-pictures are deep cultural constructions, and the "culture" may include many other types of beings than those presently living and visible on any one planet. Thus relative causality is quite binding on the individual person, on the mental, verbal, and physical levels.

Thus, the Buddhist intuition of selflessness was liberative originally from the theistic, spiritualistic worldviews that held the world a product of an all-powerful creator, and in the same way that modern rationalism was liberative from medieval theism. But it was also liberative from those who carried this liberation to the opposite extreme, the Lokayata materialistic nihilists, who held that ultimate reality was nothingness, and hence denied the coherence of relativity and causality. The most celebrated eulogy of the Buddha saluted him as the discoverer of the fact that all things arise from causes (*ye dharmāh, hetuprabhāvāh* . . .), not as the discoverer of religious truth.

The causality that has produced human beings, in the Buddhist view, is a process of evolution (*karma*) emerging from a beginningless past. This evolution is quite mechanical, just like modern biological theories, in that a certain pattern of action repeated in the course of living develops a propensity for that action, which eventually crystallizes into a physical mutation in a succeeding generation.

Therefore, in Buddhism, just as in biology, a human being is a product of an inconceivably long process of evolutionary action and represents an amazing achievement due to a process of successful adaptations. But there is this immense difference between the Buddhist and the Darwinian evolutionary theory: the Buddhist evolution is not only a physical process, it is also linguistic and mental. (It is intriguing how the verbal is conceived as a level of process somehow midway between the material and the mental.) Therefore a human being is not just the product of countless previous generations of *others*, his horde of ancestors. He or she is the product of countless previous generations of *himself* or *herself*. The mental continuum of a human being, while constantly changing even in one life, is itself a beginningless continuum.

Therefore, and this is the crucial point of the theory for our purposes, the magnificent evolutionary achievement of human embodiment is the individual human being's own personal achievement. A human person has earned his or her own humanity. Buddhist thought developed the concept of *gotra*, which I translate as "spiritual gene," to capture this sense of the individual's being literally self-made in part.

The act of conception of a living being in Buddhism involves three sets of genes, those of the mother, those of the father, and those of the person being born. The former two determine the physical characteristics of the being, the last determines the choice of that sort of physical environment and the being's spiritual or mental characteristics. This is symbolically expressed in the imagery of the Tantras as the union of three drops (*bindu*): the red drop of the mother unites with the white drop of the father and then the blue drop of the child unites with them both, emerging from the subtle realm of pure mental energy into connection with the gross realm of physical matter. In the case of a human child, it brings with it a rich treasure of instinctual propensities coded into a kind of spiritual DNA, the fruit of all its previous evolutionary actions.

By the same token, according to the theory, the mental, verbal, and physical actions committed by human beings shape the spiritual gene they take with them through death into their next generation. They are the consequences of their past actions, and they will bear the consequences of their present actions in the future. No God or nation can damn them or save them, and they cannot count on an automatic anesthesia after death. They are thoroughly embedded in an endless relativity of causes and effects, and they must take responsibility first of all for their own destinies.

This life-description of the Buddha's was hotly disputed by theists and atheists alike for thousands of years. There is a rich literature of philosophical defense and elaboration of the theory. But this is not the place to explore the metaphysical debates. Our concern is the ethical impact of this view, which we can immediately see is profound. It provides a metaphysical base for an indomitable individualism.

Those individuals who subscribe to this theory cannot feel they belong totally to their parents, tribe, nation, or even culture. They have to evaluate every compulsion from family or priest or king in terms of what the actions demanded of them by those in charge will produce by way of effects they alone must experience in the future. Not even a god can change those effects. Hence if the orders of the god, through the priest, or of the king, through the general, conflict with their own understanding of what they owe themselves, they are rationally serving their individual self-interests if they each obey the evolutionary causal law, expressed as moral injunctions, instead of the social or political regulations. Each feels a pride in the achievement of human life, and feels a rational fear of losing that achievement by perhaps acting in a sub-human manner. Each has the precious wish-granting gem of human life, in Buddhist parlance, which will not lightly be thrown away. As for their rights, while such rights are not absolutistically innate, or inherent, these individuals have earned those rights arduously, rights that are relatively innate in their humanness, not granted them by parents, gods, or kings.

This theory describes further how these individuals came to be human, rising up from the wretched states of hells, the grotesque *preta* realms, and the vicious realms of the beasts, and not being seduced into the powers and plea-sures of the manifold heavens. The human state was slowly evolved through transcending aggression by expressing love, transcending greed by expressing generosity, and transcending delusive stupidity by expressing intelligence and wisdom. These three are called the "three positive mental evolutionary paths." Verbal positive actions are analogous to the positive mental acts, pleasant speech fitting with love, pacifying speech fitting with generosity, true speech and meaningful speech fitting with intelligence; these four are called the four positive verbal evolutionary paths. And physical well-being emerges from physical acts also analogous, preserving lives expressing love, giving gifts expressing generosity, and proper sexual interactions expressing intelligence. On the other side, such individuals know that if they hate, covet, and uphold delusive beliefs, if they revile, slander, chatter, and lie, if they kill, steal, and indulge in abusive sexuality, they go against their humanity, gen-erating an evolutionary causality that will drag each one back down into the wretched states.

This whole theory is replete with the most elaborate, dreadfully vivid depic-tions of actual results of actions in experiential states, which, if contemplated by the imaginative, serve to compel compliance with these evolutionary laws. For example, the malicious liar eventually ends up in a hell for liars, in which he/she is born as a small bulbous globe of consciousness attached to a giant tongue of great sensitivity, spread over many acres of burning iron ground, with little horned devils merrily running red hot iron plows back and forth through its nerves from dawn to dusk of a multimillion-year day. Or on a less extravagant note, one who kills other beings, especially human beings, will be killed one time in a future life in a similar way, one for each being one kills.

Those who inquire into this theory more deeply begin to worry that, while each now enjoys human life as the result of previous positive evolutionary actions, each may very well face the results in the future. As the past is beginningless, there are no guarantees. Therefore, now that one has human life with its communicativeness and intelligence, one had better explore any possible ways of gaining freedom from such future terrors, attaining liberation and enlightenment, defined either as an escape from involuntary rebirth or as mastery of the causal processes to a degree sufficient to insure favorable rebirths. This terror and this ambition become the motivating drives for enlightenment, which itself is actually the tenth positive path, that of cultivating intelligence or wisdom to the transcendent degree. And so such seekers find that the Buddha's Dharma teaches that the supreme value of the human life lies in its closeness to enlightenment; hence its supreme use is in the quest of enlightenment. Importantly also, since evolution connotes ascent to us, it can be wasted as well, as one can throw away a diamond, and the terror of experiencing a hellish devolution becomes another powerful motive for self-transcendence.

In sum, individual humans who possess rights are presented as spiritual as well as physical beings of unique accomplishments and valuable opportunities. They have earned their own rights through suffering and transcending egotism in the sea of evolution, and no one can deprive them of such rights, since no one conferred these rights upon them. Their primary right is that of life, then that of liberty, then that of education. Societies are nothing but collections of such individuals, and they cease to be truly human societies when they cease to acknowledge that each individual's fulfillment is the purpose of the whole. Humans are free also to give away their rights in furtherance of the fulfillment of others. Indeed it is by the supreme generosity of giving even one's life that one evolved into a human out of lower forms. Thus talk of rights quickly passes over into talk of responsibilities, as the individual who is self-fulfilled—i.e., enlightened as to selflessness—automatically wills to share that happiness of release with others by aiding them in their own quests of enlightenment.

Self-interest and altruistic interest come into coincidence upon enlightenment (wisdom having dispelled the egocentric delusion that one's own life depends on the destruction of others' lives), and one's own life becomes immeasurably enriched by the preservation of others' lives, because of the multilife environment within which one lives. Morality becomes a matter of evolutionary causality, reason, and enlightened will having come into harmony, and there is no longer need of unreasoned obedience or rational expedience.

Such in, of course, an ideal sense, is the Buddhist worldview and ethical position on human rights and responsibilities. I have already pointed out that no so-called Buddhist society has ever yet fully realized these principles in practice. It is hardly necessary to mention that there is very little chance that the modern world will ever come (en masse) to adopt such a position. If, however, certain valuable points can be understood, it may be possible to extrapolate from them emphases and critical principles with which to buttress modern human rights ideals and responsible practices. Without totally challenging all aspects of theistic or nontheistic world views, it may be possible to move some of their impacts around to support a more compelling position on human rights and to inspire a more energetic assumption of human responsibilities.

For example, adherents of a theistic movement might argue for use of capital punishment, based on a perceived hopelessness of rehabilitation of certain types of criminals, and might employ biblical examples in a literalistic way, based on a feeling that what God giveth God can take away. They thereby avoid a sense of personal responsibility in calling for the blood of these human persons. One might find resources to temper their conviction by thinking of the support from the Buddhist position. " 'Vengeance is mine,' saith the Lord," is like the view that karmic evolution itself causally brings forth eventual retribution. The taking of the second life can then in no way be considered a compensation for the loss of the first, and will have to be faced as itself another murder, and all those members of society who feel strongly motivated to kill the criminal must themselves accumulate some form of the evolutionary action of taking life. Whether or not there is any immediate or obvious rehabilitative success through compassion, the fact that they follow Christ's teaching of "turn the other cheek" is actually much more in their own self-interest as human beings, even if they should eventually be murdered themselves, loving mind and all, by the very criminal upon escape. "Who loses his life for my sake, shall find life everlasting."

Or take a nontheistic utilitarian movement that advocates capital punishment, based on the same perception, arguing that there is no space in the prisons, there is too much expense, society must not continue to suffer needlessly beyond the original loss of a life, and the murderer himself will find release from his guilt and imprisonment in death's nothingness. One might challenge its certainty that there is nothing after death, pose the burden of explaining what it means to say "something, a personal subjectivity can become nothing," and even argue that in that case, the murderer himself can also argue he helped his victim find release in the nothingness after death.

Society's killing for expediency is only different in degree from the murderer's killing for gain or passion. The only lesson taught is that you should not kill unless there are enough of you to get away with it, and what sort of society is that? Admittedly, the convinced materialist is the most difficult person to engage, as he or she is so emotionally committed to that final nothingness, staving off as it does the terrors of hells and other such "primitive superstitions," and he or she is so well supported by the scientific materialistic worldview we inherit from the past century. But the Buddhist metaphysical tradition has rich resources, especially in the works of the great philosopher Dharmakīrti (seventh century), to assist Pascal in at least introducing doubt into such a conviction.

In sum, the points we can learn from the Buddhist thinkers are 1) that the ethical theory seeking to develop a compelling human rights position cannot dispense with analysis and a stance on the underlying metaphysical issues, as a human rights position cannot be really compelling if it is purely dogmatic or purely prudential, absolutist, or spiritually nihilistically relativist; 2) that some form of rationally plausible spiritual irreducibility of a human being may be as essential to support human rights as is a healthy this-worldly individualism suspicious of spiritual rationalizations of injustice; and 3) that human rights thought should always be conducted in interconnection with a balancing consideration of human responsibilities. Especially today, if a new and viable central way between the extremes of dogmatic religions and materialistic sciences is to be discovered, compelling to the minds and hearts of modern humans, then Buddhist thought's long experience of keeping open a center between various types of absolutist spiritualists and nihilist materialists is certainly worthy of study.

NOTES

1. Jack Donnelly. "Human Rights and Human Dignity: An Analytic Critique of Non-Western Conceptions of Human Rights," in *American Political Science Review* 76:2 (June 1982), 304.

2. Ibid., p. 304, here quoting the "United Nations International Covenant on Civil and Political Rights" and the "United Nations International Covenant on Economic, Social, and Cultural Rights (1960)."

3. Robert Thurman. "Buddhist Ethics: The Emptiness That Is Compassion," in *Religious Traditions* (November 1981).

4. H. Richard Niebuhr. *The Responsible Self* (New York: Harper, 1963).

5. Robert Thurman. "The Politics of Enlightenment," *Lindisfarne Letter* 8 (Winter 1979).

6. Robert Thurman. "Guidelines for Buddhist Social Activism Based on Nāgārjuna's Jewel Garland of Royal Counsels," in *The Eastern Buddhist* 16, no. 1 (Spring 1983).

7. Karl Jaspers. "The Axial Age," *The Origin and Goal of History*, trans. by Michael Bullock (New Haven: Yale University Press, 1953), p. 15.

8. Peter Berger, Brigitte Berger, and Hansfried Kellner, *The Homeless Mind: Modernization and Consciousness* (New York: Vintage Books, 1974).

9. *Ratnavat-karmavipāka-kṣaṇasampatmanuṣyadeha* . . .

10. See, for example, Wm. Theodore de Bary et al., *Sources of Chinese Tradition* (New York: Columbia University Press, 1960), pp. 312–326.

4

Confucian Perspectives on the Individual and the Collectivity

IRENE BLOOM

In approximately the same historical time frame there began to evolve, in the societies we recognize as ancestral to two of the world's oldest continuous cultures, India and China, distinctly different conceptions of the human—distinct perspectives on the individual and the relation of the individual to the various configurations of society. By a time well before the beginning of the Christian era in the West—during an age represented by Karl Jaspers as the "axial age"[1] of antiquity—certain fundamental attitudes concerning the person had been articulated in China, as they had in India. A religious core had been laid down that seems to have given shape and substance to subsequent intuitions concerning what it means to be human. Despite enormous changes in ideas and social practices over a long span of human history, this religious core proved remarkably vital and resilient. It still profoundly influences what many of our contemporaries believe about their own humanity and what they understand of human dignity. Given the long tenure, the inherent weight, and the continued relevance of this core of beliefs and values, it deserves to be taken seriously by those concerned with human rights.

In the first part of the essay, which deals with classical Confucian perspectives on the nature, duties, and rights of the individual, I have attempted some comparisons with the Hindu perspectives described by Joseph Elder in his essay in this volume. In the second part, which is concerned with Confucian perspectives on the nature, duties, and rights of the collectivity, the focus is primarily on China. In the conclusion certain comparisons are suggested between China and the West.

The Chinese literature on which I draw is of a different character from the Indian literature on which Professor Elder bases his analysis of the Hindu tradition. He notes a distinction between the Vedic literature recognized as the *Śruti* ("what is heard, revealed, implying a supra-human origin") and the post-Vedic literature referred to as *Smṛti* ("what is remembered, what is tradition, implying a merely human origin"). For his discussion of the doctrine of the unity of *Brahman* (World Spirit) and *Ātman* (the unconditioned self) and of transmigration, Elder draws from the literature known as *Śruti* and particularly from the *Chāndogya Upaniṣad.* For his discussion of "duties" and "correct action," he draws on the *Smṛti* literature, especially the *Manava Dharma Śāstra* or the Precepts of Manu. The reader must be struck by the difference in tone and content in the examples offered from the *Śruti* and the *Smṛti* texts.

The Confucian literature to which I shall be referring amounts to a kind of core curriculum known as the Four Books: the *Analects*, the *Mencius*, the *Great Learning*, and the *Mean*. The first of these is a record of statements and conversations of Confucius (551–479 B.C.E.) and his disciples, compiled at different times after the Master's death. The *Mencius* is a record of the teachings of Mencius (ca. 372–289 B.C.E.), one of the most influential of Confucius' successors. Like the *Analects*, the *Mencius*, while purporting to be a record of Mencius' conversations, was apparently compiled by followers.[2] The *Great Learning* and the *Mean* are chapters from a work known as the *Record of Rites* (*Li chi*), dating from the Han (206 B.C.E.–221 C.E.) period.

Though none of the Four Books has the term *ching*, or classic, in its Chinese title, they have for centuries been considered the epitome of the Chinese classics. From the early fourteenth until the early twentieth century these texts, with commentaries by the Neo-Confucian scholar Chu Hsi (1130–1200), formed the core curriculum on which the Chinese civil service examinations were based. They have been understood as repositories of an enduring wisdom, but a wisdom that is of human, not of supra-human origin. The human and the natural are not distinguished from the sacred or the divine, and an Indian-style distinction between "what is heard" and "what is remembered," or between what is revealed and what is transmitted through "merely human" bearers, has no resonance here. The Chinese classics would be both "heard" and "remembered," but, always, their source would be human. In this we may discover a clue to what must follow in our discussion of a tradition which is preeminently this-worldly and which, especially in its classical age, focuses primarily on three things: interpersonal relationships, personal cultivation in the context of those relationships, and the practicalities of ordinary life in the world.

THE INDIVIDUAL

The Nature of the Individual

The conversations in Book VI of the *Chāndogya Upaniṣad* between the sage Uddālaka and his well-tutored, if not yet wise, son Śvetaketu convey a classic Upaniṣadic statement about the nature of the person and of the self. The son has spent a dozen years studying the Vedas with a teacher and has returned, "conceited, priding himself on his learning, and obdurate." The father engages him in a discussion which involves a reflection, intended for the son's edification, on the nature of Being. As the discussion opens, the father questions the son about his experience of studying with his teacher,

> Did you also ask about that teaching by which what had not been heard is heard; what had not been thought of, is thought of; and what had not been known, is known?" (*Chāndogya Upaniṣad* 6:1).

In other words, asks the father, did you advance to the teaching that concerns itself with ultimate questions? Śvetaketu has apparently not gotten that far and replies, "Now, sir, what manner of teaching is that?" As Elder points out, the ensuing discussion moves unswervingly toward a perspective on the nature of ultimate truth and a formulation of that truth which remains central and formative in the entire Hindu tradition.

In the Confucian texts which are the nearest counterparts to the Upaniṣads, we find ourselves on ground that is more like ordinary earth. Disciples of the Confucian masters frequently inquire about learning and about establishing priorities, but their questions (normally, in a Chinese context, it is the disciples who ask the questions and the teachers who answer them) are unlike the leading question with which Uddālaka challenges the unwarranted confidence of his son. The questions posed by the disciples of Confucius and Mencius typically have to do *not* with things hitherto unheard, unthought of, or unknown, but with things already familiar, though perhaps imperfectly clarified in the mind or resolved in the will of the questioner. Questions are often aimed at finding ways of coping with the immediate challenges of life or, more obliquely, at assessing the subject's own behavioral and moral development. An "ultimate" question, when one is interposed at all, may even be consciously deferred or dismissed by a Confucian teacher as beyond the realm of secure human knowledge or as "difficult to discuss." In such a case the response may direct the student to transfer his attention from a matter essentially unknowable to one which is within his ken—or from an ultimate to a proximate sphere:

Chi-lu asked about serving spiritual beings.

The Master said, "Before you have learned to serve human beings, how can you serve spiritual beings?"

"I venture to ask about death?"

"When you do not yet know about life, how can you know about death?"

(*Analects* 11:11)

Chi-lu's questions—which probe the relation between the living and the dead, the responsibilities of the living to the dead, and the possible influence of the dead over the living—evoke issues important in the religious life of any culture. Confucius' response reflects an emergence from an "auguristic-sacrificial"[3] mentality toward values which are this-worldly and moral. Were the living to consult and appease the spirits of deceased ancestors, or should the focus be on human interactions and the capacity of the living to act as moral agents with primary responsibility for the conduct of human affairs?

The Chinese of the "axial age" did not simply relinquish their belief in ghosts and spirits or in a connectedness between the living and the dead, nor does Confucius himself appear to have done so. But the scope of human competence had begun to be reinterpreted: there was a transfer of attention from prognostication to "virtue," from external controls and influences over human affairs to self-control and "moral force" on the part of living individuals. It is probably as a consequence of this diversion of attention from the efficacy of "auspicious" actions to the efficacy of "virtuous" behavior that it becomes meaningful to speak of "individuals."

The conception of the person in the early Confucian texts is primarily biological, familial, and social. This is a worldly spirituality in the sense that neither revelation nor higher knowledge is necessary where common human experience is itself found to be so telling. One is in the first instance the product of one's parents' procreation, a son or a daughter, and likely also a sibling; eventually, a spouse; possibly, a minister to the ruler; always, a friend to others. Confucius says something about each of these relationships in the conversations recorded in the *Analects*, though he puts primary emphasis on the relations between father and son and minister and ruler. In later centuries, by the time of the *Mencius* and the *Mean*, there begins to be reference to "the five relationships" (*wu-lun*).[4] These five relationships—between parent and child, husband and wife, elder and younger siblings, ruler and minister, friend and friend—come to be understood as providing the form and structure of human existence.

While the psychological sense and experience of relatedness are obviously valued, it is more the elemental fact of relatedness, relatedness as a given, that stands out in the early texts. A person is a recipient of the gift of human life and, through a reciprocity that links generations, a giver and sustainer of that same gift. A continuum of life and a continuity of being, no doubt prefigured in the earlier religious outlook that put such stress on ancestry, are both assumed as a fact and felt as a value. This seems to represent a fundamental intuition, wherein lies the basis for the spiritual dimension in the worldly spirituality of Confucius.

Moral value is seen by Confucius and his followers to inhere in the way a person carries out the natural familial and social roles and the concomitant responsibilities of giving and sustaining life. It is in their concern with the clarity with which these familial and social roles are understood and the correctness and depth of feeling invested in their enactment that the early Confucians reveal what is most distinctive about their view of the individual. There is little in their conversations and pronouncements that resembles a metaphysics of the person, such as Uddālaka reveals to Śvetaketu. There is no inquiry into what a person ultimately *is* but, rather, reflection on how a humane person can be expected to act, or to *inter*act. Two examples may be suggestive.

While usually supportive of his disciples with their various strengths and foibles, Confucius expresses vexation with Tsai Yü, who is depicted as deficient in both discipline and devotion. In the course of one interview with Confucius, Tsai Yü inquires about the practice of mourning the death of a parent for three years; in his none too humble opinion, such a lengthy period of mourning is disruptive of productive life. When Confucius questions him on whether he would feel fully at ease were he to contemplate resuming a comfortable routine after a shorter period of mourning, Tsai Yü unhesitatingly affirms that he would. For Confucius, this betokens an unforgivable callousness:

> How inhuman Yü is! Only when a child is three years old does it leave its parents' arms. The three years' mourning is the universal mourning everywhere under Heaven. And Yü—was he not the darling of his father and mother for three years?
>
> (*Analects* 17:21)

As the child of one's parents, one is expected to nourish certain feelings and to express a sense of reciprocity toward them, the want of which casts doubt on one's humanity. This point anticipates two others to which we shall return later in the discussion. First, filiality and humanity are closely conjoined. Second, among Confucians, humanity as a descriptive category and humanity as an evaluative category may not always be clearly distinguished. What Confucius literally says here is that Tsai Yü is "inhumane." Yet this translation, which is Arthur Waley's, captures the tone of the Chinese which leaves us feeling that the absence of humane sentiment in Tsai Yü is tantamount to a want of basic humanity.

On another occasion Confucius is questioned by Duke Ching, the ruler of the feudal state of Ch'i, about proper government. His response is epigrammatic: "The ruler is ruler; the minister is minister; the father is father; and the son is son."[5] His meaning is that, given the proper understanding and enactment of these roles by each individual, the success and stability of the state are guaranteed; his tacit assumption is that the relationships between ruler and minister and between father and son represent categories which are at once primary, stable, and perspicuous. One's identity as an individual is bound up with the way one relates to others and performs one's appropriate roles; the relationships and roles are basically secure; the behavior each role entails is seen as so natural as to be transparently clear.

At the same time, I am reluctant to go so far as to say that the individual is defined entirely in terms of his role relationships or that he is the sum total of his relationships, with nothing over.[6] Confucius has an evident interest in the possibilities of *te* (variously translated as "virtue," "inner power," or "moral force") which, in his view, is something endowed in the individual by Heaven or Nature.[7] At several points in the *Analects* (12:10; 12:21; 14:5), as in other ancient Chinese texts, it is indicated that this "virtue" is something that can be "piled up" or "accumulated"; elsewhere (7:3) we find that it can be "cultivated." *Te* becomes part of one's capacity, of one's very being. Mencius speaks of accumulating or cultivating an inner capacity for rightness. Like Confucius and Mencius, the authors of the ritual texts have a sense for the self-esteem and the feeling of well-being that are a concomitant of humane interactions and right conduct. Though they are concerned with moral reciprocity, the realization that isolated acts of goodness are less potent than a conscious pattern of resolute action is one which occurs to them not in the course of moral score-keeping, but as a matter of psychological insight. They are aware of an individual identity that is clearly inward, if perhaps not utterly private, and that is the subject of an ongoing and self-conscious enterprise in self-cultivation.

The overall impression created by Confucius is that he is very much "his own person." He appears not only as a public figure—active teacher, inquirer into ritual matters, aspirant to office—but as one occupied with the cultivation of his own person. When he speaks of the value of learning "for the sake of the self" rather than to impress others (14:25), he reveals something about his own project, as he does when he offers what may be the world's briefest autobiography:

> At fifteen my heart was set upon learning; at thirty, I had become established; at forty I was no longer perplexed; at fifty, I knew what is ordained by Heaven; at sixty, I obeyed; at seventy, I could follow my heart's desires without transgressing the line.
>
> (*Analects* 2:4)

This life story could be interpreted as one of self-discipline and an acceptance bordering on resignation. Yet, in context, it appears to be more than that. Beyond simply recounting a prolonged process of socialization, Confucius seems to offer a glimpse of a self, of an individual whose achievement over the years of his life has given him cause for constant concern, occasional self-doubt, ultimate satisfaction, and possibly even, beneath the cultivated modesty of the expression, a certain pride.

These stages of development related by Confucius might be considered an analogue to the Hindu *āśramas*, or stages of life, described by Professor Elder (essay 2, this volume). However, three of the four *āśramas* are determined by the individual's relations to others and by the debts he must repay to the seers, his forefathers, and the gods respectively, while the fourth or ascetic stage is the one in which he abandons those relations and pursues his freedom. Confucius' progress through his own stages is apparently self-determined, without fixed expectations concerning the pattern of his life. At the end he remains very much involved in the world around him.

To pick up another thread of the comparison with Hindu views of the individual, wherein the relation of Ātman and Brahman is at the heart of the metaphysics of the person, it may be noted that no mention has been made of a Confucian concept of the soul. A concept of the soul *is* found in early Chinese thought; in fact, there is more than one such concept, and the relation of one to the other is in itself a fascinating subject.[8] However, the common Chinese terms for "soul" (*hun* and *p'o*) occur nowhere in the *Analects,* the *Mencius,* the *Great Learning,* or the *Mean.* Interestingly, in these core texts, the idea of "soul" is not a relevant category.

We also find no philosophically telling distinction between the categories of mind and body, no hint of a dualism involving a transient or compromising physical form harboring a pure and perduring spiritual reality. For Mencius, the mind, seen in its focused state as the will (*chih*), serves as a guide to the physical energy, but mind and body are not conceived dualistically. There is also no reference in these early texts (or, to my knowledge, in any pre-Buddhist Chinese texts) to the idea of transmigration, no hint that the project of an individual life might carry over into successive incarnations. While, as Professor Elder explains in his essay, the Hindu "search for freedom (*mokṣa*) may well span scores, if not hundreds, or thousands, of transmigrations (*samsāra*) of the soul," the Confucian project of human perfection must be carried out within the span of a single, finite lifetime. In contrast to both Hindu and Christian views of an individual life, which involve, though in different ways, a sort of metaphysical enjambment, there is in the Confucian view a physical and metaphysical end-stopping. Indeed, this may well be among the most significant facts in all of Confucian psychology and ethics.

The Hindu idea of *karma* and the idea of transmigration are part of a set, at least one aspect of the idea of *karma* being that it entails a concept of justice. The present life circumstances of individuals, born into higher or lower *varṇa* or ranks, are unequal: this present inequality is thought to be not only justified but required by the past actions of the individuals involved. Likewise, the rewards for present actions, if not evidently realized in this lifetime, must be assumed to be forthcoming in a future lifetime. While inequality among social orders is believed to have been part of the structure of reality since the sacrifice of the Primeval Man, Puruṣa, the primal event through which the varieties of human life originated, *karma*, operating over the course of an unfathomably long time, offers the prospect of ultimate justice as well as an ultimate unity of being.

The early Confucians have a metaphysics, an eschatology, a temporal sense, and a sense of justice that are different. The Confucian perspective, in contrast to either the Hindu view of successive lives or incarnations or the Christian view of an infinite career of the soul and the promise of life everlasting, might be characterized as "one person/one lifetime." In addition to placing emphasis on the physical reality of the person, on the here and now, on the immediacies of daily life, on history as a record of the completed lives of those who have gone before, and on involvement rather than freedom, the Confucian conception of the human project entails its own view of human nature.

It is a view which, in the context of the ancient world, may be seen as distinctly egalitarian. The idea of a fundamental similarity or natural equality among human beings is another new development in the period from the sixth to the third centuries B.C.E. which is closely identified with Confucius and the Confucian school. Like the evolution from the "auguristic-sacrificial" mode to a "this-worldly and moral" mode, and no doubt linked to it, it represents another momentous change in perspective during the "axial age" in China. Socially, the background to this change has been found in a marked increase in social mobility during the spring and autumn (722–479 B.C.E.) and Warring States (479–222 B.C.E.) periods of the late Chou.[9] Confucius himself, apparently a member of the lower nobility and of a family of reduced circumstances, is often thought to have been responding to the social change going on around him in the sense that he reinterpreted older aristocratic notions of nobility in line with a new conception of *moral* nobility. Thus, the *chün-tzu*—the "noble person" or "gentleman" is so designated solely on the basis of his nobility of personality rather than nobility of birth.

This egalitarian strain and commitment had its limits, however. The term *chün-tzu* in itself does not carry with it a specification of gender and need not be translated in such a way that it refers exclusively to males.[10] Tu Wei-ming, in writing about the *Mean*, adopts the gender-neutral and spiritually and sub-jectively shaded translation "profound person."[11] Yet the social realities of ancient China were such that *chün-tzu* were male. Traditional Chinese society was strongly hierarchical in terms of male-female relationships and in terms of age categories. The role of the male involved the responsibility to guide and to govern; the role of the female was to follow and submit, a social distinction echoed in the Chinese cosmology of yin and yang.[12] The elder also took prece-dence over the younger, though in this case categories naturally evolve with the cycle of life, as sons become fathers and fathers-in-law and daughters become mothers and mothers-in-law.

Within the distinct gender categories, in which social roles follow a defi-nite conception of biological differences, individuals are regarded as equal in their endowment and potential. This is a matter that Mencius and other thinkers who followed in the tradition of Confucius would discuss in relation to the notion of *hsing*—usually translated as "the nature" or "human nature."

In the *Analects* itself, there is little evidence that can be regarded as an unambiguous indication of Confucius' view of *hsing*. However, in saying that human beings are, "By nature, near together; by practice, diverging,"[13] he seems to affirm that it is enough to know that, fundamentally similar in terms of endowment, we define and refine ourselves through the quality of our cul-ture and habitual action. Both parts of the statement are significant: the con-viction of a fundamental similarity among human beings and the perception that individuals distinguish themselves through their personal development. Donald Munro has observed that a distinction can be drawn between natural equality and evaluative equality. Confucius and Mencius, he suggests, demonstrate a belief in natural equality along with a moral perspective that entails evaluative *in*equality. A corollary of the notion that human beings enter the world with a similar endowment and equal potential is that this potential is realized to different degrees. Value attaches more to the achieve-ment that a completed human being represents than to the potential with which he began.[14]

Nonetheless, both strands—that of natural equality and of evaluative inequality—remain important in subsequent thinking about the nature of the individual and the relation of the individual to the collectivity. Both have a bearing on views of education and personal cultivation. Confucius states that, "There is a difference in instruction but none in kind,"[15] implying that we are what we are educated to be. Mencius affirms that all human beings are born with a similar nature, one that involves the propensity to goodness and is subject to almost unlimited development. Every person is capable of becoming a perfected person, a sage.[16] The belief in natural equality and in the perfectibility of each individual would crucially influence Chinese social and political life not only as an ideal but as the premise of the civil service examination system that was instituted in the Han dynasty and established as the basis of recruitment of the Chinese bureaucracy from the T'ang period (618–906 C.E.) on.[17]

These, then, are the lineaments of the classical Confucian conception of the individual: this individual 1) enters the world, allowing for gender and birth-order differences, on a basis of relative equality with others; 2) exists within and is conditioned, but not wholly defined, by an encompassing familial and social structure; 3) functions as an integrated whole, unencumbered (or, unrelieved, depending on one's viewpoint) by any sense of distinct or competing physical, mental, and spiritual components; 4) possesses a nature resembling that of others and, with it, the potential for moral perfectibility; and 5) enjoys a single, finite lifetime. The individual is also evaluated or judged—in Christian terms, one might say "justified"—according to how fully the potential for perfectibility appears to have been realized during his life and at its close.

The Duties and "Rights" of the Individual

Joseph Elder has chosen to discuss the duties and rights of the individual sequentially; I shall discuss them in tandem because in a Confucian perspective they are correlative. Unlike the Hindu case, wherein certain rights of the individual may flow from special individual relationships or encounters with the gods (this volume, p. 70–72), the worldly tradition of Confucianism is such that the "rights" of individuals derive from fulfillment by other individuals to whom they are related of certain duties, either explicitly prescribed or intuitively understood. In a Hindu perspective the duties of the individual are determined by the *varṇa* or rank into which the individual is born, by the stage of life, by the historical age, and by gender. Only the last of these applies in a Confucian context, the differences in the roles and responsibilities of males and females being distinctly differentiated, especially as elaborated in the prescriptions of the *Record of Rites*.

In considering the duties and "rights" of the individual, I shall focus on a cluster of primary concepts which recur in the Four Books. The first of these is *hsiao*, meaning filiality or filial devotion. The second is *jen* (pronounced *ren*), variously translated as Goodness, benevolence, and humaneness or humanity. The third is *li*—rites, ritual, or propriety. This list does not begin to exhaust the moral vocabulary of classical Confucianism; however, consideration of these concepts should provide access to the attitudes toward human interrelatedness which underlie Confucian views of duties and rights.

Filial devotion (hsiao)

Filial devotion is less prominent as a concept in the *Analects*—or, indeed, in any of the Four Books—than the reader with a general familiarity with the Chinese tradition might reasonably expect. It was the opinion of Arthur Waley that "filial piety played a relatively small part in the teaching of the earliest Confucians."[18] In his view, the references to *hsiao* in the *Analects* would not lead one to conclude that Confucius regarded it as comparable in importance to *jen* or humanity.

I should not want to gainsay Waley's judgment in this, especially inasmuch as I find in his view helpful support for a somewhat different point I hope to be able to sustain in what follows. At the same time one may question just what significance should be attached to the fact that, philosophically, Confucius seems to have found *hsiao* a less engaging subject than *jen*. A number of scholars have noted a change in the reference of the term *hsiao* during this period. As Waley observed,

> This word seems originally to have meant piety towards the spirits of ancestors or dead parents. In the *Analects* it still frequently has this meaning; but it is also applied to filial conduct toward living parents, and this is its usual meaning in current Chinese. In this change of meaning we may see, I think, another example of that general transference of interest from the dead to the living which marked the break-up of the old Chou civilization.   (ibid.)

In the course of this transference of interest from the dead to the living and the evolution of the worldly spirituality of Confucius, certain of the values and practices of a still more ancient China were rejected; others were transmuted; still others were substantially retained or even enlarged in their significance. One plausible explanation for the fact that filial devotion sparked relatively little engagement at a philosophical level may be that, as a value in the latter category, it was not a contested issue. Confucius was not *un*concerned with filial devotion; he seems, in fact, to have assumed its centrality. To him filial devotion may have seemed at once so natural and obligatory that legitimate disagreement concerning its importance would have been difficult to imagine.

Such a explanation would tally with what has already been suggested in regard to *Analects* 17:21, where Confucius doubts the humanity of Tsai Yü when the disciple's attitude toward mourning for parents suggests dereliction in regard to what Confucius acknowledges as universally accepted claims of filiality. It is in accord with the evidence of 12:11 where Confucius associates proper government with letting "the ruler be a ruler, the minister a minister, the father a father, and the son a son." The brevity and incisiveness of this comment are such that it is only intelligible on the assumption that the hearer understands the devotion that is expected to exist between father and son and accepts that filiality has broad implications: the hearer must be receptive to the notion that the same attitudes and duties are relevant within the family and the public sphere. Asked why he is not in public service, Confucius, citing the *Classic of Documents*, replies:

> "Be filial, only be filial and friendly toward your brothers, and you will be contributing to government." There are other sorts of service quite different from what you mean by "service." (*Analects* 2:21)

He makes the strongest possible claim for family loyalty when he calls filiality conjoined with fraternity "the root of humaneness."[19] These two bonds are the source of the sensitivity, responsiveness, and moral commitment that absorbed his most philosophical reflections.

The Chinese character for *hsiao* 孝 shows a son 子 beneath an old man 耂, suggesting both support and hierarchy. The way this support is construed is important. Confucius appears concerned that the care of parents by children not be merely a matter of seeing to their physical needs, without the proper spirit, demeanor, and involvement. A number of his statements indicate that he takes the style and spirit of a son's mourning for his parents and his ability to carry on the will or intention of his deceased father to be a crucial indicator of the son's own moral character. In his repeated reversion to this theme he reveals the depth of his feeling for the value of continuity in a family line.

Filial devotion is regarded in the *Mean* as the most impressive virtue of that most exemplary of sage rulers, Shun,[20] and of the heroic dynastic founders of the Chou, King Wu and the Duke of Chou:

> The Master [i.e., Confucius] said, "How far-extending was the filial devotion of King Wu and the Duke of Chou! Now filial devotion is seen in the skilful carrying out of the will of our forefathers and the skilful carrying forward of their undertakings." (*Mean*, 19)

It would have been superfluous for Confucius to have added that sons must carry on the biological line. This is assumed. A distinction between biological and spiritual continuity would not likely have occurred to Confucius or to the compilers of these early texts.

Mencius goes beyond Confucius in reflecting on the psychology of filial devotion. Filiality is rooted in the complex of feelings with which one's personal formation begins and shaped in the complex of obligations which figure in moral education. What Confucius only hints when he asks, "And [Tsai] Yü—was he not the darling of his father and mother for three years?" is elaborated by Mencius. Perhaps his deepest conviction is that everything necessary—all the appropriate dispositions and attitudes, and, above all, the feeling of love—will be experienced at the beginning within the matrix of the family. He appears confident that all children are cherished and that they come to respect and care for their parents and siblings and then for others, in ever-widening circles. Feeling and duty are linked through the crucial sense of reciprocity, which, for Mencius, is both psychological and moral.

To many it has seemed that the influence of Chinese parents, especially fathers and heads of families, has, over the course of centuries, been the most striking fact of Chinese social history. Given a strongly hierarchical and strictly patriarchal social structure, the rights of family heads have traditionally been so powerfully asserted as to result in highly authoritarian patterns in the society as a whole. This pattern is commonly characterized as "the Confucian family system." As a general observation, broadly applicable over time, there is considerable truth in this. Yet several qualifications are warranted.

First, there is in the Four Books little to support either the idea of filial devotion or patriarchal authority as ends in themselves[21] or a notion of filiality as requiring explicit and timelessly applicable modes of performance. There is much to suggest that what is required of the devotee in terms of attitude and behavior, is, apart from the expectation of sincere respect during life[22] and appropriate mourning after death, left to the individual. More strictly hierarchical views, the authority patterns associated with such views, and highly elaborated expectations in regard to filial conduct represent a development that appears to have begun in the Han period when Confucianism became intermixed with Legalism and other currents of thought.[23] Even then the duties and rights of the individual converge in the acknowledgment of a mutuality that operates over the long term. Spared an early death, one who is now a child should in turn become a parent; one who is now a parent will in due course have the status of an ancestor. The duty to serve has as its reciprocal the right to be served in turn. This applies not only to service of the body and of physical needs but to service of the spirit, the will, and virtue. One is implicated, proximately, in the life of one's parents and ancestors, intermediately in the life of the community, and ultimately in the life of humanity as a whole.

Clearly, it is unrewarding to talk about Confucianism as if it were a monolithic and unchanging tradition or as if its fundamental premises were subject to a single foreordained pattern of development. Were we to go beyond our original focus on the Four Books and to adopt the wider perspective of social history, it would become apparent that parental "rights" vary from one period to another. Not only prevailing conceptions of filial devotion, but legal interpretations, and behavioral patterns change over time.[24] If there is an irreducible "core" of Confucian values associated with filiality throughout several millennia of Chinese social history, it will be found in the most basic elements: awe for the fact of human life and procreation; gratitude for the gift of life; a sense that the individual, having received this gift, is enduringly connected and indebted not only to parents and ancestors, but to Heaven as the ultimate source of life; respect for the continuity of life. All of these—the sense of awe, gratitude, connectedness, indebtedness, and respect—shape and condition evolving attitudes toward filial and parental duties and the filial and parental rights of the individual.[25]

Humaneness (jen) and rightness (i)

As a concept, a focus of philosophical interest and reflection, and a vision, *jen* abides at the heart of the Confucian tradition. The term is translated here as "humaneness" or "humanity" to bring out its connection with *jen* meaning "a human being" or "a person." More than being homophones, the two words are cognates. The Chinese character for "human being" 人 is "a summary picture of a walking man."[26] The character for "humaneness" or "humanity" 仁 has an added component: alongside the walking person is the number "two," suggesting a human being in company with others or "humanity towards another" (ibid.).

Confucius in speaking of *jen* was chary of categorical statements concerning its meaning[27] or even its manifestations. Disciples who questioned him about *jen*, hoping to gain his assent to awarding the designation to some actual or hypothetical candidate, invariably met with something well short of an endorsement (ibid. 14:2). He denied that he himself might be called either a sage or a humane person. When he spoke about *jen* he nearly always left its significance open for further reflection, as though he preferred his hearers to ponder it rather than to presume they could grasp it. And yet being human and being humane are so closely related that the fact of humanness and the value of humaneness may not always be distinguishable. Humaneness in the *Analects* may have to do with "the display of human qualities at their highest,"[28] suggesting a behavioral ideal, but Confucius insists that it is always within one's ken:

> Tzu-kung said, "What would you say of someone who broadly benefited the people and was capable of helping everyone? Could he be called humane?" The Master said, "How would this be a matter of humaneness? Surely he would have to be a

sage? Even Yao and Shun were concerned about such things. As for humaneness—you want to establish yourself; then help others to establish themselves. You want to develop yourself; then help others to develop themselves. Being able to recognize oneself in others, one is on the way to being humane." (*Analects*, 6:28)

What this translation rather freely renders as "being able to recognize oneself in others," is, more literally, "being able to take what is near and grasp the analogy." Beginning with an immediate awareness of oneself—one's own impulses and desires—and assuming a fundamental similarity between oneself and others, one forms an assessment of the needs and wants of the other. The empathetic response does not guarantee that one will attain humaneness, but one can be sure of moving in the right direction. One does not need to be a sage to be on course. However much it may be concerned with dignifying the ordinary,[29] humaneness remains bound up with common human experience and with the simple desire to be humane.

In addition to involving a sense of mutuality, *jen* is a project and a lifelong commitment:

Tseng Tzu said, "The man of service may not be without breadth and endurance. His burden is heavy, and his way is long. Humaneness is the burden that he takes upon himself. Is it not heavy? Only in death does his way come to an end. Is it not long?"[30]

Elsewhere Confucius says that the "determined scholar and the humane person will not seek life to the detriment of humaneness; and it may be that he has to sacrifice his life in order to accomplish humaneness."[31]

For Mencius, *jen* is the central conception. Always, as in the *Analects*, it involves human relations and, possibly because so many of his recorded conversations are with rulers, Mencius is insistent on *jen* as a form of moral practicality that works for everyone and that is more real and effective than "profit" or utility. The ruler's duty, he argues, is to act on the impulse to humaneness and to establish a humane government. No matter what his vulnerability, no matter what extremity he may face in coping with war, famine, or other adversity, the ruler may be assured that he retains the capacity for humaneness. Indeed, everyone has it, hence people naturally respond to humane rulers.

In advancing his arguments for the practicality of *jen*, Mencius articulates a view with as much moral resonance as any in Confucian teaching. Echoing and reechoing in virtually all later discourse is the idea that what ultimately matters in human interactions is the motivation of the actors and their capacity for mutual respect and regard based on recognition of a common humanity. This sense of common humanity, or *jen*, is differentially expressed by individuals performing distinct roles and confronting the different circumstances of life according to the complementary principle of *i*, rightness or appropriateness.

Mencius was the single most influential contributor to a view of human nature that ultimately became dominant, not only in China but in the rest of Confucianized East Asia, and not only in the thought of an elite, but in the value system of an entire culture. In its metaphysical weightlessness,[32] it is a view different from that found in Hinduism, which sees the individual in terms of a soul having already experienced numerous transmigrations and anticipating further transmigrations before attaining the state of ultimate perfection marked by the union of the *Ātman* and *Brahman*. In its optimism, it contrasts also with the view found in the biblical religions, which share a conception of human beings as inherently flawed and needing to reverse the distance between themselves and God which entered the definition of humanness almost at the beginning of human history. Mencius, dealing only with the here and now and with the actual lives of his contemporaries, finds that all have the potential for goodness and even for perfection in this world and in this finite lifetime.

The evidence he adduces, in perhaps the most celebrated passage in the work, rests on a single powerful example. "All human beings," he says, "have a mind which cannot bear to see the sufferings of others."

> Here is why I say that all human beings have a mind that commiserates with others. Now if anyone were suddenly to see a child about to fall into a well, his mind would always be filled with alarm, distress, pity, and compassion. That he would react accordingly is not because he would use the opportunity to ingratiate himself with the child's parents, nor because he would seek commendation from neighbors and friends, nor because he would hate the adverse reputation.   (Mencius 2A:6)

Mencius does not need to tell us what the person who sees the child teetering on the edge of the well will do. We fill this in out of our own humanity, recognizing that all human beings can be counted on to act on the spontaneous impulse to save the child by pulling it from danger. This mind or heart (the distinction is absent in Chinese) which cannot bear to see the sufferings of others is compassion. "One who lacks a mind of pity and compassion would not be human," he says. He then extends the argument considerably by adding, "One who lacks a mind that feels shame and aversion would not be human; one who lacks a mind that feels modesty and compliance would not be human; one who lacks a mind that knows right and wrong would not be human." These four—compassion, shame, modesty, and the sense of right and wrong—are the "four sprouts" or the "four seeds" of virtue. These Mencius believes to be reliably present in every human being.

As sentiments, as promptings of the mind or heart, these inclinations exist at the outset of the individual's life as a potential. The sense of compassion is the sprout of humaneness; the sense of shame, the sprout of rightness; the sense of modesty, the sprout of ritual or ritual propriety; and the sense of right and wrong, the sprout of wisdom.

> Human beings have these four sprouts just as they have their four limbs. For one to have these four sprouts and yet to say of oneself that one is unable to fulfill them is to injure oneself, while to say that one's ruler is unable to fulfill them is to injure one's ruler. When we know how to enlarge and bring to fulfillment these four sprouts that are within us, it will be like a fire starting to burn or a spring finding an outlet. If one is able to bring them to fulfillment, they will be sufficient to allow him to protect "all within the four seas"; if he is not, they will be insufficient even to enable him to serve his parents.

Cultivating the four sprouts is a matter of effort, experience, and duty. By failing to cultivate them, one injures oneself and one's intimates quite as much as others. By even expressing skepticism about the moral capacity of another one injures that person, stealing from him something that is his and that is precious.

"Humaneness is the human mind. Rightness (*i*) is the human path,"[33] says Mencius. By "rightness" he means the ways that humaneness is translated into appropriate behavior in specific situations. Far more than simply "manners," rightness is associated with a sense of personal well-being on the part of the person who is practiced in "right" conduct, suggesting a connection in Mencius' mind between morally appropriate action and self-esteem. Rightness is also bound up with a sense of human dignity, an integrity which prompts the individual to do certain things and to refrain from doing others. Mencius is confident that human beings are capable of setting certain priorities that on grounds of simple self-interest might be unintelligible.

"Humaneness is what it means to be human" (ibid. 7B:16). Here the fact of being human and the value of being humane seem to be interpenetrating categories. The consequences of such an interpenetration of fact and value for attitudes toward the duties and rights of the individual are interesting and, from a contemporary "human rights" point of view, important. In its positive aspect, this statement contains embedded within it several of the background notions which we have been observing in the foregoing discussion: 1) the Confucian belief in the idea of equality of persons (allowing for gender and birth-order differences); 2) a conviction of the capacity of each individual for perfectibility; 3) a commitment to the duty of each individual to cultivate his own capacities. In its negative aspect, the statement carries with it the implication that individuals who do *not* cultivate their own potential are guilty of violating their own humanity. They literally "throw themselves away" or "play the thief to themselves." More than being wanton with their endowment, they cease in some sense to be fully human.

The significance of this notion of humanity for Confucian views of individual duties and rights may be something like this: each individual, appreciating the humanity of others on the basis of his own humanity, has the duty to recognize and treat every other individual as fully human. Each individual has the corresponding "right" to be recognized and treated as human. But an individual who defaults on his duty, more than becoming morally reprehensible, may be described as *pu jen*—inhumane, or, *in effect*, inhuman. It maybe that, the duty and the right being correlative, the right to be recognized and treated as fully human will be considered vacated. That the individual is thus both valued and *de*valued in moral terms has significant implications in popular morality as well as in law.

Rites, ritual, or propriety (li)

If filial devotion has its origins in the sense of relatedness deriving from biological inheritance and continuity, and humaneness involves an extension of that sense of relatedness, ritual (*li*) represents the outward structure, discipline, or order through which the sense of human relatedness is expressed and celebrated.

The Chinese character for *li* 禮 is composed of a radical element 示 indicating an omen, manifestation, or prognostication, alongside an element 豊 depicting a sacrificial vessel.[34] The ritual of the later Chou period and thereafter had its roots in the most archaic strata of Chinese religious culture and represented an outgrowth of the complex of ideas and practices referred to by Waley as the "auguristic-sacrificial" mode. At some point in the Chou period the idea and practice of ritual began to incorporate a moral dimension, and may be seen in the *Analects* as the focus of the moral practice of Confucius.

Rites were understood by Confucius as a time-honored means of celebrating the momentous occasions as well as the ordinary events of human life, of ensuring balance and dignity in human interactions, of giving appropriate expression to human feelings, and of observing forms conducive to the cultivation of particular moral attitudes. Whereas *hsiao* and *jen* involved duties so encompassing as to be almost beyond definition, and moral sentiments that ideally involved all that an individual could summon forth, the *li* were specific, detailed, and often formulaic. Given the demands imposed upon individuals in this relation-oriented society, the *li*, combining specificity with beauty and the weight of tradition, must have done much to reassure practitioners that it was, after all, possible to fulfill their duties.

If the idea of the *tao*, or the Way, as understood by Confucians, is that of a human path through a moral and interreactive universe, the rituals are like signposts on that way. As the *Mean* puts it,

> How great is the path (*tao*) proper to the Sage!
> Like overflowing water, it sends forth and nourishes all things, and rises up to the height of heaven.
> All-complete is its greatness! It embraces the three hundred rules of ceremony, and the three thousand rules of demeanor.   (*Mean*, 27)

"Three hundred" and "three thousand" must be round numbers, but it is clear that a fair amount of guidance is indicated. From the evidence of the *Analects*, one learns that Confucius particularly valued ritual forms that dignified one's bearing and demeanor (vis-à-vis family members, fellow villagers, officials, the ruler), gestures, facial expressions, forms of address, giving gifts, offering sacrifices, arranging funerals, observing mourning, disposing furnishings, eating, drinking, and sleeping. In the *Record of Rites* there is discussion of rituals which serve to govern and to grace many other aspects of life as well.

Ritual is related to humaneness. Confucius responds to a question about humaneness by saying that, "Through mastering oneself and returning to ritual (or propriety, *li*) one becomes humane."[35] He insists that a commitment to humaneness is a condition for involvement in ritual (ibid. 3:3). The sense and the sentiment of human relatedness provide the moral and psychological ground in which the ritual forms are rooted. Rulers are advised that ritual is appropriately associated with government (ibid. 4:13) and that order in a community is best kept through ritual rather than punishments (ibid. 1:3). The practice of ritual creates harmony and functions to modulate the very harmony that it creates (ibid. 1:12).

Whereas the Confucian sense for a natural equality of persons comes through in filial devotion and humaneness, the hierarchical nature of Chinese society is evident in rites. Not only are the Chinese social hierarchies distinct from those of other cultures, such as the Indian, but the ritual context out of which they emerge is different as well. As described by Joseph Elder, the duties and "rights" of the individual are determined, in a Hindu perspective, by the *varna* or rank into which the individual is born, by *āśrama* or stage of life, by gender, and by *yuga* or the historical age. In China, there is no conception or institution comparable to *varna* and, prior to the advent of Buddhism, no conception strictly comparable to *yuga*. The *āśramas* or stages of life have no real counterpart, least of all the final, ascetic stage in which the individual leaves his family in search of freedom. As in Hindu society, and in other traditional societies, the roles and responsibilities of males and females are distinctly differentiated. However, in a society in which the natural equality of males is an important belief, the responsibilities of women also tend to be differently understood.[36]

In terms of duties and "rights," we might say that rites represent particular duties which are then subsumed within larger frames, as, for example, filial devotion. They include the verbal, kinesic, emotional, and physical forms by which other duties are to be fulfilled; they convey the respectful and deferential attitude with which they are to be approached. The specific rituals which an individual is duty-bound to perform are determined by that individual's gender, age, position in a family, status in the community, life situation, etc. A certain conception of "rights" enters the picture here because the status and dignity of particular individuals are recognized in rituals—as, for example, that of a deceased parent in a funeral ceremony, or that of the ancestors of an official in rituals performed in an ancestral shrine. Each individual can expect to be acknowledged and respected in specified ways by persons who stand in particular relationships to him or her. These "rights," while belonging to individuals, are very different from the rights involved in modern Western conception of human rights according to which individuals are understood to have claims deriving solely from the fact of their humanity. Here we have not human rights but human rites, a highly contextualized form of recognition and regard for the humanity of individuals and for the quality of their interrelatedness.[37]

The Collectivity

The Nature of the Collectivity

Two general points may be made about the perspective on collectivity found in the Four Books. First, we find in these texts only the barest trace of a distinction between the concerns of personal cultivation and those of government. The spheres that Western sources might distinguish as private and public are interfused; the categories of moral and political philosophy are so continuous that there appears little need to explain their relatedness. Second, the monarchical state is thought to be as natural as the patriarchal family; these are, and would remain throughout the history of traditional China, the two basic collectivities.

There is no real speculation on the part of Confucius about the nature of the Way or alternatives to monarchy. It probably would not have occurred to

Mencius to propose that the components of individual personality might serve as an analogy for the constituents of the state, as did Plato in the *Republic*, nor would he have been likely to separate a utopian vision of the state from a more quotidian realism. (The contrast between Plato's *Republic* and his *Laws* would likely have perplexed Mencius.) He makes no attempt to consider what human beings might be like prior to society or apart from it, or, like Aristotle in his *Politics*, what human beings might be like subject to different kinds of polities. Confucius, Mencius, and the authors of the ritual texts seem to take as a given that the patriarchal family and the monarchical state are constant features of social life—the one as microcosm, the other as macrocosm.

As the two primary collectivities, the family (*chia*) and the state (in modern Chinese, *kuo-chia*, or state-family) are both assumed to have moral validity and to figure in a continuous and unified world. To a reader steeped in a different value system this assumption must seem remarkable. Plato, in the *Republic*, expresses a negative view of the influence of the family as a distraction from the demands of citizenship. Socrates goes to great lengths in his design for the institution of the Guardians to propose the benefits of careful nurturing and education of a leadership elite *without* the diversion of loyalties associated with the claims of family. Aristotle, in the *Nicomachean Ethics*, differs with Plato over the influence of the family, recognizing the nurturing by parents of children and the affection of children for parents as sources for the positive bonds he refers to as *philia*.[38] Yet, in the *Politics*, he criticizes the Socrates' assertion in the *Republic* that "the greater the unity of the state the better,"[39] contending that,

> the nature of a state is to be a plurality, and in tending to greater unity, from being a state, it becomes a family, and from being a family, an individual; for the family may be said to be more than the state, and the individual than the family. So that we ought not to attain this greatest unity even if we could for it would be the destruction of the state.[40]

The Chinese family, far from being seen as a particularistic distraction from properly political, or more universal, claims, or as but one good among others, is the primary model for human existence. It is the matrix of personal development and the constant point of reference for rulers and subjects in the conduct of public as well as private life. There is no "science of politics," but rather a family ritual enacted at several levels of reality—personal, societal, and cosmic. Unity inheres not only in the individual, as Aristotle supposed, but, as the goal of the entire social enterprise[41] and the motive of the cosmic process.

There are a number of possible explanations for the Confucian sense of continuity between the private and the public spheres and the disinclination to speculate about alternative social arrangements. Perhaps the most encompassing of them may be found in the centrality of the biological conception of life. This is a conception in which fact and value may be seen as interpenetrating categories: life itself is a given and also a gift. The continuity of life and the interreactivity among all living things are experienced both as empirical reality and religious faith. The drive for survival (in China, it is never *mere* survival) involves both.

The notion of the family (associated at once with the facts of life and its ultimate values) illumines and is illuminated by a cosmological conception, at once very old and elaborately developed over the course of centuries, of a universe which is highly interreactive, orderly, harmonious, and richly productive of life, in much the way that a traditional Chinese family would ideally be. This is expressed in the "Appended Remarks," the most philosophically significant of the appendixes to the *Classic of Changes*:

> The succession of yin and yang is the Way.
> As continuer, it is good (*shan*).
> As completer, it is the nature (*hsing*) . . .
> It manifests itself as humaneness, but conceals its workings.
> It gives life to all things, but does not share the anxieties of the sage.
> Its glorious power, its great sphere of activity, are of all things the most sublime.
> It possesses everything in complete abundance: this is its great sphere of activity.
> It renews everything daily: this is its glorious power.
> Producing and reproducing, it is called change.[42]

What so profoundly impresses the Chinese consciousness is the vital capacity of the universe for creation and procreation, for the renewal and nurturing of life. The continuity of life that comes about through the interaction of yin and yang, the female and male energies, is an expression of goodness (*shan*); the completion of living things in the cycle of becoming is the nature (*hsing*).[43] Yin and yang are complementary, not contradictory, forces: all life depends, biologically, on their mutually fructifying relationship and, morally, on the appropriate balance between them. Yin and yang are also directly related to *ch'ien* and *k'un*, the Creative and Receptive forces of the universe, with *ch'ien* and *k'un* being associated with heaven and earth respectively. We see here a complementarity of male and female progenitive roles, conceptualized in distinct but related ways.

In discussing the nature of the individual, I suggested that the Confucian conception of the person was essentially biological; here it emerges that the conception of the universe is of a biosphere. In neither case, however, do these conceptions exclude a moral dimension: given the value attached to life itself, they directly entail it. The dignity as well as the duties of the individual derive from his role as a link in a biological chain; the perception of the Way as "good" and manifesting itself as "humaneness" reveals both awareness of the continuity of life and the assignment of value to life itself. The fact that the Way is perceived as simultaneously human *and* natural—a single pattern or design displayed throughout the entire fabric of biological life—may help to explain why Confucians were not disposed to think in terms of alternate ways of ordering the state. For them, the patriarchal family, guided by a loving father, the monarchical state, ruled by a humane sovereign, and the natural order, overseen by an overarching Heaven, formed a complementarity so self-evident within a universe so integrated that any other arrangement must have seemed either an absurdity or a sacrilege.

This sense of an integrated and interreactive universe seems also to have conditioned particular Confucian views of the nature of the collectivity. An example of this may be found in the idea of the Mandate of Heaven (*t'ien-ming*), an early intuition that the interreactivity among the living things of the universe is also demonstrated in history. This idea appeared in the "Announcement to the Duke of Shao" in the *Classic of Documents* or *Book of History*, which interpreted the Chou conquest of the Shang dynasty[44] as having been ordained by a transfer of the mandate of Heaven, the Heaven-ordained authority to rule, from a cruel and decadent Shang ruler to the leaders of the Chou people. The access to authority of the Chou, attributed to the moral forcefulness of their leaders, was taken as a reenactment of events which occurred in more remote antiquity when the Shang rulers themselves had inherited the right to rule following the loss of Heaven's mandate by a degenerate Hsia dynasty.[45] In the minds of the author(s) of the "Announcement," a change in the mandate testified to Heaven's concern for the well-being of its people and its sensitivity to the moral standing of rulers.[46] This idea originally had historical significance as a way of conceptualizing the way heaven (or Nature)[47] operates in human history.[48] As appropriated by later Confucians, it had continuing political significance through being invoked as a reminder to rulers of the need to remain responsive to the plight of ordinary people. Quoting another chapter of the *Classic of Documents*, Mencius affirmed that "Heaven sees as my people see, Heaven hears as my people hear."[49]

Eventually the idea attained a comprehensive moral significance, finding its way into the understanding of individual lives, as seen in the way human nature is understood in the *Mean*, which establishes in its opening lines that,

What Heaven has endowed is called the nature.
Following the nature is called the Way.
Cultivating the Way is called instruction.

The Way cannot be departed from for so much as an instant.

If it could be departed from, it would not be the Way.

Therefore the noble person is cautious and watchful about what is unseen and fearful and apprehensive about what is unheard.

There is nothing more visible than what is hidden, nothing more apparent than what is minute.

Therefore the noble person is watchful over his own solitude.   (*Mean* 1:1–3)

The individual possesses as a condition of his own being a nature endowed by Heaven, one that is ordained by Heaven (*t'ien-ming*), in the same sense that the authority to rule is ordained by Heaven in the ruler. This is an individual capacity; it is also the individual's link to the family, to the larger collectivity of the state, and to the still more encompassing reality of the biosphere.

According to the *Mean*, the individual is to follow his original nature and to pursue his education. He is not so much an individual that he is destined or directed to "find his own path" or "go his own way" because that Way has already been defined by Heaven and is unalterable, yet he is enough of an individual that it matters what he does in his solitude, what his innermost thoughts and feelings are like, and how they are regulated. The *Mean* makes clear that, owing to the commonness of human nature, the Way entails a common wisdom as much as a higher wisdom. As a human Way, it is for common people, for noble persons, and for sages;[50] as a Way of nature, it is the selfsame pattern to be seen throughout the biosphere:

The Way of the noble person originates among ordinary men and women and, at its furthest reaches, is displayed brightly in Heaven and Earth.[51]

Heaven or Nature—the term *t'ien* may be translated either way—comes to be seen as 1) representing a natural order that derives "from the primal depths of the universe";[52] 2) operating to preserve a people and to effect moral purposes; 3) protecting the cause of civilization; and 4) working itself out in individual human lives. Several strains of thought join in this powerful and enduring ideal of a protective and overarching Heaven, expressing itself in the historical process as well as the processes of nature, concerned with the course of civilization and culture, sensitive to human suffering, and constitutive of individual human capacity through the endowment of human nature.

When the *Mean* comes to talk about government, Confucius is quoted concerning the kind of government practiced by Kings Wen and Wu, founders of the Chou dynasty. He focuses not on institutions, but on the importance of having the right men in government. "Men must be active in matters of government, just as the earth is active in making things grow: the government is a growing reed."[53] The way to get the proper men in government is for the ruler to attract them through his own personality or character; the way he accomplishes this is by cultivating the Way in himself by means of humaneness (*jen*).

The duties and rights of the ruler are specified in similar ways in the *Mean* and in the *Great Learning*. The ruler is to become both a filial son and a father (and mother) to the people; the state is like an extended family. As Tu Wei-ming puts it, "Society so conceived is not an adversary system consisting of pressure groups but a fiduciary community based on mutual trust."[54]

> . . . The mode of exercising power in a fiduciary community is significantly different from that of an adversary system based upon the check and balance of pressure groups. In *Chung-yung's* [i.e., the *Mean's*] view, the ministers and officers are not only regulators of the bureaucratic process but also teachers of state ritual. The bureaucratic process is not seen as merely an objectively designed control mechanism. It is also thought to be an elaborate ritual act through which the people of the kingdom all become active participants in the community. Ideally, the ministers and officers are the ruler's messengers who, by moral exhortation, keep the masses informed of his political and educational endeavors. The government in this sense, far from being a necessary evil, is a body of persons that constitutes the moral authority of the empire.[55]

The operative word here is, of course, *ideally*. What Tu presents is an ideal model of the state, as conveyed in the *Mean*, rather than a description of a state that actually existed. Government in this, as in every other complex society, obviously involved not only "ethical education," but less edifying functions as well, such as taxation, corvée or labor service, and military conscription. To the extent that the state touched the lives of ordinary people, these other functions must have been always impressive and often oppressive. Indeed, there are many indications in early Chinese literature that the state, in exercising its functions in the areas of taxation, recruitment, conscription, and penal law, often exerted its authority in ways which seemed to its subjects to neglect, if not actually to contravene, ordinary moral sentiments. Nor is there anything to indicate that such an impression was erased in later centuries as the Confucianization of Chinese society proceeded.

Still, the "fiduciary community" remained an ideal model over the course of many centuries. Not only was it an ideal firmly implanted in the value system of philosophers who viewed the system from without, it was also one that inspired many of the scholar-bureaucrats who tried to steer the bureaucratic process and to stage the "elaborate ritual act" of the state from within. It is a matter of historical record that a vision of this kind led many such officials to insist on the importance of education, to prefer voluntarism to coercion, to favor ritual over law, and to support an approach to the economy that they hoped would satisfy the subsistence needs of the entire population. Sometimes these Confucians had their way; often they had to compromise or to adapt their vision, perhaps without fully realizing the degree to which they were absorbing other attitudes and approaches. Yet it is clear that the same ideal persisted for some twenty centuries, profoundly influencing Confucian perspectives on the state, particularly in regard to the stress on "getting the right persons" in office, i.e., on government by morally competent individuals.

The two "collectivities" that have been discussed here are the family and the state. Arguably, one might also include the more embracing collectivity of the universe or the biosphere, but I shall not press that case here. It is striking that in the texts that form the core curriculum of a culture known for its stress on the interests of the collectivity, there is so little discussion of the *nature* of these collectivities as distinct from their ideal functioning. This may recall Joseph Elder's observation that, "One of the striking features of classical Hinduism is its almost total absence of reference to collectivities *as entities*." He goes on to explain that, despite the importance of such entities in later Hinduism, there is almost complete silence about them in the classical literature, especially in terms of collective tasks, responsibilities, and obligations (see essay 2 in this volume). Such a silence in regard to collective entities other than the family and the state is even more complete in the Four Books, though the explanations for this are to be sought in different underlying religious and sociological patterns.

Ambrose King, reviewing the work of a number of Chinese and Western sociologists, who wrote over a period of about half a century, observes:

> Confucians classify the human community into three categories: *chi*, the individual; *chia*, the family; and *ch'ün*, the group. For a Confucian, the emphasis is on the family, and for this reason Confucian ethics have developed an elaborate role system on the family level. Relatively speaking, the Confucian conception of *ch'ün* is the least articulate. It should be pointed out that, conceptually, the family is also a group. For the purpose of analytic distinction, "family" might be termed "familistic group," while the *ch'ün* is "nonfamilistic group" or simply "group." Insofar as Confucian theory is concerned, there is no formal treatment of the concept of *ch'ün*. *Ch'ün* remains an elusive and shifting concept. Fei Hsiao-t'ung correctly argues that the boundary between *chi* and *ch'ün* is relative and ambiguous; in the Chinese tradition there is no group boundary as such—the outer limit of the group is the vague concept of *t'ien-hsia* [i.e., literally, "all under heaven," or the universe].[56]

King explains that even the term *chia* or family, the basic social unit, is ambiguous. The *chia* commonly includes only the members of a nuclear family but may also be defined in terms of the larger lineage or clan groupings. Depending on the determination of the individual or the self (*chi*), virtually anyone can be enfolded into a family and included among *tzu chia jen* ('our family people'). Theoretically, at least, *tzu chia jen* can be "extended to an unlimited number of people and thereby becomes what is called *t'ien-hsia i-chia* ('all the world belongs to one family')."[57]

This line of argument has a number of ramifications, only one of which can be followed up here: the considerable scope that is suggested for individual autonomy, understood in terms of "the voluntaristic nature of the self and the dynamic role of structure." Groups, especially the family group, are far more elastic than the conventional wisdom about Chinese society might suggest. Whereas many roles, such as the five relations (*wu-lun*; see p. 117) are fixed, many more in the far wider net of human relations (*jen-lun*) in which the individual is existentially involved are open, flexible, and subject to definition by the "dynamic entity" that is the self:

> . . . The individual's relations with others are neither independent nor dependent but *interdependent*. Thus the individual self is not totally submerged in the relationships. On the contrary, the individual has considerable social and psychological space for action. Indeed, apart from the preordained *lun*, for example, the father-son *lun*, in which individual behavior is more or less prescribed by the fixed status as well as fixed responsibilities, an individual has considerable freedom in deciding whether or not to enter into voluntarily constructed relationships with others at all; and the individual self is also capable of shaping, if not fixing, what kinds of relationships to have with others . . . The self is an active entity capable of defining the roles for himself and others and, moreover, of defining the boundaries of groups of which the self is at the center.[58]

The evidence from contemporary sociology, while drawn from sources different from the classical Four Books, yields a remarkably similar perspective in terms of the role of the individual in a "relation-based social system" (ibid. 63). As King emphasizes the social and psychological space left open to the relationally oriented individual, so we may also draw attention to the moral space left open to that same individual. From our texts it would appear that the individual in part accepts and in part defines the collectivities to which he relates, the scope of his view being a function of the openness and the dynamism of his conception of his own humanity.

Duties and Rights of the Collectivity

Theoretically, a discussion of the duties and rights of the collectivity could begin with either the family or the state without altering the argument in any crucial respect: again, the family and the state are considered as microcosm and macrocosm. Ideally, they are understood to operate on the same principles and to be interreactive. Just as the individual's duties to the nuclear family serve the well-being of the state, so a ruler is charged with attending at the outset to his own filiality so as to fix his own moral character and with cultivating his own humanity so as to project a paternal attitude toward his subjects. Microcosmically, the family, as the matrix of humanity, has the duty of nurturing its progeny; macrocosmically, the state, as the protector of humanity, has the duty of nurturing its subjects.

Mencius, in advising rulers, suggests a magnanimous extension of the self through human kindness or compassion;[59] the *Mean*, more measured in tone,[60] favors a similar approach to the matter of government:

> Humaneness is what it means to be human,[61] and being affectionate toward one's kin is the greatest part of it. Rightness is doing what is right, and honoring the worthy is the greatest part of it. The diminishing degree of affection due to one's kin and the different gradations of honor owed to the worthy are born of ritual. When those below do not gain the confidence of the one above, the people cannot be governed. Therefore the noble person cannot but cultivate his person. As he thinks about cultivating his person, he cannot but serve his parents. As he thinks about serving his parents, he cannot but know other human beings. As he thinks about knowing other human beings, he cannot but know Heaven.
>
> (*Mean*, 20:5–7)

Everything is connected—self, family, state, and cosmos—requiring a comprehensive effort of cultivation, expressed in terms of the "five universal duties," which are to be performed by means of the "three universal virtues."

> The universal Way of the world involves five relations, and practicing it involves three virtues. The five are the relations between ruler and minister, between parent and child, between husband and wife, between older and younger brother, and among friends. These five are the universal Way of the world. The three—knowledge, humaneness, and courage—are the universal virtues of the world. And the means by which they are practiced is oneness. (*Mean*, 20:8)

In the end, the multiplicity of duties and virtues is resolved in unity.

The intimate connection between the cultivation of the individual person, the ordering of the family, and the governance of the state and between knowledge and action is likewise the central message of the *Great Learning*. As Mencius attributes to the ancients the surpassing ability to "extend" to others what they themselves carried out in their own personal lives, the great catena of the *Great Learning* ascribes to them the awareness that peace in the world begins in the mind of the individual:

> Those in antiquity who wished to illuminate luminous virtue throughout the world would first govern their states; wishing to govern their states, they would first bring order to their families; wishing to bring order to their families, they would first cultivate their own persons; wishing to cultivate their own persons, they would first rectify their minds; wishing to rectify their minds, they would first make their thoughts sincere; wishing to make their thoughts sincere, they would first extend their knowledge. The extension of knowledge lies in the investigation of things. It is only when things are investigated, that knowledge is extended; when knowledge is extended that thoughts become sincere; when thoughts become sincere that the mind is rectified; when the mind is rectified that the person is cultivated; when the person is cultivated that order is brought to the family; when order is brought to the family that the state is well governed; when the state is well governed that peace is brought to the world. From the Son of Heaven to ordinary people, all, without exception, should regard cultivating the person as the root.[62]

Large purposes demand personal beginnings; when properly carried out, the personal cultivation of the individual is always availing. In terms of the duties of the collectivity, it is important to note that those who enact these duties on behalf of the family or the state—heads of families and rulers of the state—are individuals. The fact that they are performing their *individual* duties (learning, mental cultivation, and filial devotion) toward the fulfillment of *collective* goals is significant.[63]

Given the biological conception of the person, and the centrality of sustaining life itself, it is not surprising to find that great importance attaches to the duty of the ruler to attend to the material needs of the people. Confucius alludes to the importance of the ruler's providing adequately for their livelihood;[64] Mencius, recognizing the baneful influence of poverty on the lives of ordinary human beings, dwells on their basic needs. "Those with constant means of support will have constant hearts," he reflects, "while those without constant means will not have constant hearts."[65] For him, the basic needs include not only food, clothing, shelter, but also education. All of these needs must be met if the very existence of the people as human beings is to be possible. In the provisions he advocates for landholding, taxation, agriculture, animal husbandry, fishery, forestry, famine relief, arboriculture, sericulture, commerce, and the establishment of schools (ibid. 1A:3; 2A:5; 3A:3), he is specific about what a ruler must do in order to provide on a long-term basis for these needs. Making a case both against warfare, which entails the squandering of lives and resources, and for welfare, which involves their nurturance and conservation, he sets forth convictions about the duties of the ruler that would persist in Confucian thinking for centuries.

One final point has to do with the abiding Confucian preference, which becomes a Chinese cultural preference, for *li* or ritual as against *hsing* (punishments) or *fa* (law). Law in Chou China was understood primarily in the sense of penal law and associated with the cruel but usual punishments found in many societies of the ancient world. Perhaps because of the dominance of the family and the assumption that family and state worked in the same way, there was no break in the direction of a more abstract concept of justice such as is seen, for example, in Plato's *Euthyphro*.[66] When it came to thinking about the modes and mechanisms for ensuring order in state and society, the viable alternatives contemplated by the Chinese appear to have been law and punishments on the one hand and ritual on the other. Confucius was unhesitating in his endorsement of ritual:

> Lead them by means of regulations and keep order among them through punishments, and the people will evade them and will lack any sense of shame. Lead them through moral force (or virtue, *te*) and keep order among them through rites (*li*) and they will have a sense of shame and will also correct themselves.[67]

This brief statement encapsulates the Confucian position on the efficacy of ritual and moral force on the part of the ruler and the disincentives associated with reliance on regulations and punishments. Virtue attracts; ritual recognizes the element of human dignity which is evident in the salutary sense of shame or forbearance. Regulations repel; the coercive force of punishments crushes the sense of self-respect and mutual trust on which a "fiduciary community" is founded. Confucians, always concerned about incipiences, roots, beginnings, and potentialities, have yet another reason to favor ritual. Associated as it is with education, morality, and harmony, ritual is also consonant with the underlying purpose of government: a process of correction and rectification which extends from the individual to the family and from the family to the society as a whole. Only as late as the seventeenth century did a major Confucian thinker—the historian and philosopher Huang Tsung-hsi—take a significantly different position, arguing for a greater role for law and, above all, for laws that would serve to bring the ruler in check and to control the dynastic institution.[68] Despite the longstanding Confucian preference for ritual over law, China *was*, of course, governed over the centuries by law; every major dynasty had its law code. The Confucian influence was, overall, to try to see that legal codes supported rather than undermined the functioning of the family and that ritual had its due before the sanctions of law came into play.

Thus far the discussion has focused on the duties of the collectivity, especially those of the state (as represented in the person of the ruler) without mention of the corresponding rights. Though not expressed in the language of "rights," the prerogatives of the ruler—as Son of Heaven, father and mother of the people, and representative of the human community in the intermediation between Heaven and earth—were enormous. And just as the rights of patriarchal heads of families seem to have grown over time (see pp. 126–27), so the rights of the ruler were gradually enlarged, with an authoritarian pattern deepening over the course of Chinese history and becoming most pronounced in the Ming (1368–1644) and Ch'ing (1644–1911) periods. However, even in later periods, the right of a ruler to command his subjects was never, in the Confucian perspective, unlimited. This was above all because individuals were seen to have a direct connection with Heaven, as were the people as a collectivity. The belief that "Heaven sees as my people see, Heaven hears as my people hear," implied a kind of fundamental right, albeit a right of last resort, of the people against the ruler. Chinese rulers, however much they might wish to, could never quite forget this claim.

CODA

The concept of the human that evolved in ancient China was different from the concepts that evolved in the "axial age" in India or in the Greco-Roman or Judaeo-Christian West. First, the Chinese family, as the basic social unit, was the primary frame of reference in value formation, the most enduring values being those of biological survival, inheritance, and continuity. Second, the family was at the center of what Max Weber called the "familistic state," which was understood much in the manner of an extended family: a "fiduciary community," under the tutelage of a ruler whose role in the state was like that of the patriarchal head of a family. Third, the state in turn was understood to exist in a universe—a biosphere—which was congenial to and supportive of similar values, the complementarity and interreactivity of universal forces being understood as a confirmation of the importance of procreativity and of the harmonized tension and mutual responsiveness found in the family.

This familistic perspective, with its applicability on individual, collective, and cosmic levels, was considered so "natural" that the impulse for philosophers to reflect on alternative political institutions or arrangements did not come into play. It is a perspective so integrated that a distinction between immanent and transcendent realms, or natural and supernatural spheres, if discoverable at all, must be considered extremely weak. As the world was not divided in such a way as to distinguish a transcendent realm from the mundane world of ordinary experience, the religious realm, for ordinary people, was virtually synonymous with family life itself, so that religious functions that might in other cultures have been performed by a priesthood were largely the duty and the prerogative of family heads. In Weber's view it was significant that Confucianism "lacked any experience of disparate (religious) qualifications existing between human beings . . . and hence any concept of the differentiation in religious terms between individuals bestowed by a 'state of grace.' "[69]

The world *is* the world of ordinary experience; the events of the world are neither illusory nor discounted in their reality by the existence of a transcendent realm superior to quotidian reality. Parallel to this perspective of ordinariness is the emphasis on custom and the sublimation of custom in ritual. Related also to the beauty and solemnity of ritual is the absence of any inclination to deprecate custom vis-à-vis a concept of abstract or transcendent justice or of natural law. The Western idea of a law which is universal, perduring, and ascertainable through human reason, against which human institutions and positive law are to be tested and judged, may depend on at least two premises which Confucians did not seriously entertain: 1) the idea of a level of reality superior to that of mundane existence, or of a law-giving transcendent deity; and 2) that of a distinct rational faculty possessed by human beings which allows their access to such a higher law even while they remain existentially implicated in a social system in which that law is imperfectly realized or even contravened. The idea of natural law may also depend on the experience of significant cultural differences and a certain intuition of cultural relativism to which the assertion of the higher authority of a universally applicable law represents a response. China, being *the* high civilization in the East Asian culture area, had no experience of another such civilization prior to the introduction of Buddhism in the first century. One might say that the "problem" to which natural law represented a solution was never faced in China's premodern experience.

Developing at a time when feudal society was in decline and social mobility was on the rise in China, early Confucianism asserted the fundamental similarity of human beings, their "natural equality." Just as the Chinese world was a continuum, without separate levels of reality, each individual could be seen an integrated whole, similar by nature to every other, and endowed with comparable potential. In a sense China in antiquity was already quite "modern" inasmuch as equality and fraternity were commonplace ideas as far back as the "axial age." Yet liberty had no real purchase in any premodern Confucian conception. The theme of "liberty, equality, fraternity" would, of course, be asserted in the West only in the eighteenth century. When it was, it would be asserted over against an older monarchical and aristocratic tradition and with an energy or authority which derived in part from earlier struggles for religious liberty and the freedom of individual conscience. Its adherents would deploy an individual who, even before religious liberty took shape as a modern issue, and before the surfacing of "individualist" currents in the eighteenth century, could be imagined or construed as existing unto himself, independent of the bonds and supports of family. The Chinese knew of such an individual primarily through Buddhist influence but were always uneasy about the biological decontextualization.

Confucianism has been described here as a worldly spirituality that focused on the education and moral cultivation of individuals who have one lifetime to lead in this world—who pass this Way but once. Human beings were not thought of as created by God, or in the image of God, nor were they seen as possessing a soul with a career projected in terms of countless future incarnations, as in classical Hinduism, or with an infinite career, as in Christianity. They were, however, related to Heaven or to Nature through a human nature that, according to the *Mean*, was ordained by Heaven and that accounted for their status in the universe, their moral potential, and their dignity, which was a dignity of moral capacity.

It is often maintained that Confucian China had no room for the individual but only for the collectivity, that the tradition dictated that individuals subordinate themselves to the interests of the family and the state. What I have tried to suggest involves a substantial modification of that view, which I take to be inadequate to express the spirit of classical Confucianism. Far from ignoring the individual or the experience of subjectivity, the writers of the Four Books focused on the individual and saw that individual as involved in and fulfilled through human interactions. These human interactions began, both biologically and educationally, in the nuclear family and extended outward toward the larger kinship groups of lineage and clan toward the still larger unit of the "fiduciary community" or state. Spared the misfortune of lacking male progeny, this individual, at the close of his life, would assume the status of an ancestor and endure, not exactly immortal, but still unobliterated, as part of a biological/historical chain, ultimately absorbed and enfolded into the continuum of being.

Of the greatest consequence for the political development of China over the long course of history is that, while Confucianism did attach importance to the individual—it was, after all, the individual who possessed all potentialities, duties, and "rights,"—he possessed "rights" not *against* the family, community, or state, but *within* them. There being no basis for an adversarial relationship between the individual and the family, there was also no basis for an adversarial relationship between the individual and the state.

With only a few exceptions,[70] dissidents and reformers, from earliest times to the nineteenth century, rather than conjuring up alternative visions of the state, differently constituted, would continue to discover the primary solution to political problems where Confucius and Mencius had found it centuries earlier: in correcting the minds of individuals so as to return to a time-honored and humane pattern of human interaction. Failing that, the impulse was usually to remove corrupt individuals from office and replace them with incorruptible ones.

This does not mean that basic institutions did not change from the fifth or fourth centuries B.C.E. or that there was some Confucian "ideological" inhibition in regard to change. Rather, the idea that political responsibility, like family responsibility, rested with individuals was so powerful that the idea that radical institutional change would be required to preserve Chinese life intact required an equally powerful challenge to the system.

That challenge ultimately came by way of the Western incursion into China. Much has happened to change China radically in "the Western age," including the wrenching experience of Western and Japanese imperialism in the nineteenth century and two major wars and two revolutions within the first half of the twentieth century. Yet despite the radical changes that have occurred in our own century, including those involved in the Communist revolution of 1949, there remain certain consistent patterns in Chinese thinking.

These have to do not with the form of government, with institutions, or with law, where the changes have been profound, but with more primary patterns of human interaction, which continue to reassert themselves even in the midst of cataclysmic changes. These go back to some of the earliest conceptions of what it means to be human and to intuitions that call for mutual protection ahead of the individual assertion of self-interest, for the survival and continuity of life before everything else. In the course of the twentieth century, China has already borrowed a great deal from the West, and some advocates of human rights would like to see her borrow more, and perhaps from different sources.

It is not by way of disagreeing with them but, rather, of calling attention to the value of indigenous Chinese resources that I wish to emphasize the weight of human experience involved in the Chinese perspective on human dignity and the respect this experience should command. Being cognizant of this experience is essential to effective communication between Westerners and Chinese. It may also serve to enhance our own humanistic awareness (a more old-fashioned word for which is wisdom) and our understanding of human rights as a broadly human and still evolving undertaking. Facing the twenty-first century when resources will be more scarce on an ever more crowded planet, the West in turn may have much to learn from the Chinese—about them, about ourselves, and about ultimate survival.

Notes

1. Karl Jaspers, "Die Achsenzeit," in *Vom Ursprung und Ziel der Geschichte* (Zurich: Artemis Verlag, 1949), ch. 1. Trans. by Michael Bullock as *The Origin and Goal of History* (New Haven: Yale University Press, 1953). The concept of the "axial age" is discussed in Benjamin I. Schwartz, "The Age of Transcendence," in the symposium, "Wisdom, Revelation, and Doubt; Perspectives on the First Millennium B.C." in *Daedalus*, Spring 1974. See also Benjamin I. Schwartz, *The World of Thought in Ancient China* (Cambridge: The Belknap Press of Harvard University Press, 1985), pp. 2–3 and p. 423, note 2.

2. That Mencius himself may have been involved in the work of compilation of at least part of the work is a possibility.

3. Arthur Waley, *The Way and Its Power: A Study of the Tao Te Ching and Its Place in Chinese Thought* (London: George Allen and Unwin, 1965), p. 21.

4. See *Mencius*, 3A:4:8 and *Mean*, 20:8.

5. *Analects*, 12:11. An alternative translation would be, "Let the ruler be a ruler, the minister be a minister, the father be a father, and the son be a son."

6. Though I deeply admire Henry Rosemont's work in comparative philosophy. and especially his recent work on the bearing of Confucianism on modern Western human rights thinking, we differ slightly here. In his stimulating essay, "Why Take Rights Seriously? A Confucian Critique," Professor Rosemont suggests (typescript, p. 22) that, "for Confucius, I *am* my roles," and (p. 23) " . . . The early Confucians would insist that I do not play or perform, but am and become the roles I live in consonance with others, so that when all the roles have been specified, and their interconnections made manifest, then I have been specified fully as a unique person, with no discernible loose threads with which to piece together a free, autonomous, choosing self."

For reasons I shall indicate in what follows, I am inclined to the view that individuals have more social, psychological, and moral space in which to move than the language of Professor Rosemont's analysis might seem to imply. We are, however, in agreement on the issue of choice, which seems not to play a significant role in Confucian moral discourse or in the concept of the person.

7. *Analects*, 7:22.

8. Yu Ying-shih, " 'Oh Soul, Come Back!' A Study in the Changing Conceptions of the Soul and Afterlife in Pre-Buddhist China," *Harvard Journal of Asiatic Studies* 47:2 (December 1987), 363–95.

9. Hsu Cho-yun, *Ancient China in Transition: An Analysis of Social Mobility, 722–222 B.C.* (Stanford: Stanford University Press, 1965). See also Donald J. Munro, *The Concept of Man in Early China* (Stanford: Stanford University Press, 1969), pp. 5–11.

10. Thomas A. Metzger overstates the case perhaps when he says, "Given the sexist bias integral to traditional Chinese culture, many of the apparently universal traditional concepts about human life implicitly refer only to males, or perhaps better, to a mode of existence shared by males and females but attaining its fullest realization only in the case of males. That a woman could become a sage was inconceivable to the typical Confucian . . . and we do not need to translate *chün-tzu* as 'true gentleman or lady.' " *Escape from Predicament; Neo-Confucianism and China's Evolving Political Culture* (New York: Columbia University Press, 1977), p. 237, note 3. My main concern about this way of stat-

ing the issue is that the reference to "a sexist bias integral to traditional Chinese culture" might be construed to mean that such a bias is more typical of traditional Chinese culture than of most other traditional cultures, which would surely be erroneous. Just to preserve the essential ambiguity of the term *chün-tzu* (in recognition of the fact that in later times the term *chün-tzu was* sometimes applied to women), I shall translate it, Professor Metzger's comment notwithstanding, as "noble person" or "morally noble person."

11. Tu Wei-ming, *Centrality and Commonality: An Essay on Chung Yung* (Honolulu: University Press of Hawaii, 1976), esp. ch. 2.

12. See Theresa Kelleher, "Confucianism," in *Women in World Religions*, ed. by Arvind Sharma (Albany: State University of New York Press, 1987), p. 140.

13. *Analects*, 17:2.

14. Munro, *The Concept of Man in Early China*, esp. chs. 1 and 4.

15. *Analects*, 15:38.

16. *Mencius*, 4B:32 and 6B:2.

17. Volumes have been written about the nature and extent of social mobility in China in different periods; suffice it to say here that there endured over the course of centuries a distinctly Confucian confidence: any male, given hard work, effort, and access to education, might succeed in the civil service examinations and enter the power structure by becoming an official.

18. Arthur Waley, trans., *The Analects of Confucius* (New York: Vintage, n.d.), Introduction, p. 38.

19. *Analects*, 1:2.

20. *Mean*, 17.

21. This is in contrast to the *Classic of Filial Devotion* where Confucius is quoted as saying, 'Filiality is the first principle of heaven, the ultimate standard of earth, the norm of conduct for the people." See Mary Lelia Makra, trans., *The Hsiao Ching* (New York: St. John's University Press, 1961), p. 15.

22. Confucius in the *Analects* refers generally to "respect" or "reverence" and to "proper behavior," without getting into specific prescriptions.

23. Some scholars suggest that it is with the *Classic of Filial Devotion* that the five relationships take on a different cast and that a more hierarchical or "asymmetrical" view replaces an earlier one characterized by greater mutuality and regard for the party who later became the "inferior" in a given relationship.

24. See Paul Chao, *Chinese Kinship* (London: Kegan Paul, 1983), esp. chs. 1–2.

25. In his fascinating study, *Chinese Kinship*, Paul Chao observes (p. 43) that, "In contrast to conditions in ancient Rome, where the *pater familias* has '*jus vitae et necisque*', the Chinese father has no absolute power over the life and death of his children unless he is grossly insulted and attacked." Whereas the first emperor of the Ch'in dynasty (221–207 B.C.E.) could command his son to commit suicide and expect obedience, he could do so only as sovereign. (Even so, one might add, the infamous Ch'in Shih huang-ti could never be free of the stain of sordidness and inhumanity that clung to him and to his culpable ministers ever after in the Chinese memory.) Professor Chao cites the Han dynasty text *Pai-hu tung*, which explains that another father would himself be liable to execution for killing his son: "Why should a father be executed for killing his son? Human beings are most important in the nature of heaven and earth; they are produced by heaven merely through the

medium of their parents. And the ruler provides a living for them and educates them. Therefore the father can have no claim on them." *Pai-hu tung*, SPTK ed., 4:5a; cited in Chao, p. 43.

Again, the continuity of life figures importantly here, as does the direct relationship that each individual has with Heaven.

26. Bernhard Karlgren, *Analytic Dictionary of Chinese and Sino-Japanese* (Paris: Librairie Orientaliste Paul Geuthner, 1923; New York: Dover reprint, 1974), p. 271.

27. *Analects*, 12:3.

28. Waley, trans., *The Analects of Confucius*, p. 28.

29. *Analects*, 12:2.

30. *Analects*, 8:6 (or, in some versions, 8:7). The word *jen* meaning humaneness and the word *jen* meaning a burden or responsibility are homophones. Karlgren explains the latter word to mean "to carry a weight on the shoulder . . . a carrying pole supported in the middle part and having one object attached at either end, as always done in China." *Analytic Dictionary of Chinese and Sino-Japanese*, p. 271.

31. *Analects*, 15:8.

32. What I mean by this is that, in contrast with the kind of discussion found in the Upaniṣads, very little is asserted by Mencius at a metaphysical level. His observations are essentially psychological, and most discussions in the text are concerned with how people actually behave in relation to how they ought to behave.

33. *Mencius*, 6A:11.

34. Karlgren, *Analytic Dictionary of Chinese and Sino-Japanese*, pp. 175, 260.

35. *Analects*, 12:1.

36. See Katherine F. Young, "Hinduism" and Theresa Kelleher, "Confucianism" in Arvind Sharma, ed., *Women in World Religions*, pp. 59–104 and 135–59.

37. See Wm. Theodore de Bary, "Human Rites: An Essay on Confucianism and Human Rights," in Irene Eber, ed., *Confucianism: The Dynamics of Tradition* (New York: Macmillan, 1986), pp. 109–32.

38. *Nicomachean Ethics*, Book 8, ch. 12 (1162a). In Richard McKeon, ed., *The Basic Works of Aristotle* (New York: Random House, 1941), p. 1073.

39. *Politics*, Book 2, ch. 2 (1261a). In Richard McKeon, *The Basic Works of Aristotle*, p. 1146.

40. *Ibid.*, pp. 1146–47. I am grateful to Lenn Goodman for alerting me to the relevance of this passage to the point being made here.

41. See especially *Mean* 20:8.

42. *Chou I cheng-i*, 7:7a-8a. Cf. the translation in Richard Wilhelm and Cary F. Baynes, *The I Ching or Book of Changes* (Princeton: Princeton University Press, 1967), pp. 297–99.

43. *Chou I cheng-i*, 7:7b; Wilhelm and Baynes, *The I Ching*, p. 298.

44. By modern dating, mid-eleventh century B.C.E.

45. According to traditional dating, in the late twelfth century B.C.E.

46. See the *Book of History*, "Announcement to the Duke of Shao," in James Legge, trans., The Chinese Classics (Oxford: Clarendon Press, 1893), vol. 3, pp. 420–33.

47. Again, the fact that the same term, *t'ien*, may be translated into English as both Heaven (having, for us, a religious sense) and nature (having primarily a philosophical or scientific sense) is indicative of a distinction which is central to a modern Western view but which had no purchase in the Chinese frame of reference.

48. Obviously it must also have had ideological or propagandistic significance in legitimating the Chou conquest of the Shang.

49. *Mencius*, 5A:5, quoting the *Classic of Documents*, "T'ai-shih."

50. *Mean*, 12:2. Translation adapted from James Legge, *Chung Yung*, The Chinese Classics, vol. 1 , pp. 391–92.

51. *Mean*, 12:4.

52. Wilhelm/Baynes, *The I Ching*, Introduction, p. 4.

53. *Mean*, 20:3.

54. Tu Wei-ming, *Centrality and Commonality: An Essay on Chung-yung* (Honolulu: University Press of Hawaii, 1976), p. 67.

55. Tu, *Centrality and Commonality*, pp. 93–94.

56. Ambrose Y. C. King, "The Individual and Group in Confucianism: A Relational Perspective," in Donald J. Munro, ed., *Individualism and Holism: Studies in Confucian and Taoist Values* (Ann Arbor: University of Michigan Press, 1985), p. 61.

57. King, "The Individual and the Group in Confucianism," p. 61, citing Fei Hsiao-t'ung, *Hsiang-t'u Chung-kuo* (Peasant China) (Taipei: Lu-chou ch'u-pan she, 1967 reprint), p. 29.

58. King, "The Individual and Group in Confucianism," pp. 63–64.

59. See, for example, the exchanges with King Hui in *Mencius* 1A:1–5 and with King Hsüan of Ch'i in 1A:7.

60. Mencius does not omit the more measured approach based on the definition of specific human relations, however. See, for example, *Mencius*, 3A:4:8.

61. This may appear, but is *not*, tautological: as in *Mencius* in 7B:16 and 4A:12, the author of the *Mean* uses the cognate terms *jen* (meaning humane, benevolent, or good) and *jen* (meaning a human being).

62. *Great Learning*, text. Translation by Wing-tsit Chan, *A Source Book in Chinese Philosophy* (Princeton: Princeton University Press, 1963), pp. 86–87.

63. See also Hung-chao Tai, "Human Rights in Taiwan: Convergence of Two Political Cultures?" in James C. Hsiung, ed., *Human Rights in East Asia: A Cultural Perspective* (New York: Paragon House, 1985), p. 88.

64. *Analects*, 12:7 and 13:9.

65. *Mencius*, 3A:3.

66. See Irene Bloom, "On the Matter of the Mind: The Metaphysical Basis of the Expanded Self," in Donald J. Munro, ed., *Individualism and Holism: Essays in Confucian and Taoist Values*, p. 295.

67. *Analects*, 2:3. Translation by Arthur Waley, *The Analects of Confucius*, p. 88.

68. See *Waiting for the Dawn—A Plan for the Prince*, by Huang Tsung-hsi, trans. by Wm. Theodore de Bary (New York: Columbia University Press, 1993).

69. Max Weber, *Confucianism and Taoism*, trans. by Max Alter and Janet Hunter (London: London School of Economics, 1984), pp. 47–48.

70. One of the exceptions is Huang Tsung-hsi. See above, note 68.

5

The Individual and the Collectivity in Christianity

JOHN LANGAN, S.J.

Human Rights and Christian Norms

In a recent defense of what he calls postmodern bourgeois liberalism, Richard Rorty draws a contrast between two groups of philosophers and social and legal theorists. The first group believes that there is a "supercommunity one had to identify with as such." Rorty calls them "Kantians," and he observes: "These are the people who think there are such things as intrinsic human dignity, intrinsic human rights, and an a-historical distinction between the demands of morality and those of prudence."[1] He contrasts them unfavorably with the "Hegelians," who "say the 'humanity' is a biological rather than a moral notion, that there is no human dignity that is not derivative from the dignity of some specific community, and no appeal beyond the relative merits of various actual or proposed communities to impartial criteria which will help us weigh those merits." Rorty rejects the project of finding what he calls an "a-historical backup" for loyalty to particular communities, and he replaces the notion of human dignity with "the comparative dignity of a group with which a person identifies herself." Rorty makes it clear that he does not object to "the institutions and practices of the surviving democracies;" his difficulty is with the kind of justification that most social philosophers think it necessary to provide for them. One of the objections to his view which he considers is "that on my view a child found wandering in the woods, the remnant of a slaughtered nation whose temples have been razed and whose books have been burned, has no share in human dignity." Rorty admits that this is indeed so. But he holds that this does not authorize our treating her as an animal. He explains:

> For it is part of the tradition of *our* community that the human stranger from whom all dignity has been stripped is to be taken in, to be clothed with dignity. This Jewish and Christian element in our tradition is gratefully invoked by free-loading atheists like myself. . . . The existence of human rights, in the sense in which it is at issue in this metaethical debate, has as much or as little relevance to our treatment of such a child as the question of the existence of God. I think both have equally little relevance.   (ibid.)

This position, which in effect turns from the search for foundations for human rights to the partial affirmation of traditions favoring human rights, is of particular interest for several reasons.

First, it ignores one of the most important functions of human rights norms, which is to regulate the ways in which people who come from different traditions, ideologies, and cultures may deal with each other. Such cross-cultural contacts and the conflicts to which they often give rise are not the contrived counterexamples of metaethical theorists, but are part of the daily bread of contemporary world politics, whether we are dealing with economic development in the interior of Brazil or the status of the Palestinians or communal violence in India.

Second, it focuses on the task of preventing *our* violation of other persons from outside our culture, and evades the task of setting up mutually or universally recognized norms for the protection of all, including ourselves.

Third, it makes the interesting but not very plausible claim that human rights concerns about the treatment of others are adequately captured by norms from the basic religious traditions of our culture about the treatment of those likely to be excluded.

Fourth, and what is most important for the purposes of this essay, Rorty's position suggests that the basic contribution to the shaping of our norms for the treatment of others comes from our religious traditions and that this has a continuing strength and validity even after religious truth-claims are dismissed. It is the atheistic philosopher who is the free-loader, in sharp contrast to those positions in which the religious believer is dismissed as the victim of illusion and, at best, the confused purveyor of truths which he provides through a symbolic system whose real meaning and social function he does not grasp.

Ironically, Rorty here comes into agreement with those religious apologists who contend that not secular reason but religious faith provides the only lasting support for humane values in our civilization. Indeed, if one thinks in terms of the historical continuity and social impact of moral norms on large numbers of people in a society, as one has to do when the whole issue of moral norms is put in terms of tradition and social change, then one has to give a central place to religion, regardless of one's views on the ultimate metaphysical and epistemological questions and regardless of the fair to poor record of many religious groups in articulating and observing human rights.

THE CONTINUITY OF THE CHRISTIAN CHURCHES

My own intention here is not to work over the familiar battleground between belief and unbelief in Western culture, but to explore some aspects of the understanding of individual and collectivity in Christianity and to indicate some of the ways in which these both aid and hinder the development of human rights. How are we to understand the connections between Christian views of the individual and the collectivity and those elements in the Western tradition that lead to the affirmation of human dignity and human rights? This can never be an easy question to answer, since one of the most fruitful sources of sectarian division among Christians down through the centuries has been precisely the question of how individual and collectivity are to be integrated both in the case of the Christian community itself and in the case of the larger civil society.[2]

A basic reason for the multiplicity of views in this area and for the ensuing divisions among Christian groups has been the fact that Christianity has stood in four different relationships to the larger societies within which it found itself.

First, it has had the status of an intermittently persecuted religious minority, which was far from the centers of power (political, economic, military, cultural). From quite early on, the Christian church had a certain number of wealthy and even prominent converts; but the sense of distance from "the powers that be" is pervasive throughout the New Testament. In times of persecution this was combined with a passionate desire for divine deliverance and vindication; in more peaceful times it was combined with a more positive appreciation of the benefits of Roman order and peace.

Second, it has had the status of a comprehensive and established church, whose members comprised the great bulk of society and which expected both to have relations of mutual support with other centers of power in society and to exercise significant controlling functions, particularly with regard to education and the dissemination of ideas but also with regard to marriage and family life, the keeping of records, and the relief of poverty.

Third, it has had the status of being one of a number of legally recognized and protected free associations coexisting and competing peacefully with each other in a situation of religious and intellectual pluralism as in the United States over the last two centuries.

Fourth, it has had the status of being divided in such a way as to imperil public order and so to require political, legal, and sometimes military intervention.

There is a certain tendency to regard the first three conditions as progressive stages in the history of the Christian church from its beginnings in late antiquity through the medieval period to modern times. But that would be inaccurate. The first status can be found in contemporary China and prevailed until recently in most of Eastern Europe and the Soviet Union. The second status was dominant well into the twentieth century in Spain and most of Latin America. The third status can be found coexisting with significant holdovers from the second status, e.g., the established churches of Britain and Scandinavia. The fourth status occurs at different times, either when Christianity is locked in combat with one or more rival groups (not always religious) or when the Christian church is divided into hostile groups as, for instance, in the course of the Reformation or in contemporary Ulster. The fourth status is the least stable and produces movement in the direction of one of the other three.

Each of these conditions, however, brings with it a different set of practical problems and a different set of normative reflections and expectations with different issues in dispute and different sources of religious authority being drawn on. But in all the welter of historical information and theological dispute which has to be examined in reviewing Christian thought about the proper relationship between the church and society and the state and in tracing Christian norms about the rights and duties of individuals, both Christian and non-Christian, there seem to me to be three constants.

The first is the normative role of Scripture. Thus all Christian groups, no matter how they may be divided on other theological issues, acknowledge the authority of the New Testament, which serves as both the religious record of the life and teaching of Jesus and the foundation of the community and as a guide for prayer and theological reflection in the community. They also acknowledge the continuing authority of the Hebrew Bible precisely as the Old Testament, the record of God's dealings with His people in Israel in preparation for the fulfillment of his covenant with them through the life, death, and resurrection of Jesus.

Second, they assume that the group of those who accept the Christian message constitutes an extensive and exclusive community. This means two things: first, that it is appropriate, normal, and even obligatory for those who accept the good news of salvation in Christ Jesus to join together in forming a community of worship and life. Only a small minority of Christian congregations over the centuries has attempted to live precisely in the manner proposed in the famous description of the Jerusalem church in Acts 2:44–47:

> And all who believed were together and had all things in common; and they sold their possessions and goods and distributed them to all, as any had need. And day by day, attending the temple together and breaking bread in their homes, they partook of food with glad and generous hearts, praising God and having favor with all the people. And the Lord added to their number day by day those who were being saved.[3]

The practice of most of the communities referred to in the New Testament falls short of this fullness of community life, but it is clearly more than the gathering of a group for occasional ritual observances. Rather, it is a community of mutual support, from which those who lead openly immoral lives are to be excluded. Paul, for instance, urges the Corinthians:

> I wrote to you in my letter not to associate with immoral men, not at all meaning the immoral of this world, or the greedy and robbers or idolaters since then you would need to go out of the world. But rather I wrote to you not to associate with any one who bears the name of brother if he is guilty of immorality or greed, or is an idolater, reviler, drunkard, or robber—not even to eat with such a one. For what have I to do with judging outsiders? God judges those outside. Drive out the wicked person from among you.   (1 Corinthians, 5:9–13)

The community, then, is extensive in its concern for the way of life of its members, even though it does not generally aspire to form a closed society or a total institution.

At the same time, the community is exclusive in the sense that while it is open to people of all nations, races, and conditions, it operates on the assumption that a person may legitimately belong to and participate in the activities of only one religious community. In this respect, it is similar to Judaism and Islam and differs from Hinduism and Buddhism. In making this assumption, Christianity continues the exclusionary demands of the Lord in the Hebrew Bible, in particular the prohibition of idolatry in Exodus 20:3–6. Paul tells the Corinthians: "You cannot drink the cup of the Lord and the cup of demons. You cannot partake of the table of the Lord and the table of demons." (1 Corinthians 10:21) This is a formulation which rules out participation in idolatrous worship. It does not address the question of whether a person could be simultaneously active in Christian and Jewish religious communities. This was a possibility which was envisaged in Acts 2:46 and which lies behind the demand of some that all Christians are to observe the Mosaic law (cf. Acts 15), but it was a possibility which came to be rejected by both Judaism and Christianity.

Thus, Christians of all sorts acknowledge the authority of Scripture, though they disagree on how this is to be defined and on some of the writings which are to be included in the canon. They also acknowledge that they are called to form a community in the name of Jesus, a church, even though they have had many intense and profound disagreements about how the church is to be organized and what its legitimate powers and practices are.

The third decisive point or constant is the conviction that is contained in the New Testament and that animates the life of all the churches in the Christian tradition, the conviction that the God of Israel has, in the person and teaching of Jesus, entered into a new relationship with humanity at large. This point has been a matter of controversy, not merely between Jews and Christians, for whom it is clearly a fundamental point of division, but also among Christians who have offered many different accounts of how to formulate the relationship between Jesus and the one whom He called Father. Early Christian theology proclaimed that Jesus was not merely the Messiah, the royal figure expected to bring redemption to Israel and the nations, but the unique son of God (Hebrews 1:2). The main Christian tradition formulated in the early ecumenical councils affirmed the divinity and humanity of Jesus and the union of three persons in one God. But, even for those Christians who have questioned the classic creedal formulations, Jesus, conceived as teacher or as exemplar of love, has remained of central importance, an importance which is affirmed in secularized societies in ways ranging from the Western system of chronology to the place of Christmas in secular social life.

One issue about Jesus which does not exactly coincide with customary denominational or theological divisions, but which is of very great importance for understanding the development of Christian attitudes to society and its problems, is the question of how the coming of Jesus in Palestine at the beginning of our era is to be linked with the end of the present world.[4] There was clearly an early Christian expectation that Jesus would return to earth to bring about the fullness of God's kingdom within the lifetime of most members of the community (cf. Thessalonians 4:13–18; 1 Corinthians 7:17–31) and that the present order of things would pass away. Even after the expectation of an imminent end declined, a certain eschatological emphasis in Christianity has survived because of the continuing relevance of death and judgment to the lives and choices of individuals. Collective eschatological expectation, moreover, has been revitalized from time to time, and eschatological themes have never completely disappeared from mainstream Christianity. This eschatological expectation can be conjoined with either a profound devaluation of existing social institutions or with a patient acceptance of their negative and presumably temporary aspects. Thus Paul urges the Corinthians to remain in their present condition, whether it be slavery or freedom (1 Corinthians 7:25–40); and he also urges them not to marry before the second coming unless it is necessary, "since the appointed time has grown very short."

But the main Christian bodies have been able to build on the New Testament's acknowledgment of the uncertainty of "the times and seasons," which are determined by the Father (Acts 1:7). They have also been able to develop a conception of the Christian era as a long-term transitional stage between the old dispensation and the coming of the kingdom in its fullness and with a need to develop institutions that are sustainable over time. They have also been able to develop the indications of a realized eschatology particularly in the Gospel of John, according to which the decisive elements of the end of time are already present in the life of the Christian community and eternal life is already begun.[5] "This is eternal life that they know thee the only true God and Jesus Christ whom thou hast sent" (John 17:3). This is a position which can lead either to a concentration on the inner life of the Christian community accompanied by a strong sense of separation from and opposition to "the world" (John 15:18–27) or to a concern for the transformation of the institutions of society that they may be appropriate to a kingdom of justice and peace.[6]

If these points are taken together, we have an understanding of a Christian church (that is, any Christian church) as a group of persons forming a distinctive and exclusive religious community guiding itself by the Scriptures and taking Jesus as central in its understanding of morality and history and looking forward to his second coming and the full manifestation of God's justice. This characterization applies to vast organizations present in widely separated cultures, such as Roman Catholicism and the Anglican communion as well as to independent congregations in towns in the southern United States or Zaire or Guatemala. It, of course, falls short of the full theological claims made about Christ and the church in the major traditions; and it is intended to do so. But it enables us to see the central place of the church both in continuing Christianity over the generations and in occupying a middle ground between the believing individual and the collectivity which is the larger society with its norms and its conception of itself. At different times the church may function as an ideological factor promoting the cohesion of the larger society, or it may regard itself as the supreme and ultimate collectivity, the earthly manifestation of the City of God, carrying on the prophetic task of a religious leadership which the Lord sets "over nations and over kingdoms, to pluck up and to break down, to destroy and to overthrow, to build and to plant" (Jeremiah 1:10).[7]

The Christian church thus stands athwart the contrast that Rorty proposes between the Kantian effort to found universal norms for humanity on universal moral reason and the Hegelian focus on particular communities rooted in specific histories and proposing their own standards. The universalization of the particular in Christian thinking about the fulfillment of humanity in Christ can be taken as evidence of conceptual confusion or religious arrogance, or it can be seen as a decisive breakthrough in the articulation of human aspirations. But whatever assessment one finally makes of it, one has to see it as a fundamental and recurrent characteristic of Christianity's effort to speak its message to humanity.

THE SALVATION OF THE INDIVIDUAL

In what is by common consent of the scholarly world the earliest of the canonical Gospels, that according to Mark, Jesus begins his ministry in Galilee with the simple and direct proclamation: "The time is fulfilled, and the kingdom of God is at hand; repent, and believe in the gospel" (Mark 1:15). On one level the call to repentance, to a change of mind and heart with an appropriate alteration of one's way of life, had been taken as addressed to individuals. This should not blind us to the fact that the New Testament reports mass conversions, notably in the Acts of the Apostles (Acts 2:41, 4:4) and that conversions could involve groups and households (Acts 10:44). The crucial point is that while conversion can affect groups it can also affect individuals, who leave the religious and also in many cases the social groups with which they were previously associated.

Thus the early Christian community is composed of believers who have been called to follow Jesus and who have made the decision to do so, a decision that cuts them off both from the Jewish community and from the idolatrous Gentiles. In the Gospels there are numerous passages which stress the responsibility of individuals to hear and to respond to God's call and which present an individualized and non-collective interpretation of salvation. So, for instance, in the eschatological discourse in Matthew 24, Jesus warns the disciples about the coming of the Son of man: "Then two men will be in the field; one is taken and one is left. Two women will be grinding at the mill; one is taken and one is left" (Matthew 24:40–41). The individual character of the gift of salvation depends on the actions of the persons who are being called, as in the famous contrast between those who aid persons who are hungry, thirsty, naked, sick, or imprisoned and those who fail to do so (Matthew 25:31–46).

It is also manifest in the contrasts and conflicts that the proclamation of Christ's message sets up even in families; as Jesus says in his discourse sending forth the twelve apostles to preach: "I have come to set a man against his father and a daughter against her mother, and a daughter-in-law against her mother-in-law" (Matthew 10:35). The disciples, however, have been reassured by Jesus: "But even the hairs of your head are all numbered. Fear not, therefore; you are of more value than the sparrows" (Matthew 10:30–31). Individual persons then are addressed by the preaching of Jesus; they are the objects of God's concern and God's judgment; they do or fail to do the things that God commands or urges. In this regard, the New Testament takes as given the affirmation of individual responsibility for wrongdoing that is found in Ezekiel 18.

The call to the individual also cuts across the standard lines of division in society, lines which have a strong normative content. Thus one of the twelve disciples, Matthew, is a tax collector, a person pursuing an occupation that was not merely politically unpopular but was also likely to involve sustained contact with Gentiles which would make observance of many details of the law difficult if not impossible (Matthew 9:9). Jesus, nonetheless, draws a contrast between the penitent publican or tax collector, who is justified, and the self-righteous pharisee, who is not (Luke 18:9–14). Jesus himself is criticized both for eating with "tax collectors and sinners" (Matthew 9:11) and for allowing a prostitute to touch him (Luke 7:39). The subordination of social divisions and expectations to the working of God's grace is dramatically illustrated in the parable of the Good Samaritan (Luke 10:29–37) as well as in the continuing presence of women in the group around Jesus (Luke 8:1–3).

Unquestionably, the most important division that the early Christian community crossed was that between the Jewish and the Gentile worlds. Jesus himself is depicted as unwilling to deliver the Canaanite woman's daughter on the grounds that "I was sent only to the lost sheep of the house of Israel" (Matthew 15:24). But he also heals the servant of a Roman centurion, observing that "not even in Israel have I found such faith" (Matthew 8:10). The Acts of the Apostles is mainly taken up with tracing the change in orientation of the early Christian community from its Jerusalem origins to its full acceptance of Gentile members. A key stage in this development is marked by the affirmation of Peter in dealing with the Roman centurion, Cornelius: "Truly I perceive that God shows no partiality, but in every nation anyone who fears Him and does what is right is acceptable to Him" (Acts 10:34–35). Paul, who plays a decisive role in spreading the gospel among the Gentiles of the Mediterranean world is then able to interpret baptism, the rite of initiation into the Christian community, as the establishment of a new identity in Christ, which transcends the principal social divisions. Thus he writes to the Galatians: "For as many of you as were baptized into Christ have put on Christ. There is neither Jew nor Greek, there is neither slave nor free, there is neither male nor female; for you are all one in Christ Jesus" (Galatians 3:27–28).

This comes close to the proclamation of a single-status society, a notion that Kenneth Minogue has pointed to as a central assumption of a doctrine of human rights.[8] But we should recall that the context for Paul's statement is the internal life of a religious community, and we should not conclude from this affirmation of fundamental equality that the early Christian communities organized themselves along strictly egalitarian lines. There are clearly both leaders and led in these communities, even though contemporary biblical scholarship warns us against equating the patterns of these communities with the subsequently developed polities of the various Christian churches.[9] What is clear in the New Testament material is that leadership and authority are connected with grace and the gifts of the Spirit (1 Corinthians 12) and with service to the community (Matthew 20:25–28), not with the use of power to dominate or with hereditary distinctions.

The New Testament also provides us with interesting examples of individuals acting against established authority in both the religious and secular spheres. In an episode that had special resonance in the period of the Reformation, Peter and the apostles, having been arrested for teaching in the name of Jesus, reply to the demand of the Jewish high priest that they should cease and desist with the famous words: "We must obey God rather than men. . . . And we are witnesses to these things, and so is the Holy Spirit whom God has given to those who obey Him" (Acts 5:29, 32). Here speaking out boldly is not so much an exercise of freedom, which it is with regard to earthly authority, but it is an act of obedience to God, and so it cannot be waived or surrendered at one's own discretion. In taking this stance, the apostles are following the example of John the Baptist, who denounced Herod for marrying his brother's sister (Mark 6:14–29) and of Jesus himself, who offered scathing criticism of the scribes and the Pharisees, the religious teachers of Israel (Matthew 23). In early Christianity, disobedience to authority is justified on religious grounds and for religious objectives. Such an attitude can both serve as an example for the exercise of human rights and as a limit on the exercise of rights, since a divine warrant or authorization is required.

Some of the early Christians, as the Apocalypse shows, could find reassurance in the expectation that Rome, the great harlot "drunk with the blood of the saints and the blood of the martyrs of Jesus" (Apocalypse 17:6) would be overthrown. At the same time, Jesus is not represented as a political adversary of Roman rule.[10] And he certainly does not appear before Pilate as a defiant revolutionary. But for Jesus and for the Christian community as well as for his Jewish contemporaries, there can never be any question of accepting the rule of Rome or of any worldly power with regard to religious matters. The word of Jesus with regard to the legitimacy of paying taxes to Romans remains of decisive importance even while it cries out for more specific interpretation: "Render to Caesar the things that are Caesar's and to God the things that are God's" (Mark 12;17).

Paul offers his famous admonition to the Romans:

> Let every person be subject to the governing authorities. For there is no authority except from God, and those that exist have been instituted by God. Therefore he who resists the authorities resists what God has appointed, and those who resist will incur judgment. For rulers are not a terror to good conduct, but to bad.
>
> (Romans 13;1–3)

The ruler, Paul goes on to say, is God's servant "for your good" and "to execute God's wrath on the wrongdoer." Particularly in the Anglican and Lutheran traditions, this position led to a doctrine of "passive obedience,"[11] according to which Christian subjects could not legitimately challenge their rulers, much less rebel against them.

On a more intimate level than the Christian's relationship to the state are the relationships to family members and neighbors. These are addressed in the sections of the Pauline epistles containing ethical exhortations, which customarily come after the doctrinal exposition. We may take chapters 4–6 of Paul's letter to the Ephesians as a particularly comprehensive and illuminating example of this material.

Paul there begins by stressing the factors that maintain the "unity of the Spirit in the bond of peace." Among these are "one hope that belongs to your call, one Lord, one faith, one baptism, one God and Father of us all, who is above all and through all and in all" (Ephesians 4:3, 5–6). He proceeds to acknowledge the diversity of gifts in the community and their positive contribution to "building up the body of Christ" (Ephesians 4:12). He warns the Ephesians not to "live as Gentiles do" and to "cut off their old nature" (Ephesians 4:17, 22). They are to avoid licentiousness, uncleanness, lust as well as dishonesty, anger, theft, and evil talk. They are not to associate with the children of darkness, and they should take particular care to avoid fornicators and idolators (Ephesians 5:5). He then goes on to the famous exhortation to husbands and wives, comparing their union to the union of Christ and the Church. He gives similar injunctions about obedience and mutual respect to parents and children as well as to masters and slaves (Ephesians 6:19). He concludes by urging them to "put on the whole armor of God," a metaphor which is developed to provide a catalogue of the virtues as well as to inculcate a strongly adversarial conception of the religious-moral life of the Christian (Ephesians 6:10–20).

This way of presenting the moral duties of Christians, which lightens the emphasis on adherence to traditional norms in the family and in social institutions with repeated calls to mutual forbearance and forgiveness, is not hospitable to the demands and the hopes of radical individualism or revolutionary anarchism.[12] The respect and the religious significance given to traditional institutions and the priority given to internal cohesion in the face of hostile spiritual powers and a social environment that could be persecuting or enticing ruled out a favorable response to those who proposed to toss traditional norms aside. Paul was particularly vehement in rejecting antinomian interpretations of the Christian Gospel, even while he strongly affirmed that justification was to be found through faith in Christ, and not by the works of the law (Galatians 2:15–21). The freedom of the Christian individual is, as Luther much later insisted, not to be equated with the overturning of the established social order or with arbitrary and amoral assertions of the individual's desires.[13]

Individuals are responsible and have duties, but they are not seen in the New Testament as subjects of rights, as persons advancing claims that should be honored. Rather, the stress in the human relationship to God is on God's gracious forgiveness and love. This is put in most moving terms in the parables of forgiveness in Luke 15, of which the most famous is the parable of the prodigal son. But the worth of the individual comes out most clearly in the parable of the lost sheep, which concludes with Jesus' affirmation that "there will be more joy in heaven over one sinner who repents than over ninety-nine righteous persons who need no repentance" (Luke 15:7). In the relationships of human beings to each other the stress is on love and mutual support, as well as on the call to imitate the forgiveness shown by the Father (Matthew 5:43–48; 18:23–35). In fact, Paul writes at one point to the Corinthians in a way that suggests that the exercise and defense of rights through resort to the courts is wrong for Christians in their dealings with one another. He writes: "To have lawsuits at all with one another is defeat for you. Why not rather suffer wrong? Why not rather be defrauded?" (1 Corinthians 6:7). This is an application to conflicts arising within the Christian community of the attitude of patient forbearance taught by Jesus in the Sermon on the Mount: "But I say to you, do not resist one who is evil. But if any one strikes you on the right cheek, turn to him the other also; and if anyone would sue you and take your coat, let him have your cloak as well" (Matthew 5:39–40).

This, of course, was an attitude which the early Christian community did not merely hear as a teaching but also saw as a norm carried out in an exemplary way in the passion and death of Jesus and as a challenge accepted by those who gave their lives as martyrs or witnesses for the Christian faith. This is a challenge which is put in particularly clear and pressing terms in the words of Jesus after Peter has both confessed his faith that Jesus is "the Christ, the

Son of the living God," (Matthew 16:16) and rejected Jesus' prediction that he would suffer and die in Jerusalem. In a passage which makes it clear that entering into the kingdom is not in any way comparable to the seizure of power or the accomplishment of personal ambition, Jesus says to the disciples:

> If any man would come after me, let him deny himself and take up his cross and fol-
> low me. For whoever would save his life will lose it, and whoever loses his life for my
> sake will find it. For what will it profit a man, if he gains the whole world and for-
> feits his life? For the Son of man is to come with his angels in the glory of his Father,
> and then he will repay every man for what he has done.   (Matthew 16:24–27)

Texts of this sort, which have played a central part in defining the requirements of Christian discipleship down through the centuries, point us in the direction of a concern with the salvation of the individual through renunciation of selfish and vengeful desires and through acceptance of sufferings inflicted by others. They leave us with a picture of Christians as resigned, passive, otherworldly—quite different from the questioning, active, socially oriented persons who are needed for the exercise and defense of human rights. Such a contrast has been made by many modern critics of Christianity as well as by the critics of pietism and the proponents of the Social Gospel in nineteenth century Protestantism and by liberation theologians and the Catholic bishops at Vatican II who would move Christianity to a more activist encounter with the modern world.[14]

But it should be remembered that the cluster of attitudes that we have been considering constitutes a profound and appropriate response to the necessary and irreversible evils which human beings encounter in life. This response, the taking up of the cross, has been found to be sustaining and consoling for millions of Christians in times of suffering and moments of agony. It is, however, inappropriate when the evils in question are preventable or removable by human agency and social cooperation. Judgments about what evils can be remedied and prevented and what the likely consequences will be for a range of religiously significant values, and about what means are justified in resisting evils, are not easily arrived at if they are made carefully and honestly.

Our ability to make them in a realistic and liberating way depends on a great deal of personal and social experience. The development of this ability by members and leaders in a Christian community is a complex and uneven historical process, which different Christian communities have articulated and practiced in different ways. But theologians, social activists, and secular observers should not underestimate the importance of the imaginative and effective connections that ordinary Christians make in their devotional lives between the cross of Christ and the sufferings and evils they have to bear in this life. This is exemplified in *The Imitation of Christ* from the Netherlands in the fifteenth century and in the stigmata of Saint Francis of Assisi as well as among the peasants of Colombia and the Philippines.

THE BODY OF CHRIST AND UNIVERSAL SALVATION

It would, however, be a major mistake to interpret the moral and social teaching of early Christianity along purely individualistic lines. In addition to the call to repentance and conversion with which Jesus begins his ministry in Mark, there is also the proclamation of God's kingdom, which is preeminently a social reality. The kingdom is often spoken of in the New Testament in negative terms: that is, it is the denial of what is evil or burdensome or troubling in the present order of things. There is an absence of sin, of tears, of condemnation, of suffering and of death. Paul writes to the Philippians: "But our commonwealth is in heaven, and from it we await a Savior, the Lord Jesus Christ, who will change our lowly body to be like his glorious body" (Philippians 3:20–21). This is a text which nicely gives a sense of the shared eschatological expectation of a new social reality, which will at the same time be a transformation of the old. The central figure in this expectation is Jesus Christ, who is "the head of the body, the church" (Colossians 1:18).

A development of decisive importance in early Christian theology is the working out of "high" christology, in which the central place of Jesus in the church, in humanity, and in the cosmos is given a metaphysical expression.[15] So, in the letter to the Colossians, Jesus is affirmed to be "the image of the invisible God, the first-born of all creation" (Colossians 2:15). His mission of proclaiming God's forgiveness and effecting reconciliation is then of universal value: "For in him all the fullness of God was pleased to dwell and through him to reconcile to himself all things, whether on earth or in heaven, making peace by the blood of his cross" (Colossians 1:20–21). In the theology of St. Paul, Christ, like Adam, the first man, serves as the point of concentration, the effective center for God's transformation of human from sin and death to righteousness and life. He writes to the Romans:

> If because of one man's trespass, death reigned through that one man, much more will those who receive the abundance of grace and the free gift of righteousness reign in life through the one man Jesus Christ. Then as one man's trespass led to condemnation for all men, so one man's act of righteousness leads to acquittal and life for all men. For as by one man's disobedience many were made sinners, so by one man's obedience many will be made righteous. (Romans 5:17–19)

Similar connections between the unique place of Jesus before God and his role of universal savior can be found in the Gospel of John and in the Epistle to the Hebrews, where Jesus is seen as the unique and eternal high priest. When the claims of this sort of high Christology are accepted, Jesus is affirmed to be the Savior of all humanity in principle. This is a theology which brings all individuals into one common destiny which both separates them from existing forms of collective life and offers them ultimate fulfillment. It affirms that human beings are to be brought together into one religious collectivity, the body of Christ, "that is, the church" (Colossians 1:24).

At the same time, this universalist theology gives rise to a profound tension between two conceptions of Christianity as a religion of salvation. The first conception requires explicit confession of the divinity of Jesus and conscious acceptance of the gift of God's forgiveness as conditions which are absolutely indispensable for salvation, while the second conception explores ways of interpreting the human search for the good and the different expressions of religious aspirations as partial, incomplete, implicit, hypothetical, or parallel ways of satisfying these conditions. The first conception can be found in both Catholic and Protestant forms. When joined with a loving concern for the well-being of those who have not come to faith in Christ, it becomes a powerful incitement to missionary activity.

So Christianity, along with Islam and Buddhism, has been one of the great missionary religions of the world. The church as a matter of historical fact is a particular and exclusive institution with its own history and limits; at the same time it proclaims a message of universal salvation and so it is committed to being inclusive. The obvious way to overcome the tension between these two points is to follow the parting injunction of Jesus in Matthew's gospel:

> Go therefore and make disciples of all nations, baptizing them in the name of the Father and of the Son and of the Holy Spirit, teaching them to observe all that I have commanded you; and lo, I am with you always, to the close of the age. (Matthew 28:19–20)

Accordingly, missionary activity has commonly been carried on in a spirit of benevolent paternalism or authoritarianism, a combination which has an inherent instability and which can sanction many human rights abuses for the sake of a higher good. This is true even before the possibility of corruption by secular temptations and pressures is considered, and before the negative possibilities created by adversarial relations with other religious bodies are brought into the picture. Benevolent authoritarianism can turn persecutorial, as when Thomas Aquinas holds that heretics may be put to death or when Augustine authorizes forced conversions,[16] and the church can at different times hand over the recalcitrant to the state or allow itself to become the instrument of an expansive imperialism. The step from regarding people as guilty and damned because of their resistance to God to disregarding their rights is not logically required, but it is easily taken when anger or greed comes to have the upper hand.

The view that "outside the church there is no salvation" has provoked uneasiness and controversy within the Christian community. We should compare the negative and rather strident assessment that Augustine offers of the virtues of the pagan Romans as *splendida vitia*[17] with the humility and the comity that Dante experiences with Virgil in the *Inferno* and the *Purgatorio*. The sages of the classical world are, in Dante's grand scheme, accorded a place of dignified retirement and are neither saved nor damned. In this century the Vatican condemned and excommunicated Father Leonard Feeney, a Boston Jesuit, for holding that those who did not adhere to the church could not be saved.[18]

The second view, which points to the ways in which God's grace works outside the Christian community, is an effort to reconcile the dictum in the letter to Titus traditionally attributed to Paul that "the grace of God has appeared for the salvation of all men" (Titus 2:11) with the evident fact that large numbers of persons have never heard the Gospel and with the reasonable judgment that many people of good moral behavior and virtuous disposition either do not accept the Gospel when it is preached to them or, given what we commonly believe about the social and cultural factors influencing the formation of beliefs, are very unlikely to accept it.

This is not a trivial problem from a theological standpoint, for it is very difficult to affirm that God is loving and just if he creates intelligent beings to whom he offers no realistic chance of salvation and on whom he then inflicts an eternity of torment or, at the very least, an eternity of frustration. Various ways of resolving this problem by appealing to the doctrine of original sin, according to which human beings are born into a situation of alienation from God and with a powerful inclination to disorder in their moral lives, or by regarding failure to accept the Gospel as a sin of pride and disobedience or by appealing to a mystery of divine election[19] have proved less than satisfactory on empirical, theoretical, or moral grounds. The Christian churches have, especially in this century, shown a strong tendency to give a more favorable estimate of non-Christian religious traditions (as well as of each other) and to look for more flexible ways of handling the theological problem of understanding the salvation of non-Christians (as well as of Christians with erroneous beliefs or deviant practices).

In doing this, they have been able to build on a long-standing tendency in Christianity to offer favorable appraisals of some aspects of the pre-Christian culture of the Græco-Roman world. This tendency goes back to the sermon of Paul to the Athenians in Acts 17. It is present in the early apologists for Christianity in the Roman empire, in Clement of Alexandria at the turn of the third century, in Thomas Aquinas, and various Renaissance humanists. A similar openness of mind to the presence of God in non-Christian cultures is also to be found in the Jesuit missionaries in India and China in the sixteenth and seventeenth centuries.[20]

Even those thinkers who were most scathing in their assessment of classical culture, such as Tertullian, St. Jerome, and St. Augustine relied heavily on the classical instruments of rhetoric and logic; they were the products of a classical education which they found both culturally attractive and religiously deficient. The vehemence of their polemic has to be understood in terms both of the effort to maintain a check on their own attraction to classical culture and in the light of their belief that the gods of the ancient world were not mere fictions but were powerful demons encouraging grossly immoral behavior. The battle against paganism, at least in the forms it assumed in the ancient world, is no longer a live issue. Many Christians today are inclined to think in adversarial terms of atheistic communism, secular humanism, and hedonistic materialism and to have less combative attitudes to other religious traditions. Harshly negative attitudes, however, still persist in some parts of fundamentalist Protestantism.

The attitude that is now predominant in Roman Catholicism and in the older Protestant denominations is expressed in the beginning of Vatican II's Declaration of the Relationship of the Church to Non-Christian Religions (*Nostra aetate*):

> The Church is giving deeper study to her relationship with non-Christian religions. In her task of fostering unity and love among men, and even among nations, she gives primary consideration in this document to what human beings have in common and to what promotes fellowship among them.
>
> For all peoples comprise a single community and have a single community and have a single origin, since God made the whole race of men dwell over the entire face of the earth (cf. Acts 17:26). One also is their final goal: God. His providence, His manifestations of goodness and His saving designs extend to all men.[21]

The council then goes on to deal with the major non-Christian religious traditions in positive terms, noting the points of difference in a way which avoids syncretism but also affirming that "the Catholic Church rejects nothing which is true and holy in these religions" and acknowledging that their different rules and teachings "often reflect a ray of that Truth which enlightens all men" (ibid. par. 2). The council also makes quite explicit that it rejects religious discrimination as well as "every theory or practice which leads to a distinction between men or peoples in the matter of human dignity and the rights which flow from it" (ibid. par. 5).

This document, along with the council's even more important affirmation in the declaration on religious liberty, illustrates one decisive resolution of the problem presented by the tendency on the part of the religious collectivity to subordinate religious freedom and the rights of conscience of the individual to its own sense of mission and its vision of religious truth. The liberal resolution of this problem, which affirms both the religious freedom of the individual and the right of the religious collectivity to exist, while depriving it of coercive power, is here accepted by the largest of the Christian churches, a church which had a long history of intimate involvement with political power and of opposition both to liberal tendencies in the modern world and to the affirmation of private judgment in religious matters. This resolution of the problem of religious liberty has effectively cleared the way for Roman Catholicism to become an active proponent of a comprehensive range of human rights.[22] In doing this, it showed a readiness to challenge secular collectivities in their oppression of the individual in ways that echoed the opposition of the prophets to injustice in Israel. This change lies behind the readiness of Catholic hierarchies in such disparate places as Poland, Chile, the Philippines, South Korea, and Haiti to take a strong stand in favor of human rights. This is also a theme which readily draws ecumenical support since the Protestant churches have had significantly less difficulty in accepting human rights norms than has Roman Catholicism.

CHRISTIANITY AND THE HISTORY OF HUMAN RIGHTS

The social transformations accompanying the collapse of the Roman Empire in the West, along with the conversion of Constantine to Christianity and its establishment as the Roman state religion under Theodosius I (379–395), were particularly significant and led Christianity away from functioning as a separate community in a larger society to which individuals adhered by conversion to serving as the party of order in medieval Christendom and its early modern successor societies. Christian theology, at least until the emergence of the radical wing of the Reformation, showed much greater interest in articulating the hierarchical order of cosmos and society than in encouraging individuals to structure society according to the norm of consent. The opportunity to exercise significant political power, which came to the hierarchy of the church throughout Western Europe; the desire to exercise an ideological monopoly in societies in which the clergy provided both many of the royal officials and most of the university professors; and the development of a hierarchical and transnational administrative apparatus with its own legal system combined to produce a situation in which the Roman Church, and especially its leadership, developed patterns of thought and behavior which expressed a profound distrust of human freedom and individual initiative.[23]

At the same time the church was recurrently corrupted by the opportunities for the acquisition of wealth and the abuse of power which its favored position in society opened up to it but which its own normative teaching condemned. Reformist movements which were deeply critical of the privileged position of the church developed in the West from the time of the Waldensians in eleventh-century Italy. The Roman church was fighting for its independence against imperial and royal power in the West and thus for the liberty of the church. At the same time it was willing to use the instruments of coercion to further what it conceived to be its mission and its interests.

Its reformist critics, who ranged from artisans to theologians and cardinals, developed positions that ranged from anarchism to a more stringent and purified version of the status quo. The quite different history of Christianity in the East was not without profound church-state tensions, particularly when the Byzantine emperors attempted to suppress the veneration of icons in the eighth century. But the church never developed the strong tradition of independence that is decisive for the normative thinking of Western church groups that are as different from each other as Calvinists, Catholics, and Anabaptists. The church in much of the East had to bear the burdens of oppressive domination either by the Islamic power of the Ottoman empire or by the developing Russian state. The Eastern Church did not serve as a protagonist in the intellectual developments of medieval scholasticism, the Renaissance, the Reformation, and the Enlightenment; and, particularly in Greece, it retained an abiding memory of the rapacity and violence of the Crusaders.

Not all reformist movements, not even all aspects of the Protestant Reformation, were favorable to the long-term development of human rights. For, in large parts of Europe, the Reformation led to the consolidation of royal absolutism, and to the effective subordination of the religious collective to the political. This development occurred in a less explicit form in Catholic states as well. It was the struggle against monarchical absolutism in Western Europe and its clerical allies that was the setting for the formulation of human rights and for the shaping of societies that would consciously aim at combining respect for personal liberty with the rule of law.

This movement developed after the Catholic and Protestant wings of Western Christianity had inflicted enormous damage on each other during the period of intolerance and religious warfare that extended from 1530 to

1690. This period of profound religious conflict led such thinkers as Grotius and Descartes and Hobbes to turn to classical antiquity, to law, and to philosophy in order to resolve deeper issues of cognitive and moral and political authority. The demands for rights made in connection with the English civil war, the "Glorious Revolution" of 1688, and the great French outburst of 1789 were made in a culture that was becoming more individualistic and more secularized, more open to transformation by entrepreneurs and intellectuals, many of whom, especially in France, were not merely anticlerical but were also antireligious. These elements in society were often perceived as hostile by established church groups, whether Protestant or Catholic. Churches often resisted the affirmation and extension of human rights, whether this was a matter of giving the franchise to Catholics and to Jews in Great Britain or of acknowledging freedom of worship for Protestants in Spain and Italy.

So for much of the period from the Reformation to World War II, we are confronted by the paradoxical prospect of churches that traced their origins back to a community of freely converted persons living in separation from the centers of political power but that had come to rely in various ways on coercion and state support and to acquiesce in various forms of state control. This was a situation found from Moscow to Lisbon and from Madrid to Manila and Quito. The churches, at least where they were in an established and protected position, had developed a profound ambivalence on the topic of human rights. This was a position that put them in tension with the universalistic, egalitarian, and nonviolent elements found in the New Testament. On the other hand, it is not justifiable, either as a matter of theology or of intellectual history, to cite some of these elements in the New Testament as an endorsement for a contemporary political philosophy. For the social contexts envisioned by the authors of the New Testament and by contemporary human rights activists and political philosophers are very different, and the systematic implications of similar expressions in these different contexts are bound to be different. In addition, the body of ethical norms within the New Testament and in the traditions of the Christian community is too diversified and contains too many potential contradictions which are in need of theological and practical resolution to admit of one universal interpretation and application to contemporary society. Furthermore, the history of the church and of its efforts to understand the life and teaching of Jesus, which is its central theme, is itself a part of the history of salvation, a part of God's action in the world. It is also a part of the history of human sinfulness and of the rejection of God's grace. It can be interpreted as progressive steps to an ultimate fullness or as illustrative failures to be faithful to the original revelation. But Christianity, like Judaism, is a religion of history, of memory and tradition, of promise and hope.

In its history, Christianity has both obstructed and contributed to the realization of human rights. A significant aspect of human rights theories and movements has been their rooting in such Christian values as universal love, the equality of all persons before God, the freedom of the person in the face of secular authority, the eternal worth of the individual person, the sense of a realm of values which ought to guide action and which are not to be subordinated to the political collectivity. But a significant aspect of human rights theories and movements has been their criticism of Christian churches and institutions in so far as they collaborated in and benefited from the repression of human rights. For these and other reasons it is seriously mistaken to accept Rorty's reduction of human rights to a surviving element in the Judeo-Christian tradition.

The major Christian churches have come to terms with a future in which they will provide one of several voices on questions of ultimate value and meaning, and not necessarily the loudest or the most persuasive voice. An essential part of this coming to terms has been the acceptance and endorsement of human rights norms which are to govern a pluralistic society and a pluralistic world. The articulation and grounding of these norms is a task for human reason working in a social context with legal structures and an intention of building civil peace. Doing this is an exercise of human dignity trying to protect itself from human sinfulness, greed, and violence. It serves as a check on the claims and practices of Christian churches and movements at the same time that it needs the support and blessing of the God of universal love that Christianity proclaims.

For Christianity offers an understanding of human individual and social collectivity that, when refined and clarified by the experience of history, is compatible with human rights and with the social solidarity that is often lost sight of in contemporary individualism. It also offers an understanding of human and cosmic destiny that links us all together despite our differences and affirms that our actions and sufferings matter before the One who is and is love.

Notes

1. Richard Rorty, "Post-Modernist Bourgeois Liberalism," in *Objectivity, Relativism, and Truth: Philosophy Papers,* I (Cambridge: Cambridge University Press, 1991), pp. 197–202. Subsequent quotations are from this source.

2. The classic treatment of this issue is the massive study of Ernst Troeltsch, *The Social Teachings of the Christian Churches,* 2 vols., translated by Olive Wyon (New York: Macmillan, 1931).

3. The Scripture translations in the following text are taken from *The Oxford Annotated Bible with the Apocrypha*, ed. Herbert Hay and Bruce Metzger (New York: Oxford University Press, 1965).

4. Here the studies by Rudolf Bultmann, *History and Eschatology* (New York: Harper, 1962), and Oscar Cullman, *Christ and Time: The Primitive Christian Conception of Time and History* (Philadelphia: Westminster, 1964 rev. ed.) are very useful.

5. See, for instance, the discussion of "eternal life," in C. H. Dodd, *The Interpretation of the Fourth Gospel* (Cambridge: Cambridge University Press, 1960), pp. 144–50.

6. This corresponds to the final and preferred type, namely, Christ the transformer of culture, in the very influential work of H. Richard Niebuhr, *Christ and Culture* (New York: Harper, 1951).

7. This text was used for many centuries as the entrance antiphon or introit in the Common Mass of Popes in the Latin rite.

8. Kenneth Minogue, "The History of the Idea of Human Rights," in *The Human Rights Reader*, ed. Walter Laqueur and Barry Rubin (New York: New American Library, 1979; rev. ed. 1989), p. 4.

9. See, for example, such works of Raymond Brown as *Priest and Bishop* (New York: Paulist, 1970) and *The Church the Apostles Left Behind* (New York: Paulist, 1984).

10. A recent overview of this subject, which has been particularly controversial in the last two decades, can be found in *Jesus and the Politics of His Day*, ed. Ernest Bammel and C. F. D. Moule (Cambridge: Cambridge University Press, 1984).

11. A famous exposition of this view is the essay, "Passive Obedience," by George Berkeley, who was Bishop of Cloyne in the (Anglican) Church of Ireland as well as a very able philosopher. See his *Works*, ed. George Sampson (London: George Bell, 1897), vol. 1. pp. 253–90.

12. John Howard Yoder, *The Politics of Jesus* (Grand Rapids: William B. Eerdmans, 1972), ch. 9, "Revolutionary Subordination," makes this point clearly.

13. See Luther's famous treatise, "The Freedom of a Christian" (1520), in *Martin Luther: Selections from His Writings*, ed. John Dillenberger (Garden City: Doubleday Anchor, 1961), pp. 42–85.

14. This is a major theme in Vatican Council II, particularly in its pastoral constitution on the Church in the Modern World, which is usually referred to by the opening words of its Latin text, *Gaudium et spes*.

15. See Reginald Fuller, *The Foundations of New Testament Christology* (New York: Scribner's, 1965), pp. 203–42.

16. St. Thomas Aquinas, *Summa Theologiae* II-II, 11, 3. For the development of Augustine's views on religious coercion, see Peter Brown, *Saint Augustine* (Berkeley and Los Angeles: University of California Press, 1967), pp. 233–43.

17. St. Augustine, *De Civitate Dei*, V, 19.

18. See *Enchiridion Symbolorum*, ed. Henricus Denzinger. S.J. and Adolfus Schonmetzer. S.J.. 33d ed. (Freiburg: Herder, 1965), nos. 3866–3873.

19. As, for instance, John Calvin, *Institutes of the Christian Religion*, Book III, chs. 21–23.

20. Jonathan Spence, *The Memory Palace of Matteo Ricci* (New York: Viking Penguin, 1984).

21. Vatican II. Declaration on the Relationship of the Church to Non-Christian Religions (*Nostra aetate*). Par. 1.

22. Acceptance of the fullest range of human rights, including religious freedom, is first manifest in the encyclical of John XXIII, *Pacem in terris* (1963). Affirmations that the protection of human rights is a fundamental task for all societies abound in the writings of John Paul II and have been made by him in the face of figures as different as Wojciech Jaruzelski (1987) and Augusto Pinochet. In his encyclical *Sollicitudo rei socialis* (1987), he uses the protection of human rights as the criterion for authentic development (par. 37).

23. This tendency was given magesterial and imaginative expression in two classic documents: The Syllabus of Errors, issued by Pius IX in 1864, and in Fyodor Dostoyevsky, *The Brothers Karamazov*, part 2, book 5, chapter 5, "The Grand Inquisitor."

6

THE INDIVIDUAL IN ISLAMIC SOCIETY

RICHARD W. BULLIET

Ever since the Iranian Revolution was discovered by a nonplussed and apprehensive world to be firmly in the hands of Shi'ite clerics and laymen intent
upon creating an Islamic republic, contemporary Islamic belief and practice
have been subjected to intense scrutiny. While scholars have concentrated
upon organizational and ideological developments of the last few decades,
general commentators have called public attention to issues of individual
behavior ranging from courtroom procedure and corporal punishments to
women's clothing regulations and bans on different forms of entertainment.

The upshot of this scrutiny has been to create an image of Islam as a faith
that is intolerant of individual deviation from social norms. This unattractive
reputation has hurt and offended many Muslims around the world who do
not see their religion in this light and who feel they have been misunderstood
and maligned. Yet specific instances of seemingly intolerant behavior in the
name of Islam have received great publicity, as witness the affair of Salman
Rushdie. My purpose in this essay will be to offer an explication of the role and
status of the individual in Islam that will make it easier to understand the complexities that lead to these contradictory appreciations of Muslim behavior.

No religiously denominated societies in the world are so consistently
approached through reference to a presumed normative uniformity as those
described as Muslim. Whatever the reality of social relations among Muslims
today or in the past, observers repeatedly invoke an ideal social order which

they characterize as being either intrinsic to Islam, or so important as a historical model as to have forever stamped societies of Muslims as first and foremost Islamic. Whatever the social issue—permissibility of birth control, legitimacy of slavery, appropriate punishment for crime, proper behavior of women—the search for an answer normally follows a set pattern: analysis of the status of the issue in Islamic law, followed by an investigation of the practice of the earliest Muslim community in seventh-century Arabia, followed by a notation of any accommodations to modernity made in the nineteenth and twentieth centuries. Finally, any loose ends are accounted for by granting that actual social behavior obviously differs in detail according to time and place.

Each of these four areas of inquiry is discrete from the others; but the hierarchy of significance among them is as important as any of them is individually. Islamic law is always privileged above the others, and social praxis is always attended to last, as if it were relatively unimportant how Muslims actually live their lives in comparison with how they should live them. From a legist's point of view, of course, social praxis contrary to the law can simply be defined as deviant or un-Islamic and consequently be dismissed as unimportant to any consideration of what Islam *is*. But other religions have laws claiming roots in the divine, too, yet none has succeeded so well as Islam in persuading scholarly believers and unbelievers alike that the law must be considered before all else.

Primers explaining Islam to non-Muslims typically set forth certain home truths about the individual and society deriving from the Qur'ān and embodied in the *sharī'a*, the religious law.[1] They explain that every individual is responsible for his or her actions in this life and will face a final accounting in the hereafter. Every individual faces God personally in prayer without priestly intermediation. Becoming a Muslim is not a mystery or a sacrament, but personal witness by voice and in the heart that there is no God but God, and Muḥammad is the Messenger of God. In making this testimony (*shahāda*), the believer performs an act of submission (*islām*) to God's will. He or she also undertakes, as part of that submission, to pray five times daily; to contribute an annual alms tax for community prescribed charitable purposes; to refrain, if physically able, from food, drink, and sex during the daylight hours of the month of Ramadan; and to perform the pilgrimage to Mecca at least once during his or her lifetime.

The believer also becomes by the act of submission a member of the community of all believers, the *umma*. As a member of the *umma*, the believer shares in certain additional obligations to varying degrees, such as fighting "on the path of God" to defend the faith or expand its territory and, more generally, "commanding the good and reproving the forbidden." While duties of this sort do not overrule the personal obligations mentioned above or subor dinate the individual to the society of believers, they have served to legitimize, at various times, a wide array of group activities that have intruded upon the lives of individual believers: migration from lands governed by unbelievers, breaking of wine jars and musical instruments as implements of unbelief, concern with the moral probity of neighbors, control of prices and standards in the marketplace, etc.

This balance between the individual and society is usually portrayed as emphasizing the dignity and status of the individual insofar as the primary manifestations of faith consist of unmediated individual acts devoid of mystery, sacrament, or priestly mediation while at the same time emphasizing community membership and establishing community rights vis-à-vis the individual. Each major point is well buttressed by Qur'ānic verse and, in most cases, the personal example of the Prophet, but the elaboration of each point is spelled out in detail in the *sharī'a*, which evolved over a period of many generations.

In writing the sort of primer that portrays Islam and Muslims in this way, authors have traditionally relied very heavily upon the elaborations contained in the *sharī'a* on the plausible assumption that the religious law represents normative Islamic behavior and that norms are more important to understand than the vagaries of personal or localized practice. The law, it is frequently explained, deals with the entirety of a Muslim's existence in this world and the hereafter. It recognizes no separate domain for Caesar, but rather shelters all political, commercial, criminal, ritual, and social concerns under its holy umbrella.

Given this ubiquitous and quite inflexible understanding of what Islam is and, supposedly, always has been, the tendency to revert first to the *sharī'a* in seeking to understand actual Muslim behaviors is understandable. But this construction of Islam, while true to an important body of literature, can also be seen as the product of an unspoken collaboration between the legists who, over the centuries, developed and maintained the *sharī'a*, and those non-Muslim scholars who have accepted their interpretation as canonical. The fact is that despite the apparent normative force of the law, the vast preponderance of the world's Muslims have always been, at least to some degree, out of step with the letter of the *sharī'a*, when they have not, indeed, marched to the beat of a different drummer altogether.

Therefore the law's claim to primacy or exclusivity as the vehicle for understanding Islam is one that historians and social scientists should view with some skepticism. How did it arise? When and how did the law achieve hegemony in the area of personal behavior? Some answer to these questions is essential to any attempt to appraise the actual position of the individual in Islamic society.

The surviving stories dealing with the earliest period of Islam in seventh-century Arabia do not permit definitive conclusions to be drawn respecting social praxis at that time. The stories are mostly anecdotal and often of questionable reliability. Common sense points to certain strong likelihoods, however. Within two years of the Prophet Muḥammad's death in 632, the fledgling caliphate established by his successor Abū Bakr at Medina in western Arabia had achieved dominance over most of the Arab tribes spread over the million square miles of the Arabian peninsula. During the succeeding few decades, hundreds of thousands of these tribespeople migrated from their homelands in Arabia into the regions they helped to conquer: Iraq, Egypt, Syria, Iran, and North Africa. A few of them joined the conquering armies after a sojourn in Mecca or Medina where they might have gained firsthand acquaintance with the social milieu of the Prophet's own community, but surely most did not.

Were these Arabs, then, practitioners of a social code governed by Islam? This hardly seems likely. The ecstatic utterances of Muḥammad were not definitively collected in the Qur'ān until a decade after his death, and chapters of the Qur'ān were transmitted almost exclusively by word of mouth since literacy was a rare accomplishment. Moreover, most of the Qur'ān, including those portions included in prayers, was of nonlegalistic import; and there were probably few Qur'ān reciters who knew the complete text, not to mention few listeners who attended their recitation long enough to hear it in its entirety. In the absence, then, of other written sources of an authoritatively Islamic character, the Arabs of the tribes must have depended for guidance on Islamic personal behavior upon whatever fragments of the Qur'ān they happened to hear, and possibly memorize, and upon the example of whichever companions of the Prophet they happened to encounter or hear of. If the portions of the Qur'ān they knew did not deal with personal behavior or law, and if they did not have personal exemplars of pious Muslim behavior to pattern their actions on, they most likely continued to follow the customs of their own tribes.

It can be argued, therefore, that what the Arabs brought to the vast territory they conquered was for the most part a tradition of Arabian tribal social praxis. Occasional nodes of self-consciously Islamic behavior would have existed whenever and wherever the companions of the Prophet, who knew of his example at first hand, happened to live and hold forth, and these nodes were important seeds for the later growth of a Muslim pattern of behavior; but it seems practically impossible for there to have existed a single, caliphate-wide, Islamically based social praxis at the outset of Muslim imperial rule. Moreover, since Muslim tradition and Western historians agree that Islam had neither ecclesiastical structure, nor organized missionary effort, nor system of coordinating decisions on social issues over the vast expanse of the caliphate, it seems almost certain that different regional groups of early Muslims gradually came to engage in a wide variety of activities that they considered proper for them as Muslims.

The *sharīʿa* emerged during the following three centuries and eventually came to be accepted, with certain mutually tolerable variations according to different approaches to deriving positive law from the Qurʾān and the example of the Prophet and his companions, as the universal normative standard for judging the behavior of Muslims. Earlier local or regional differences either disappeared or became subsumed within the body of minor variations tolerated by the *sharīʿa*. While this development of the law is unquestionably important for understanding the normative religious background of contemporary Muslim societies, the position of the individual is better understood by looking at some of the concomitants of this legal development.

The absence of an Islamic ecclesiastical structure or hierarchical system for propagating and enforcing authoritative determinations of ordodoxy is of crucial importance. From the earliest times Muslims looked not to religious officials or canonized regulations for guidance in matters of religion, but to unofficial persons of manifest piety. And piety could be manifested in many ways: ascetic behavior such as night vigils and supererogatory fasting, cultivation of a modest and God-fearing style of life, descent from the Prophet Muḥammad or his closest companions, capacity to achieve mystic transports complete with poetic utterances and apparent miracles, command of sacred lore in the form of the oral traditions relating to the Prophet's sayings and actions, and so forth.

The original Arab tribespeople of the conquest period may have had few queries to bring to the manifestly pious individuals in their tribe or territory because the social code of tribal society satisfied most of their needs for guidance. Once settled in urban environments, however, their tribal social structures tended to dissolve, and they sought more guidance. By the beginning of the ninth century, however, the increasingly detribalized Arabs became a minority in a Muslim community that was more and more populated by converts from Judaism, Christianity, Zoroastrianism, and other smaller faiths. And since the higher religions of that era had become almost the sole source of law, education, moral leadership, and community regulation for their communicants, the converts came to the Muslim faith with myriad questions about personal behavior. They, even more than the Arabs, exerted the pressure that caused Islam to develop its legal, educational, and social institutions.

In every community pious people tried to respond to the needs of their coreligionaries, particularly of the new converts who needed guidance the most, and in return the community vested their unelected, unanointed, unofficial religious elites with power and authority. While some types of piety became less important, others flourished. Religious learning, particularly in the field of law and of the traditions of the Prophet, proved the most important; and by the eleventh century the ulama, or people of religious knowledge, had achieved a position of social, moral, and religious leadership that they continue to have to the present day. But the mystics, the Sufis with their claim of direct experience of the God, also prospered. By the fourteenth century organized Sufi brotherhoods were as important to the life of most local Muslim communities as were the ulama who interpreted and sacred law.

The population of a sizable Muslim city of the sixteenth or seventeenth century might well be divided into two to four groups according to people's school of legal interpretation, into a half dozen or more Sufi brotherhoods, and possibly into sects if some people recognized the authority of one or another of the Shi'ite imams, who might be either living individuals or occluded presences that might imminently return to human society and reclaim their position of spiritual leadership.[2] For an imperial government, or even a local government, to attempt to enforce one or another of these socioreligious identities upon everyone was comparatively rare; and the tolerance of diversity that had grown up within Islam after the twelfth century made serious discord between even radically opposed versions of Islam comparatively uncommon.

This social evolution from the small band of devotees around Muḥammad in the seventh century to a world religion equally marked by dedication to a fairly homogeneous religious law and by remarkable tolerance of diversity in religious behavior is fairly well understood. But one characteristic built into most of the patterns of Islam that early modern Muslim societies inherited is not often enough stressed: in the absence of generalized authoritative institutions, Islam makes it easy and honorable for individual Muslims to choose their own source or sources of spiritual authority. The hallmark of individualism in Muslim society is more often than not the free decision of a Muslim to follow a spiritual leader of his or her choice—or no one at all.

It should be noted that this description of toleration within Islam diverges somewhat from the portrayal often given to the religion in introductory books. The same texts that emphasize the attainment of legalistic homogeneity in Islam focus their attention historically upon the first three centuries during which mutual toleration was rare and doctrinal disputes frequently led to violence. Shi'ism, which began largely as a political movement backing the rights of the family of Muhammad's son-in-law 'Alī to the caliphate, evolved distinctive religious attitudes within a generation and provided the seed for numerous revolts in the seventh to tenth centuries aimed at gaining political power for some member of the family then recognized by the Shi'ites as the imam, the divinely ordained leader of the *umma*. Kharijism, originally an offshoot of Shi'ism but subsequently unconnected with the family of 'Alī, similarly fueled revolts in the seventh to ninth centuries. Within the mainstream of Islam that subsequently came to be called Sunni, the ninth century saw a strenuous persecution launched by the caliphate to enforce universal belief in the Muʿtazili theological interpretation of Islam,[3] and in the following century a leading Sufi mystic, al-Ḥallāj, was executed for the heresy some saw in his ecstatic utterances. Even the Sunni law schools, which later were models of mutual toleration, fought fierce doctrinal and political battles in the tenth to twelfth centuries.

In short, Islam achieved its extraordinary level of toleration after the twelfth century, but along with tolerance came a diminution of doctrinal innovation and polemic. Consequently, historians of the Islam's evolution usually emphasize the struggles of the first few centuries and glide past the much longer later period during which mutual toleration was the prevalent mode of interaction within the *umma*. For present purposes, however, it is precisely the later period that provides the background for our consideration of the individual and society in Islam today.

Many religions, of course, have sects or denominations or pious brotherhoods, but none has the multiplicity, simultaneity, and mutual toleration of such entities that Islam characteristically has had in its later centuries. Not only have Sufi brotherhoods numbered in the hundreds over the last few centuries, but many people have belonged to more than one, and many new ones have come into being because the followers of a particularly saintly figure simply desired to bind themselves to his name and pious practice. But people have also bound themselves to the spiritual leadership of legal authorities, most notably within the mainstream of Shiʿism where, in the absence of an "occluded" imam, the most honored of the ulama have been increasingly looked to for guidance. Yet at no point has it been *necessary* for most Muslims to make this sort of commitment to an individual spiritual guide. As mentioned earlier, Islam requires little of the individual believer beyond prayer, the giving of alms, abstention from pork and alcohol, and observation of Muslim conventions in such matters of personal status as marriage and inheritance. Millions of Muslims have lived their lives in observation of only these things, and millions more have done even less. Indeed, one of the tendentious explanations some Christians have given for the incredible spread of Islam in various parts of the world is that it is such a simple religion with so few credal demands that people who are poor in spirit—or eager to marry more than one wife—find it an easier faith than Christianity. Following this canard, however, would lead one into the paradoxical observation that the apparently easy religion of Islam has generated far more zealous devotion to a greater number of spiritual leaders espousing a greater variety of doctrines over the past two centuries than any other faith. From Africa, to the Middle East, to India, to

China, to the Philippines, Islam has repeatedly served as a magnet for social and political movements, usually based on very specific doctrines propounded by particular Sufis, ulama, or, nowadays, lay activists.

Clearly, such partisan attacks miss the point by focusing exclusively on credal matters as if they should be as important in Islam as they historically were in the development of Christianity. Once the unity of God is affirmed and Muḥammad is accepted as His messenger bringing His word, the Qur'ān, to mankind, credal matters are more or less taken care of. To be sure, some specific variants of Islamic belief go far beyond this minimum, particularly in Shi'ism where a supernatural role for the Prophet's cousin 'Alī and some of his descendants is often an article of belief. But for all Muslims noncredal matters make their faith potentially as demanding as any other religion.

An investigation of three areas of noncredal religious practice will go far toward clarifying the issue of the role and status of individuals in Muslim societies. Those areas are law, authority, and custom.

We have already noted the primacy of law in most accounts of Muslim practice, but we have also suggested that the law arose as a historical artifact along with a class of unofficial and nonsacramental religious specialists whose legitimacy in social matters depended heavily upon popular acceptance of the preeminence of law. These religious specialists controlled the content, and often the structure, of Islamic education and through this control defined the religious law and repeatedly declared its universality. Since governments were, according to this legal theory, bound by the law, they depended upon the religious specialists for a measure of their legitimacy. In the absence of government controlled social institutions, which was normal prior to the nineteenth century, the government also depended upon the religious specialists to service many of the social welfare needs of the population and keep it content.

The religious specialists, on the other hand, depended upon the government to maintain order, since they rightly feared anarchy, and to validate the religious law through at least partial enforcement. In the colonial era many legists, such as Sir Sayyid Ahmad Khan in India and Muḥammad 'Abduh in Egypt, even came to accept non-Muslim rule as legitimate as long as the *sharī'a* was to some degree preserved in force by the government. The primacy of law in Islam, therefore, evolved in the later centuries in large measure as the product of the interdependency of governments seeking legitimacy and passive public acceptance and nongovernmental religious specialists seeking the same things in their own social arena. Governance over large territories lay with the rulers; popular allegiance and social leadership lay locally with the ulama.

Yet for a vast number of Muslims the law meant very little, and the myth of its inherent primacy in the Islamic faith has served to distort their reality.

Until the twentieth century only a modest percentage of Muslims lived in cities, where the ulama dominated moral and social life, and an even smaller percentage were sufficiently educated to understand legal issues. As in Western society, most people had few contacts with courts of law. While the law theoretically governed their ritual practices, most Muslims were taught whatever they practiced by family members without legal contextualization.

As a result, it is simply misleading to seek the actuality of Muslim social praxis in books of law. And it is equally misleading to declare that Muslims who fail to observe legal norms are by definition "bad" Muslims or members of marginal groups. Over the centuries, particular jurists deeming some particular social behavior to be lax have time and again led attacks against that behavior, but the fervor of reform inevitably dies down after a while.

If we define a Muslim as any person who believes there to be but one God, of whose word Muhammad was the bearer, and who recognizes that there are some behaviors that people holding such a belief should subscribe to, whether or not he or she personally engages in those behaviors, then we must accept the fact that most Muslims do not regulate their lives in accordance with Islamic law and did not do so in past centuries. The actual social praxis of Muslims, so defined, has always been enormously varied. It varies from region to region, from city to village, from village to tribe, and, most importantly, from individual to individual. Today, as in the past, individual Muslims have a tremendous amount of leeway, and exercise great personal responsibility, in deciding how to act religiously, despite the myth of the all-encompassing law. By and large, Muslims have never been "excommunicated" for being "bad" according to *shari'a* standards. Excommunication, in fact, is very nearly a meaningless concept in Islam.

The priority of Islamic law in the examination of matters pertaining to individual Muslim behavior should therefore be seen as the outcome of a particular social-religious-political evolution that left so powerful an imprint upon urban literary culture that the notion that the law was, in fact, the inevitable touchstone of Muslim behavior still comes easily to the mind of anyone educated to that culture, whether a Muslim student in a *madrasa*, or religious college, or a Western orientalist. This accounts for the widespread clichés that *normal* Muslims, that is, Muslims acting in accordance with their holy law *as their religion demands*, cut off the hands of thieves, marry four wives, practice seclusion of women, kill apostates, and see the world as permanently divided into an Abode of Islam and an Abode of War which must permanently remain in conflict until everyone in the world accepts Islam. Manifestly these have not been the practices of most Muslims over the past fourteen centuries. Muslim rulers have not systematically mutilated thieves; most Muslim men have had only one wife; the practice of secluding women has been followed only in certain areas and among certain classes; and apostasy has rarely been punished by death. In short, these legal strictures, despite their normative appearance, have not actually functioned as norms. They are ideas that have gained ascendancy, though in some times and places, such as contemporary Saudi Arabia, indeed been put into practice, as well, because of the achievement of literary cultural hegemony by religious legal specialists.

Turning to the second level of analysis usually adopted in seeking to explain Muslim views, the example of the Prophet and his companions, we encounter a more complex phenomenon than is immediately apparent. The issue of the particular religious authority of the practices, or *sunna*, of these revered individuals leads unavoidably to the question of the religious authority of the practices of other revered Muslims who lived at later periods, including our own.

Throughout history individual Muslims, and groups of Muslims, have displayed an unusual propensity to fix upon a pious individual as their moral leader and behavioral model. This phenomenon is quite distinct from the reverence and obedience adherents to other faiths give to their clerical leaders—rabbis, priests, bishops, etc. In the absence of an ecclesiastical structure, a sacramental vesting of individuals with religious leadership, or a concept of religious hierarchy, Muslims have not only been unusually free to dispose of their own moral allegiance, but also unusually prone to do so. The result, in the legal sphere, has been to embed within the *sharīʿa* the moral example of the Prophet and his companions. But equally important results have been the proliferation of Sufi brotherhoods in which obedience, even to the point of antinomian defiance, is owed to the leader of the brotherhood, and a multitude of millenarian movements utilizing the charisma assumed to inhere in the person of someone claiming to the *mahdi*, the person whom Sunnīs and Shiʿis alike believe will appear at the end of time, suppress evil and sinful ways, and preside over a millennium of peace and perfect justice until the world actually ends. In recent times a newer phenomenon reflecting the same proclivity has been the growth of myriad activist movements, ranging from the fanatically revolutionary to the piously meliorative, based upon the leadership of lay individuals with few, if any, formal qualifications for their role.

From the point of view of the role of the individual in Islam, the freedom and proclivity to dispose of one's moral allegiance, generally without censure or penalty, is probably more important than the specific content of the doctrines and behaviors ordained by the chosen leader. On the one hand, this quality has contributed to Islam's enormous variety and has facilitated its spread into every type of social milieu; on the other, it is one of the principal reasons that it is so difficult to define Islam in a manner that actually includes most people who regard themselves as Muslims. Despite its importance, however, this tendency evolved for specific historical reasons and is not intrinsic to the faith.

We discussed earlier the steps by which the unofficial but enormously influential class of religious specialists known as the ulama came into being. Muslims often point with pride to the capacity of their faith to grow, adapt, and serve the needs of the faithful without reliance upon an ecclesiastical structure. This understandable pride conceals, however, a genuine question as to why no such structure emerged. Was it because Islam became the religion of rulers almost from the start, and therefore Muslims never needed to organize to resist persecution? Was it because the early identity between Muslim and Arab made an ecclesiastical structure otiose since most Muslims led their lives within the traditional framework of tribal custom? Or was it because Muḥammad himself took no steps to designate groups of followers as the performers of specific duties associated with the religion?

In all likelihood, historians will never resolve this question. But it is important to ask it because it highlights the fact that most people who converted to Islam in the early centuries were thoroughly accustomed to some such structure of authority and moral guidance and looked for its analogue within their new faith. The ulama eventually filled this role, using the *sharīʿa*, through increasingly fixed modes of interpretation, as their dogmatic authority. But by the time this happened, Muslims had grown accustomed to having a choice of authorities. While many followed the ulama in their adherence to the law, many others did not. Yet those who did not follow the ulama often did follow someone else.

Most early Islamic sects were structured through personal loyalty to a leader rather than to a doctrine. Indeed, they are almost always named for their leaders. Sects split frequently when leaders died and their followers disagreed on whom to follow next. Followers of each pretender to leadership developed doctrines to justify their allegiance, but doctrine tended to follow loyalty rather than govern it. Rarely was there any compulsion in these sectarian developments. One distinctive Shiʿite sect, the Fāṭimid Ismāʿīlīs, ruled Egypt successfully for two centuries from 969 to 1171 and sponsored active proselytization, but it never succeeded in implanting its doctrines among the Egyptian population. The idea of forcing Muslims to adopt the beliefs of the rulers never arose. Force was later used in Iran after 1500 to implant Shiʿism there, but that is the exception that proves the rule.

Against this background we can more easily approach the question of how a person should live as an individual Muslim. We have already discussed the law as an answer to this question, but the law is not always adequate and many, if not most, Muslims have deviated from or been ignorant of the law in leading their lives. The *sunna* or behavioral example of the Prophet and his companions provides another answer, and, indeed, the answer that is most acceptable in the eyes of the law. Though law schools may differ on which early behaviors are to be seen as binding, they concur in the importance they assign to the example of the earliest community. It is worth noting that the largest and most extensive Muslim organization in the world at the present time, the Tablighi Jam'at, which originated earlier in this century as a movement for moral improvement in a single district in India, requires that its adherents govern many of their daily actions according to a manual based on the *sunna* of the early community.

For Shi'ites, however, the behavior of the imams, the descendants of Muḥammad through his cousin 'Alī and daughter Fāṭima, takes on this special quality of authoritative example even though different Shi'ite groups have recognized different imams from time to time. For the primary branch of Shi'ism, which today holds sway in Iran and has millions of supporters in Lebanon, Iraq, Pakistan, and India, the last authoritative imam became occluded from human society toward the end of the ninth century. Consequently, individual Shi'ites and their religious specialists, nowadays commonly termed *mullas*, had wide latitude to debate how Shi'ites should act in the absence, presumed temporary, of the Hidden Imam. Many avenues were explored, but increasingly in the nineteenth century the dominant answer came to be that the faithful were to regard the most highly educated and esteemed mullas of their own times as authoritative, though they might individually choose which of these recognized figures to follow. For this reason important Shi'ite mullas in modern times, such as Ayatollah Khomeini, have written minutely detailed manuals of behavior.

Sufi leaders have similarly instructed their followers. One early manual by the twelfth-century Sufi Abū Najīb Suhrawardī, the eponymous founder of an important early order, illustrates the tendency of Muslims to dispose of their allegiance on an individual basis particularly well. His manual sets down detailed rules for people who wish to follow the Sufi way.[4] For example:

109. When the Sufi enters a town, he should visit the Sufi *shaykh*, if there is one. If not, he should go to the meeting place of the Sufis. If there are several such places, he should go first to the most important of them. . . .

110. When he enters a convent [Sufi meeting place], he should turn aside and take off his shoes beginning with the left in taking off and with the right in putting on. Then he should turn to the washing place [to perform the ritual washing] and then perform a prayer of two *raq'as* [prostrations]. . . .

111. The guest should be served whatever food is available without formality. Nice manners with guests are: to begin with greeting, then to express respect, then to give food, and after that, conversation. In conversation the Sufi should not ask

about worldly affairs but about the *shaykhs* and the companions and brethren.

(pp. 53–54)

After listing these and many other rules, Suhrawardī closes with a chapter on dispensations or exceptions designed for people who do not have the dedication or ability to lead a full Sufi life but nevertheless want to behave somewhat like the Sufis. "Whoever adopts the dispensations is one of the beginners, and he should strive to enhance his inner state. . . . Whoever falls below the level of the 'dispensations' thereby renounces Sufism and is forbidden to enjoy the gifts and endowments which are made for the Sufis" (p. 82). Typical of these rules are the following:

> 175. There is a dispensation allowing one to joke. The rule in this matter is to avoid slandering, imitation, and nonsense. 'Alī said: "When the Prophet saw one of his friends distressed, he would cheer him up by joking." It is improper, especially for persons of high rank, to do much jesting. It is said: "Do not jest with a noble man lest he bear malice against you, and do not jest with a base person lest he behave impudently toward you."
>
> 179. There is a dispensation allowing one to love leadership. The ethics of this matter are that one should know one's own capability and should not have aspirations beyond it. Anonymity is better for the ignorant than fame. . . .
>
> 181. There is a dispensation allowing one to revile insolent persons by disparaging their ancestors. The rule is that one may resort to this dispensation only in retort to ill-behavior, and it should be done by indirect expressions and not by explicit ones. (pp. 75–76)

Suhrawardī's strictures, of course, were not the same as those laid down by other Sufi leaders. Today members of one of the Sufi brotherhoods that play such an important role in the life of Muslims in West Africa may be held to very different behaviors from those required of the devotees of different brotherhoods in Turkey or India. But in every case the rules go beyond, or better, alongside, the legal stipulations of the *sharī'a*. What Suhrawardī makes very clear, however, through his dispensations is that even people who are not truly members of a Sufi brotherhood may choose to pattern their lives somewhat in accordance with the Sufi way.

Turning now to the third conventional step in analyzing Muslim behavior, namely, any efforts made in modern times to accommodate Muslim practice to contemporary conditions, certain topics have been discussed again and again. In the nineteenth century, slavery and polygamy were paramount issues. Today, unequal access to divorce and the use of corporal punishment loom large. The underlying issue remains the same, however. If Muslims are viewed as people who govern their behavior according to Islamic law, and the law preserves strictures or calls upon the faithful to emulate behaviors that were appropriate to the seventh century but are generally regarded by non-Muslims as inappropriate, inequitable, or inhumane today, then what is the process by which the law can be adapted or amended to bring it into accord with modern sensibility?

The legal answers to this question have been outlined by a number of scholars.[5] They range from drafting new law codes to supersede all or part of the *sharī'a*, to reinterpreting questionable parts of the *sharī'a*, to recombining doctrines from several different law schools to make the law more palatable, to rejecting the need for modernization altogether. What underlies all of these approaches, however, is the idea that the law is paramount. Yet, in fact, even if legal changes are made, Muslims may choose to act differently. Despite the powerful influence of the Western notion of the dominance of law, and the forceful repudiation of alternative sources of binding authority—mainly that of the Sufis—made by the ulama in the nineteenth century, many Muslims persist in choosing their own authoritative code.

The contemporary Islamic world is strewn with Muslim activist groups from Morocco to Indonesia, and from Nigeria to West Germany, not to mention those in the United States. Some groups continue old Sufi practices, but many others are newly created. Some, like the Tablighi Jam'at, mandate strict compliance in social behavior but are politically quietist.[6] Others, like at-Takfīr wa'l-Hijra in Egypt, reject the Egyptian state and its laws as non-Islamic and endorse violence as a means for bringing society back into conformity with Islam, as they understand it.[7] Altogether, membership in these groups represents only a minority in the world Muslim population, but even among the millions of Muslims who formally adhere to no group at all there is often a tendency to respect what at least some of them stand for, and to modify one's behavior at least somewhat in accordance with the sensibility they reflect. Take the example of a Muslim student from a country in which certain Muslim activist groups require that their male adherents grow beards and government authorities consequently view beard-wearing as subversive. Once he has arrived in the United States, such a student not infrequently chooses to grow a beard. Doing this does not necessarily signify adherence to an activist movement, but it is an indicator of the degree to which such movements provide attractive behavioral models, just as the Sufis did in the days of Suhrawardī.

The modernization or supplanting of Islamic law, therefore, is important to the realm of law, and clearly, in specific instances, affects the status of the individual Muslim before the law. But just as it would be mistaken to conceive of the role of the individual in Muslim society solely or predominantly in legal terms, it would be equally mistaken to overstress the importance of legal modernization. The course of Westernization, or Western cultural imperialism, may ultimately make the law, however transformed from its original religious form, truly predominant in Muslim society, just as the ulama have always maintained it should be. However, at present Muslims around the world seem to be reinvigorating the countertradition of choosing their own models of authority from leaders who do not necessarily adhere to legalistic approaches.

The final line of interpretation of Muslim behavior mentioned at the outset is a fallback position conveniently termed local custom. Once the scholarly analysts of a specific problem have cited the *sharī'a*, brought forward the most plausible traditions relating to the Prophet's personal example, and taken note of any legal accommodations to modern tastes and standards over the last century or so, they are more often than not left with the problem that some or all of the Muslims they are studying act differently. If these analysts are uncharitable, they might say that the people involved are bad or ignorant Muslims. More commonly, such deviations from the putative legal and/or Prophetic norm are described as local custom, or folk Islam, or products of a "little tradition," as opposed to the "great tradition" of literate, legalistic Islam.

This unfortunate practice has the effect of diminishing the religious status of the actual behavior of millions of Muslims. It amounts to a kind of religious disenfranchisement. To argue that whatever specific groups of Muslims or Muslim individuals say is Islam is, therefore, for them, Islam may be pointlessly tautological. But it is a better thing to do than arbitrarily to adopt one version, or one set of versions, of Islamic belief and practice as authoritative and to devalue all others when there is nothing in the history or intrinsic character of the faith to justify that adoption.

The individual in Muslim society, throughout history, although inevitably socialized into some specific understanding of his or her religion through family and community upbringing, has intrinsically enjoyed the freedom to choose his or her authoritative definition of Islam, whether it be grounded in the law, or in the practice of a pious or political leader, or in the traditional usages of his or her community. Throughout the later centuries of Islam, this uncommon freedom has normally been exercised without severe penalty; diversity of practice and tolerance of diversity of practice have been normative over broad areas and periods of time. Sects have fought one another, of course, from time to time, but they have not generally contested for absolute authority in the way various Christian groups fought throughout much of European history.

Today, an individual Muslim may be whatever he or she chooses and still claim allegiance to Islam. Millions of secular and religiously antinomian Muslims are nevertheless proud of their religious heritage. Yet along with this diversity and tolerance goes a persistent and ever reappearing tendency for some individuals to choose some sort of authoritative guide or example upon which to model their behavior.

At the top of the scale of social and political importance one finds the twelfth-century Almohad movement of North Africa beginning with a single pious enthusiast going to towns where he was previously unknown and reproving people for their sinful behavior, thereby gaining a devoted band of disciples who heard him and chose to bestow on him their moral allegiance.[8] At the lower end one finds the fictional scoundrels of the medieval *Maqāmāt* stories by al-Ḥarīrī and al-Hamadhānī who repeatedly gull people into following them, and donating money to them, by feigning piety and decrying moral lapses.[9] In our contemporary period, whether the issue is as mundane as sexual segregation of university cafeterias or as weighty as calling for Salman Rushdie's execution, more and more Muslims are conferring their moral allegiance and trust upon leaders, official or unofficial, whom they judge to be pious.

Muslims remake their religion in every generation at both the individual and the community level, and they do so by exercising an uncommon degree of personal choice inherited as part of the template of religious practice that slowly emerged in early centuries of Islam. The *sharī'a* cannot be ignored because it gradually developed into the most intellectually dominant version of Islamic observance, and because the status of the individual is involved in many of its particulars. But to overstress the law, particularly at the present time, can only mislead and cause one to disregard or marginalize the many millions of Muslims who lead secular lives, or voluntarily follow the guidance of a particular leader, or adhere to traditional community usages that do not find a place in the legal treatises of the ulama.

NOTES

1. See, for example, H. A. R. Gibb, *Mohammedanism* (New York: Oxford University Press, 1962) or John Esposito, *Islam: The Straight Path* (New York: Oxford University Press, 1988).

2. Shi'ism is the branch of Islam that recognizes one or another descendant of Muḥammad's cousin and son-in-law 'Alī as the Imam, or divinely ordained rightful leader of the Muslim community. Different Shi'ite sects disagree, however, about which descendant should be the imam. Some (Zaidis and Nizari Isma'ilis) follow imams who are living amongst them, but the largest Shi'ite sect (Imamis or Ithna'asharis) believes that the last Imam disappeared from human society ca. 873 and will remain in occlusion until he chooses to return and establish a truly just and pious society.

3. During this episode, known as the *mihna* or inquisition, officeholders and religious leaders were required to swear adherence to the doctrine that the Qur'ān was created in time and not co-eternal with God. While the three caliphs who enforced this rule may have

had personal theological interests in the doctrines of the Muʿtazilis, the reason for the inquisition was more deeply rooted in their desire to impose centralized caliphal authority in areas of religious belief. This desire was thwarted when so many important religious leaders refused to take the oath that it had to be discontinued.

4. *A Sufi Rule for Novices*, tr. Menahem Milson (Cambridge: Harvard University Press, 1975).

5. J. N. D. Anderson, *Islamic Law in the Modern World* (New York: New York University Press, 1959).

6. The Tablighi Jamʿat organization was founded in rural India to teach Muslims who followed many local folk practices how to be better Muslims. It has now spread worldwide and attracted millions of followers. The organization's stress is on living daily life in accordance with the practice of Muḥammad and the early Muslim community as known from collections of traditions. The organization has no political agenda.

7. Gilles Kepel, *Muslim Extremism in Egypt: The Prophet and Pharaoh* (Berkeley: University of California Press, 1986), ch. 3.

8. Roger Le Tourneau, *The Almohad Movement in North Africa in the Twelfth and Thirteenth Centuries* (Princeton: Princeton University Press, 1969), ch. 1.

9. al-Ḥarīrī, *The Assemblies*, tr. T. Chenery (London, 1867); continued by F. Steingass (London, 1898).

Part Two

Religion, Secularity, and
Religious Tolerance

7

RELIGION AND LOCKEAN NATURAL RIGHTS

RICHARD ASHCRAFT

In this essay, I propose to discuss the relationship between religion and human rights as it is presented in the political thought of John Locke. On the basis of that discussion, I will offer a few observations as to how some of our human rights came to be established, and the role played in that achievement by (Lockean) liberalism as a political theory. Before offering a more detailed account of the specific theses I wish to defend, however, it would be helpful to sketch, briefly, the general dimensions of a widely held perspective which calls into question the presumptive validity of the endeavor I have described.

At first glance, it might seem odd that one should speak conjunctively of religion *and* human rights. To many in the West, the historical record of the relationship between religion and human rights is far from being an unequivocally positive one. Indeed, not a few juridical claims which we now recognize as "rights" were first advanced *against* the intolerance and persecution practiced by those imbued with religious authority. And, in a larger sense, the development of our modern concept of "rights" appears to be an outgrowth of those same beliefs and social forces which are generally associated with the process of secularization. The language of rights, that is, establishes a *prima facie* case for the importance of political and legal relationships, and might, therefore, best be viewed as part of a comprehensive historical shift away from a reliance upon a network of meanings drawn from the sphere of religion toward a viewpoint more centrally rooted in the practical concerns of social life. Political theories focused upon the rights of individuals, in other words, emerged during a historical period shaped by industrialization, urbanization, and democratization on the one hand, and by rationalism, science, and a materialist-oriented ethics on the other. Since these are the sociological and intellectual mainsprings of the development of modern secular society, it could be argued that we gained the political rights we enjoy as benefits of and in proportion to the declining influence of religion as a dominating force in society.[1]

The establishment of religious toleration, for example, is generally viewed as the consequence of a drift toward reason, enlightenment, and an attitude of skepticism toward the epistemological claims of theology.[2] The social importance accorded to individual property rights, to cite another example, is explained in terms of the privatization of religious principles in conjunction with a materialistic ethos of accumulation fostered by industrialization and the emergence of a capitalist society.[3] Free speech, the growth of a free press, the right to vote—these and many other specific rights seem bound up with the pluralistic conditions of urban life, the spread of literacy, the social mobility of individuals, and the rise of a powerful secular state which gradually assisted and/or succumbed to those tendencies which promoted the development of democracy. Moreover, from the standpoint of the aspect of the argument which emphasizes the "intellectual secularization" of the modern world, John Locke figures prominently as a progenitor of the ideas which helped to mobilize support for both the specific rights claims mentioned and for a rationalistic, scientific, and materialistic attitude toward life. Locke's "thoroughgoing rationalism," his "narrow individualism," and his assertion of the autonomy of politics and the importance of its divorce from the sphere of religion, made him, according to Harold Laski, the first important English thinker whose argument is primarily framed in secular terms.[4] George Sabine, in his influential *A History of Political Theory*, agreed with Laski that "the whole intellectual temper" of Locke's thought was secular, rationalist, skeptical, and individualist.[5] Later scholars added emphasis to certain features of this interpretive perspective, stressing Locke's defense of property rights and capitalist appropriation, and the degree to which he was responsible for the relativization of moral values and the materialistic preoccupations which characterize a civilization dominated by beliefs nourished in an atmosphere of "intellectual nihilism."[6]

To summarize the position I have outlined, it would appear that in any general discussion of individual rights as they exist in modern Western societies, religion is one of the least important explanatory factors to be considered, and Locke is one of the most important thinkers with respect to any account which attempts to provide evidence in support of this assertion. To suggest not only that religious beliefs exercised a positive influence upon the development of a notion of rights, but also that confirmation of this point can be established through an examination of Locke's political thought thus seems to be an ill-fated venture from the outset.

The general viewpoint I have described is familiar enough to any student of sociology, history, or political science, but, if we ask why this is so, and, on what grounds is it challengeable, the answers to these questions require that we bracket for the moment the substantive content of the propositions cited above in order to concentrate attention on certain methodological problems which have supplied the fuel for a long-standing controversy concerning the nature and purpose of the social sciences. Thus far, we have approached the subject of this essay from the standpoint of broad typological generalizations, characteristic, as Max Weber noted, of a sociological perspective. Though not divorced from historical evidence, such ideal typical portrayals of secularization, rationalism, individualism, etc., do tend to establish their credibility over the long term at the expense of a more complicated, concretely textured picture of social reality as it appears within a much more limited time frame. Even if one does not accept Weber's attribution of "uniqueness" to the configuration of social phenomena disclosed by a historically structured approach, it is nevertheless true that there is a shift in perception as one moves from one explanatory level to the other. The plausibility of the argument I wish to make in this essay, in other words, depends upon adopting a methodological approach in which the political ideas of Locke are viewed in relation to the specific historical and social context within which they were formulated, rather than as elemental pieces of a large-scale theoretical generalization advanced by twentieth-century social scientists.

This historically grounded argument is not offered solely in the interest of a more accurate portrayal of Locke's intentional objectives as a theorist. After all, to be fair, a number of scholars who linked Locke's name with the development of secularization were perfectly willing to concede that, in his own personal beliefs, Locke was a devout Christian. His responsibility, at least in some instances, for the uses which eighteenth- or nineteenth-century thinkers made of his ideas was therefore inadvertent. Nevertheless, if the actual complexities of Locke's thought were sacrificed to the theoretical imperatives attached to the construction of a network of simplifying abstractions, this methodological practice did not lack for its intellectual defenders amongst social scientists. Yet, in order to appreciate the degree to which a later restructuring of the emphasis Locke placed upon his assumptions and arguments affects our conception of "rights" and their definition within the framework of liberalism, the issue of historical accuracy cannot be so easily discounted.

Beyond the interpretive reparations owed to Locke, however, a more important aspect of the approach adopted here is its ability to disclose the darker side of liberalism and the struggle for human rights. That is, the tendency of scholars to direct their attention toward the universalizing claims for equality, liberty, and justice which are characteristic of liberalism has obscured the extent to which its practical success in winning the battle for human rights was dependent upon a set of specific prejudices, erroneous beliefs, and an attitude fed more by conspiratorial fear than rational enlightenment. This point leads to what I believe is a major weakness in any approach which is not focused upon the historicity of the phenomena under investigation; namely, the failure to provide an account of the dynamics of political change. The reliance upon ideal types as sociological categorizations of experience leads to a notion of social change as functional displacement. That is, science displaces magic, utilitarianism displaces puritanism, secular attitudes displace religious beliefs, and so on. At best, it can be said that there is an implicit theory of evolutionary change underlying this approach, but the actual character of any of the political struggles which helped to bring about changes, either with respect to belief systems or institutions, is generally omitted from the discussion. From the standpoint of political theory, it should be obvious that such an approach will not do. I would go even further, arguing that the failure to develop a theory of social change is a fatal impairment to the claims of certain twentieth-century social scientists that their approaches to the study of society can supply the methodological standards for the social sciences. I shall not pursue this point here,[7] however, it being sufficient for my purposes to stress the theoretical linkage between a historically grounded approach and an understanding of the dynamics of political change.

In this essay, therefore, I shall attempt to provide not only a more historically accurate interpretation of Locke's political thought, or a better understanding of the particular limitations of liberalism as a political theory, but also some appreciation of the relationship between the recognition of human rights and the practical dimensions of the political struggle necessary to achieve that recognition. Having sketched the broad parameters of the substantive and methodological issues in relation to which my argument in this essay is formulated, let me now turn to a more precise statement of the points I wish to make with respect to Locke's political thought. The three interpretive claims I shall make are that, for Locke: 1) *all* rights exercised by individuals are grounded in and derive their ultimate justificatory meaning from religious beliefs; 2) these rights, with one special exception, are meaningful to the individual only in the context of his membership in a moral community, which is posited by Locke as a necessary condition for the existential exercise of such rights; and (3) both presuppositions are incorporated into Locke's critique of the politicization of religion. Following an attempt to establish the importance of these propositions to Locke's thought viewed as a whole, I will focus upon Locke's argument for religious toleration as a specific illustration of how these assumptions were, in Locke's view, applicable to the solution of particular political problems. Both Locke's argument for toleration and the political achievement of toleration will be considered in relation to the ideas and activities of his contemporaries which helped to institutionalize this right of religious freedom.

> There is [Locke declares] one science incomparably above all the rest . . . I mean the-ology, which, containing the knowledge of God and his creatures, our duty to him and our fellow creatures, and a view of our present and future state, is the compre-hension of all other knowledge directed to its true end, i.e., the honor and venera-tion of the Creator, and the happiness of mankind. This is that noble study which is every man's duty, and everyone that can be called a rational creature is capable of."[8]

This point is reaffirmed by Locke in the *Essay Concerning Human Understanding*, where he characterizes "the main end" of his writing that work as providing support for "the knowledge and veneration" of God, because that is "the chief end of all our thoughts and the proper business of all under-standings."[9] The importance accorded by Locke to religious beliefs supplies the foundation for his discussion of morality, since "the true ground of moral-ity . . . can only be the will and law of a God" who exercises authority over individuals.[10] As Locke states repeatedly throughout his writings, the Law of Nature, which is "the decree of the divine will," establishes the framework for any definition of moral action by human beings.[11] Hence, for Locke, "all obligation leads back to God," and no moral claim could be advanced for which any independent justification can be provided.[12] That is, every moral claim made by one individual in relation to or against other individuals must, in the end, be traceable to these divinely decreed duties. In other words, Locke has so structured his argument that any notion of natural or human rights can be justified if, and only if, it can be shown to be derivative from some obliga-tion individuals owe to God, as stipulated by natural law. Without this pedi-gree, the particular claim may be reasonable viewed in terms of its practical convenience or for other specific reasons, but it will not, by Locke's definition, be a "right" to which individuals are morally entitled. It is in this sense, given a rather tightly structured argument linking religion, morality, natural law, obligations, and rights, that I wish to argue that all Lockean natural rights are premised upon a religious belief in God.

Since Locke's "rationalism" is so frequently stressed, it might be thought that there is a loophole in this argument through which individuals can escape, provided they make use of their rational faculties. That is, if it is pos-sible simply by employing human reason to arrive at a clear understanding of our moral duties, then it could be maintained that reason, in an essentially secular sense, is a sufficient basis for a system of moral rules. From this, it would follow that a defense of individual rights framed in terms of rational arguments would, in itself, supply some part of the evidence for a general argument in which rationalism, secularization, and human rights are inextricably conjoined. Locke could then be subsumed within the general sociological categories mentioned at the beginning of the essay, and, as I suggested, this is, in fact, the standpoint from which his ideas have been interpreted by a number of influential scholars.

There are three assumptions made by Locke which lend credence to this interpretive viewpoint. First, Locke does assert the rationality of human beings, and it is no exaggeration to say that this assumption is crucial to every aspect of his thought.[13] Second, he often describes the Law of Nature as a "law of reason," and, more important, maintains that a knowledge of its precepts is possible for individuals who make use of their reason.[14] Third, Locke insists that the principles of morality are as demonstrable and self-evident as are the principles of mathematics, and both the proposition and the analogue contained within it appear to suggest that, whatever Locke may believe personally and for psychological reasons, the tie between God, morality, and reason cannot be described as a logically necessary one.[15] The problem with this reading of Locke is not that it is without any evidential basis in his writings; as I have indicated in the notes, there are statements by Locke which confirm his belief in each of the three propositions which constitute the core of this rationalist perspective. Rather, the point is that the argument is formulated in such a way that it assumes what it ought to prove, namely, that these propositions are, from Locke's point of view, independent of his religious beliefs and assumptions. That is, Locke's statements regarding reason and morality are extracted from the larger context in which they appear in his thought, and then, precisely because they have been so extracted, it is argued that they can stand on their own, i.e., independent of any (religious) context. This contention is all the more plausible because we know that, as a matter of fact, other thinkers beside Locke can be found who did defend these propositions without reference to God or religion. Nevertheless, as an interpretation of Locke's thought, this viewpoint is seriously misleading.

Let us take up the first point. That Locke believes that individuals are created rational beings is true enough, but he also stipulates that anyone "who would pass for a rational creature" must believe in God.[16] "In fact it seems to me to follow . . . from the nature of man that, if he is a man, he is bound to love and worship God," and that, failing to do so would, in Locke's judgment, mean that the individual has not "fulfilled" his "rational nature."[17] Thus, not only is the belief in a Deity "the foundation of all morality," but without this belief, "a man is to be counted no other than one of the most dangerous sorts of wild beasts and so incapable of all society."[18] It is obvious that Locke includes not only a belief in God but also the fulfillment of a natural law obligation to love and worship Him, in his definition of "rationality." Nor is this an innocuous stipulation, for, without this belief, Locke will not permit an individual to be a member of political society.[19] Indeed, those familiar with the *Second Treatise of Government* will recognize in the passage cited above the bestial language Locke employs in that work to describe the person who has transgressed against the Law of Nature.[20] In other words, without a belief in God, the individual (a) cannot be counted a rational being; (b) is no better than a dangerous wild beast which is the terminology Locke uses to describe those who deny the divinity of or who transgress against the Law of Nature; and (c) is incapable of all society or fellowship with other human beings. Far from standing on its own, therefore, Locke's assertion of human rationality is embedded in a network of religious and moral assumptions which supply much of its meaning.

Locke sometimes speaks of natural law as a law of reason, but this popular phraseology exists within a much more technically defined conception of law. For, according to Locke, "without a notion of a law-maker, it is impossible to have a notion of a law, and an obligation to observe it."[21] Hence, that "there is a law-maker" who is directly responsible for the existence of a "law" is a fact which is "necessarily presupposed in the knowledge of any and every law."[22] This voluntarist definition of law is of course especially important to Locke's conception of natural law, since the latter is a law precisely because it is the expression of a "divine will."[23] Without God as the lawmaker, it would be meaningless, from Locke's perspective, to speak of natural law as a "law," however reasonable its precepts are assumed to be. If Locke does not dwell on this point, it is only because he "takes for granted" the proposition that God is the author of the Law of Nature, and that the latter is the direct declaration of "the will of God."[24] Thus, neither the origin, obligatory force, nor legalistic status of natural law can be accounted for in terms of reason; rather, these features of natural law require a belief in God.

Moreover, Locke maintains that "human reason unassisted" has never "made out an entire body of the 'law of nature.'" In fact, "all the moral rules of the philosophers" past and present do not add up, when collected together, to the precepts contained in natural law.[25] If these endeavors by individuals most skilled in the use of reason cannot provide an adequate account of the Law of Nature, the meaning of natural law as "a law of reason" must be severely circumscribed within much narrower limits than is generally assumed by those who emphasize Locke's "rationalism." These limitations are explained by Locke in terms of the superiority of a specifically Christian morality, as stated in the Scriptures.

> The Gospel contains so perfect a body of ethics, that reason may be excused from that inquiry, since she may find man's duty clearer and easier in revelation than in herself.[26]

This also explains why Locke did not pursue the claim that morality was as demonstrable as mathematics, despite the urgings of his friend William Molyneaux to do so. It might be of some benefit to have such a demonstration, but since "knowledge and science in general is the business only of those who are at ease and leisure," Locke never believed that such a contingent relationship could possibly be substituted for a divine obligation laid upon every individual, regardless of his education or social position.[27] It might be true that certain practical obstacles—e.g., a life devoted to work and drudgery, lacking in leisure—stood in the way of an individual's exercise of reason through a long train of deductions necessary to demonstrate the certainty of natural law, but no such practical limitations could excuse an individual from "engaging his thoughts in religion" or from "framing the general notions relating to religion, right."[28] Thus, Locke affirmed, we are under "an obligation . . . an absolute and indispensable necessity" to study the Scriptures.[29] Once again, the obligatory force of the individual's duties with respect to natural law stand on a much higher (religious) plane than that supplied by human reason.

What I have tried to show is that while "reason" may have considerable latitude to operate within the boundaries of Locke's thought, the foundations and basic structure of that thought are supplied by certain presuppositions Locke draws from his Christian faith.[30] And, since the ethical validity of natural rights claims depends, for Locke, upon locating a Scriptural or natural law source for such claims, reason may confirm the existence of such a source, but it cannot of itself provide the obligatory force to support the Lockean argument for natural rights. It is this distinction, important to Locke, which is obscured when Locke's commitment to "rationalism" is lifted out of its context. Locke's religious beliefs are not simply subjectively held opinions to be added onto a rationalistic structure of natural rights; rather, they are the constitutive a priori conditions for there *being* any such thing as "natural rights" at all. I return, therefore, to my original proposition, that all natural rights are for Locke dependent upon the existence of some specific command of God. It will be noticed that this is a stronger formulation than the initial proposition which maintained that rights claims were dependent upon a belief in the Deity. This is because, as we have seen, such a belief, according to Locke, entails the recognition that we are under moral obligations. In other words, the individual's expression of a belief in God is not merely a subjectively defined action, it is also a tacit assent on the part of the individual to an objective structure of moral obligations decreed by God.[31]

Indeed, this point leads directly to my second thesis, namely, that Locke assumes that individuals are members of a natural moral community, precisely and in so far as they have recognized their relationship to God and the Law of Nature. This is because, Locke explains, "according to the law of nature all men alike are friends of one another and are bound together by common interests."[32] Hence, "the more rational part of men" have always recognized that there is in man "some sense of a common humanity, some concern for fellowship."[33] In describing the natural condition of mankind in the *Second Treatise*, Locke argues that the individual is subject to the Law of Nature, "by which law common to them all, he and all the rest of mankind are one community, make up one society distinct from all other creatures."[34] It is "this great and natural community" which constitutes the moral starting point for Locke's discussion of political relationships between individuals.

In fact, according to Locke, the individual only has a "political" power in so far as he acts as an executor of natural law, which wills the preservation of mankind. Because violations of the Law of Nature are, in effect, crimes against the community and not merely a particular victim, Locke maintains that the violator has committed "a trespass against the whole species" and is therefore "dangerous to mankind." Thus, every man, "by the right he has to preserve mankind in general" is authorized to punish the criminal. It is the language of "rights" which, as Locke admits, sounds "strange" in this argument, since it is clear that Locke's meaning is that every individual has an obligation to obey and to enforce the Law of Nature, which is established for the benefit of mankind.[35] It is "the preservation of all mankind," Locke declares, which is "the true principle to regulate our religion, politics, and morality by."[36] Because Locke conceives of morality in terms of the collective responsibilities which individuals owe to each other, the individual's "right" is not only derivative from a natural law duty, it is also legitimated in terms of its being consonant with the general good of the community of which the individual is a member. Hence, any claim for the recognition by others that the individual, or any other body, is exercising political power is dependent upon that action being consonant with the purposes of natural law, i.e., the realization of the common good.[37] For, Locke observes, the municipal laws of countries "are only so far right, as they are founded on the Law of Nature, by which they are to be regulated and interpreted.[38]

If the "right" to exercise political power is itself dependent upon the execution of a duty referable to the Law of Nature which is in the collective interest of the community, then, I am arguing, all rights claims advanced by the individual *within* a political community must conform to this Lockean standard. There is one exception to this statement, namely, the right to freedom of religious worship. "No man," Locke declares, "has power to prescribe to another what he should believe or do in order to the saving [of] his own soul, because it is only his own private interest and concern. . . . God has nowhere given such power to any man or society, nor can [any] man possibly be supposed to give it to another."[39] Since Locke believes that "it is out of the power of any man to make another a representative for himself in matters of religion," it is obvious that this "natural right" cannot be mediated through the interest of the community or any other person.[40] There is a collective responsibility to enforce morality, but not salvation. It is "part of my liberty as a Christian and as a man," according to Locke, "to choose of what church or religious society I will be of, as most conducing to the salvation of my soul, of which I alone am judge, and over which the magistrate has no power at all."[41] In short, "the care of each man's salvation belongs only to himself," and "every man . . . has the supreme and absolute authority of judging for himself" in the matter of fulfilling his natural law obligation to worship God.[42] The natural right to religious toleration therefore stands above and outside of the moral or political authority of the community, and, in this respect, it is on a different plane from other Lockean natural rights.[43]

The third thesis I propose to defend is, in effect, an application of the first two arguments in the form of an attack on the politicization of religion. Locke's general separation of the sphere of religion from the sphere of politics is, as was noted above, included in his definition of political power which is placed in the hands of the community, whereas the "care of each man's soul" is placed in the custody of the individual. Both rights claims, as we have seen, flow from a common source, natural law, which, in turn, presupposes a belief in God and a recognition that we are his "workmanship . . . sent into the world by his order and about his business."[44] Thus, while all political rights have a religious foundation in Locke's thought, the individual's religious right to freedom of worship has no political derivation whatsoever, at least in so far as its exercise does not violate the basic moral rules which regulate the life of the community as a whole.[45]

Locke's separation of religion and politics as spheres of authority pertaining to the individual's religious worship has generally been viewed as part of a larger trend toward religious skepticism, secularization, and a decline in the importance of religious commitment. Thus, for Laski, Locke's privatization of religion reflects the social subordination of the religious life to a predominant concern for politics and economic interests.[46] While this view, as I have suggested, cannot be simply dismissed as one way of reading the evidence, it does not, I think, accurately reflect Locke's intentions nor does it accord sufficient importance to the context within which his arguments were formulated. If Locke's epistemological arguments against spurious claims for "knowledge" in matters of religion are seen as part of a strategy to undermine the political authority of the clergy, then the defense of "faith" in an egalitarian sense might better be viewed as an attempt to radicalize religion, very much in the spirit of some of the leading thinkers of the Reformation itself. In attacking the claims for hierarchical authority exercised by either the civil magistrate or the clergy with respect to matters of religion, in other words, it is possible to maintain either that no special knowledge is required (religious truth is available to all equally), or that some knowledge (whether one has gained personal salvation) is not available to anyone in this world. Locke, I believe, advanced both arguments at various times in the *Essay Concerning Human Understanding*, the *Reasonableness of Christianity*, and the *Letter Concerning Toleration*.[47] The effect of these epistemological arguments was to reinforce the anti-authoritarian strains of Protestant thought.

This deeply held anticlerical aspect of Locke's thought has been little appreciated because, from the standpoint of a conception of Locke, the philosopher, it appears to be, at best, merely a historically rooted characteristic of Locke, the individual. Yet, this dismissal plays a significant role with respect to the ease with which Locke is assimilated into a rationalist tradition of thought, seen from the perspective of the later development of philosophy. To view Locke as a defender of a radicalized version of Christianity, on the other hand, is to link his thought, historically, with certain intellectual developments within religion in the sixteenth century, in the context of which the simplification of religious beliefs and duties did not in the least imply religious skepticism, nor, for example, in the case of the anabaptists, any concession of importance to the state.

In Locke's view, it was not only the magistrate who was likely to cross the boundaries separating religion from politics; more frequently, it was the clergy who did so in seeking to enforce particular religious beliefs by coercive means, which included their indirect use of governmental power. This misuse of clerical authority might appear to be little more than a deplorable fact which adds nothing to Locke's theoretical argument with respect to politics, religion, or natural rights. Nevertheless, there is a problem to be confronted because the natural right to toleration, during the period of Locke's writing, did not, in fact, exist. If this right was to become a reality, therefore, it must gain the support of the community. That is to say, toleration must be recognized as a political right, even though, as Locke had structured his argument, it was not essentially a political right, but a pre-political natural right. In this sense, the community as a political entity stood in the way of the individual's fulfillment of his natural law obligations, rather than, as in all other cases, supplying the means by which these obligations may be fulfilled. It was not really the community or the majority of mankind, however, which was at fault; rather, according to Locke, it was the clerical minority, in collusion with the magistrate, who were responsible for the misuse of political power. Somehow, therefore, the political power of the clergy must be defeated, and this could only be accomplished through the use of political power. Hence, a political struggle was necessary in order to institute a natural right of toleration which, in essence, was not a "political" right at all. What we are addressing in the case of the third thesis are the practical dimensions within which the presuppositions of Locke's argument concerning religion and natural rights must operate. And, it is precisely because *Locke* did not believe that "reason" or logic alone was sufficient to establish the right to toleration—however committed some of the interpreters of his thought may be to the view that toleration is simply the product of enlightened reason—that this specifically political problem must be raised.

Toleration has so often been viewed as the logical outcome of an enlightened liberal perspective that it has been forgotten what a distinctly unpopular political act it was to offer a defense of this policy during the period in which Locke wrote his *Letter Concerning Toleration*. The dissenters were a small but vocal minority of the total population. They had repeatedly been accused of political subversion, and some of them had in fact been involved in various plots, conspiracies, and rebellions that characterized Restoration England. While a few members of the Anglican establishment entertained ideas which might have made it possible for some moderate Presbyterians to be included within a more loosely and comprehensively defined Anglican church, the toleration of all sectarian religious beliefs was not a policy which drew support from the established clergy.[48] Locke certainly recognized this, and in the *Letter Concerning Toleration* he showed no hesitation in attacking their "ambition," their "worldly interests," and their desire for "temporal dominion," which, in his view, explained their opposition to toleration.

> For who does not see that these good men are indeed more ministers of the government than ministers of the Gospel, and that by flattering the ambition and favoring the dominion of princes and men in authority, they endeavor with all their might to promote that tyranny in the commonwealth which otherwise they should not be able to establish in the church.

Thus, for "a participation of the spoil," the Anglican clergy have used the political power of the magistrate as the means "to increase their own power."[49]

It was an important practical dimension of Locke's argument for toleration, therefore, to engage in an ideological unmasking of the self-interested motives of the chief opponents of toleration. Through such a political attack, he hoped to undermine their authority with respect to religious beliefs and practices.

At the same time, Locke defended the use of political power to exclude Catholics from any policy of toleration. Catholics, according to Locke (and most of his contemporaries), owed their primary allegiance to a foreign power, the pope. They subscribed to beliefs that were destructive of all human society: that faith was not to be kept with heretics (Protestants), that kings could be deposed for religious reasons, that dominion was founded in grace, and other propositions which made Catholics the "irreconcilable enemies" to any Protestant government. In Locke's view, Catholics were not to be trusted, since they represented a "secret evil," a conspiracy which made them "ready upon any occasion to seize the government and possess themselves of the estates and fortunes of their fellow subjects."[50] As violators of the precepts of natural law, Catholics stood outside of Locke's natural moral community as individuals who had forfeited their claims to be treated as other human beings.[51] Whereas the sphere of religious belief was, in general, governed by persuasion, reason, and the individual's own conscience, Locke nevertheless endorsed the application of force to Catholics as a means by which they might be "converted" to the truth of Protestantism.[52]

Locke was certainly not alone in holding such opinions. On the contrary, deep fear and hatred of Catholics was a hallmark of seventeenth-century English political life.[53] This anti-Catholicism was an especially important aspect of the argument for toleration because both Charles II and James II had attempted to institute a policy of toleration which included Catholics within its purview. The political opposition to this inclusion of Catholics was sufficiently powerful and widespread to defeat any attempt to legitimize a toleration which exceeded the limits of this cultural prejudice. Locke's *Letter Concerning Toleration* stood within this framework, and indeed, actually contributed to the efforts to foster and justify the anti-Catholic fear shared by his countrymen, which, in its extreme form, had manifested itself as a national hysteria during the "popish plot" crisis a few years earlier.[54] Even during the debate to secure a Declaration of Rights for the nation in the wake of the Glorious Revolution, the participants often seemed more concerned with insuring that no Catholic sat on the throne than they were with enacting certain rights for the benefit of individuals.[55]

In other words, the political argument for religious toleration while it obviously made all possible use of appeals to individual reason, natural law, etc., depended for its practical success upon appeals to the prejudices, fears, and hatreds shared by the community and directed against Catholics, and, to a lesser extent, atheists, who were also excluded from membership in political society, as defined in Locke's *Letter*. The latter not only incorporated these shared beliefs, but also formulated an ideological critique of the Anglican clergy who were accused of having politicized religion. It was not so much an indifference to religion as the unifying effect of a fear of Catholicism which prompted the practical alliance of Protestants, and thereby made possible the enactment of toleration. The limited form in which toleration gained acceptance, leaving intact the penal laws against dissenters but suspending the application of their penalties, indicates just how politically fragile and contingent this Protestant unity was. Nor should one confuse anticlericalism with religious skepticism. Locke certainly espoused the first, and just as certainly rejected the second in his writings.[56] That an established church was likely to fall victim to the corruption of "worldly interest" and that religion might very well be reduced to a few basic beliefs subscribed to by individuals through faith were two central propositions of Locke's thought; they were also essential elements of Luther's thought and, in a larger sense, of the entire Protestant Reformation. Of course, it is a relatively easy task to bring Locke's thought within the compass of our modern world, and it is comparatively difficult to accomplish this feat in the case of Luther. Nevertheless, as I have argued, there are crucial respects in which Locke stands closer to Luther and his world than he does to ours, and, in the case of his argument for natural rights in general and for the right of religious toleration in particular, it is essential to recognize this fact. It is the primary importance of religious belief, not its secondary status in relation to philosophy or politics, which underlies the structure of Locke's moral and political thought.

Quite apart from the hierarchy of values ascribed to Locke, however, I have argued that a consideration of the historical circumstances under which human rights such as the right to free exercise of religious worship gain political recognition may lead us to a fuller appreciation of the contingencies which govern the practice of rights. If we continually insist upon rooting human rights in such impersonal phenomena as industrialization, urbanization, or secularization, we may come to believe that these rights are as stable or as far beyond the capabilities of organized human action as the social forces with which we have identified them. To see such rights as the products of the cultural prejudices of the community, or a fragile political alliance, or fear of a common enemy, etc., may place these rights within a less attractive framework, but, at the same time, it reinforces our consciousness that such rights are impermanent, that they are the products of a political struggle, and that organized human action is necessary to guarantee their preservation. Indeed, the very recognition that such rights and the political values of Lockean liberalism generally depended upon certain shared religious beliefs which are no longer constitutive of our political society ought to make us more, not less concerned with the problematic character of the contemporary rights claims advanced by the individual against the state. In the end, therefore, it is perhaps most salutary to grasp the meaning of human rights in terms of a cumulative political struggle comprised of many concrete victories, each of which needs to be understood in terms of its historical, sociological, and political dimensions.

Notes

1. Alastair MacIntyre, *Secularization and Moral Change* (London: Oxford University Press, 1967); Harvey Cox, *The Secular City* (New York: Macmillan, 1966); R. H. Tawney, *Religion and the Rise of Capitalism* (New York: Mentor Books, 1954), pp. 14–17, and passim.

2. Franklin L. Baumer, *Religion and the Rise of Skepticism* (New York: Harcourt Brace, 1960); Robin Attfield, *God and the Secular* (Cardiff: University College Cardiff Press, 1978).

3. Tawney, *Religion and the Rise of Capitalism*, pp. 15, 222–23; Sheldon Wolin, *Politics and Vision* (Boston: Little, Brown, 1960), p. 338ff.

4. Harold J. Laski, *Political Thought in England: Locke to Bentham* (London: Oxford University Press, 1920), pp. 42, 47, 52; Sterling P. Lamprecht, *The Moral and Political Philosophy of John Locke* (New York: Columbia University Press, 1918), p. 21.

5. George H. Sabine, *A History of Political Theory*, 3d ed. (New York: Holt, Rinehart and Winston, 1961), pp. 518–19, 526; Tawney, *Religion and the Rise of Capitalism*, pp. 160–61; Baumer, *Religion and the Rise of Skepticism*, pp. 57–58, 94–95.

6. C. B. Macpherson, *The Political Theory of Possessive Individualism* (Oxford: Oxford University Press, 1962), pp. 194–262; Leo Strauss, *Natural Right and History* (Chicago: University of Chicago Press, 1953), pp. 202–51; Wolin, *Politics and Vision*, 337–40.

7. I have discussed this point with specific reference to Weber elsewhere. See my "Marx and Weber on Liberalism as Bourgeois Ideology," *Comparative Studies in Society and History* (March 1972), pp. 130–68.

8. *The Works of John Locke*, 12th ed., 9 vols. (London: 1824), vol. 2, p. 360.

9. John Locke, *An Essay Concerning Human Understanding* (hereafter cited as *ECHU*), ed. Peter Nidditch (Oxford: Clarendon Press, 1975), 2:7, 6; cf. Introduction, 5; 1:3, 12; 2:23, 12; 4:12, 11.

10. *ECHU*, 1:2, 6, 18; 2:21, 72; 2:28, 8.

11. John Locke, *Essays on the Law of Nature*, ed. W. von Leyden (Oxford: Clarendon Press, 1954), pp. 111, 113, 187; *Two Treatises of Government*, ed. Peter Laslett (Cambridge: Cambridge University Press, 1967), II, par. 135.

12. *Essays on the Law of Nature*, pp. 183, 187.

13. *Essays on the Law of Nature*, pp. 113, 115, 127; *Two Treatises*, II, pars. 61, 63.

14. *Essays on the Law of Nature*, pp. 125, 127, 149, 199; *Two Treatises*, I, par. 101; II, par. 57. Nevertheless, even these passages, I believe, must be read in the context of Locke's emphasis (II, pars. 59, 60) upon the individual's possession of "a capacity of knowing that Law." Thus, Locke's assertion is that he must "be supposed *capable* of knowing the Law"

(italics added) which entails a presumption of rationality on the part of individuals, but leaves open the empirical question as to whether, and under what conditions, individuals actually *do* attain a knowledge of natural law through the use of their reason. Hence, in the state of nature, "though the Law of Nature be plain and intelligible to all rational creatures," yet, "for want of study of it," or for reasons of biased interests, such knowledge may be lacking. II, par. 124.

15. *ECHU*, 3:11, 16; 4:3, 18; 4:4, 7; 4:12, 8.

16. *Journal*, July 29, 1676, Locke MS. f.1 (Bodleian Library, Oxford); *ECHU*, 1:3, 9; 2:17, 17; 4:10, 8.

17. *Essays on the Law of Nature*, p. 199; *Two Tracts on Government*, ed. Philip Abrams (Cambridge: Cambridge University Press, 1967), *Second Tract*, pp. 215–16; *Journal*, September 1, 1676, Locke MS. f.1; Lort King, *The Life of John Locke*, 2 vols. (London, 1830), vol. 2, p. 101.

18. Locke, *Essay Concerning Toleration (1667)*, cited in John Gough, *John Locke's Political Philosophy* (Oxford: Clarendon Press, 1950), appendix, p. 197.

19. "The taking away of God, though but even in thought, dissolves all . . . the bonds of human society." *Works*, vol. 5, p. 47.

20. *Two Treatises*, II, pars.8, 10, 11, 16, 172, 181, 182.

21. *ECHU*, 1:3, 8; cf. 1:2, 12; 2:28, 5–6.

22. *Essays on the Law of Nature*, pp. 151, 173.

23. *Essays on the Law of Nature*, pp. 111, 187; *Second Tract*, p. 222.

24. *Essays on the Law of Nature*, p. 109; *ECHU*, 2:28, 8.

25. *Works*, vol. 6, pp. 140–41.

26. *Works*, vol. 8, p. 377; vol. 9, p. 306.

27. *Works*, vol. 2, p. 342. Locke insists that "every one has enough" time or leisure "to get as much knowledge as is required and expected of him," p. 384. This minimal egalitarianism is a necessary structural element of Locke's thought because, without it, the lowest social classes would stand condemned theologically as a consequence of the social actions taken by others. "I cannot imagine that God . . . would put poor men . . . under almost an absolute necessity of sinning perpetually against Him," *Journal*, March 20, 1678, Locke MS. f. 3; *Works*, vol. 6, p. 147; *ECHU*, 4:20, 2–3.

28. *Works*, vol. 2, p. 342. "No man is so wholly taken up with the attendance on the means of living, as to have no spare time at all to think of his soul, and inform himself in matters of religion." *ECHU*, 4:20, 3.

29. *Works*, vol. 6, p. 408; vol. 5, p. 41. It is the moral status of this "necessity" which supplies the foundation for Locke's anticlericalism. Thus, "those things that every man ought sincerely to inquire into himself, and by meditation, study, search, and his own endeavors, attain the knowledge of, cannot be looked upon as the peculiar profession of any one sort of men." *Works*, vol. 5, p. 25.

30. For a more extended discussion of this point, see "Faith and Knowledge in Locke's Philosophy," in John W. Yolton, ed., *John Locke: Problems and Perspectives* (Cambridge: Cambridge University Press, 1969), pp. 194–223.

31. "For it seems to me that certain duties arise out of necessity and cannot be other than they are. . . . [and] since man has been made such as he is . . . there necessarily result from his inborn constitution some definite duties for him, which cannot be other than they are." *Essays on the Law of Nature*, p. 199; *Works*, vol. 6, p. 112.

32. *Essays on the Law of Nature*, p.163.

33. *Essays on the Law of Nature*, p. 205.

34. *Two Treatises*, II, par. 128; cf. par. 6.

35. *Two Treatises*, II, pars. 7–13.

36. *Works*, vol. 8, p. 113.

37. *Two Treatises*, II, par.3.

38. *Two Treatises*, II, par. 12; *Essays on the Law of Nature*, pp. 119, 189.

39. "Toleration," Locke MS. t.1, f.125.

40. Locke MS. c.34, f.122. "Liberty of conscience is every man's natural right." *Works*, vol. 5, pp. 47–48.

41. Locke MS. c. 34, f. 74.

42. *Works*, vol. 5, p. 41.

43. It might be objected that the natural right to property also stands outside and above the moral authority of the community. This is a complicated issue, which cannot be entered into here. Suffice it to say that, insofar as "natural right" is associated with the individual's "person" and the subsistence necessary to preserve himself, property in this limited sense is as absolute a right as is the individual's liberty of conscience. *Two Treatises*, II. pars. 27, 194. Property in the sense of the ownership of goods, however, is not absolute, and is subject to the authority of the community. II, pars. 50, 120, 121, 138. See pars. 190–92, where Locke draws the distinction between the two forms of property and their respective juridical status.

44. *Two Treatises*, II, par. 6.

45. *Works*, vol. 5, p. 33.

46. Laski, *Political Thought*, p. 42; Wolin, *Politics and Vision*, pp. 337–40.

47. *Works*, vol. 5, pp. 20–21, 23, 27, 36, 53. Locke's anticlericalism is also evident in the *Two Treatises*. See the preface, and I, pars. 3, 10.

48. Henry Kamen, *The Rise of Toleration* (New York: McGraw-Hill, 1967), p. 204. For a general review of the situation in Restoration England, see Charles F. Mullett, "Toleration and Persecution in England, 1660–1689," *Church History* (March 1949), pp. 18–43; Gerald R. Cragg, *Puritanism in the Period of the Great Persecution, 1660–1688* (Cambridge: Cambridge University Press, 1957).

49. *Works*, vol. 5, p. 54.

50. *Works*, vol. 5, pp. 45–46.

51. In Locke's view, there were a number of doctrines associated with Catholicism which justified his assertion that any subscriber to these doctrines "breaks the great bond of humanity" and fellowship between individuals. *Essays on the Law of Nature*, p. 175. On Locke's lifelong aversion to Catholicism, see Maurice Cranston, *John Locke*, (London: Longmans, Green, 1957), p. 45.

52. The use of force against Catholics was no more "than what the cruelty of their own principles and practices are known to deserve." Locke not only attacked Catholics for holding principles which are "absolutely destructive of all governments," he also criticized their "blind obedience to an infallible pope" and the absurdity of their religious beliefs which appeal primarily to those with "unstable minds." *Essay Concerning Toleration* (1667), in H. R. Fox-Bourne, *The Life of John Locke*, 2 vols. (London: 1876), vol. 1, pp. 187–89.

53. John Miller, *Popery and Politics in England, 1660–1688* (Cambridge: Cambridge University Press, 1973).

54. William Penn, for example, who included Catholics among his notion of toleration, complained against the "panic fear . . . now animated more than ever against popery" by those who, like Locke, opposed James II's policy of extending toleration to Catholics. *Some Free Reflections Upon the Occasion of the Public Discourse About Liberty of Conscience* (1687), p.16.

55. Lois G. Schwoerer, *The Declaration of Rights, 1689* (Baltimore: Johns Hopkins University Press, 1981), p. 284. The actual circumstances surrounding the marshaling of support for the Toleration Act of 1689 are still something of a mystery, but it is clear that anti-Catholicism was a primary factor in securing the fragile legislative consensus in Parliament. Henry Horowitz, *Parliament, Policy, and Politics in the Reign of William III* (Manchester: Manchester University Press, 1977), pp. 28–29; G. V. Bennett, "Conflict in the Church," in Geoffrey Holmes, ed., *Britain After the Glorious Revolution* (London: Macmillan, 1969), pp. 155–75.

56. Locke specifically denied that his defense of toleration was in any sense linked with skepticism. *Works*, vol. 5, p. 415. Also see the work cited in note 30 above.

8

HUMAN RIGHTS AND THE WORLD'S RELIGIONS: CHRISTIANITY, ISLAM, AND RELIGIOUS LIBERTY

DAVID LITTLE, ABDULAZIZ SACHEDINA, AND JOHN KELSAY

Adamantia Pollis and Peter Schwab conclude their essay, "Human Rights: A Western Construct with Limited Applicability," by expressing a familiar objection to ethnocentrism.

> Unfortunately not only do human rights as set forth in the Universal Declaration reveal a strong Western bias, but there has been a tendency to view human rights ahistorically and in isolation from their social, political, and economic milieu.[1]

This criticism is frequently applied to statements of rights concerning private property, vacations with pay, the status of women, marriage arrangements, forms of punishment, and some particular political and civil guarantees, such as voting procedures, that are contained in various "internationally recognized" human rights documents. The complaint is that these are so many manifestations of a highly parochial cultural and historical experience that, at certain points, neither does have nor ought to have anything definitive to say to peoples with other experience and traditions.

The charge is a serious and challenging one. Human rights advocates need to face it squarely and respond to it with precision and care. Are all the rights contained in the documents equally binding upon all peoples everywhere? Or, are some rights (more than others) subject to national and cultural discretion?

Which ones? And how much discretion? Ought it simply be up to each government and each culture to pick and choose among the catalogues of rights and decide which ones are binding and which ones not? Or, are some rights (at least) indefeasible and absolute whatever particular governments and societies, in accord with their cultural traditions, may decide? In short, are human rights—all, or in part—the measure of governments and cultures, or are governments and cultures the measures of human rights?

These are staggeringly large questions. They go to the heart of political, legal, and moral theory, including the study of comparative ethics. We do not begin to have a comprehensive answer, and we doubt that such an answer is even possible at this rather primitive stage of reflection on human rights questions. But it is necessary to make some preliminary attempts. We propose to do that by considerably narrowing the range of inquiry, and by taking up particular charges of Western bias and cultural discrimination that have persistently been lodged by Muslims and by Western students of Islam against the statements in various human rights documents concerning "the right to freedom of thought, conscience, and religion." By examining and evaluating in detail the disagreements between Islamic culture and proponents of the Western tradition over just one of the alleged human rights—the right to freedom of conscience and religion—we may begin to see how we might go at the bigger problems.

Many of the Muslim objections were first registered in 1948 during the deliberations that surrounded Article 18 of the Universal Declaration, which states:

> Everyone has the right to freedom of thought, conscience, and religion; this right includes freedom to change his religion or belief, and freedom, either alone or in community with others in public or in private, to manifest his religion or belief in teaching, practice, worship and observance.[2]

In response, a number of Islamic countries (in particular, Saudi Arabia) attempted to delete this article. Failing that, they blamed others, e.g., Lebanon, for supporting it because, they contended, the rights of Lebanese Muslims would be compromised by such wording.

Objections were raised by some of the same countries against the somewhat more elaborate version of the right to religious freedom contained in the draft of the International Covenant on Civil and Political Rights, which was later adopted, and which stated: "No one shall be subject to coercion which would impair his freedom to have or to adopt a religion or belief of his choice" (Article 18, sect. 2). And Article 26 added another new stipulation which guaranteed equal protection of the law against any form of discrimination "on any ground such as race . . . sex . . . [or] religion."

More recently, objections from much the same quarter were again raised in reaction to the Draft Declaration on the Elimination of All Forms of Intolerance and of Discrimination Based on Religion or Belief. The dissenting views that were advanced in the discussions of the Human Rights Commission actually had some limited effect on the final version of the Declaration. In that version, which the United Nations General Assembly adopted on November 25, 1981, some of the wording that referred to a right to choose, adopt, or change one's religion was deleted, although by no means uniformly. In any case, in Article 8 of the Declaration, the General Assembly made clear it considered the earlier statements of the right to choose and change one's own religion contained in the Universal Declaration and the Covenant on Political and Civil Rights to be fully binding.

Furthermore, Article 2 of the Declaration adds some new stipulations of its own.

1. No one shall be subject to discrimination by any State, institution, group of persons, or person on grounds of religion or other belief.

2. For the purposes of the present Declaration, the expression intolerance and discrimination based on religion or belief means any distinction, exclusion, restriction, or preference based on religion or belief and having as its purpose or as its effect nullification or impairment of the recognition, enjoyment, or exercise of human rights and fundamental freedoms on an equal basis.

The reactions of Muslim political officials and religious leaders to the idea that human beings have a basic right to follow their consciences, change religion as they see fit, and be free of discriminatory treatment based on religious belief are, for the most part, well summarized as follows:

> [A] major area of disagreement is freedom of religion. The Qur'ān vigorously denounces those who renounce Islam, for "the Devil has seduced them" away from the true faith (67:25). The major historical example is the revolt of the tribes after Muhammad's death in 632 A.D. Abu Bakr, and jurists since then, condemned secession from Islam (*ridda*) as doubly heinous: It not only is a violation of the compact of submission made with Allāh, but it is also a breach of contract with his representatives on earth. It is, then, an offense both against God and against the state: it is both apostasy and treason. Far from having the right to become a non-Muslim, the Muslim faces the death penalty as a sanction for such a change.[3]

The message of the Qur'ān is preoccupied with what might be called the political threat of religious unbelief. Muhammad's campaign to solidify and extend his political authority depended on religious as well as political loyalty from the contending factions. His struggle to subdue Medina and Mecca by creating an intricate confederation was wrought out of severe and constant struggles against these religious-political factions, and stability was constantly threatened by one or another of them.

These facts help explain the intensity of some Qur'ānic utterances concerning apostasy, and the reasons for recommending the use of force in some cases against apostates.[4]

> [The disbelievers] wish that you should disbelieve as they disbelieve, and then you would be equal; therefore take not yourselves friends of them, until they emigrate in the way of God; then, if they turn their backs, take them, and slay them wherever you find them; take not to yourselves any one of them as friend or helper.   (4:90)
>
> This is the recompense of those who fight against God and His Messenger, and hasten about the earth, to do corruption there: they shall be slaughtered, or crucified, or their hands and feet shall alternately be struck off, or they shall be banished from the land. That is a degradation for them in this world; and in the world to come awaits them a mighty chastisement.   (5:35f.)
>
> Fight against such of those who have been given the Scripture as believe not in Allāh nor the Last Day, and forbid not that which Allāh hath forbidden by His messenger, and follow not the religion of truth, until they pay the tribute readily, being brought low.   (9:29; trans. by Pickthall)

These passages are supplemented by certain statements of Muḥammad, as reported in the *ḥadīth* literature (sayings of Muḥammad or narratives concerning him): "He who changes his religion must be killed," and by other reports from the same source that apostates were occasionally punished by losing hands and feet before being killed. Accordingly, apostasy has come to be included in Islamic law as one of the *Ḥudūd*, or capital crimes, along with adultery, defamation and slander, alcoholism, theft, brigandage, treason and armed rebellion. The conflict at this point between conventional Islamic interpretation and the prescriptions of the human rights documents concerning a "right not to be subject to coercion which would impair [one's] freedom to have a religion or belief of his choice" would appear to be acute.

There is also the question, in the words of sections 1 and 2 of Article 2 of the Declaration on Intolerance, of legal discrimination "on grounds of religion and other belief," that is, of "any distinction, exclusion, restriction, or preference based on religion or belief." Even though, as is well-known, non-Muslim monotheists (*dhimmīs*), namely Jews, Christians, Zoroastrians, and some others, are traditionally treated more tolerantly than polytheists and other kinds of "disbelievers," they are hardly accorded full and equal rights. So long as they live peaceably, they may practice their religion (in a subdued manner), but they are nevertheless required to pay a tax (*jizya*) to the Islamic state—described by one scholar as "a discriminatory poll tax for unbelief."[5]

What is more, Muslim authorities may prohibit the *dhimmīs* from marrying Muslims, conducting certain forms of business, and the *dhimmīs* may be required, according to traditional Islamic law, to wear distinctive clothing and to live in houses smaller than Muslim houses. Finally, in certain Islamic states non-Muslims are prevented from occupying high public office, as, for example, in Pakistan and most Arab states where the head of state must be a Muslim. In short, the record shows that "non-Muslims in Muslim countries did not enjoy the same basic rights as the Muslims." Or, as Majid Khadduri puts it, "as a subject of the Muslim state, [the *dhimmī*] suffered certain disabilities which reduced him to the status of a second-class citizen" (ibid.).

The conflict, then, seems clear. The freedom of religion and conscience articles in various human rights documents appear to run afoul, at important points, of much established and official Muslim teaching about the treatment of apostates and protected non-Muslims. There are at least four possible strategies we might adopt in face of this conflict.

First, we might simply advocate retracting all statements in favor of freedom of religion and conscience (or, we might accomplish the same purpose by rewriting existing statements so as to make them innocuous). There are problems with this response. Are all human rights statements to be retracted or emasculated whenever they encounter opposition? But, more to the point, there is actually little interest in the international community, even among Muslims, in taking such a radical step. Muslims, like others, seem committed to giving human rights status to freedom of religion and conscience, so long as those rights are properly restricted according to traditional teaching.

Second, we might try to argue that devotion to existing freedom of religion statements entails allowing Muslim states, along with everyone else, discretion to define religious tolerance and its limits in whatever way they see fit. We would then, would we not, be allowing Muslims the right to follow their own consciences, and thus act on their internationally guaranteed right to religious liberty? There are two problems here. One is that tolerating all views, even the most intolerant ones, yields a contradictory policy, especially when intolerance toward certain beliefs can be enforced. Equally troublesome is the fact that existing statements of the right to religious liberty explicitly include prohibitions that contradict certain Muslim policies.

Third, we might cling to existing statements of the right to religious liberty and attempt to enforce them internationally by means of the same devices that the United States, for example, has from time to time employed in trying to enforce other civil, political, and economic rights. There are no doubt special problems of feasibility in this case. Moreover, without agreeing that a belief in freedom of religion entails tolerating any belief, even those that enforce intolerance, it does seem that the cultural differences over this question create some subtleties and perplexities for human rights advocates that are not present in respect to the more notorious violations, like gross mistreatment of prisoners, political opponents, etc.

Fourth, we might use the contemporary debate between Westerners and Muslims over freedom of religion and conscience as an occasion for reconsidering the foundations and character of a belief in such freedom both in the West and in the Islamic tradition. If, upon careful, critical examination, the conflict between Western and Islamic views concerning something so important and so basic as a right to freedom of religion and conscience turns out to be much less clear and consistent that has been alleged, then we shall, it seems, have some reason to begin to call into question the "limited applicability" of human rights declarations.

In this essay, we adopt the fourth strategy. We are convinced that the subject of human rights in general and the right to freedom of religion and conscience in particular has suffered in the West from a fashionable but unconvincing belief in relativism, and in the Islamic world from a failure to subject the Qur'ānic foundations of Islamic faith to rigorous and sympathetic reexamination, as well as to acknowledge the internal complexity of the Islamic tradition as regards those matters.

In what follows, then, we shall indicate what we take to be the main features of the notion of religious liberty as it has developed in the West. Following this, we shall make some proposals concerning similar features in the tradition of Islam. Our argument will be that the existence of such similarity is at least as important as those differences between the West and Islam which have heretofore been emphasized, and that the possibilities for fruitful discussion of matters of human rights in general and religious liberty in particular ought not be overlooked.

The Western Tradition Concerning Religious Liberty and Freedom of Conscience

There is no doubt that the right to freedom of religion and conscience as formulated in human rights documents is the product of Western experience and belief. The political strife and conflict caused by contending religious groups in sixteenth-, seventeenth-, and eighteenth-century Europe, England, and America eventually made toleration very desirable. Against that historical background, there is special poignancy in the words of the Preamble to the Declaration on Intolerance:

Considering that the disregard and infringement of human rights and fundamental freedoms, in particular the right to freedom of thought, conscience, or whatever belief, have brought, directly or indirectly, wars and great suffering to mankind.

On the other hand, there is no understanding the emergence of these ideas apart from the moral and religious tradition in which they germinated for so long.

The right to freedom of religion and conscience, as we have it today, arose out of a complicated interweaving of classical Greco-Roman and Christian notions. The Greek and Latin terms for conscience, *syneidesis* and *conscientia*, respectively, were not limited, as in our understanding of conscience, to reflection on moral and religious matters. The terms also denoted what we would call consciousness.[6] In fact, while a view of conscience as doing normative work was important in the thought of Roman philosophers like Cicero and Seneca,[7] and was decidedly important in popular Greek culture, it did not occupy an important place in the thought of Plato and Aristotle.[8]

There are three noteworthy characteristics of the Roman and popular Greek view of conscience as a center of normative reflection. First, it is a "private monitor."

> [It reviews,] the quality of a man's own acts, and, it follows, of his own character . . . [It] is not concerned with the acts, attitudes or characters of others . . . [T]he knowledge or awareness that a man has, the witness that he is in a position to bear—is internal. No external authority need be consulted: he knows, and is his own witness to himself; and his knowledge and witness are private to him alone.   (Ibid. 42)

Implicit in this view, of course, was the idea that human beings had implanted in them "by nature" a set of general requirements and standards of behavior, both formal and substantive, according to which the internal appraisal of one's own acts and character is conducted.

Second, the conscience referred to specific acts—it is practical in being preoccupied with the circumstantial details of action. And third, the regnant image is exclusively judicial. The reference is always to reviewing *past* acts in order to determine guilt or innocence (ibid. 42–43). The judicial image extends to the function of sentencing for culpable misdeeds, and the punishment is, of course, the "pangs" of conscience.

These characteristics underlie Paul's appropriation of the concept in his Epistles, as they underlie the entire Western tradition. But, as Eric D'Arcy points out, Paul innovated in two crucial respects.[9] In his discussion in 1 Corinthians of the pros and cons of eating meat, Paul suggests, first, that the conscience is not only judicial—after the fact, but also "legislative" (deliberative), or before the fact. One now is understood to struggle with one's conscience in anticipation of future action. Second, conscience is, as Paul's mention of a "doubtful, uneasy conscience" (1 Corinthians 8:7) implies, taken to be subject to error. The condition of fallibility leads to the idea of "erroneous conscience" that was to become so important in the later development of tolerance and freedom of conscience, as we shall see.

In addition, Paul reinforces and fills out somewhat the assumptions that were packed into the Roman and popular Greek notion of conscience. In Romans 2:14–15, he stresses the natural-moral grounds of conscience that are available to all human beings, Jew and Gentile alike. For example, in Romans 3:19 Paul emphasizes that these grounds are assumed to be objective and universal: according to him, "every mouth may be stopped and the whole world may be held accountable to God." Finally, Paul draws attention to some of the particular requirements of what, out of the Western tradition, we have come to call "conscientiousness," namely the virtues of sincerity, veracity and perseverance (see, for example, 2 Corinthians 2:12ff).[10]

Much of significance in the development of the idea of conscience took place during the Middle Ages. The Catholic Scholastic disputes[11] laid the groundwork for the influential analysis of conscience by Thomas Aquinas. Two major features of his view need to be highlighted: his description of conscience, and the kind and degree of freedom or sovereignty he believed it to have.

As to its character, Thomas Aquinas (henceforth for convenience referred to simply as Thomas) argued that conscience consisted essentially of *a rational act* by which an individual undertakes to apply the first principles of the natural-moral law—what he called *synderesis* (borrowing from the Greeks)—to particular circumstances in which an individual is called upon to do or not do something. Thus, the conscience has a *cognitive and logical feature*: It assumes and draws upon indubitable first moral principles, and it has the capacity to identify and distinguish among objects and relations in the world, and it is able to apply the principles to the world according to commonly available canons of rationality. Moreover, since the conscience, so to speak, addresses and seeks to guide the will, it also has a *conative feature*. Finally, as the conscience in its judicial role can convict its owner of wrong-doing and cause remorse and the experience of guilt, it has an *affective feature*.[12]

Now it is important to note that Thomas intentionally provides us with at least the outlines of a normative model of the conscience. That is, if one's first principles are in order, if they are conscientiously, correctly and consistently applied to the circumstances of a given case, and if the will, having heard the recommendation of the conscience, knowingly and deliberately—which is to say, freely—acts upon it, and, next, if the affections register favorably as they should, then this is an example of a righteous act, one conducted fully in accord with conscience. And, as he says, a correct conscience "binds absolutely."[13]

But of course deviations and mistakes at various points are possible. If, for example, one reasons conscientiously, accurately, and consistently from first principles, but for some reason, chooses not to act on the recommendation despite the visitation of pangs of guilt, one has what Thomas called a "weak conscience." Or, a person may make cognitive and logical mistakes in instructing the will. One may, in one of his more outrageous examples, properly intend to observe the moral rule against adultery, but in the act of sexual intercourse mistake another woman for one's wife! Or a person may mistakenly believe with the heretics that God regards all oaths as wrong, or, still again, one may do something under the false impression that it will have good effects. Finally, one may reason fallaciously in arriving at certain practical conclusions.

People who make mistakes of this sort have erroneous consciences. The error involved may be *culpable* or *inculpable*, depending on whether it is the result of negligence or willfulness of some kind. If it is, then the mistake is inexcusable and the person making it is held responsible. But if it is not then the person in error is held to be in "invincible ignorance," and is excused from blame. The difficulty of knowing for sure when someone is acting willfully or negligently in face of error has some important consequences for his attitude toward religious liberty and freedom of conscience, as we shall see (ibid. art. 2).

In any case, an inculpably erroneous conscience is morally binding and must be respected as such. In other words, from an observer's point of view, a person judged to have an erroneous conscience is still bound to follow that conscience, so long as the observer is convinced that the alleged ignorance is invincible.

This point is important for understanding the sort of freedom Thomas Aquinas extends to those who hold conscientious beliefs. For him, it seems that a person's will is totally dependent upon the recommendations for action put to it by the conscience. The will is above all morally bound to act upon such recommendations, providing of course the person is conscientious. In fact, for Thomas, this sort of choice by the will is the only truly *free* choice. But that means, as D'Arcy points out, that:

> if reason presents an [inculpably] false picture, the will cannot be blamed; there is only one standard for judging it: the good as apprehended [by reason]. If [the will] fails to live up to that, its only standard, its performance is bad. But if it is faithful to its only standard, its performance is surely good.[14]

The argument obviously moves in the direction of tolerating conscientiously held beliefs and actions with which one may profoundly disagree.

The argument becomes sharpened somewhat in specific reference to religious belief. To begin with, Thomas claims that unbelievers who have never been Catholics must not be coerced into joining the church (ibid. 160).

> The argument is very simple. The act of faith is essentially a free act; without an interior, free choice of the will there is no valid act of faith at all. It is therefore not lawful to use compulsion in any way to force Jews or pagans to accept the Christian faith. With regard to making the initial act of faith, St. Thomas accepts St. Augustine's principle, "A person can do other things against his will; but belief is possible only in one who is willing." A man may sign a contract, join a firing-squad, pronounce an oath of allegiance, without any interior consent; but *unwilling belief is an impossibility. The only valid act of faith is that which proceeds from a free, interior choice.* (ibid. 153–54; italics added)

And Thomas Aquinas is thoroughly consistent on this point:

> Belief in Christ is, of itself, something good, and necessary for salvation. But if one's reason presented it as something evil one's will would be doing wrong in adopting it. (ibid. 156)

This is a particularly arresting statement. He clearly asserts that it is conceivable for someone to reject Christian belief *blamelessly*, at least from a human point of view, because of invincible ignorance. The Christian will not agree with the nonbeliever, but he should, nevertheless, honor the conscientiousness of unbelief, and forbear from any coercive intervention. Deep matters of conscience are beyond a human outsider's control; they are so profoundly private and personal that they are strictly between the individual and God. It ought to be added that Thomas does permit force against uninitiated unbelievers, but only as defensive counterforce against persecution. Unprovoked coercion against peaceful unbelievers would not be justified. (ibid.)

In many ways, this is a remarkable view for the intellectual leader of the Church of the High Middle Ages to have held. Its implications are quite radical. But he did not see those implications through. In fact, he seems to have contradicted them at several points. In a way that is reminiscent of much Islamic teaching, Thomas Aquinas drew a sharp distinction between uninitiated unbelievers, on the one hand, and apostates and heretics, on the other. While the first group might not be coerced against their consciences, the second group could be. Heretics and apostates, he writes, "at one time professed the faith and accepted it; they must be compelled even by physical force, to carry out what they promised and to hold what they once accepted" (ibid. 159). The argument (in part like the Muslim one) is that promises once made may be enforced by the state, if necessary. This case therefore constitutes an exception in his mind to tolerating ordinary unbelievers. It is important to notice, in passing, that his argument in favor of this sort of exception is not very convincing. If it is wrong, as he argues, to will to believe, or to act as though one did believe in Christ, when one's reason presents that belief as something mistaken, then it is surely wrong, on his own terms, to go on willing in that way if for some reason one has ceased to believe, or has changed one's beliefs.

The matter of freedom of religion and conscience is left in this state of ambiguity up through the Renaissance and Reformation. It was the leftish Protestants in France, Holland, England, and (later) America in the late sixteenth and seventeenth centuries who led the way in working out the modern notions.

Of all those struggling for religious liberty in the early modern period, Roger Williams was especially significant. He was so significant both because he elaborated and developed the Catholic tradition of freedom of conscience, and because he had such an influence on the formulations of the American documents of religious liberty, such as the Constitution and the Virginia Statute for Religious Freedom (1786). Documents like these provided, of course, the models for contemporary international statements.

Williams' views, which led to his experiment in religious liberty at Rhode Island, were the source for Isaac Backus and the Separate Baptists in their drive to provide for the separation of church and state in the United States Constitution. Moreover, the similarities and parallels between Williams' views and those of John Locke, especially in respect to religious liberty and freedom of conscience are incontestable, and Locke, in turn, directly influenced Thomas Jefferson and others in these matters.[15]

Although he was a Puritan, and thus a child of the Reformed or Calvinist side of the Reformation, Williams, like his Puritan associates, shared many of Thomas Aquinas' convictions concerning the conscience. He simply pushed the more liberal arguments we have sketched to their inevitable conclusions. To begin with, Williams, like Thomas, believed that conscience was the seat of individual freedom and sovereignty. Conscience properly acted as a private monitor in respect to the basic beliefs and the practical guidance that followed from those beliefs. Again like Thomas, one is truly free only when one's will is allowed to be bound by the dictates of conscience. In fact, conscience is not something one can altogether help. It constrains a person often beyond one's immediate wishes and preferences. And yet, conscience compels with the force of authority; it has in some deep sense the individual's final and free consent. It is not, therefore, like other compulsions that pathologically drive us against our "better judgment." As with Thomas, conscience involves and integrates all aspects of self: reason, will, and affections.

Accordingly, there is established a presumption against outside interference, especially of a coercive sort. Williams' view is thoroughly (liberal) Thomist here: 'Unwilling belief is an impossibility.' To try to determine an individual's basic commitments, or to disturb the practical inferences conscientiously drawn from them, by means of compulsion, is an affront to the fundamental structure of the self.

As we see, none of this is particularly new. Williams' signal innovation in respect to modern formulations of liberty of conscience is to tie all this to a crucial distinction between morality and religion. Initially, even this move is not totally at odds with Thomas. Williams affirms the existence of certain fundamental moral truths that he assumes are objectively and universally binding. They constitute the natural law that is imprinted upon the human psyche. Thomas would have called these the constitutive features of *synderesis*. For Williams, they are the fundamental requirements of social cooperation: non-maleficence, truth-telling and promise-keeping, at least limited beneficence (duty of mutual aid), and a standard of justice and reciprocity. In addition, Williams assumes some standard canons of reasonableness and conscientiousness, according to which the application of these basic moral duties may be assessed. These natural-moral duties are, so to speak, the inalterable conditions of conscience and will. The systematic repudiation of any one of them could not be an act of conscience or of "free will." Deliberately to inflict severe suffering and injury upon an innocent person for fun of it, or for other purely self-serving reasons, has to be regarded as always and everywhere wrong. The interpretation and application of these basic duties may of course vary, but Williams assumes a fixed, commonly recognizable core.

For this reason, these duties may properly be enforced by the state. They establish what Williams calls the basis for the "law civil and moral." By undertaking to enforce these duties, the state is not, on Williams' view, interfering with conscience. It is rather keeping the fences in repair within which conscience may do its job. The state may perform this function well or poorly, but if it did not do the job at all, there could be no freedom of conscience.

Now with religion things are different. Religion concerns a person's fundamental beliefs about the world, and about life and destiny, which are peculiarly intimate and "self-involving." Religion, as Williams understood it, calls upon the deepest dedication and commitment of each individual. Religious devotion is something no one else can supply for another. It was precisely out of his respect for the importance of religious belief and commitment as the mark of an individual's self-conception that Williams sought both in theory and in practice to hedge it about against coercive interference, and against depriving citizens of their "natural civil rights and liberties" on account of their religious convictions (ibid. esp. 13–14).

Actually, Williams was doing little more here than tightening up and taking the consequences of Thomas' notion of erroneous conscience. Williams had his own decided theological convictions—they were strongly, if sometimes deviantly, Calvinist. He did not agree with the religious views of the American Indians or "pagans," as he called them, nor with the "Mohammedans" (as he called them), nor "Papists," nor many other Protestants, such as the Quakers. He frequently and in detail made known his objections to some of these groups; he regarded many of them as seriously in error. But for all the above reasons they had a right to their error; they were excused from punishment and compulsion in matters of religious belief and practice. As Williams puts it in an interesting remark: "This conscience is found in all mankind, more or less [more or less erroneously, that is] in Jews, Turks, papists, Protestants, pagans, etc.," and it ought to be respected accordingly.[16]

Williams was not altogether insensitive to the points of possible difficulty in deciding just when a practice inferred from a religious belief was no longer simply erroneous, and therefore excusable and permissible, and when it was an impermissible violation of the basic moral duties of the natural law. He mentions, for example, that child sacrifice, even though practiced on grounds of conscience in Peru, constitutes such an impermissible violation (ibid.). Williams was probably not as attentive as he should have been in this regard to providing guidelines for distinguishing permissible from impermissible acts in hard cases. Still, one clear and usable prescription does emerge from Williams' thought in this context. It is that, given the character of conscience, the burden of proof rests with those who would compel the conscience. They must show cause for their coercion; they must provide reasons that live up to very demanding standards. They must, in short, be exceptionally conscientious in justifying compulsion in religion, for the presumption is strongly against them.

THE ISLAMIC TRADITION AND RELIGIOUS LIBERTY: COMPARATIVE REFLECTIONS ON THE QUR'ĀN

We may now proceed to compare with some care these observations concerning the Western Christian tradition with Muslim teaching. We shall try to show that contrary to first appearances, Muslim teaching is not by any means systemically antagonistic to the Western concepts of liberty of conscience and religion. In fact, there is strong evidence that this tradition assumes and operates according to some of the key ideas we discovered in Thomas Aquinas and Roger Williams. We shall further try to show that many of the differences between the Western human rights tradition and Islam can be accommodated and illuminated within the framework provided by the idea of erroneous conscience.

As we saw, the Western Christian notion of conscience assumes the existence of certain objective universal and commonly or rationally available moral duties that make up what is regarded as natural law. These are, of course, believed to exist independent of God's special revelation and to be apprehensible by human beings apart from it. Indeed, unless a natural law as a fixed basis for conscience were presupposed, one important reason for risking freedom and diversity of conscience would be eliminated. Moreover, the Western tradition assumes some degree of logical as well as cognitive capacity in determining and applying these natural-moral requirements. As we know, the words, "some degree," are important. The idea of erroneous conscience rests on the belief that human beings are rational enough to be held accountable, but fallible enough frequently to be mistaken in their judgments.

Similarly, the Islamic tradition confirms the existence of a natural or non-scriptural knowledge in matters of ethics, and asserts the capacity of human beings to reason and act in accordance with this knowledge—to "some degree." The Qur'ān itself points to such knowledge in a text such as 91:7–8, which speaks of the soul or self and God who "perfected it and inspired it (with conscience of) what is wrong for it and (what is) right for it."[17] Perhaps less directly, though no less significantly, the Qur'ān often uses moral terms in ways that suggest that the ordinary language of its hearers would recognize the meanings. For example, in speaking of the wrongness of *zulm*, or "injury," the Qur'ān appears to assume that ordinary persons will understand the claim being made and the type of action intended.[18] The purpose of the Qur'ānic appeal in such cases does not seem to be the revelation of new moral knowledge; rather, the text points to the relationship between what is already known and the one God who creates the world, judges it, and demands true faith.

Perhaps more significantly for our discussion, there is ample evidence from the developed tradition of Islam to support this contention. Just as notions of natural law and conscience may be traced throughout the Western-Christian tradition, so in Islam one finds that the "natural law" tendencies in the Qur'ān have been the subject of intense debate throughout the centuries. One might characterize the development of an idea of religious liberty in the West as the product of an ongoing conversation between the "basic texts" of the New Testament and various interpreters responding to the texts, as well as to one another. Similarly, the tradition of Islam includes conversations between various thinkers and schools attempting to respond to and understand the Qur'ānic text throughout the centuries.

To illustrate this, one can refer to the debate over the nature of "guidance" (*hudan, hidāya*), particularly as it developed in the classical period of Islamic culture, but also in relation to important figures in modern Islam.[19] The classical period was dominated, with respect to this debate, by the discussions within and between the two great movements centered on *Kalām* or "dialectical theology": i.e., the Mu'tazila and the Ash'ariyya.[20] Of particular importance for our comparative reflections are the ways in which important figures within these schools of thought reflected on the Qur'ānic text through the medium of the *tafsīr* or "Qur'ān commentary."[21] As is well known, the Mu'tazili approach to such interpretive activity was based on a metaphorical approach, developed in connection with certain dogmatic positions. These may be summarized as (1) the thesis that human beings, as free agents, are responsible before a just God; and (2) the thesis that good and evil are rational categories which can be grasped independently of revelation. According to the Mu'tazila, God created the human intellect in such a way that it is capable of distinguishing good and evil, even without the aid of a Scripture or "Book." For the Mu'tazila, this is a fact required by the first thesis, for God's justice depends on good and evil being "objective"—i.e., available to reason, and not subject to changes or alterations by the will of moral agents—even that of the Divine Lawgiver. This position, as a way of responding to the Qur'ānic text, was best developed by Maḥmūd b. 'Umar al-Zamakhsharī (d. 1144 C.E.).[22] His commentary has exercised great influence in the tradition of Islam, although a number of his theological inferences have typically been regarded as suspect (as have those of the Mu'tazili school in general).

The Mu'tazili position was bound to be challenged. As a contemporary student of Qur'ānic ethics, the late George Hourani, pointed out, the question of just how extensive the notion of "natural guidance" is in the Qur'ān, is a difficult one to adjudicate.[23] It is not surprising, then, that the Ash'ariyya would develop a position opposed to the Mu'tazila, arguing that natural reason is an inadequate source of knowledge in matters of ethics. They maintained, instead, that good and evil are as God decrees them to be, and that it is presumptuous to judge God on the basis of any 'independent' or 'non- revelational' standards. For the Ash'arite there is no way, within the bounds of ordinary logic, to explain the relation of God's power to human actions. It is more realistic just to maintain that everything that happens is the result of God's will, without explanation or justification. Lest human action be stripped of its moral significance, however, the Ash'ariyya developed the notion of *kasb* or 'acquisition.' According to this notion, God alone creates all actions. But in some actions (those which have a moral component) a special quality is added (by God's will) which makes the agent responsible. The success of the notion may be debated; for our purposes, what is most significant is that even with this notion, which appears to be an attempt to safeguard freedom and responsibility, the sovereignty of the Divine Will is stressed.[24]

Guidance, in terms of human knowledge and motivation, is the result of this Will. And it is this Will which is the basis of any notion of value. Subsequently any Qur'ānic notion of 'natural guidance' would appear to be undermined, as the stress is on the way(s) that God, in His mercy, has made a declaration of His Will in the text of the Qur'ān. In terms of Qur'ānic commentary, the leading exponent of these notions during the classical period was Fakhr al-Dīn al-Rāzī (d. 1209 C.E.). His commentary marks the high point of Ash'arite exegetical work, and is remarkable in the breadth of its scholarship and influence.[25]

With respect to the question before us, namely, "Does the Islamic tradition witness to the existence of a 'natural law' which can be helpfully connected with 'conscience'?" the position of the great commentators of these two schools may be discovered in their treatment of the problem of "guidance." The central points for this discussion may be outlined in a diagram.

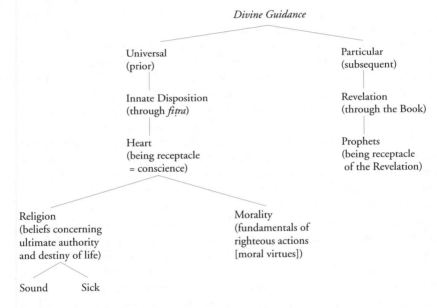

The first point to be made, following the outline in the figure, is that the great commentators of both schools distinguished two forms of guidance. One notes, for example, their discussions of 2:2: "that is the Book wherein is no doubt, a guidance to the godfearing." Why, the commentators ask, should the Book (that is, the Qur'ān) be described as "a guidance to the godfearing"? Such persons have already apprehended guidance in some form, else they could not be "godfearing." According to al-Rāzī and al-Zamakhsharī, the Book is God's provision for believers; a guidance which aids them as they encounter unbelievers and hypocrites. There is a guidance which is "prior" to faith, however; and this guidance is given to human beings *as such*. Whether one is a member of a community addressed by the Book or not, one cannot escape the claims of this "universal," even "natural" guidance.[26]

The source of this universal guidance in human beings the Qur'ān calls *fiṭra*, by which is indicated that aspect of humanity which makes one a responsible creature, capable of choice.[27] At 30:30, the Qur'ān addresses Muḥammad:

> So set thy face to the religion, a man of pure faith —
> God's original [*fiṭra*] upon which he originated mankind.

According to al-Rāzī and al-Zamakhsharī, *al-fiṭra* denotes the capacity of human beings to affirm the oneness of God—though they differ as to the nature of this capacity in connection with the theological tenets of their respective schools. The point that there is a universal guidance which is known to humanity through "natural" means (the *fiṭra* being human nature as created by God) cannot, however, be denied.

In one sense, what is spoken of in connection with *al-fiṭra* is closely akin to the Thomistic *synderesis*. The *fiṭra* is interpreted, especially by al-Zamakhsharī, as equivalent to *al-khilqa*, a "natural disposition" or "capacity" to affirm fundamental truth. There is a concurrence, he says, between the *fiṭra* and reasoning, especially the reasoning indicated by "sound opinion" (*al-naẓar al-ṣaḥīḥ*). One grasps the "first principles" of reasoning through *al-fiṭra*—or one might say that *al-fiṭra* indicates the inherent ability of human beings to reflect on their experience and to arrive at a knowledge of the truth.

For that ability to be actuated in any given case, however, human beings must reason from "first principles" to conclusions. Or, to put it another way, they must bring together two types of data—that of their experience, and that of *synderesis* or *fiṭra*. For Thomas Aquinas, the making of this connection is an act of *conscientia*. For the Qur'ān, as understood by al-Rāzī and al-Zamakh-sharī, it is *al-qalb*, "the heart." Thus, the heart, which is technically the "seat" of consciousness of thoughts, volitions and feelings, indicates the way in which persons draw upon those capacities signified by *al-fiṭra* and undertake to reflect on experience.

Of course, for Thomas, *synderesis* indicates the first principles of *practical* reason, and *conscientia* is the procedure by which one reaches *practical* judgments. It is not speculative or scientific truth that is the aim of *synderesis/conscientia*, but judgment in the sense proper to ethics. Similarly with *al-fiṭra/al-qalb* as developed in the commentaries of al-Rāzī and al-Zamakhsharī, the "universal guidance," which is available to humanity by virtue of *al-fiṭra* and which comes to consciousness in relation to particular experiences through the "heart," is ethical. It has to do with that which is the right or the good in human conduct—as the Qur'ān has it, with that which characterizes the "successful" or the "godfearing" person.

The general Qur'ānic position as to the good in human conduct is clear. Over and over again, the "successful," the "godfearing," are described as those who "believe and do good works." "Belief" or *al-īmān* is, at its most basic level, an assent to the oneness of God—a "reckoning of God as righteous," or as "truthful." And "good works" express those types of action which are or ought to be conjoined with such belief, as in 2:177:

> . . . righteous is he who believeth in Allāh and the Last Day and the Angels and the Scripture and the Prophets; and giveth his wealth, for love of Him, to kinsfolk and to orphans and the needy and the wayfarer and to those who ask, and to set slaves free; and observeth proper worship and payeth the poor-due. And those who keep their treaty when they make one, and the patient in tribulation and adversity and time of stress. (translated by Pickthall)

As has been said, this general description of the "good" seems clear enough. It becomes less so if one asks how the particular attributes of the righteous mentioned here are connected with that universal guidance symbolized in *al-fiṭra*, however. In particular, al-Rāzī and al-Zamakhsharī disagree over the relation of universal guidance to a knowledge of those *moral* virtues which are included in the description of the righteous—giving to kinsfolk, for example, and keeping of treaties. This disagreement, which is characteristic of the Ashʿari-Muʿtazili schools as a whole, is of great significance, especially given our earlier assessment of the connection between natural law morality and ideas of religious liberty in Western Christian thought.

Thus, al-Rāzī (and the Ashʿariyya in general) view the guidance given through *al-fiṭra* as that which compels a person to faith.[28] Reflection on the creation—its order, and in general its existence—indicates the power and wisdom of a Sovereign Creator and Governor who is unique in being one and eternal. Further reflection leads to the affirmation that this Being is ever-speaking and ever-willing, demonstrating its continuous Lordship over creation. The proclamation of this Lordship, the demonstration of the all-encompassing will of God through a uniquely authoritative word or speech—this is prophecy, such as was given to Muḥammad in the Qur'ān. And one's reasoning capacity (*al-qalb*) working in connection with universal guidance (*al-fiṭra*) compels one to acknowledge that the Qur'ān is authoritative.

The significant point for our discussion is that this view makes no connection between universal guidance and basic moral understanding. Indeed, the Ashʿarite position on this is quite explicit: *al-fiṭra* leads to the affirmation that God is one, and that Muḥammad is God's prophet. But the values which serve to establish and evaluate rightness in action (i.e., *al-ahkam*) are the result of God's willing, and are apprehended when one hears God's speech. Revealed texts, not natural reason, are the measure of rightness in action.[29]

The Mu'tazili view is quite different. For al-Zamakhsharī and others, faith must be connected with justice (*al-'adl*). Indeed, a basic understanding of justice is prior to any true affirmation of faith, since God is just by definition, and faith ought not be put in any revelation that does not point to this. Revelation such as that found in the Qur'ān is, by and large, construed as confirming that which is known by natural reason, or as enhancing the appeal to follow natural guidance by proclaiming that Divine sanctions are attached to it. There is, of course, some sense in which revelation establishes criteria of rightness in actions previously unknown to reason. This is so in the sense that a text like the Qur'ān, given to a particular community, establishes a set of practices which help to cultivate a disposition to do the good. In this connection, primarily thinking about religious disciplines such as *al-ṣalāt* (obligatory prayers) or the fast of Ramadan, the Mu'tazila could speak of revelation as establishing the goodness of an act which, while natural reason alone could not perceive it, nonetheless commends itself to reason as good upon reflection on the purposes of revelation.[30]

Which position one takes in this debate is of crucial import in questions of religious liberty, as shall be shown below. Before proceeding to such discussion, however, it is worth noting the predominance of the Ash'arite theory during the classical period. For reasons which cannot be elucidated here, the Mu'tazili version of the nature of guidance came to have the character of a "minority report" in classical, Sunnī Islam.[31] Nevertheless, it has had a significant impact on a number of Muslim reformers in the nineteenth and twentieth centuries— one might say this view has enjoyed a revival, especially among important Sunnī thinkers such as Sayyid Ahmad Khan of India and Muḥammad 'Abduh in Egypt. Speaking of the nature of guidance, the former expresses a view which is quite consonant with the Mu'tazili emphasis on natural reason:

> There is no lawgiver other than He. Yet this does not imply that He blindly issues nonsensical and useless laws. Thus it is an absurd belief to hold that the recompense or punishment for good or bad or any actions is by reason of the order of God and His command or prohibition. Rather the goodness or badness of things and the recompense or punishment of any action is founded on the . . . law of nature and the commandments of God are what this law of nature declares. Thus there are actions the goodness or badness of which human reason can recognize straightaway and there are others, the goodness or badness of which reason accepts only after (having heard) the news from the messengers sent by God Most High."[32]

In a more complex way, Muḥammad ʿAbduh argues for a distinction between four types of guidance: that given through instinct, as for example in the propensity of infants to avoid pain and seek survival; that given through sensory perception; that given through reason, which enables human beings to live in an ordered society; and that given through prophecy. Of special interest to us are the third and fourth types, and the relations between them.[33]

Specifically, ʿAbduh indicates that the guidance which comes through reason is relevant to the social life of human beings—it includes what one might call "moral" and "political" understanding. It is basic to humanity as such, and therefore is equivalent to the universal guidance we have been speaking of. Such guidance is not infallible, however. The reason is as capable of error as the senses, and one can wrongly direct one's reason toward the lesser appetites. It is when this misdirection becomes characteristic of a people that revealed guidance becomes important, says ʿAbduh. In effect, it comes to their aid by demonstrating their error. It is the light which brings a people out of their self-created darkness. In addition, revelation enhances one's awareness that there is more to one's behavior than current rewards and punishments—the future resurrection and the Day of Judgment add force to the guidance available to reason. Revealed guidance is 'particular" in being addressed to specific peoples; it is "subsequent" in following on that guidance which is universal. Yet it is necessary for human flourishing, so that one ought to pray: "Guide us in the straight path" (1:5), meaning "Help us by divine aid so that we remain protected from being misguided and committing errors" (1:62–65).

Having established the existence of an idea of universal guidance/conscience in the Islamic tradition parallel to the natural law/conscience idea of Western Christianity, we may now proceed to a discussion of the *status* of personal conscience in Islam. Are there ways in which the Islamic tradition establishes the right of conscience in matters of religion?

The evidence of the Qurʾān and of significant contributors to this tradition indicates that our answer must be "yes." No reader of the Qurʾān can possibly escape the message, repeated again and again, that faith and unfaith, belief and unbelief, are matters which are properly the concern of God, not of any human authority. To the Prophet, concerned with the lack of response to his preaching, the Qurʾān speaks:

> And if thy Lord had willed, whoever is in the earth would have believed, all of them, all together. Wouldst thou [O Muḥammad] then constrain the people, until they are believers? *It is not for any soul to believe save by the leave of God;* and He lays abomination upon those who have no understanding.   (10:99–100)

Thus, even the prophet, the bearer of revelation, is not to use his power (in particular, his military-political power) to compel faith. It is *God* who grants or withholds the gift of faith, either making the heart (or "conscience") receptive, or hardening it. This being the case, it is correct to say that, for the Qur'ān, as for Western Christianity, religious devotion is something nobody can supply for anyone else. In its most succinct statement of this theme, the Qur'ān declares: "There is no compulsion in religion" (2:256).

It is this verse, and the general theme crystallized in it, that give rise to strong tendencies in Islam toward freedom of conscience in religion. For the Mu'tazilite al-Zamakhsharī, for example, 10:99 (see above) indicates that persons are to choose freely in the matter of faith.[34] Indeed, all humanity is considered to stand before God, responsible for choices made in the light of universal guidance working through conscience. That is also true for neo-Mu'tazili thinkers such as Muḥammad 'Abduh and Sayyid Ahmad Khan. For the former and certain of his disciples, the Qur'ān and the tradition it has engendered suggest the formation of a polity which, while informed by Islam, certainly allows for religious pluralism.[35] And the thought of Sayyid Ahmad Khan almost certainly lies behind certain statements made by the Pakistani foreign minister at the United Nations in 1948. Regarding Article 18 of the Universal Declaration of Human Rights, which establishes rights to freedom of conscience in religion, the representative of the new state declared that

> neither faith nor conscience which gave birth to it, could have an obligatory character. The Koran expressly said: "Let he who chooses to believe, believe, and he who chooses to disbelieve, disbelieve," and it formally condemned not lack of faith but hypocrisy.

Contrary to Saudi Arabia and other Islamic nations, Pakistan would thus vote for Article 18, and would "brook no lessening of its provisions."[36]

However, it must also be said that Islam as a tradition also contains elements which contradict this evidence of respect for the right of conscience in religious matters. Or, perhaps more accurately, there are strong tendencies in Islam to restrict the right of conscience by means of a variety of institutions. Among these one would include the *dhimmī* system and the laws regarding apostasy (see above). Where did these provisions come from, and what is their status, given the evidence that exists for a doctrine of freedom of conscience in Islam?

In order to understand such tendencies to limit the right of conscience in matters of faith, one may recall our earlier discussion of the Mu'tazilite–Ash'arite schools and their dominant tendencies. Even with the agreement of such leading exegetes as al-Rāzī and al-Zamakhsharī on such notions as the two types of guidance (universal and particular) and the existence of conscience (*al-qalb*), very important differences remain between the two schools. For al-Rāzī and the Ashʿariyya, universal guidance is that which *compels* a person to acknowledge the oneness of God. And that acknowledgement is, as has been shown, the very foundation of moral knowledge, since it is the command of God given through particular, revealed guidance that constitutes the criterion by which good and evil may be distinguished. That being the case, the conscience which professes faith in a true prophet is "sound" (see diagram), and is the guarantor of personal justice—and thus, of the possibility of social order. Those who do not profess faith in the oneness of God have consciences which are "sick," and they must be coerced to a true confession — for their good and the good of the state.

It is in this vein that al-Rāzī and others have placed limits on the "no compulsion" theme summarized in 2:256. Al-Ṭabarī, for example, argues on the basis of several reports of Muḥammad's policy (*sunna*) that an Islamic state must tolerate the "People of the Book" so long as they accept "protected" (*dhimmī*) status.[37] As those who profess faith in God's oneness, these are of a "sound" conscience—though their failure to acknowledge Muḥammad as the Prophet of God means their judgment is only partially sound. For al-Ṭabarī and al-Rāzī, however, "associationists" or polytheists and apostates are in a different category. These have consciences that are "sick," and they are to be coerced into a profession of faith. Religion is the guarantor of morality, and thus to make faith a matter which is beyond the influence of the state, is to make the state's existence precarious.

These arguments have a distinctly Thomist ring about them, especially when one recalls the great doctor's discussion of heretics and apostates. According to Thomas, one may have an "erroneous" conscience due to various flaws in the process of reasoning about one's acts. Such flaws may be "inculpable," as in the case of Jews or pagans who cannot accept the truth of Christianity, and persons whose error is of this type are to be tolerated. On the other hand, there are culpable errors which ought not be tolerated; e.g., apostasy, which is a violation of a contract (with God) and involves a breach of moral truth so basic as to be unquestionably blameworthy. For al-Rāzī and al-Ṭabarī, one substitutes the "sick heart" for "erroneous conscience," so that the conclusion is: certain kinds of "sickness," as in the case of Jews or Christians, can be tolerated within any Islamic state. But the sickness of a polytheist or an apostate is different. Polytheism is a failure to recognize truths so basic as to destroy or negate *al-fiṭra*. And apostasy involves a breach of contract and therefore of a moral law revealed by God.[38]

Al-Rāzī and al-Ṭabarī certainly have their followers in the Islamic world today, and there is no denying their power. In the discussions of Article 18 of the Universal Declaration of Human Rights, the arguments of the Saudi ambassador have the distinct sound of this traditional heritage. This is particularly so in view of the version of Islam propagated by the Wahhābī movement, so significant in the religious and moral life of Saudi Arabia. Further, in the writings of such a widely read thinker as the Pakistani Abu'l- 'Alā Mawdūdī, one finds ideas very congenial to the traditional limitations on conscience in matters of religion.[39]

The point of this discussion is to say that the Ash'arite heritage in such matters is not the *only* one available to the tradition of Islam. Given the indisputable evidence for ideas of religious liberty in the Qur'ān and in important contributors to Islamic discussion of its verses, one can imagine a doctrine which emphasizes the moral aspects of universal guidance, and which views the existence of such knowledge as the possibility for good public order. Profession of God's oneness, while not an indifferent matter from the point of view of the Muslim community, could be affirmed as "beyond the competence" of the state. In this way, the "soundness" or "sickness" of the conscience could be viewed in *moral* terms—i.e., the "sound" conscience would be one which acknowledges and adheres to certain basic moral obligations (no murder, no theft, etc.), and the "sick" conscience would be one which fails to do so. Certainly, the "sick" conscience would still be subject to the power of the state.

But such power would be exercised vis-à-vis basic moral beliefs, whereas religious faith would be a matter beyond the state's control, with disagreement to be viewed in terms of an error which cannot be corrected by coercive force. That is, while it is not necessary to become "latitudinarian" or "indifferent" in religious matters, an Islamic state would emphasize that true faith is a gift of God, the outcome of God's work in the heart and thus beyond the reach of the power of the word. Such a position is in fact implied by al-Zamakhsharī when he argues, *contra* al-Rāzī and al-Ṭabarī, that the "no compulsion" theme which resounds in 2:256 applies to human beings *as such*, and cannot be limited to those "People of the Book" accepting *dhimmī* status.[40]

We do not suggest that this sketch of a doctrine of religious liberty is widely held in the Islamic countries at present; nor are we ignorant of its controversial nature. But it does seem to us to exhibit a greater respect for the Qur'ānic proclamation of religious liberty than does the Ash'arite doctrine; at the same time it allows for another element which is equally important to the Qur'ānic witness: the concern for a just public order. What we are suggesting is that "religion" and "morality" may be distinguished in Islam at least vis-à-vis state authority. And this fact leads us to believe that there is more of a basis for an Islamic affirmation of the right to religious liberty than has usually been acknowledged.

While descriptions of human rights documents as culturally biased and ethnocentric need to be taken seriously, we believe we have indicated some reasons for regarding such charges skeptically, or at least critically. There is a good deal of loose talk in the human rights field, and sometimes, it appears, the talk is as loose from the critics as from the advocates. This is no doubt understandable, but we need to begin to move to new levels of precision. We need to take up specific human rights prescriptions and test them in detail in relation to different cultural and political attitudes and responses. Then, perhaps, we can identify with some confidence specific points of divergence and similarity, and go on to figure out what in particular we should do about them.

We do not pretend that our account of deep and surprising parallels between the Western and the Islamic traditions has magically removed all tensions and strains. Even if we are right that the Islamic tradition, like the Western one, implies a strong burden of proof upon political authorities to show cause for compulsion in religious affairs, we are not so naive as to overlook the fact that there will still be deep differences, among other things, over what is to count as a sufficient justification in given circumstances for excusing the imposition of compulsion. What is regarded as a mortal threat in an Islamic society may not be so regarded in a Western liberal society. All that needs, in its own right, the most careful sort of exploration.

But our central point still stands, we believe: both traditions share a common framework within which to think about freedom of conscience and religious liberty, and many of the categories are mutually applicable in a most illuminating way. Thus, current human rights formulations, along with the important notions that underlie them, are by no means necessarily irrelevant to cultures outside the West. Granted, a comparison between two traditions does not prove anything to be universally true. But it is a start.

One last word about natural law. It is by now tedious to keep reminding ourselves that descriptive conclusions about cross-culturally shared values and modes of practical reasoning do not logically show that they are worth something. Still, anyone who is already committed on other grounds to a natural law view, is bound to be perplexed, if not undone, by encountering an elaborate and persistent cultural tradition that systematically denies and rejects what are taken in the natural law tradition to be moral requirements constitutive of being human—requirements such as Thomas Aquinas and Roger Williams espoused, like nonmaleficence, beneficence, truth-telling, promise-keeping, etc. It is therefore reassuring (though we admit, not conclusive) to discover in a tradition as apparently divergent as the Muslim one, so much underlying consensus on these basic requirements.

Notes

1. Adamantia Pollis and Peter Schwab, *Human Rights: Cultural and Ideological Perspectives* (New York: Praeger, 1979), p. 17.

2. Human Rights Documents, 98th Cong. 1st sess., 1983, Committee Print, 66.

3. James Piscatori, "Human Rights in Islamic Political Culture," *Moral Imperatives of Human Rights*, ed. Kenneth W. Thompson (Washington, D.C.: University Press of America, 1980), p. 145.

4. Qur'ānic citations in this essay are usually from Arberry, *The Koran Interpreted* (New York: Macmillan, 1955). When another edition is used, it is indicated. The authors have, on occasion, altered Arberry in accord with a more suggestive rendering of certain Arabic terms. In some instances they cite the translation of Mohammed Marmaduke Pickthall, *The Meaning of the Glorious Koran* (New York: Penguin Books USA, n.d.).

5. Majid Khadduri, *War and Peace in the Law of Islam* (Baltimore: John Hopkins University Press, 1955), 198.

6. C. A. Pierce, *Conscience in the New Testament* (London: SCM Press, 1955), pp. 21–22.

7. Eric D'Arcy, *Conscience and Its Right to Freedom* (London: Sheed and Ward, 1961), pp. 7–8.

8. C. A. Pierce, *Conscience in the New Testament*, pp. 21–22.

9. D'Arcy, *Conscience and Its Right to Freedom*, pp. 9–12.

10. John Kelsay, "Thoughts on the Pauline Understanding of Conscience," unpublished paper.

11. See Timothy C. Potts, *Conscience in Medieval Philosophy* (Cambridge: Cambridge University Press, 1980).

12. Thomas Aquinas discusses his theory of conscience in three places: his *Commentary on the Sentences* of Peter Lombard; *De Veritate*, Questions 16 and 17; and *Summa Theologica* 1.79. Eric D'Arcy's analysis of Thomas' theory of conscience in *Conscience and Its Right to Freedom* is most illuminating and helpful. This essay is indebted to D Arcy's account, though the framework just suggested is our own. For the distinction between *synderesis* and conscience in Thomas, cf. Potts' study (cited note 11). According to Potts, all the Catholic Scholastics made use of the Greek *sunteresis* (most often translated as *synderesis*) to indicate that element of conscience which is "natural" or "habitual" in human beings, and therefore cannot pass away. Thomas connects this knowledge of the first principles of the natural-moral law. As Potts puts it: "Aquinas regards [*synderesis*] as an innate rational disposition by which basic deontic premises are known to us without reasoning" (p. 46).

13. *De Veritate*, Question 17, art. 4.

14. D'Arcy, *Conscience and Its Right to Freedom*, pp. 117–18; italics added.

15. For a discussion of the connection between Roger Williams and Thomas Jefferson (author of the *Virginia Statute*) via both John Locke and Isaac Backus, see David Little,

"Roger Williams and the Separation of Church and State," *Religion and the State*, ed. James E. Wook, Jr. (Waco, Texas: Baylor University Press, 1985).

16. *Complete Writings of Roger Williams* (New York: Russell & Russell, 1963), 4:508–9.

17. Here, we use Pickthall. Arberry reads: "By the soul, and shaped it and inspired it to lawlessness and godfearing!"

18. See George Hourani's essay, "The Ethical Presuppositions of the Qur'ān," *The Muslim World* 70 (1980): 1–28.

19. *Hudan* and *hidāya* are identical in meaning except that in the usage of the Qur'ān *hudan* usually implies revelational guidance, i.e., regarding the Book and the religious ordinances (*al-Sharī'a*). *Hidāya* is more general in meaning and includes guidance in all matters, i.e., social, moral, and so on. It is used in the sense of *'arf* in its second form (*'arrafa*), meaning to apprise. This form is not used in the Qur'ān but was common in the Hijaz where the Qur'ān was revealed. See al-Turayhi, *Majma'al-bahrayn*, 1 (Najaf: 1959), p. 472; al-Zabidi, *Taj al-arus*, 10 (Kuwait: 1969), p. 406.

20. For historical information, see W. M. Watt, *The Formative Period of Islamic Thought* (Edinburgh: Edinburgh University Press, 1973). For an interpretation of certain aspects of the Mu'tazilite and Ash'arite movements in terms relevant to this discussion, see John Kelsay, "Religion and Morality in Islam: A Proposal Concerning Ethics in the Formative Period," Ph.D. dissertation, University of Virginia, 1985; these two movements emerged during the eighth and ninth centuries C.E.

21. For an introduction to *tafsīr*, see Mahmoud Ayoub, *The Qur'ān and Its Interpreters* (New York: State University of New York Press, 1984), vol. 1.

22. Zamakhsharī's commentary is known as *al-Kashshāf* (Cairo: al-Babi al-Halabi, 1968).

23. For example, in his essay on "The Ethical Presuppositions of the Qur'ān," see note 18.

24. See Kelsay, "Religion and Morality."

25. al-Rāzī, *al-Tafsīr al-Kabīr* (Cairo: al Babiyya al Misriyya, 1938).

26. This is so even for al-Rāzī, though "natural" guidance in the Western Christian sense, seems "foreign" to him at times. His terminology is often more suggestive of what Western theologians call "general" and "special" revelation. See *al-Tafsīr al-Kabīr*, 1:9 ff. Nevertheless, he can speak of natural faith (*al-īmān al-fiṭrī*), ibid., 25:120.

27. *Fiṭra* means "creation." The verb *fṭr* is used with this signification in the Qur'ān in 11:51: "O my people! I ask of you no reward for it. Lo! my reward is the concern of Him who created me (*faṭaranī*)" (Pickthall).

It has the meaning of "bringing something into existence, newly, for the first time." *Fiṭra* in the Qur'ān and *ḥadīth* literature signifies the natural constitution with which a child is created in its mother's womb; it also signifies the faculty of knowing God with which human' beings were created, and whereby a person acquires an "inherent capacity" or "innate disposition" to accept the religion of truth. See E. W. Lane, *Arabic-English Lexicon*, vol. 1, part 6, p. 2416.

28. *al-Tafsīr al-Kabīr* 25:121 ff.

29. Kelsay, "Religion and Morality."

30. Kelsay, "Religion and Morality," and the literature cited there.

31. On its relation to Shi'i doctrine, cf. A. A. Sachedina, *Islamic Messianism* (Albany: State University of New York Press, 1981).

32. From the translation given by Christopher W. Troll in *Sayyid Ahmad Khan: A Reinterpretation of Muslim Theology* (New Delhi: Vikas, 1978), p. 274.

33. 'Abduh's commentary was originally published in the journal *al-Manār* and was edited by his disciple, Rashīd Riḍā. See *Tafsīr al-Manār* (Cairo: 1968).

34. Zamakhsharī, *al-Kashshāf*, 1/387.

35. See Hamid Enayat, *Modern Islamic Political Thought* (Austin: University of Texas Press, 1982).

36. *U.N. Official Records*, 3d Session, 1948–49, Plenary 889–91. N.B.: In these *Records*, the foreign minister is quoted as speaking about Article 19, which has to do with freedom of speech. The numbering of the various articles was altered at several points during the committee and plenary discussions. It seems clear from the comments that the argument refers to the article on freedom of conscience (Article 18 in the final version). Certainly the Qur'ānic citations are referring to the issues of freedom of religion embodied in Article 18. Some interpreters of this discussion have noted that M. Zafrullah Khan was himself a member of the Ahmadiyyat sect, which many Muslims consider heterodox. For a discussion of the relationship between Ahmadiyyat views and themes in Sayyid Ahmad Khan's thought, see David Little, John Kelsay, and Abdulaziz Sachedina, *Human Rights and the Conflict of Cultures: Western and Islamic Perspectives on Religious Liberty* (Columbia: University of South Carolina Press, 1988), esp. pp. 33–52.

37. Al-Ṭabarī, *Tafsīr al-Ṭabarī*, 3:10–12. For al-Rāzī's comment, see *al Tafsīr al-Kabīr*, 4:15–16.

38. That there are also differences between Thomas Aquinas and al-Rāzī or al-Ṭabarī is clear. Thomas, for example, justifies the use of force against non-Christians in language that suggests defensive or counterforce strategy. al-Rāzī and al-Ṭabarī could, evidently, justify the use of offensive force to extend Islamic hegemony under certain conditions.

39. On this, as well as many other points in the present essay, see the authors' *Human Rights and the Conflict of Cultures: Western and Islamic Perspectives on Religious Liberty*. In addition, readers may wish to compare aspects of the argument presented here with Ann Elizabeth Mayer, *Islam and Human Rights: Tradition and Politics* (Boulder: Westview Press, 1991); Abdullahi An-Na'im, ed., *Human Rights in Cross-Cultural Perspectives: A Quest for Consensus* (Philadelphia: University of Pennsylvania Press, 1992); LeRoy Rouner, ed., *Human Rights and the World's Religions* (South Bend, Ind.: University of Notre Dame Press, 1988); and the ongoing work of the Project on Religion and Human Rights, based at Emory University in Atlanta, including *Religion and Human Rights*, ed. John Kelsay and Sumner B. Twiss (New York: 1994). See also the discussion of Mawdūdī's thought by Miriam Cooke and Bruce B. Lawrence, essay 12 in this volume.

40. Zamakhsharī, *al-Kashshaf*, 1:387.

Part Three

~

Religion and Rights in the
Contemporary World

9

HINDU NATIONALISM AND HUMAN RIGHTS

MARK JUERGENSMEYER

The rise of Hindu nationalism in India in the last decade of the twentieth century has been the occasion for a spirited public discussion of human rights. Within this discussion are questions about whether a concept that originated in the secular political theories of the Enlightenment has a home in the discourse of traditional religion, and whether it is compatible with an ideology of nationalism based on indigenous non-Western culture.

Before we can enter into this discussion, however, we have to be clear about what we mean by human rights and, for that matter, what we mean by Hindu nationalism. Regarding the former phrase, not only is "human rights" fuzzily defined in English, it does not easily translate into other languages. The term evolved in the West to indicate a respect for life and a resistance to oppression, and it has also come to mean a host of other things: legal due process, equal opportunities for minorities and women, freedom of the press, freedom of religion, free speech, and much more. When seen from a non-Western perspective, at the very most it means a libertarian attitude endorsing any expression of individual tastes, feelings, or desires, as obscene or heretical it might appear to the pious public eye. At the very least, from a non-Western point of view, it means those things that Amnesty International watches out for: the right to live free from physical intimidation and incarceration on account of one's political position or ethnic and religious affiliation. If this minimum definition is what is meant by "human rights"—the notion that people should be able to reside peacefully alongside each other, in dignity and with personal security—then virtually every religion embraces this ideal, albeit in its own terms.[1] One might find, as David Little has, "deep and surprising parallels" between other religions' notions of tolerance and one's own.[2]

The problem that many religious leaders have is not so much with the humane virtues implied by the term "human rights" as with the idea of rights itself: the notion that individuals possess, on their own, rights that do not come from the community or from God. Religious leaders in many parts of the world find unacceptable the notion that rights can be held by individuals rather than by groups. Such an idea connotes a society made up of individuals who are granted authority and independence, and whose "rights" are possessed at the expense of the integrity of the communal whole. Rather than using the term "rights," then, many religious leaders would rather describe the relationship between the individual and society in communitarian terms, as one of moral responsibility. As one religious conservative put it, "we have no rights, only duties and obligations."[3]

In a way the discussion over the term "human rights" is moot if societies respect the personal security and dignity that is at the heart of both secular "human rights" and the humane values of religion. It makes little difference if religious leaders give religious rather than secular reasons for their motivations as long as they affirm that a nation is obligated to uphold basic freedoms and regard everyone with dignity—the sorts of things that are listed in the United Nations Universal Declaration of Human Rights.[4]

The question is how deep this apparent compatibility goes. No matter how similar religious values and human rights might seem, the ideological basis for traditional religious values is not ultimately the same as the humanistic secular version. From a traditional communitarian point of view, the stark individualism and the laissez faire attitude toward personal expression run fundamentally counter to the spirit of collective loyalty and disciplined demeanor that is typically found in the religious life. It is unlikely, therefore, that religious traditionalists will ever fully adhere to the more extreme libertarian view, even though in many other ways they may look and talk like human rights advocates anywhere in the world. The fact is that the values of communal life that most traditionalists revere make most Westerners uncomfortable, and in some cases make them outraged. The differences are deep and abiding, and not easily resolved.

HINDU VALUES

The "human rights" espoused by Hindu nationalists provides a case in point. On one level Hindu nationalists can and do affirm the values of human rights.

Yet secular Indians, Westerners, and members of minority religious communities (Muslims, Christians, and Sikhs) remain suspicious.

The reason for their suspicion is well founded, for the concept of human values that Hindu nationalists affirm is invariably Hindu in character. Hindu nationalism is, after all, not just a political movement, but a political ideology based on a tradition of human values that runs deep in India's cultural history. Some would claim that these values define Hinduism itself. In traditional India, as in most traditional societies, there was no clear distinction between religion and the general culture of the region. Even the words "India" and "Hindu" are etymologically linked. Both terms were coined by outsiders to refer to the land and the people along the Indus River.[5] Today, of course, one can speak of "Hindus" as one among several religious communities in India, and the census takers can confidently state that 83 percent of the population is Hindu, 11 percent Muslim, 2.6 percent Christian, and slightly over 1 percent Sikh, with small communities of Jains, Parsis, and Buddhists. Yet all people and aspects of life in the subcontinent are affected by traditional Indian values.

The Indian term for these values is *dharma. Dharma* is sometimes compared with the Western notion of natural law, but there are several important differences. One, as we have just mentioned, is that the Hindu view lacks the Western emphasis on individualism. Another is that *dharma* emphasizes obligations that one holds rather than rights that one possesses or rules that one should follow. A third difference has to do with universality. Unlike rights, which are typically imputed to all persons at all times and places, dharmic obligations are particular: they vary from one stage of life to the next, and from one social group to another. At the heart of *dharma* is the notion that the individual's ethical responsibilities depend upon particular circumstances: age, gender, family connections, and so forth. In any social circumstance, *dharma* gives guidance as to what should be done.

We usually think of *dharma* in connection with caste, but there are other social roles that carry dharmic weight as well. Rulers, for example, are expected to observe *rajdharma*, the special obligations of those who rule, and the legitimacy of a ruler is in jeopardy if he or she is perceived as having abandoned dharmic standards.[6] There also exists the notion that each individual has his or her own dharma: *svadharma*, a sense of personal responsibility that sometimes—as in the *Bhagavad Gītā*) appears as a sort of moral conscience.[7] *Svadharma* is the heroic ideal of one's moral destiny. There are also dharmic codes underlying an individual's ordinary day-to-day moral behavior. South India's *Tirukkural*, for example, is a manual for individual morality.[8]

Hence *dharma* includes such a diversity of moral standards and ethical expectations that it can apply to virtually everyone, even those who are not Hindu, or even religious in a pious way. Even Muslims and Christians in India retain a sense of adherence to dharmic virtues. Dharmic Hinduism has remained unscathed in its cultural contacts in part because of its "tolerance"— a stance which is, in fact, an ability to absorb other points of view and ultimately to dominate them. What Ainslie Embree calls the "Brahmanical ideology" of high caste Hinduism has a way of swallowing up other ideologies and making them its own.[9]

Some scholars in India have argued that this cultural unity—which some call "Hindu," some "Hindutva," and others "traditional Indian values"—is the cultural base on which a noncolonial view of India's unity may be constructed. Ashis Nandy, for instance, looks to traditional Hindu values, not just as a faith but as "a way of life" that permeates traditional Indian culture.[10] T. N. Madan has made something of the same point in his critique of secularism in India. Although wary of "the real dangers of Hindu communalism," Madan has said that he and his fellow intellectuals in India have to "overcome our distrust of India's indigenous religious traditions."[11] His hope is that this substratum of traditional culture can become the basis for a new Indian unity. A similar hope has been expressed by Partha Chatterjee.[12] Thus some of India's leading intellectuals—virtually all of them Hindu—have yearned to embrace at least some aspects of Hindu cultural unity in India, albeit one shorn of stridency and intolerance. Not surprisingly, they have been deeply criticized by their colleagues, especially secularists, Westerners and Indians from minority Muslim backgrounds.[13]

The scholars' position is surprising to many modern Indians since modernity and secularism have been touted as being virtually synonymous. The Nehru legacy in independent India has been one of staunch opposition to the intrusion of religion into public life, and Nehru himself had regarded "communalism" along with superstition as one of the great threats to modern India and an impediment in its quest to become a developed state. Yet India's independence movement, although officially secular, preached nationalist loyalties in terms that carried echoes of Hindu cultural concepts, including dharmic obligations to society. The nationalist devotion to "mother India" incorporated some of the characteristics of worship of Hindu goddesses. Mohandas Gandhi attempted to forge a compromise between the religious and secular wings of the independence movement by applying Hindu ethical values to the nationalist movement. He adhered to a form of Hinduism that had wide appeal beyond its sectarian origins and he successfully applied religious concepts to political tactics in his use of what he called *satyagraha* ("the force of truth") and *ahimsa* ("nonviolence") in political conflict.

Not all Indian political leaders were enthusiastic about Gandhi's compromise with religion: Nehru and other secular nationalists, for example, felt uncomfortable with it, while Muslim leaders felt betrayed by it. Mohammad

Ali Jinnah and his Muslim League, suspicious of what they regarded as Gandhi's Hinduization of the nationalist movement, demanded that the British create a separate nation for Muslims. When the British withdrew from India in 1947 they carved Pakistan out of portions of Bengal in the east and sections of Punjab, Sindh, and other areas in the west. Jinnah was named Pakistan's first governor-general. Not all Muslims in the remainder of India moved to the areas designated as Pakistan, but eight million people did move from one side of the borders to the other, and as many as a million lost their lives in the communal rioting that occurred during the transition. Gandhi strongly protested the partition of the country and the communal hatred it unleashed. Militant Hindus felt that he had capitulated to the Muslims, and a former member of a radical Hindu organization, the Rashtriya Swayamsevak Sangh (RSS), assassinated Gandhi in 1948.

THE RISE OF HINDU NATIONALISM

Hindu nationalism kept a low profile in the first forty years of India's independence, but in 1991 the new, Hindu-leaning Bharatiya Janata Party (the BJP, or Indian People's Party) made a remarkable showing. It gained over 120 seats, making it the largest opposition party in India's parliament. It also gained control over several state governments, including the largest, Uttar Pradesh. These impressive gains were the crowning achievement of almost seventy years of Hindu nationalist efforts.

The major group supporting the BJP, the RSS, was founded in 1925 by middle-class Hindus in Maharashtra and Madhya Pradesh, many of whom had been associated with the Hindu reform movement, the Arya Samaj. The main mission of the RSS was to train young Hindu men to stand up to the temptations of secular society and revive the traditional values of Hindu India.[14] For years its chief activities consisted of weekly meetings in urban homes and summer camps that were similar to Boy Scout outings except for their nationalist religious ideology and training sessions in self-defense. Despite their Hindu rhetoric, the leaders of the movements were not priests and holy men and other traditional Hindu leaders, and the RSS did not—until recently—become a part of mainstream Indian society.

Nonetheless, the RSS set the standard and defined the terms of Hindu nationalism so effectively that they continue in force today. The ideas were shaped by the writings of Vinayak Damodar Savarkar, who called upon "the undying vitality of Hindu manhood" to assert itself "so vigorously as to make the enemies of Hindudom tremble."[15] Savarkar advanced the concept of *hindutva*, the idea that virtually everyone who has ancestral roots in India is a

Hindu and that collectively they constitute a nation.[16] It is on the basis of this idea that the RSS, in its Constitution, called upon all Hindus to "eradicate differences" and realize "the greatness of their past" in the "regeneration of Hindu society."[17] The RSS, like the Indian National Congress, opposed British rule, but never supported Nehru and his emphasis on secular nationalism.

When India became independent in 1948, Nehru proclaimed it a secular state and exhorted India to "lessen her religiosity and turn to science.[18] But the tension between secular and religious nationalism remained.[19] The gnawing suspicions about Hindu influence persisted among Sikhs, Muslims, and members of other minority communities, but the government appeared eager to dispel these and treat all religions equally. It protected and maintained religious institutions of all faiths; it allowed colleges sponsored by Sikhs and Muslims, as well as Hindus, to be incorporated into state universities; and it permitted aspects of traditional Islamic law pertaining to marriage, divorce, and inheritance to be applied to members of Muslim communities. Christians, and other minority religious communities were also given legal sanctions similar to those given the Muslims.

Despite the government's claims of impartiality, Hindu political leaders began to charge that the government was only "pseudo-secular," for it bent over backwards to support Muslims, Sikhs, and other minorities.[20] Members of minority religious communities, however, saw the situation the other way around: they felt that the government was implicitly Hindu. During the 1980s many Sikhs regarded Mrs. Gandhi and her Congress party as pandering to the interests of the Hindu right, and the rise of militant Sikhism during that decade was, in part, a response to what many Sikhs saw as the increasing Hinduization of Indian politics.

For their part, Hindu activists in the 1980s were devoted to the politicization of Hinduism. In 1981 they began organizing protests against what were reported to be mass conversions of lower caste Hindus to Islam at Meenakshipuram in South India. Allegedly large sums of money from the Islamic states in the Persian Gulf had been sent to India to encourage what was portrayed as raids on Hindu society. The secular government became a target for the Hindu leaders' wrath, since the state's policy of religious neutrality was read as being protective of these Muslim assaults. In 1983, a great "Procession for Unity" was organized by a group closely related to the RSS, the Vishva Hindu Parishad [World Hindu Council] or VHP. It brought over a million people to New Delhi in what has been proclaimed one of the largest political rallies in history.

The Hindu momentum expanded with another issue: control over the alleged birthplace of the god Ram. For many years, conservative Hindus had been incensed over the government's protection of a number of mosques which Mogul leaders over three centuries ago had built on the sites of Hindu temples. In 1984 the VHP called for a reassertion of Hindu control over a dozen of these. Chief among them was the Babri Mosque, built by a lieutenant of the emperor Babar on the location of a Hindu temple in the city of Ayodhya, which is traditionally identified as the home and capital of the God-king, Ram. At some point in history—exactly when is a debated issue—the site of the Babri Mosque was identified as none other than the birthplace of Ram. Soon after India's independence, during a time of Hindu–Muslim tensions, it is said that an image of Ram magically manifested itself in the abandoned mosque, so some Hindus insisted on worshiping there. Riots broke out between Muslims and Hindus over the use of the place and the government barred them both. In 1986, after the VHP demanded that Ram be liberated from what they called his "Muslim jail," a judge again opened the site for worship. Violent encounters between Muslims and Hindus soon ensued, with the VHP calling for the mosque to be destroyed or removed, and a new temple built in its place. By 1986 the VHP claimed to have over three thousand branches throughout India and over a million dedicated workers. It targeted for defeat politicians who it felt were unfaithful to the Hindu cause, and lobbied for pro-Hindu legislation.

It was largely through the Ayodhya issue that the Bharatiya Janata Party became directly linked to the VHP. There had been a relationship between the two for years through the RSS, whose workers supplied the organizational energy for both the party and the movement. The old Hindu political party, the Jan Sangh, had merged with the Janata party in a united front against the Congress in 1977. When the Janata party broke up, the leaders of the Jan Sangh regrouped in 1980 to form the BJP. The general secretary of the party was Atal Behari Vajpayee, a former leader of the Jan Sangh; the vice president was Vijaye Raje Scindia, a rather remarkable and outspoken woman who was a member of the former ruling family of the princely state of Gwalior; and as president, the BJP named Lal Krishna Advani.

Advani's background indicates much about the character of the BJP. He was born in 1928 and raised in Karachi, but was forced to flee in 1947 when Pakistan was created. He was educated in Catholic schools and worked as a lawyer and a journalist and has been a member of the RSS. He seldom worshiped in a temple or performed Hindu religious rites, and at one time he ate meat, contrary to the usual upper caste Hindu preference for vegetarianism. When asked why the BJP had become so phenomenally popular, he said it had nothing to do with religious sentiment; it was purely a matter of "nationalism," or rather, as he put it, "patriotism."[21]

When Advani and other BJP leaders came into power they seemed eager to demonstrate that they could be good citizens and responsible politicians. The party attempted to present a more moderate face to the Indian electorate. In 1992, at the party's annual caucus, it claimed to have adopted a Gandhian approach, and attempted to employ the Mahatma's reputation for moderate Hindu politics on its behalf. In the fall of 1992, the Indian press spoke of a "honeymoon" between Congress and BJP leaders, including an agreement over how to deal with the sensitive Ayodhya matter: the BJP pledged to uphold the constitution and the rulings of the Supreme Court. In a meeting with a group of American academics in Berkeley in October 1992, Advani spoke of the virtues of Hindu tolerance, and claimed that his party's policies would fit easily into the mainstream. In fact, he asserted that the electoral success of his party would help to foster harmony among competing religious groups because it was sensitive to religious concerns. This kind of talk, coupled with inaction regarding Ayodhya, made Advani's party appear too moderate for the radical tastes of a good number of his old supporters. Many Hindu activists began to turn against the BJP, asserting that the party had sold its soul to secular political interests.

By giving verbal support to the Ayodhya demands, and allowing preliminary construction of a Hindu temple adjacent to the mosque, the BJP could appease its radical followers without doing anything that would offend the more moderate public. Over half of the Hindu population in North India was in favor of replacing the mosque with a Hindu temple, so the BJP had no choice but to offer plans for some sort of temple to be built on the site.[22] The design that they offered was ingenious. It involved the eventual destruction of the mosque, but it also called for the temple to be built in stages. For some years—perhaps indefinitely—the mosque and the partially constructed temple could sit side-by-side. This was a useful compromise for the BJP, since it allowed it to support the temple and protect the mosque at the same time.

As it turned out, the Hindu forces proved to be beyond Advani's control. Despite his alleged assurances to Prime Minister Narasimha Rao that he could control the crowds and no harm would come to the mosque, the walls came tumbling down.

On December 6, 1992, following a Supreme Court ruling that forbade the government from completing the construction of a temple that would eventually replace the mosque, an angry mob of 200,000 Hindu *kar sewak* (action servants) and lower-class Hindus from nearby towns descended on the ancient edifice with iron bars taken from an adjacent fence and hacked the mosque to rubble. The nation was shocked, and within days the four state governments controlled by the BJP were suspended under the emergency powers vested in the central government. In the weeks that followed, some 3,000 people were killed in riots involving Hindus, Muslims, and the police. BJP leaders, including Advani, were jailed.

The critical question for those concerned about human rights is whether Hindu politicians were to blame for the acts of angry Hindu mobs. Initially the BJP leaders appeared to be surprised by the destruction of the mosque. The day following the attack, Advani publicly took responsibility for the debacle and resigned as leader of the opposition in parliament; the BJP chief minister in Uttar Pradesh resigned as well.[23] Advani, who is said to have personally assured Prime Minister Rao that his party would uphold the decision of the Supreme Court, appeared "visibly shaken," and India's most popular Hindu politician, A. B. Vajpayee, said that the Ayodhya incident was the BJP's "worst miscalculation."[24]

At first glance their expressions of displeasure seemed to be credible, for it appeared that the BJP had little to gain from the attack on the mosque. Although Advani had built his political career on Hindu emotions fanned by the Ayodhya situation, it is likely that he thought that his party would have been better off with the mosque intact. Advani needed to prove that once his party was in power it could act responsibly, and he needed a continuing symbol of opposition to secular politics. The mosque filled both of these needs. As along as the mosque existed, and the secular national government continued to protect it, he had a ready symbol of how the secular government was willing to pander to Muslim interests at the expense of Hindu pride.

For the first few days, then, the Ayodhya tragedy could be seen as a setback for the BJP. By the middle of January 1993, however, the harsh measures of the ruling Congress party against the BJP had backfired against the Congress, and made martyrs out of the BJP leaders. According to a poll in the January 15, 1993, edition of *India Today*, the majority of the public disapproved of the Congress government's action of arresting BJP leaders, banning Hindu nationalist organizations, and dismissing the four BJP-controlled state governments. Moreover, the poll indicated that if new parliamentary elections were held, the BJP would gain over 50 seats (from 119 up to 170), and the Congress would lose 12 (from 245 down to 233; the other BJP gains would come from losses in other parties).[25] The rise of BJP popularity in the wake of the destruction of the mosque made many observers wonder whether the party might not have orchestrated the destruction after all.

HINDU VALUES AND MINORITY RIGHTS

Does Ayodhya demonstrate that Advani and his Hindu nationalist colleagues are opposed to minority rights, especially the rights of Muslims? The Hindu nationalists assert that it does not. In fact, they claim that theirs is a movement for unity—a claim made most dramatically by the BJP's "unity march" from South India to Kashmir early in 1992. They insist that all Indians—including Muslims, Jains, Christians, and Sikhs—are welcome in Indian society. But of course they are welcome only if they recognize Hindutva—traditional Indian values—as the unifying force in Indian culture.

Many Indians regard this as a preposterous notion, but perhaps even more, including many who do not directly support the BJP, do not. They reason that a nation has to be unified by some sort of ideological principles if it is to be unified at all. Increasingly nationalists in formerly colonized countries are coming to regard the Western notion of a social contract among individuals, an ideology with which they were saddled at the time of their independence, as one that is incompatible with their own traditional values. This rejection of Western secular nationalism has led to modern movements of religious nationalism such as the BJP, which claim to subcribe to democratic political processes, but which also attempt to find a legitimation for modern politics in traditional laws and ideas. Hence the return of *dharma* as a political ideology.

Yet Muslims, Sikhs, and members of other minority communities watch the rising tide of Hindu nationalism with great apprehension. What they are concerned about is not just *dharma*, but the possibility that a religious state will favor the majority religious community at the expense of the minorities. Moreover, they worry that a Hindu government will give preferential treatment to the majority community members in government hiring and policies, and that minorities will be required to submit to Hindu religious laws. Beyond that is an even more apocalyptic fear: that they will eventually be driven away from their homelands, or persecuted or killed if they remain.

Regarding the worst fear: the Ayodhya incident does not give conclusive evidence that Hindu nationalists are systematically attempting to kill Muslims or drive them from their homes. An analysis of a thousand people killed in the two weeks immediately following the December 6, 1992, destruction of the Ayodhya mosques indicates that although the majority killed were Muslims, most of them were killed not by Hindu militants but by policemen dispatched by the secular government to nip the demonstrations in the bud. The violent incidents were almost solely an urban phenomenon. The following is a state-by-state compilation of these incidents, taken from press reports:[26]

Maharashtra: 259 dead. Almost all were young male Muslims killed by police in Bombay when they were protesting or in a crowd near the demonstrations.

Gujarat: 246 dead. Most of these were in the city of Ahmedabad when the police fired on Muslim protesters.

Madhya Pradesh*: 120 dead. Rioting between Hindu and Muslim activists; Muslims were killed with police complicity.

Uttar Pradesh*: 201 dead. Mostly in towns such as Kanpur and Varanasi; Muslim demonstrations and Hindu/police attacks.

Rajasthan*: 48 dead. Most were Muslims killed by police firing, but police claim that without it, the numbers killed in direct riots would have been far worse.

Bihar: 24 dead. Most were police firings when the Chief Minister was determined to show strength to keep riots from occurring.

West Bengal: 32 dead. In Calcutta, police were slow to respond to Hindu-Muslim riots between poor shopkeepers.

Assam: 100 dead. Most were Hindus killed by Muslim immigrants from Bangladesh who went on rampage.

Kerala: 12 dead. Most from police firings after Muslim League announced a general strike.

Andhyra Pradesh: 12 dead. In the Muslim city of Hyderabad the Muslim protests were generally orderly and the police response moderate.

Karnataka: 60 dead. Most were killed when Muslim protesters showed up in larger numbers than the police could handle, and the police fired on them in desperation.

Tamil Nadu: 2 dead. Muslim response was muted, in large part because of the lack of BJP strength in the state.

Haryana: 0 dead. Relatively few Muslims live in the state (most migrated to Pakistan in 1948).

Punjab: 0 dead. Few Muslims live in the region, which is virtually a police state already because of the Sikh unrest.

Himachal Pradesh*: 0 *dead.* There are few cities in this mountainous region.

Interestingly, the numbers killed in BJP-controlled states were less than in other regions—especially the area of western India around Bombay and Ahmedabad, where Hindu–Muslim tensions have been rife for years. In this area, communal rivalries are linked to economic ones: poor Muslim villagers coming to cities in search of work have found themselves confronting mobs of lower-class Hindu workers who desperately attempt to hold on to what little they have.

Perhaps the most impressive statistic in the list is Bihar's. It is a state rife with communal tensions, but the chief minister of Bihar, Laloo Prasad Yadav—who is neither BJP or Congress, but a leader of the Janata party—met with Muslim leaders immediately after the demolition of the mosque to work

---

* indicates states with BJP-controlled government

out a strategy of moderation and police intervention that would reduce violence on both sides. It is a model of communal cooperation that BJP leaders claim is possible only if one recognizes the communal nature of Indian society. Put another way, they claim that all religious communities receive stature when the majority religious community receives its due.

Hindu activists observe that communal tensions already exist in India, and secular politics have failed to change what religious nationalists regard as natural predilections to religious loyalties. This makes the religious nationalists both dangerous (if one feels that communal identities are morally repugnant to a healthy society) and honest (if one believes that these identities exist, whether or not one wants them to). The BJP claims that honesty about communal identities is an advantage in dealing with minority groups, and that tensions between the government and the unhappy Muslim and Sikh minorities would be eased if the government were commanded by leaders who appreciate communal identities and try to find a way of integrating Muslims and Sikhs into society as Muslims and Sikhs, rather than as faceless individual members of a secular state. Advani said that if his party came into power nationally "the Muslims will be happy" within "a couple of months."[27]

Most Muslims dispute that assertion, however, and the question remains as to how Hindu nationalists should deal with the issue of minority rights if and when a religious state is established. In general, they have proposed two solutions. One is to provide a separate status (or even a separate state) for minority communities—essentially the British solution of providing reserved constituencies for minorities. A variation on this solution is the idea of creating an upper house or other branch of government composed of representatives of collectivities, including religious and ethnic groups.

The other solution is to accommodate the communities into the prevailing ideology—primarily by regarding the dominant religious ideology as a general cultural phenomenon to which a variety of religious communities are heir. This is the Hindutva approach of the BJP, which claims all of Indian tradition to be Hindu tradition—including Sikhism, Buddhism, and Jainism—and allows for religions from outside India, such as Christianity and Islam, to be affiliated as syncretic Christian-Hindu and Muslim-Hindu branches: "uniting the country," the BJP claims, "with its cultural heritage."[28] In a curious way, this Hindu nationalist solution has a historical Muslim parallel: the Delhi Sultanate in fourteenth-century India allowed for non-Islamic behavior, including the maintenance of Hindu temples and priests, as long as Islam was recognized as the state religion.[29] The Mogul Emperor Akbar is fabled for his tolerance of non-Muslim religions, and although scholars dispute just how open-minded he was, Akbar is familiarly portrayed in art surrounded by religious counselors of various faiths, including a Jesuit.

HUMAN RIGHTS AND THE HATRED OF HINDU NATIONALISTS

Shortly after the destruction of the Ayodhya mosque, in a series of measures that one journalist described as "too much, too late," the government suspended the four state governments controlled by the BJP, arrested Advani and hundreds of other BJP leaders, and banned five organizations: the RSS, the VHP, the Bajrang Dal, the Islamic Sevak Sangh, and the Jama't-i-Islami Hind. The ban would have involved sealing up the organizations' offices, freezing their bank accounts, and detaining key members of the associations. In the case of the RSS, this would have been an enormous task: it has 35,000 branch organizations and over two million members, and is linked with a great number of other organizations that could quickly step in if the RSS offices' doors were closed. The ban was never effectively implemented, and soon was lifted. Most of the leaders were also soon released from jail.

In the zealousness of their response, the Congress leaders had given Advani a great gift of martyrdom which he was quick to exploit for his purposes. The actions of the Congress leaders also caused them to lose the moral high ground. By abrogating democratic processes and dictatorially silencing the opposition, they seemed hostile to the very rights and freedoms they were pledged to protect, and which they claimed the religious nationalists were undermining. It is a pattern that has occurred in other parts of the world where the threat of religious activism has caused otherwise sensible governments to discard their faith in democratic procedures: in Algiers, the 1992 elections were suspended when a preliminary round of voting indicated that the Islamic party would be victorious; in Israel, followers of Hamas were ejected from the country and for almost a year languished in a no-man's-land between Lebanon and Israel.

Are such measures warranted? The example that is usually given to justify these measures is Nazi Germany, which was initially vaulted into power through a democratic election. Put simply, are the BJP leaders Nazis?

Some Indians think that they are. In a full-page editorial in the January 15, 1993, edition of *India Today*, the editors of India's most influential middle-class magazine claimed that "the parallels between the rise of Nazism and the tactics of the Sangh [the RSS and what they describe as its political front, the BJP] are difficult to ignore."[30] Articles in the same issue that purport to be straight reporting rather than editorials carry the same theme; when BJP leaders state that they are concerned about minorities or saddened at the destruction of the mosque, these statements are reported as acts of deception.

The harsh rhetoric against the BJP is one symptom of the ideological polarization that has emerged between secularists and nonsecularists in India. When the editors of *India Today* assert that "the greatest enemy of the BJP is not liberal democracy . . . but secularism," they are no doubt correct: the battle front in India is being drawn along a religious-secularist line. What is happening in India is what is happening in many other parts of the world, where what I describe elsewhere as a "new cold war" mentality has emerged between secular and religious politicians.[31]

In India, this new cold war has a home front, where it is waged largely as an urban battle between two modern groups, both of which claim the middle class. The religious activists include a surprising number of the newly emerging educated middle class, although they lean linguistically toward Hindi rather than English, and are often on the lower end of the middle-class range. Still, they share enough of yuppie values for *India Today* to have branded them as "scuppies"—saffron-clad yuppies. They see in Hindu political parties a stabilizing influence on the country and not a narrow dogmatism.[32] Allied with these urban scuppies are a great number of Hindu shopkeepers, lower middle-class workers from India's towns, and the often ragtag band of religious mendicants who help get out the vote. In a wider sphere, their allies are supporters of religious nationalism elsewhere in the world, and in that sense there is a curious collusion between Hindu nationalists in India and Islamic nationalists in the Middle East.

On the other side are the supporters of secular nationalism, who might be characterized as "antifundamentalists."[33] In India, antifundamentalists consist of educated members of urban upper middle-classes and their allies. The secularists are often English-speaking, college-educated, and pursue urban careers—in brief, the readers of magazines such as *India Today*. Allied with them are many poorer Muslims, but few Sikhs: although they have equal reason to oppose the rise of Hindu nationalism, Sikhs (who have the advantage of living primarily in one region of India, the Punjab) have developed a religious nationalism of their own. Members of the lowest classes in India—the Untouchables—are sometimes also allied with antifundamentalists, although not for ideological reasons; in some areas of the Punjab and western Uttar Pradesh they have economic and political reason to make common cause with the BJP.

Indian antifundamentalists are represented politically by the Nehru camp in the Congress party, and gain a great deal of ideological support from English-language journalists and academics.[34] They are often encouraged by their counterparts in America and Europe.[35] A common theme of the antifundamentalist critique is the inability of religious imagination to include ideas of tolerance.

For instance, in the introduction to a volume of essays on the Ayodhya controversy, Sarvepalli Gopal presented the topic by claiming that the very reputation of India as a modern nation was at stake. To his mind, "the separation of the State from all faiths," was a fundamental attribute of modernity and was characteristic of "a modern outlook anywhere." Only "secularism of this type," he claimed, was appropriate to "an egalitarian, forward-looking society."[36] This would appear categorically to exclude religion from any form of participation in modern politics no matter how democratic it might be.

Although antifundamentalists are consistent in warning about fundamentalists' violation of human rights, we might also ask whether antifundamentalists themselves pose a threat to human rights. In India, for instance, the extreme measures taken by the Congress party following the destruction of the Ayodhya mosque made it appear as if the party leaders were indeed violating the rights of Hindu nationalists. In part for that reason, the measures were soon reversed. The antifundamentalist rhetoric of magazines such as *India Today*, however, could be used to justify the return of such measures if the BJP gains greater electoral strength. If new elections were held, and the BJP were vaulted into the position of forming a national government, these could be the justifications for proclaiming a national emergency and preventing the BJP from taking office.

If the BJP leaders are in fact Nazis, then the suspension of human rights is warranted. It is difficult, however, to assess whether or not this is the case. The BJP leaders themselves have repeatedly affirmed their support for democracy, claiming that as long as the country has a clear sense of national identity and moral purpose, they are satisfied with the existing political framework and policies of the state.[37] In the state governments they have controlled, the policies of BJP have been remarkably similar to those of the Congress and other secular political parties, and Advani has stated that despite his affirmation of Hinduism as the ideological glue that holds the nation together, he has no intention of "running a Hindu government."[38]

If he is right, then the BJP leaders are not Nazis, but politicians of a familiar sort looking for whatever support they can find. Their religious ideology responds to a genuine desire of many in India that the Indian political system should rest on a foundation of cultural legitimacy and indigenous values. That desire is not necessarily dangerous, but a zealous affirmation of it could indeed lead to the sort of violent excesses that the world witnessed on December 6 in Ayodhya. There is no question that Hindu nationalists hold the potential of threatening human rights; alas, secular antifundamentalists have that potential as well.

HINDU VALUES AND CIVIL SOCIETY

Beyond the dispute over the BJP and how dangerous it may be is a more basic question: whether religious ideology can embrace a civil society that protects what the West regards as basic human rights. The attempts of Nandy, Madan, and others to develop an indigenous cultural basis for Indian unity are, as they put it, antisecular—but they are not narrowly Hindu. These scholars view the traditional character of Indian religion as unified: the various religious traditions in India, as Madan has put it, are "members of one family."[39] Madan goes on to specify the similarities that underlie popular Hinduism, Sikhism, Jainism, and presumably even Indian Islam: "they share crucial metaphysical presuppositions," and their followers "share many attitudes and have many social practices in common" (ibid.)

The point Madan makes is that there is a shared core of cultural sensibilities that undergird all religious communities in India. Although Peter van der Veer has claimed that the proponents of traditional syncretism have exaggerated the degree of cultural unity that has existed in the past, there is sufficient anthropological evidence to suggest that there is at present indeed an Indian "style" of religiosity.[40] L. A. Babb, writing about three seemingly marginal religious movements in contemporary North India, has detected strands of religious sensibilities common to all three that have nothing to do with creeds or beliefs in a narrow sense. Rather, they are about notions of a fluid sense of self, a spiritual physiology, the interpenetration of sacred and secular realms, human abilities to convey spiritual power, and the like.[41] Following Babb's line of reasoning, one could say that most Indians possess a kind of common spiritual reflex as part of their cultural heritage.

Whatever this core of Indian religious sensibilities might be, however, it probably would not be wise to call it "Hinduism," for that term now has definite doctrinal and partisan associations. As Nandy and Madan have argued, the Hindutva proponents have coopted the authentic, inclusive Indian cultural tradition; and though some may call it Hinduism, it plays no favorites among Hindu, Muslims, Sikhs, Jains, Buddhists, and Christians in contemporary Indian society. It is this authentic cultural core that provides an alternative to the Hindutva-secularism dichotomy, allowing for the cultural integrity of the former and the tolerance of the latter. The challenge now, as Partha Chatterjee has stated, is for nationalism in India to launch its "most powerful, creative and historically significant project: to fashion a 'modern' national culture that is nevertheless not Western."[42] This proposal is hopeful indeed, for if it could be achieved, it would provide a way around the theoretical impasse between religious chauvinism and secular notions of human rights.

NOTES

1. For a discussion of human rights in comparative perspective see David Little, John Kelsay, and Abdulaziz Sachedina, *Human Rights and the Conflict of Cultures: Western and*

Islamic Perspectives on Religious Liberty (Columbia: University of South Carolina Press, 1988); Max L. Stackhouse, *Creeds, Society, and Human Rights: A Study in Three Cultures* (Grand Rapids, Mich.: W. B. Eerdmans, 1984); Arlene Swidler, ed., *Human Rights in Religious Traditions* (New York: Pilgrim Press, 1982); Leroy S. Rouner, ed., *Human Rights and the World's Religions* (Notre Dame, Ind.: University of Notre Dame Press, 1988); and Kenneth W. Thompson, ed., *The Moral Imperatives of Human Rights— A World Survey* (Washington, D.C.: University Press of America, 1980).

2. David Little, "The Development in the West of the Right to Freedom of Religion and Conscience: A Basis for Comparison with Islam," in Little, Kelsay, and Sachedina, *Human Rights and the Conflict of Cultures*, p. 30. See also essay 8 by Little, Kelsay, and Sachedina in this volume.

3. Speech given by Meir Kahane, Jerusalem, January 18, 1989 (the English translation was supplied to me on that occasion by Ehud Sprinzak and his students). See also the transcript of an interview with Kahane in Raphael Mergui and Philippe Simonnot, *Israel's Ayatollahs: Meir Kahane and the Far Right in Israel* (London: Saqi Books, 1987), pp. 33–34.

4. See the chapter on human rights in my book, *The New Cold War? Religious Nationalism Confronts the Secular State* (Berkeley: University of California Press, 1993), pp. 171–92. Some of the arguments employed in this article and background information used in it have been taken from the book.

5. See John S. Hawley, "Naming Hinduism," in *The Wilson Quarterly* (Summer 1991), pp. 20–34.

6. An accessible introduction to traditional Indian political concepts, along with excerpts from relevant texts, are found in Mackenzie Brown, *The White Umbrella* (Westport, Conn.: Greenwood Press, 1981).

7. This notion and its development in Buddhist and Jain thought is explored by Padmanabh Jaini, "Swadharma and the Ethics of the Individual," paper presented at a conference of the Berkeley/Harvard Program for the Comparative Study of Social Values, held at the Center for the Study of World Religions, Harvard University, June 1979.

8. The classic translation is by G. U. Pope, *The Sacred Kurral* (New Delhi: Asian Educational Services, 1984; orig. pub. in 1886). See also *The Tirukkural: A Unique Guide to Moral, Material, and Spiritual Prosperity*, trans. by G. Vanmikanathan (Tiruchirapalli: Tiruchirapalli Prachar Sangh, 1969).

9. Ainslie T. Embree, "Brahmanical Ideology and Regional Identities," in his *Imagining India: Essays on Indian History*, Delhi: Oxford University Press, 1989), pp. 9–27. For the way Brāhmaṇical Hinduism encapsulates its competition, see Ainslie T. Embree, "The Question of Hindu Tolerance," in his *Utopias in Conflict: Religion and Nationalism in Modern India* (Berkeley and Los Angeles: University of California Press, 1990), pp. 19–37. As early as the mid-1960s, Arend van Leeuwen proclaimed that Hinduism was becoming the national ideology of India in *Christianity in World History: The Meeting of the Faiths of East and West* (New York: Scribner's, 1964), p. 365.

10. Ashis Nandy, "Hinduism versus Hindutva: The Inevitability of a Confrontation," *Times of India*, February 18, 1991. See also his *The Intimate Enemy: Loss and Recovery of Self Under Colonialism* (Delhi: Oxford University Press, 1983); and "The Politics of Secularism and the Recovery of Religious Tolerance" in Ashis Nandy and Veena Das, eds., *Mirrors of Violence* (Delhi: Oxford University Press, 1990).

11. T. N. Madan, "Whither Indian Secularism?" *Modern Asian Studies* 27, no. 3 (1993), p. 696. See also his *Non-Renunciation: Themes and Interpretations of Hindu Culture* (Delhi: Oxford University Press, 1987); and "Secularism in its Place," *Journal of Asian Studies* 46, no. 4 (Fall 1987), pp. 747–59.

12. Partha Chatterjee, *The Nation and Its Fragments: Colonial and Postcolonial Histories* (Princeton: Princeton University Press, 1993), p. 6. See also his *Nationalist Thought and the Colonial World: A Derivative Discourse* (Minneapolis: University of Minnesota Press, 1986).

13. See, for example, Tapan Raychaudhuri, "Shadows of the Swastika: Historical Reflections on the Politics of Hindu Communalism," *Contention* 4, no. 3 (Spring 1995); and Brian Smith, "Reenvisioning Hinduism and Evaluating the Hindutva Movement," *Religion*, forthcoming. See also my response to these and other articles, "The Debate Over Hindu Nationalism," *Contention* 4, no. 3 (Spring 1995).

14. On the history of the RSS, see Walter Andersen and Shridhar Damle, *The Brotherhood in Saffron* (Boulder: Westview Press, 1987).

15. V. D. Savarkar, "Foreword" to Savitri Devi, *A Warning to the Hindus* (Calcutta: Hindu Mission, 1939).

16. V. D. Savarkar, *Hindutva: Who Is a Hindu?* (Bombay: Veer Savarkar Prakashan, 1969).

17. Quoted in Ainslie T. Embree, "The Function of the Rashtriya Swayamsevak Sangh: To Define the Hindu Nation," in *Accounting for Fundamentalisms*, ed. Martin E. Marty and R. Scott Appleby (Chicago: University of Chicago Press, 1993).

18. Jawaharlal Nehru, *The Discovery of India* (New York: John Day, 1946), p. 531.

19. For an analysis of the persistence of what the author calls "Hindu fundamentalism" in South Asia, see Robert Eric Frykenberg, "Revivalism and Fundamentalism: Some Critical Observations with Special Reference to Politics in South Asia," in *Fundamentalism, Revivalists, and Violence in South Asia*, ed. James W. Bjorkman (Riverdale, Md.: Riverdale, 1986).

20. See Peter van der Veer, "Hindu 'Nationalism,' and the Discourse of 'Modernity': The Vishva Hindu Parishad," in Marty and Appleby, eds., *Accounting for Fundamentalisms*.

21. Quoted in Bernard Weinraub, "A Hindu Nationalist Stirs and Scares," *New York Times*, International edition, June 9, 1991, p. A10.

22. According to a poll in *India Today*, 54% of all North Indians (including 10% of the Muslims) favored demolition of the Babri Mosque. *India Today*, January 15, 1993, p. 16.

23. Yubaraj Ghimire and Rahul Pathak, "Too Much, Too Late," *India Today*, December 31, 1992, p. 50.

24. Inderjit Badhwar, "Masters of Deception," in *India Today*, December 31, 1992, p. 35. The reporter expressed a good deal of skepticism over the genuineness of Advani and Vajpayee's comments.

25. *India Today*, January 15, 1993, p. 14.

26. Information culled from reports in *India Today*, December 31, 1992, pp. 40–43.

27. Quoted in Mark Fineman, "Riding the Crest of India's Hindu Revival," *Los Angeles Times*, June 11, 1991, p. H1.

28. Prabhu Chawla, "Ambitious Alliances," *India Today*, April 30, 1991, p. 44.

29. Carl W. Ernst, "The Symbolism and Psychology of World Empire in the Delhi Sultanate," a paper given at a conference, "Religion and Nationalism," at the University of California, Santa Barbara, April 20, 1989, p. 15. Ernst is quoting the chronicle of the Muslim historian, Ziyamal-Din Barani.

30. "Fight the Menace Politically," *India Today*, January 15, 1993, p. 9.

31. Juergensmeyer, *The New Cold War?* p. 2.

32. Madhu Jain, "BJP Supporters: Invasion of the Scuppies," *India Today*, May 15, 1991, pp. 18–19.

33. See my "Anti-Fundamentalism," in Martin E. Marty and R. Scott Appleby, eds., *Fundamentalisms Comprehended*. I have coined this term to describe the ideological position of those who label as "fundamentalist" any religious activism with which they disagree.

34. See, for example, Tapan Raychaudhuri, "Shadows of the Swastika: Historical Reflections on the Politics of Hindu Communalism," *Contention* 4:3 (Spring 1995).

35. See, for instance, Harold Gould, "Fascism Wrapped in Saffron Robe," *Times of India*, July 1, 1993, p. 3; Stanley Wolpert, "Resurgent Hindu Fundamentalism," *Contention* 2, no. 3 (Spring 1993); and Brian Smith, "Re-Envisioning Hinduism and Evaluating the Hindutva Movement," *Religion*, forthcoming.

36. Sarvepalli Gopal, "Introduction," in Sarvepalli Gopal, ed., *Anatomy of a Confrontation: The Babri Masjid-Ramjanmabhumi Issue* (New Delhi: Penguin Books, 1991), p. 13.

37. See Embree, "The Function of the RSS," p. 5.

38. Zafar Agha, "BJP Government: What Will It be Like?" *India Today*, May 15, 1991, pp. 20–21.

39. Madan, "Whither Indian Secularism?" p. 696.

40. Peter van der Veer, *Religious Nationalism* (Berkeley: University of California Press, 1994), p. 201.

41. L. A. Babb, *Redemptive Encounters: Three Styles in the Hindu Tradition* (Berkeley: University of California Press, 1988).

42. Chatterjee, *The Nation and Its Fragments*, p. 6.

10

Catholicism and Human Rights in Latin America

MARGARET E. CRAHAN

Religion and human rights in Latin America have been strongly linked particularly since the 1960s. Many of the principal human rights actors, including the Vicariate of Solidarity in Chile, the Office of Legal Assistance of the Archbishopric in El Salvador, and the Justice and Peace Commission in São Paulo, Brazil, were started by churches during periods of severe repression and survived in large measure because of national and international ecclesial support. It is frequently assumed that the connection between churches[1] and human rights was initiated by the Second Vatican Council (1962–1965) and the Conference of Latin American Catholic bishops in Medellín, Colombia in 1968. While both these gatherings encouraged the contemporary churches' focus on human rights there was a historical base for it as far back as the early sixteenth century when Dominican and Franciscan friars denounced the exploitation of Native Americans by Spanish and Portuguese colonists. Even with the close identification of ecclesiastical and secular elites in Latin America, there has always been an outspoken sector of church people that called for an end to the exploitation of the poor and greater respect for human rights.

This tendency was reinforced in the late nineteenth century by Pope Leo XIII's landmark encyclical *Rerum Novarum* (1891) which urged that there be an end to the exploitation of workers by industrial capitalism. Using a critique similar to that of Marx, Leo held that capitalism tended to regard labor as a commodity to be bought and sold according to market forces. Leo further argued that it was more moral for economic and political elites to act according to the common good and pay wages that would allow workers and their families to live with dignity. While strongly critical of capitalism's excesses, Leo was also clearly not enamored of socialism, regarding it as liable to result in too great a concentration of power in the state. At the same time he counseled workers to ignore the appeals of those who called for class struggle, as he felt it would lead to violence and instability.

Leo's encyclical, together with growing pressures for socioeconomic and political change in Latin America, contributed to increasing activism on the part of church people in the early twentieth century—a period of considerable societal ferment and experimentation. There was a proliferation of reformist groups in the 1920s and 1930s, including church-initiated organizations such as Catholic Action, Young Christian Workers, Young Christian Students, as well as Christian Democratic parties. These organizations tended to further legitimate calls for greater commitment to human rights and increased attention to reducing poverty and political and social marginalization. The strategies of these groups were largely reformist, and they enjoyed increasing support from the 1930s to the 1960s.

CATHOLICISM AND HUMAN RIGHTS IN THE MODERN WORLD

The Catholic Church's current agenda was hammered out at the Second Vatican Council (1962–1965) held in the aftermath of World War II and the Holocaust and amidst a growing sense that the church was not well adapted to meet the challenges of the modern world. These included increasing conflict generated by poverty within and between nations and escalating repression by authoritarian governments. Prelates from Asia, Africa, and Latin America succeeded in increasing the focus on gross violations of human rights and unequal relations between industrialized and industrializing countries. The Brazilian bishops, in particular, lobbied their colleagues to pay more attention to social justice issues. The prelates gathered in Rome concluded that the church should emphasize the promotion of peace, justice and human rights, as well as modernize their institution theologically, bureaucratically, liturgically, and pastorally in order to make it more effective in promoting that agenda. In 1968 the Latin American hierarchy met in Medellín, Colombia, for the Second General Conference of Latin American Bishops (CELAM II) to translate the conclusions of the Vatican Council into Latin American realities.[2]

Influenced by position papers drafted largely by social scientists and progressive theologians, the bishops concluded that the promotion of peace, justice, and human rights required a preferential option for the poor, that is, greater involvement of the church in the struggle of the majority of Latin Americans for liberation from poverty, exploitation, and repression. The Medellín conclusions, cast in the general terms of consensus statements, stimulated a great deal of debate both within and without the church and were interpreted by some as justifying support for revolutionary movements, including Marxist ones. Critics began organizing, coalescing around the Colombian prelate Alfonso López Trujillo, who succeeded in 1972 in being elected secretary general of CELAM, albeit with only a narrow numerical majority. From 1972 until the next General Conference in Puebla, Mexico in 1979, there was intense debate focusing on the implications of the preferential option for the poor, liberation theology, new pastoral forms such as Base Christian Communities (CEBs) and the direct involvement of priests and religious in politics.[3]

Puebla reasserted the church's commitment to a preferential option for the poor, avoided rejecting liberation theology, supported CEBs as a useful tool of evangelization and criticized clerical involvement in politics, holding that the latter was the responsibility of an evangelized laity.[4] After Puebla debate continued, stimulated, in part, by the attempted imposition by Pope John Paul II (1978-) of greater theological and doctrinal orthodoxy and more centralized authority. In addition, increased emphasis was placed, particularly at CELAM IV in Santo Domingo in 1992, on a theology of reconciliation in a conscious effort to compete with the theology of liberation.[5] Given this, it is remarkable that the Catholic Church has maintained the level of consensus it has concerning the necessity of substantial societal change to accomplish its goals of peace, justice, and human rights.

By regarding the church as a community of believers, engaged in a struggle for salvation via the promotion of the common good, defined as peace, justice, and human rights, Vatican II raised the issue of the criteria for the legitimate exercise of political and economic power. Those systems that resulted in violations of human rights, poverty, exploitation, and repression, for example, were categorized as sinful. Both capitalism and socialism were criticized for such defects. It was argued, however, that there were individuals of good will in both the socialist and capitalist camps with whom the church could work to promote reform and therefore the common good.

The very general nature of the conclusions of Vatican II allowed for considerable latitude in interpretation, which was quite evident at the Medellín conference. There capitalism, colonialism, and underdevelopment were sharply criticized. This made the church appear somewhat partisan; at the same time the hierarchy was attempting to establish itself as a nonpartisan promoter of change. The utilization of Medellín by some church people to legitimize specific movements, theologies, or ideologies contributed to controversy over the actual intent of the conclusions. They became the object of intense debate in the period prior to the general conference at Puebla in 1979. This was at the same time that the institutional reforms of Vatican II were being implemented. The creation or activation of national bishops conferences, national associations of religious, and a variety of lay groups provided numerous arenas for debate. There issues were raised concerning the magisterium or teaching authority of the hierarchy, as well as theological and doctrinal orthodoxy. The impact on the public was mixed—disquieting some and energizing others.

THE OPTION FOR THE POOR AND THE UNIVERSALITY OF THE CHURCH

A critical issue was the relation of the preferential option for the poor to the universality of the church's mission. Insistence that the option was intended to be inclusionary rather than exclusionary and referred not just to the materially poor, but also to the poor in spirit, did not eliminate the fears of those who saw in the preferential option an acceptance of the inevitability of class conflict. Liberation theologians, such as Gustavo Gutierrez, held that recognition of class struggle did not mean advocating it, rather, he insisted:

> Those who speak of class struggle do not "advocate" it—as some would say—in the sense of creating it out of nothing by an act of (bad) will. What they do is to recognize a fact and contribute to an awareness of that fact. And there is nothing more certain than a fact. To ignore it is to deceive and to be deceived and moreover to deprive oneself of the necessary means of truly and radically eliminating this condition—that is, by moving towards a classless society. Paradoxically, what the groups in power call "advocating" class struggle is really an expression of a will to abolish its causes, to abolish them, not cover them over, to eliminate the appropriation by a few of the wealth created by the work of the many and not to make lyrical calls to social harmony. It is a will to build a socialist society, more just, free, and human, and not a society of superficial false reconciliation and equality. To "advocate" class struggle, therefore, is to reject a situation in which there are oppressed and oppressors. But it is a rejection without deceit or cowardliness; it is to recognize that the fact exists and that it profoundly divides men, in order to be able to attack it at its roots and thus create the conditions of an authentic human community. To build a just society today necessarily implies the active and conscious participation in the class struggle that is occurring before our eyes.[6]

In spite of such disclaimers, the utilization of concepts such as class struggle aroused fears of church identification with Marxism and armed struggle. This gave rise to efforts to modify some of the conclusions of Medellín, as well as liberation theology.

These efforts were directed, in part, against groups of progressive clergy such as the Priests for the Third World in Argentina, the National Office for Social Information (ONIS) in Peru and Christians for Socialism in Chile, as well as against priests participating directly in politics and some liberation theologians including Gustavo Gutierrez and Leonardo Boff. Also targeted were some foreign missionaries whose numbers increased substantially in the 1960s and 1970s.[7] Disagreements between those who supported reformist modernization and those who supported socialism intensified in church organizations, theological schools, and within dioceses, parishes, and CEBs.

Puebla and Santo Domingo attempted to restate the church's agenda by reaffirming support for peace, justice, and human rights, but cautioned that they should be promoted via evangelization rather than direct political action on the part of the church or its personnel and without identification with a particular system. The conclusions of these meetings were sufficiently general to allow for continued latitude in interpretation and hence little was resolved. The legitimation of change by Vatican II and Medellín had already had its impact and there was no strong antichange lobby. The debate was focused essentially on how to accomplish it, whether through conflict, including revolution, or through reform.

Efforts to rein in some of the more radical sectors of the church have been interpreted by some as evidence of a waning commitment to change. However, the institutional weight of the church continues to be largely in favor of change. Having repositioned itself, it would be exceptionally difficult for the church totally to reverse itself. Hence, while some of the hierarchy may not have fully realized the possible impact of Vatican II and Medellín, their support for peace, justice, and human rights set in motion processes that would make abandonment of the new emphasis of the church difficult. Much of the current debate focuses on the authority of those arguing for specific strategies for change. As a consequence, the actions of a good number of church advocates for change have become highly controversial.

There have been a variety of attempts to identify and categorize agents for change in contemporary Latin America. Among the most intriguing is that of Isaac Cohen and Gert Rosenthal, analysts for the United Nations Economic Commission for Latin America (ECLA). In their view agents for change fall into three general categories: paternalists, social engineers, and vanguardists. Church people appear in each. Paternalists, include traditional entrepreneurs, emerging business elites, professionals, senior military officials, officers of national and international enterprises, and a portion of the church hierarchy. Cohen and Rosenthal posit that paternalists accept the need for limited change in part to avert violent confrontations in highly inegalitarian societies. The social engineers include some middle sectors, including government technocrats, leaders of the democratic left, and sectors of the military. The authors locate the majority of the clergy in this category. The main resources of the social engineers for influencing change are knowledge and technical expertise. Their objective is the creation of a species of welfare state via evolutionary change and they reject violence as a policy instrument. Emphasis is on building consensus through dialogue with influential sectors. In the view of Cohen and Rosenthal, social engineers are vulnerable because of a lack of mass support, as well as openness to cooptation.

The vanguardists are basically professionals, intellectuals, and students who believe in the need to radically transform society through revolution. They include some clerical and lay activists identified with liberation theology. The group as a whole reflects some of the traditional differences among revolutionaries including disagreement between those who counsel waiting for the propitious objective conditions and those who argue for hastening revolution via armed struggle. Cohen and Rosenthal argue that none of these groups enjoy mass support.[8]

Other analysts tend to place the majority of church people in a category committed to gradual reform to achieve pluralistic welfare states and competitive non-Marxian politics. The remainder are categorized as traditionalists or radical activists.[9] The latter have been the focus of a great deal of media and scholarly attention, in part because of their high concentration in the intellectual elite of the church. This has given them considerable access to the national and international media, as well as publishing outlets and scholarly networks. In addition, their arrogation to themselves of greater moral authority than the hierarchy or the Vatican increases their visibility as challengers to the traditional magisterium of the church. The combination of their questioning of both the secular and ecclesial order has sometimes resulted in their repression by both civil and church officials. This has contributed to the waxing and waning of the more radical sectors within the church. Other factors which have contributed are limited success in mobilizing mass support and changes in the internal dynamics or leadership of such groups due to factors such as ideological or personal discord, cooptation, or lack of political skill.

Such factors, among others, contributed to the fading of the Priests for the Third World in Argentina, Christians for Socialism in Chile, the Golconda Group in Colombia, Priests for the People in Mexico, and ONIS in Peru, as well as lay groups such as the Christian University Students (JUC) and Young Christian Workers (JOC) in Brazil in the 1960s and 1970s and revolutionary CEBs in Nicaragua and El Salvador in the 1980s. This has not, however, meant the disappearance of change-oriented sectors within the church; instead it has increased their appreciation of the difficulties of implementing substantial societal change and the most effective means of accomplishing it. Ultimately the struggle for societal change by a variety of sectors within the church has tended to encourage acceptance of the need for change. It has been the long-term involvement of church people, rather than the particular strategies of groups or individuals, that appears to have had the most impact. As agents of change, church people have had the advantage of the impetus of moral principles which has helped them transcend some institutional and secular impediments, but not others.

Constraints on the Promotion of Human Rights

A principal constraint on the church's promotion of human rights has been the division between those who believe that change can be accomplished by transforming individuals and their values and those who believe it can only occur by changing social conditions. This difference exists not only within the Catholic Church, but also within society. Traditional evangelization is regarded by some as insufficient unless accompanied by action. Hence, while the church has indicated its intention to abandon its traditional political alliances, it continues to be heavily involved in politics. At Puebla and Santo Domingo attempts were made to clarify the limits of ecclesial political involvement by asserting that the role of the church was to animate the laity to participate politically, not to act itself. The maintenance of the distinction is extremely difficult, especially in highly conflictual and repressive societies. While the church regards religious beliefs as politically neutral, their implementation since Vatican II encourages political activity given the objective conditions of many societies.

The Catholic Church has always attempted to mold the normative values and communal reactions of the faithful toward the institutional bases of society. This can encourage political partisanship, and attempting to exclude clergy and religious from such partisanship is virtually impossible. Some analysts have seen the distinction as one of activation versus activism. The former focuses on evangelization to inspire lay people to do justice, while the latter involves all church people, including priests and religious, acting to achieve justice. Studies have shown that ecclesial leaders regard activation as more consonant with the proper role of the church.[10] In practice where activation ends and activism begins is not clear either in terms of institutional or individual behavior. In crisis situations justification for exceeding the limits of activation often has been morally sanctioned.

Liberation theology has helped stimulate activism as its methodology encourages individuals to take action. According to liberation theology, one must analyze reality, reflect upon it in view of social doctrine and scriptures, and act. The Christian is required to participate in the struggle for liberation within a historical context, thereby reducing the traditional separation between the sacred and the secular. The methodology of liberation theology also reinforces the vision of the church as a community of believers, thereby legitimizing new pastoral forms such as CEBs and challenging highly central-ized secular and ecclesiastical decision making. As a consequence, the church's promotion of societal change, together with the concomitant emergence of such innovations as liberation theology and CEBs in the 1960s and 1970s, raised several critical issues, as yet unresolved, such as: the morality of violence to accomplish liberation and societal justice, the democratization of the church, as well as the limits of its politicization.

Although liberation theology has been criticized for promoting revolution-ary violence to accomplish change, its chief proponent, Gustavo Gutierrez, denies the charge. He argues that "to be committed to struggle for justice is not to advocate class struggle or some other form of social conflict. On the contrary, it tries to eliminate this confrontation."[11] In spite of such denials the theology has been used to justify armed struggle. That, and its utilization of elements of Marxist analysis, led to its being officially criticized by the Vatican's Congregation for the Doctrine of the Faith in 1984 and 1986. The Vatican censured it for an allegedly partisan conception of truth and confus-ing the spiritually poor with the proletariat of Marx. The theology was also seen as challenging the magisterium of the hierarchy. The Congregation did admit some positive aspects of the theology, endorsed CEBs, and confirmed the church's historical position that armed struggle was legitimate in the face of long-standing tyranny.[12]

The impact of liberation theology on contemporary Latin America, how-ever, is virtually impossible to measure, although there are a good number of commentators who assert that it has been substantial. A multinational survey commissioned in the 1980s by the United States Information Agency con-cluded that it was not as widely disseminated as had been supposed and pri-marily influenced clerical and lay intellectuals, as well as students.[13] In addi-tion, research has shown that reactions to liberation theology have been highly varied. In some instances, it has stimulated more attention to strictly pastoral work, rather than political activism. In addition, there are in Latin America many other liberationist impulses which make the measurement of the spe-cific impact of the theology difficult.[14]

Liberation theology does appear to have helped reinforce the attention that the institutional church has been paying in recent years to popular sectors which has resulted in a proliferation of grass roots activities and their greater identification with the church. The utilization of lay deacons and preachers in areas where there have been chronic shortages of clergy and religious has also opened up the church to more popular input. Such individuals tend to bring to the mission of the church their own vision which may bear little resemblance to formal theological views, including those of liberation theology.[15] Grassroots religious work has taken on a dynamic of its own in recent years that suggests that the agents for change are not limited to innovating elites. Ultimately, in order better to understand the nature and extent of ecclesial-stimulated change the focus must be broader than such innovations as liberation theology and CEBs.

CHANGE AND THE CHURCH AS AN INSTITUTION

As a complex bureaucratic institution with a hierarchical superstructure, it is difficult for the Catholic Church to make the internal modifications necessary for the effective promotion of substantial societal change. For such complex organizations effectively to promote change, certain conditions are generally required. These include a relatively high degree of internal consensus and commitment, a clearly defined agenda or set of policy goals and sufficient autonomy to legitimate them, the resources necessary to convince a critical mass within society to accept change or at least not to be strongly opposed, the expertise to devise recommendations and strategies adequate to the effective promotion of change and its implementation, as well as the maintenance of such a commitment over the long term in the face of fluctuating circumstances both within and without the institution. While there has been considerable consensus in support of the promotion of peace, justice, and human rights through substantial structural change, not all the institutional resources necessary for the long-term pursuit of that agenda have been present.

For example, even with the influx of young ecclesial "technocrats" in the 1960s, '70s, and '80s, the devising of adequate programs and policies, together with the generation of resources for them, has been difficult. In addition, when such policies or programs have been perceived as threatening by secular authorities, church leaders have sometimes downplayed them out of fear for the long-term survival of the institution and the security of its personnel. Overall, however, since the 1960s the Catholic Church has acted, particularly in human rights crises, with remarkable disregard for institutional concerns. Such pressures, however, do occasionally erode internal consensus in support of change. This exacerbates the usual gap between stated objectives and implementation. The situation is made even more complicated because while the church has committed itself to distancing itself from secular authorities and elites, it has not abandoned its desire to incorporate them into its salvific mission. As a consequence, the church continues to insist that its message is inclusionary rather than exclusionary. This has been reflected in increased emphasis on societal conciliation and the elaboration of a theology of reconciliation.

Ideological and political divisions within Latin American society make reconciliation difficult. Since they are reflected within the church they have given rise to considerable ideological and political tension within it. This was particularly clear in Nicaragua in the 1980s. The moral certainty that strong religious belief inculcates further complicates the situation. The internal diversity of a church such as the Catholic Church makes the maintenance of its commitment to universality difficult. Since Medellín there has been some competition between the universality of the salvific mission and the preferential option for the poor. Irrespective of repeated assertions that the option is inclusive rather than exclusive and relates to both the spiritually and the materially poor, the realities of Latin America have made it difficult to reconcile them.

This has been especially true given the survival within the church of some inclination toward elite insertion and cultivation, reinforced by the church's continuing desire to play a mediating role in society. The hierarchy, at times, continues to formulate policy in the context of their participation in elite circles. While alternative or dissident ecclesial elites have emerged, they generally have less direct control over the church as an institution.

Competition among these elites has focused on questions of ideological and theological orthodoxy, as well as authority. Ultimately, debate has centered on strategies for the promotion of peace, justice, and human rights. The utilization of Marxist concepts in some of these strategies has revived, to a degree, historical fears within the church. For some the increased identification of Catholicism with the poor has been cause to abandon or attack the church. This has further challenged the institutional church's commitment to the promotion of nonconflictual societies.

Involvement of the church in the promotion of human rights through societal change has also clearly mobilized some secular opposition. This has resulted, at times, in the repression or assassination of church people. Under such circumstances it is logical for clerical and lay activism to diminish. On the other hand, the creation of martyrs such as Archbishop Oscar Romero of El Salvador has helped to stiffen the resolve of some, as well as to attract newcomers. Overall, direct repression of the church has helped reduce internal divisions.

The preoccupation of Pope John Paul II with the radicalism of some change-oriented sectors of the church has also had some impact, particularly in moderating the utilization of Marxist analysis and clerical involvement in partisan politics. The positions of the national churches in Latin America with respect to change, however, appear to be more influenced by local conditions than by pressures from Rome. This is also true with respect to other pressures from abroad. Dependency on foreign resources, particularly from western Europe and North America, has sometimes given rise to allegations that external actors are determining the church's positions concerning change.[16] In reality a good number of external sources of aid, as well as missionary groups, have been strong promoters of change-oriented ecclesial programs, especially those focused on human rights.

Granted that the leadership of the Catholic Church, particularly at Vatican II and Medellín, supported the promotion of peace, justice, and human rights via political and socioeconomic change, the precise impact is not clear. Official statements emanating from Rome, CELAM, national bishops conferences, and organizations of priests, nuns, and brothers, as well as others, seem to indicate considerable consensus, but few studies have documented the specific impact of such declarations. Some prelates at Medellín signed the conclusions without fully realizing their implications or the degree to which they would be used to legitimize radical activism. This helps explain the efforts to clarify the Medellín conclusions particularly at Puebla and Santo Domingo. Even with a strong consensus in favor of change, there is the question of whether or not the church has sufficient resources and expertise to promote it effectively. The post-Vatican II renovation of clerical and religious education did not guarantee the agenda's successful implementation. The history of the church since 1968 has clearly indicated a wide variety of limitations within the church and strong disagreements which cut across class and generation. Given this, it has obviously been difficult to mobilize the institution in a specific direction. Nevertheless, some feel that there are greater possibilities for the promotion of change than there were twenty-five years ago.[17]

Divisions within the church basically reflect generalized political and ideological differences within Latin American society over how to accomplish change and thereby greater societal justice. Responding to the debate over reformist modernization versus revolutionary socialism the Catholic Church and church people have reacted in a variety of ways. While the official stance has been that the church does not favor a particular economic or political system, its distaste for violence and materialist atheism has inclined it toward reform of capitalism. Within the church, however, there are influential sectors that have claimed class struggle to be a necessity and have regarded socialism as more moral than capitalism. The church's attempt to mold normative values and encourage societal transformation has clearly been somewhat limited by its being enmeshed in such debates. Perhaps its greatest contribution has been to legitimize change in general and contribute to the opening of political space to debate ways to accomplish it.

This has occurred at the same time that the church has been trying to extricate itself from its historical identification with elites, which has tended to reduce its influence with governments. On the other hand, support for the Catholic Church appears to have increased at the grassroots in large measure because of its championing of human rights and socioeconomic justice.[18] By and large, the church has not attempted directly to mobilize such sectors on a broad scale save in a few exceptional cases in Brazil, Chile, and El Salvador. Such efforts have modified the church's view of its role in society, as well as the public's perception of it, but ultimately, while they may reinforce secular movements for change, they do not appear to ensure change.[19]

One of the most interesting developments resulting from the Catholic Church's involvement in the promotion of change has been the creativity unleashed within the church, particularly at the grassroots which has stimulated considerable experimentation. This has contributed to the revitalization that was part of the agenda of Vatican II. However, it has also raised a number of contentious issues related to authority. Furthermore, a portion of the progressive church elites does not appear to have fully realized the degree to which the poor may have their own agendas.[20]

Overall, as the process of promoting change has evolved in the last thirty years in Latin America there has been an intensification of societal conflict which is inimical to the Catholic Church's traditional view that society ideally should be nonconflictual. This has caused some to question the involvement of the church in the promotion of change. Nor has the church always foreseen the consequences of some of its positions or actions. At times it set in motion processes that it was unable to control. It also generated more pressures for greater involvement in secular politics on the part of priests and religious than it appears to want to tolerate. This raises the contentious issue of whether the commitment to change required the partisan participation of the church. Related to this are debates over the morality of revolutionary violence and redistribution through expropriation. The church leadership has attempted to deal with these by justifying armed struggle only in extreme cases of tyranny, such as Somoza's Nicaragua, and sanctioning both private and social property so long as they are supportive of the common good.

The repression leveled at the church, particularly in the 1970s and 1980s, raised the question of whether such positions should be abandoned because they jeopardized the survival of the Catholic Church. The evidence suggests that repression helped fortify the church in crisis situations, reducing internal divisions and increasing its moral sway. In Central America and Chile, for example, participation in and esteem for the church increased.[21] Certainly, the church has succeeded in accomplishing one of its Vatican II objectives, namely the reassertion of stronger moral leadership.

The ferment of these years has also raised questions concerning competing models of church among church people. None of the traditional models, nor the people's church model, has emerged as dominant.[22] Indications are that they will continue to compete. This has contributed to a certain confusion in the church's identity which affects the image it projects, as well as its programmatic priorities and capacities. What is clear is that the image of the church as a monolithic support of the status quo is not accurate.

All this makes the growth of religious competition particularly challenging. The very ferment within church and society has stimulated some growth, particularly among fundamentalists and spiritists who may offer greater moral certainty and psychological release than a change-oriented Catholic Church. Competition has generated some fear and regression within the church and has, at times, undercut ecumenism. It would appear that the Catholic Church is somewhat more inclined to accept political and ideological pluralism than religious. The growth of religious competitors is a further indication of the more autonomous behavior of some sectors of Latin American society particularly at the base.

The task the Catholic Church set itself in the 1960s in Latin America was nothing less than the reordering of society to ensure the common good, defined as that "combination of specific conditions which permit all people to reach standards of living compatible with human dignity. Thus the essential characteristic of the common good is precisely that it be common for everyone, without discrimination of any kind whether it be cultural, social, religious, racial, economic, political, or partisan."[23] Such an undertaking implies major structural change which could undercut the interests of some sectors of church and society. This sometimes appears at odds with the Catholic Church's desire to maintain the universality of its appeal. As a consequence, it has attempted to promote change, while at the same time reasserting the importance of building community, solidarity, and reconciliation within societies. The difficulties involved make the accomplishment of its stated objectives—peace, justice, and human rights—as difficult as it is transcendental.

NOTES

1. Because of constraints of space, this essay will emphasize the Roman Catholic Church with which approximately 90 percent of Latin Americans identify. However, beginning in the late nineteenth century mainline Protestant denominations began to penetrate Latin

America. Since the 1950s fundamentalist groups have grown substantially, as have African and European derived spiritist groups, particularly in Brazil and the Caribbean. One of the reasons for this is ferment within the Catholic and mainline Protestant denominations, as well as within society more generally. Fundamentalists and spiritist communities often offer moral certainty and psychological release from the pressures of rapid societal change. It should also be noted that Catholic and mainline Protestant congregations that have vibrant leadership and are responsive to community needs have also experienced strong growth. Accurate statistics on current denominational membership are difficult to establish in large measure because they are rarely based on actual censuses. In addition, there is considerable variation as to what constitutes a member, with the latter sometimes being defined as anyone who may have participated in any of the activities of the church. Furthermore, recent research on fundamentalist growth suggests that there are substantial retention problems with many "members" leaving within a year or two.

See, for example, Timothy E. Evans, "Percentage of Non-Catholics in a Representative Sample of the Guatemalan Population," paper presented at the XVI International Congress of the Latin American Studies Association, April 4–6, 1991, Washington, D.C. More optimistic estimates of fundamentalist growth are contained in David Martin, *Tongues of Fire: The Explosion of Protestantism in Latin America*, Foreword by Peter Berger (Cambridge, Mass.: Basil Blackwell, 1990) and David Stoll, *Is Latin America Turning Protestant? The Politics of Evangelical Growth* (Berkeley: University of California Press, 1990). On spiritists see David J. Hess, *Spiritists and Scientists: Ideology, Spiritism, and Brazilian Culture* (University Park: Pennsylvania State University Press, 1991) and Jim Wafer, *The Taste of Blood: Spirit Possession in Brazilian Condomblé* (Philadelphia: University of Pennsylvania Press, 1991). Useful sources for statistics on religion in Latin America include the *World Christian Encyclopedia*, as well as the *Annuario Pontificio* and *Statistical Abstract for Latin America*.

2. For the elements of Catholic theology and social doctrine that informed Vatican II, see Donal Dorr, *Option for the Poor: A Hundred Years of Catholic Social Teaching* (Maryknoll, N.Y.: Orbis Books, 1992) and Joseph Gremillon, *The Gospel of Peace and Justice: Catholic Social Teaching Since Pope John* (Maryknoll, N.Y.: Orbis Books, 1976). On Vatican II see Peter Hebblethwaite, *Pope John XXIII: Shepherd of the Modern World* (New York: Doubleday, 1985), as well as Austin Flannery, ed., *Vatican Council II: The Conciliar and Post-Conciliar Documents* (Northport, N.Y.: Costello, 1975). On Medellín see Latin American Episcopal Conference (CELAM), *The Church in the Present Transformation of Latin America in the Light of the Council*, 2 vols. (Bogotá: General Secretariat of CELAM, 1968).

3. The theology of liberation was first widely disseminated via a background paper for Medellín drafted by a Peruvian priest, Gustavo Gutierrez, who subsequently published a revised version as *Teología de la liberación: Perspectivas* (Lima: CEP, 1971). In it Gutierrez was highly critical of capitalism and liberal democracy as they had developed in Latin American and was supportive of socialism. His analysis made use of some Marxist concepts, particularly class struggle. In his more recent works, particularly *La verdad los hará libres: Confrontaciones* (Lima: Instituto Bartolomé de las Casas, 1986), he has moderated somewhat his criticism of liberal democracy, as well as his support for socialism. For the evolution of the theology of liberation since the 1960s see Arthur F. McGovern, *Liberation Theology and Its Critics: Towards an Assessment* (Maryknoll, N.Y.: Orbis Books, 1989). Base Christian Communities (CEBs) are groups of approximately 10 to 30 people who come together regularly to engage in spiritual reflection related to their daily lives.

4. Philip Berryman, "What Happened at Puebla," and Renato Poblete, S.J., "From Medellín to Puebla: Notes for Reflection," in *Churches and Politics in Latin America*, ed. Daniel H. Levine, Preface by John P. Harrison (Beverly Hills, Calif.: Sage, 1979), pp. 41–86; John Eagleson and Philip Scharper, eds., *Puebla and Beyond*, trans. by John Drury (Maryknoll, N.Y.: Orbis Press, 1979) and Edward Cleary, O.P., ed., *Path from Puebla: Significant Documents of the Latin American Bishops since 1979*, trans. by Philip Berryman (Washington, D.C.: United States Catholic Conference, 1989).

5. On Pope John Paul II, see Giovanni Caprile, *Karol Wojtvla e II Sinodo del Vescovi* (Rome: Libreria Editrice Vaticana, 1980); Peter Hebblethwaite, "Changing Vatican Policies, 1965–1985: Peter's Primacy and the Reality of Local Churches," in *World Catholicism in Transition*, ed. Thomas M. Gannon, S.J. (New York: Macmillan, 1988), pp. 36–53; J. Bryan Hehir, "Papal Foreign Policy," *Foreign Policy* 78 (Spring 1990), pp. 26–48; Bruno Secondin, "Santo Domingo: An Interpretation," *LADOC* 23, no. 6 (July/August 1993), pp. 1–13.

6. Gustavo Gutierrez, *A Theology of Liberation: History, Politics and Salvation*, trans. and ed. Sister Caridad Inda and John Eagleson (Maryknoll, N.Y.: Orbis Books, 1973), p. 274.

7. In response to requests from Latin America between 1963 and 1965, U.S. religious in the area increased 50 percent to 4,000. Missionaries from Canada, Italy, Spain, France, and Ireland also increased, as did financial support, especially from Germany. Luigi Einaudi, Richard Maullin, Alfred Stepan, and Michael Fleet, *Latin American Institutional Development: The Changing Catholic Church* (Santa Monica: Rand Corporation, 1969), pp. 33–34.

8. Isaac Cohen and Gert Rosenthal, "International Aspects of the Crisis in Central America," paper presented at Workshop on Central America, Wilson Center, April 2–3, 1981, Washington, D.C.

9. E.g., Daniel H. Levine, "The Meaning of Politics to Catholic Elites in Latin America," paper presented at the IX World Congress of the International Political Science Association, August 19–25, 1973, Montreal, Canada, pp. 11–12; Einaudi et al., *Latin American Institutional Development*, pp. 49–50.

10. Daniel H. Levine, "Church Elites in Venezuela and Colombia: Context, Background, and Beliefs," *Latin American Research Review*, 14, no. 1 (1979), p. 62.

11. Gustavo Gutierrez, "Liberation Theology: Gutierrez Reflects on 20 Years Urging Option for the Poor," *Latinamerica Press* 20, no. 26 (July 4, 1988), p. 5.

12. Congregation for the Doctrine of the Faith, "Instruction on Certain Aspects of the 'Theology of Liberation,' " *Origins: NC Documentary Service* 14, no. 13 (September 1984), pp. 193–204 and "Instruction on Christian Freedom and Liberation," *Origins: NC Documentary Service* 15, no. 44 (April 17, 1986), pp. 714–28.

13. The survey was commissioned ostensibly because of fear that liberation theology was encouraging Marxist revolutionary movements throughout Latin America. It found that the theology was not necessarily contrary to U.S. interests and concluded that "practitioners of liberation thought had actually aided the U.S. agenda throughout the region, as well as the transition in many Latin American countries to democracy." William Bole, "Conclusions of 1987 U.S. Information Agency Study Contradicted Official Government Line on Liberation Theology," *Religious News Service* (June 25, 1990), p. 1 .

14. John Burdick, *Looking for God In Brazil: The Progressive Catholic Church in Urban Brazil's Religious Arena* (Berkeley: University of California Press, 1993): W. E. Hewitt, *Base*

Christian Communities and Social Change in Brazil (Lincoln: University of Nebraska Press, 1991); Daniel H. Levine, "Assessing the Impacts of Liberation Theology in Latin America," *The Review of Politics* 50, no. 2 (Spring 1988), pp. 241–63; N. Patrick Peritone, *Socialism, Communism, and Liberation Theology in Brazil: An Opinion Survey Using Q Methodology* (Athens, Ohio: Ohio University Center for International Studies, 1990); Ofelia Schutte, *Cultural Identity and Social Liberation in Latin American Thought* (Albany: State University of New York Press, 1993).

15. John Burdick, "Who Are the People in the People's Church."

16. E.g., Dan C. McCurry, "U.S. Church-Financed Missions in Peru," in *U.S. Foreign Policy and Peru,* ed. Daniel A. Sharp (Austin: University of Texas Press, 1972), pp. 402–3. See also Claude Pomerleau, "The Missionary Dimension of the Latin American Church: A Study of French Diocesan Clergy from 1963–1971," Ph.D. dissertation, n.d., University of Denver.

17. Bishop Jorge Hourton, Comment at the Conference "500 Años del Cristianismo en America Latina," July 19, 1990, Santiago, Chile.

18. Daniel H. Levine, *Popular Voices in Latin American Catholicism* (Princeton: Princeton University Press, 1992).

19. Cornelia Butler Flora and Rosario Bello, "The Impact of the Catholic Church on National Level Change in Latin America," *Journal of Church and State,* 31 (Autumn 1989), pp. 527–42 and Scott Mainwaring, *The Catholic Church and Politics in Brazil, 1916–1985* (Stanford: Stanford University Press, 1986).

20. Scott Mainwaring, "Grass-roots Catholic Groups and Politics in Brazil," in *The Progressive Church in Latin America,* ed. Scott Mainwaring and Alexander Wilde (Notre Dame, Ind.: University of Notre Dame Press, 1989), pp. 176–83.

21. CERC (Centro de Estudios de la Realidad Contemporánea), *Informe preliminar sobre primera encuestra nacional* (Santiago de Chile: CERC, 1988); and Teresa Whitfield, *Paying the Price: Ignacio Ellacuría and the Murdered Jesuits of El Salvador* (Philadelphia: Temple University Press, 1994).

22. Three major models of the Catholic Church have been debated in recent years by both scholars and church people. They are 1) the Christendom model in which society is conceived as properly being rooted in and molded by religious principles and in which a strongly hierarchical church and state cooperate; 2) the neo-Christendom model in which society is infused with Christian beliefs and values and the church serves as the sacramental mediator between the individual and God and has major influence over secular institutions, but is not allied with the state; 3) the people's or popular church model in which the church is seen as allied with the poor majority in a struggle for liberation that will transform society. In this process the church, itself, becomes more communitarian and egalitarian. Variation among these models suggests the diversity of tendencies within the Catholic Church, as well as distinct phases in their evolution. The Christendom model is most closely identified with the colonial period and nineteenth century in Latin America while the neo-Christendom model more adequately describes its twentieth-century evolution. The model of the people's church flows out of the ferment of the last thirty years and best reflects the fact that the church is both an institution and a community of believers.

23. Brazilian Episcopal Conference, "Christian Requirements of a Political Order, February 17, 1977," *LADOC 'Keyhole' Series,* 16 (Washington, D.C.: United States Catholic Conference, n.d.), p. 59.

II

Russian Orthodoxy
and Human Rights

PAUL VALLIERE

This essay describes the situation and orientation of the Russian Orthodox Church with respect to human rights. Along the broad spectrum of rights I focus mainly on the civil rights of individuals and nonstate associations rather than the subsistence rights and rights to social services that figure so prominently in socialist theories of rights. By this I do not mean to suggest that the rights with which socialists are concerned are of secondary importance. It is simply a question of accepting the demands of my subject. Ever since the disestablishment and disenfranchisement of the Russian Orthodox Church as a result of the Russian Revolution the rights with which the church has been concerned are the rights of individual believers and of the church as an institution. These concerns were stimulated not by theology or ideology but by the harsh facts of life in the Soviet period: widespread persecution of religious believers and the virtual absence of civil rights respecting religion. The extent to which prerevolutionary Russian Orthodoxy may have helped to prepare the ground on which Soviet socialism was built is an issue that exceeds the scope of this essay.

Whether the Russian Orthodox Church is concerned about human rights at all has been a matter of debate. The view that the church is little more than a tool in the hands of whatever state governs Russia at a given time is widespread in the West and may not be much affected by the qualification that "Russian Orthodox Church," in this essay, means not just the hierarchs who represent the church on the national or international level but the whole company of Orthodox believers who accept the church of the Patriarch of Moscow as their own. But even sympathetic observers of the Russian Orthodox Church would agree that the church has been more passive in social and political terms, and more subservient to the state than many churches in the West in modern times. In recent years the contrast has been highlighted by the example of the Roman Catholic Church of Poland, which managed to establish itself as a kind of surrogate civil society in a Communist state well inside the zone of Soviet hegemony.

To explain the relative passivity of the Russian Orthodox Church some observers have pointed to special characteristics of Eastern Orthodoxy, others to the legacy of the tsarist state church, still others to the brutalization of the church by the Soviet state in the 1920s and 1930s. Each of these factors is important, although the last deserves attention first because it is the most obvious cause of the social and political weakness of the church in present-day Russia.

In 1914 the Russian Orthodox Church was the largest Christian church in the world after the Roman Catholic Church and the largest of all national churches. It supported 68 dioceses, over 50,000 priests, more than 60,000 deacons and psalmists, almost 100,000 monks and nuns in more than 1,000 monasteries, 57 theological seminaries, and 4 graduate schools of theology.[1] The vast majority of the Russian empire's 100,000,000 Great Russians, Ukrainians, and Belarusians as well as significant numbers of minority peoples were baptized members of the Orthodox Church.

This huge church was also an institution struggling to renew itself. A reform movement had begun in the early years of the twentieth century and acquired new strength after the February Revolution of 1917. The restoration of the Patriarchate of Moscow in November 1917 after a lapse of more than two centuries was the signal accomplishment of the movement. However, the disestablishment of the church by decree of the Soviet government in January 1918, the dislocations of the civil war and the violent repression of the hierarchy and clergy in the early 1920s left the church in a state of distress by the time Patriarch Tikhon died in 1925. The refusal of the Soviet government to allow the church to hold a national council to elect a successor to the deceased patriarch further weakened the institution. The declaration of loyalty to the Soviet state in 1927 by the *locum tenens* of the patriarchal office, Metropolitan Sergii, brought the church no secular benefits and precipitated a schism in the Orthodox community. What remained of the institution was consumed in the general holocaust of the 1930s. By 1939 the Russian Orthodox Church was one of the weakest churches in Christendom. It had no head, no diocesan administration, few priests or bishops at liberty, and very few functioning parishes.

The revival of the Russian Orthodox Church began during World War II. It was a spontaneous phenomenon at the local level as well as the result of the wartime government policy of fostering traditional Russian patriotism. Metropolitan Sergii was elected patriarch by a small meeting of bishops in 1943, and after Sergii's death in 1945 Metropolitan Aleksii of Leningrad was chosen to replace him. Diocesan administration was restored, and a few theological schools and monasteries were reconstituted. The restored church was not comparable in size, much less in power, to the prerevolutionary church.[2] Nevertheless, the postwar situation represented a dramatic change for the better.

Unfortunately the church's gains proved vulnerable to the caprices of Communist policymakers. In the early 1960s the Khrushchev government launched a new antireligious campaign that led to the closing of about half the parishes reopened during the war. After Khrushchev's fall in 1964 the government discontinued the campaign but did not restore what had been wrested from the church. In this sense the campaign was a victory for the state. However, it produced an unintended and unprecedented side effect: the Orthodox rights movement.

The Orthodox rights movement is a natural focal point for the discussion of Russian Orthodoxy and human rights. However, to appreciate the sigificance of the movement one must consider the ecclesiastical and civil contexts in which it arose. The ecclesiastical context was shaped by Eastern Orthodox tradition. The civil context was shaped by Soviet law.

Orthodox Tradition and Human Rights

Historically Eastern Orthodox tradition has been less disposed to defending human rights than Roman Catholic or classical Protestant traditions. The Roman Catholic Church, while often antagonistic to individual liberty, has always defended its rights as an international ecclesiastical polity standing above secular polities and having certain claims on them. The church's claims serve to limit the power of the state over persons in Roman Catholic countries. Protestantism, while lacking the international structure and legalist genius of the Roman Catholic Church, provides a hospitable ground for the cultivation of rights by according individual conscience a central role in the religious value system. The configuration of values in Eastern Orthodoxy shares something with both Roman Catholicism and Protestantism, but not those aspects that most prompt an interest in rights. Like Roman Catholicism, Eastern Orthodoxy propounds a highly corporate and sacramental view of salvation and so does not encourage individualism on religious grounds.

Like Protestantism, however, Eastern Orthodoxy never tires of preaching that Christianity is a religion of grace, not law, for which reason it rejects the counter-secular legalism of Roman Catholicism.[3] The result is a theological conceptuality less promising for the cultivation of rights than one finds in the Western Christian traditions.

Yet it would be wrong to deny the possibility of a rights orientation arising in Eastern Orthodoxy. Like all great faith traditions, Orthodoxy comprises concepts of human dignity which can at least support, if they do not necessarily generate, the idea of human rights. Furthermore, under the pressure of historic challenges people often find new meaning in traditional ideals. Thus, while some of the most important ideals of Orthodoxy tend to discourage individuals from viewing themselves as rights-bearers over against the community, and discourage the community from viewing itself as distinct from the state, these ideals did not prevent a lively Orthodox rights movement from developing in the very untraditional circumstances of the Soviet Union.

The Orthodox view of the relation of the individual to the community has been profoundly shaped by the ideal of wholeness. In the Orthodox vision salvation in Christ comes about through incorporation into his sacramental community, the church or "body of Christ." The church achieves public definition through its liturgy, dogmas, and canons; but its essential quality is the mystical wholeness which these forms are meant to embody. For Orthodoxy "the church" means the whole company of saints seeking to embrace the whole of humankind and reconcile it with the whole cosmos.[4] The Russian word for this wholeness is *sobornost'*. It comes from a root meaning "gather." "Conciliarity" and "catholicity" are specialized ecclesiastical translations of the term. *Sobor* also means "cathedral," which suggests perhaps the best picture of *sobornost'*. One imagines a crowd of worshipers of all ages and stations of life gathered for liturgy under the dome of a cathedral. As the liturgy unfolds, the choral music, the colorful icons of saints and angels, the smell of incense and wax and the hieratic vestments, postures, and processions of the clergy conspire to induce a powerful sense of incorporation into a great, pulsating whole. Indeed, the Orthodox liturgy offers more than a picture of *sobornost'*; it actualizes it.

Orthodox thinkers are careful to distinguish *sobornost'* from collectivism or egalitarianism. They see the church as a community of persons, each with a unique contribution to make to the whole. *Lichnost'*, "personhood," stands close to *sobornost'* in the Orthodox hierarchy of values. It is reflected, for example, in the group portraits of traditional iconography in which the artist typically accords to each individual some distinguishing feature of dress, coiffure, expression, posture, or function.[5] The structure of the liturgy, too, offers the laity ample opportunity to direct their attention to individual needs, concerns, and sources of inspiration. Still, in classical Orthodoxy the individual is not regarded as the telos of the community. The idea of *lichnost'* suggests personalism but not individualism. To the Orthodox mind the whole appears greater, more estimable, more secure than the parts.[6] The tendency of Orthodox thinkers is to synthesize, not analyze; to integrate, not isolate. This is especially true of modern Orthodox thinkers, who have had to defend the Orthodox ethos against material and spiritual threats from the West.[7] Most Russian Orthodox thinkers in modern times, such as Khomiakov, Kireevsky, Dostoevsky, Leontiev, Fyodorov, and Solzhenitsyn, have held a community based on *sobornost'* and *lichnost'*, wholeness and personhood, to be ethically superior to a community based on the social contract and individual rights. Hand in hand with this view went a "tradition of the censure of law" in Russia, an anti-legal prejudice which inevitably impeded the development of modern conceptions of human rights.[8]

If the ideal of wholeness discouraged individuals from viewing themselves apart from the community, it also made the Orthodox Church slow to distinguish itself from the state. The political dependency of the churches in the Orthodox East contrasts sharply with the pattern of church-state relations that developed in the West. Since the Reform Papacy of the eleventh century the Roman Catholic Church has defined itself juridically as a counterstate or superstate distinct from secular sovereignties. While Rome was by no means always successful in enforcing its claims, the ideal took root. Also, the need to arbitrate between ecclesiastical and secular sovereignties was one of the chief motivations for the development of law in the West, including the language and methodology of rights. Among the theological disciplines canon law played a particularly dynamic role. In the Orthodox East, by contrast, the pattern of church-state relations took shape much earlier, in the fourth and fifth centuries, and embodied the ideal of harmony (*symphonia*) rather than dualism. Church and state were seen not as competing jurisdictions but as two aspects, sacramental and lay, of an organic whole. The ideal left little room for concepts of conflict or prophetic tension between church and state. Canon law was a conservative discipline.

To be sure, there were conflicts between church and state in the Christian East, including fierce confrontations such as the Iconoclastic controversy in eighth-century Byzantium and the Schism (*Raskol*) in seventeenth-century Muscovy. But these episodes did not inspire creative new concepts of church-state relations. The chief effect of the Russian Schism, for example, was to weaken the established church and cause it to accept an even more subservient role in the Russian state system on the eve of modern times.

The ascetical ideal also presents an obstacle to a rights orientation in Orthodoxy. The most esteemed form of religious virtuosity in Orthodoxy is not that of the prophetic emissary, militant reformer, crusader, or preacher, but that of the monk. The monk is a kind of religious individualist, but his individualism is inspired by the call to leave the world, not transform it. This ideal played a fateful role in the structuring of the Orthodox clergy. In Orthodoxy the parish clergy are mostly married men, but bishops must be monks. While this arrangement has its advantages (e.g., clerical celibacy has not been the divisive issue in Orthodoxy that it has been in Roman Catholicism), it has unquestionably limited the capacity of the clergy to mobilize in defense of the secular rights of the church. Parish priests have been too enmeshed in the economic and familial networks of "this" world to challenge it in the name of the next.

The hierarchy, on the other hand, while bearing the chief responsibility for the government of the church in "this" world, has all too often failed to value this responsibility in positive terms. Practicing ascetical renunciation at the expense of the church, so to speak, Orthodox hierarchs have often accepted oppression by secular authorities as a test of patience rather than of power. Commenting on this informal "cooperation of tradition and oppression," Vladimir Zelinsky rightly observes that "in Orthodoxy it is not weakness of the will as such but precisely a zealous piety that demands a spirit of boundless submissiveness."[9]

Along with a weak parish clergy went a weak parish structure. In tsarist Russia the Orthodox parish was a sleepy, unprophetic place because it was too much a part of its environment. Religious and social community were basically identical. The local priest usually inherited his position from his or his wife's father. The concept of the parish as a unit of social, political, or missionary mobilization rarely arose, and the concept of the church as a voluntary association did not arise at all. These ideas were absent during the Soviet period, too, although for the opposite reason: religious and social community were too sharply divorced. Because gatherings of believers outside liturgy were prohibited, people who prayed together had little opportunity to work or even talk together. Also, since open churches were few, far apart, and crowded, worshipers usually did not get to know each other or their clergy very well. The Orthodox parish became an impersonal and diffuse community despite the fervent piety which no observer could fail to note.[10]

The ideal of national religious establishment also contributed to the passivity of the Orthodox Church toward the state. In tsarist Russia religious establishment dulled the church's awareness of the extent to which it was a captive of the state system. The Russian Revolution swept away the establishment but not the cultural and ecclesiastical mentality underlying it. To this day most Russian Orthodox clergy and laity cherish the ideal of a national church. Russian Orthodox people do not think of their church as one denomination or sect among others but as the Church of Russia, a church whose destiny is tied to that of the Russian people.[11] This view disposes the Orthodox community to be more patient with the Russian people and their state than religious groups that see themselves as a prophetic minority.

The continuing hold of an establishmentarian, antisectarian mentality helps to explain some of the episodes of accommodation to the state in the Soviet period beginning with Metropolitan Sergii's declaration of loyalty in 1927. Father John Meyendorff has written about this controversial event:

> The goal of Metropolitan Sergii was to preserve not himself, but *the church*, with all its liturgical order, buildings and central administrative organs. He consciously refused to limit his thinking to "the salvation of the minority, not the majority," as was done by Bishop Damaskin and others who went "underground." In his view the Church—with its essential apostolic succession in the episcopate and its (sometimes burdensome) heritage of divine services, theology and canons—could not exist for long as a sect. The historical example of the Russian Old Believers had confirmed this.[12]

Such an interpretation of the church's accommodation to the state is more satisfying than one focusing on political terror, moral cowardice, or the infiltration of the hierarchy by state agents, for it takes the Orthodox value system into account. Metropolitan Sergii was speaking about Orthodoxy, not other churches, when he asserted that "only impractical dreamers can think that such an immense community as our Orthodox Church, with all its organizations, may peacefully exist in this country while hiding itself from the government."[13] One may question the wisdom of Metropolitan Sergii's policy on tactical grounds, for it brought the church no real gains. But one can scarcely fault the Orthodox Church for trying to remain itself.

At the same time, the ideal of a national church can make a positive contribution to the consciousness of rights in a country to the extent that it fosters a sense of legitimacy on the part of the religious community. The sense of legitimacy is typically long-lasting. To put it another way, if the negative side of Orthodox patience is passivity in the face of oppression, the positive side is endurance. Despite decades of Communist propaganda and repression, countless Russians persist in the conviction that the Orthodox Church has a rightful place in their land and a self-evident claim to its alienated monuments. These people may not express their view in legalistic terms. Moreover, the rights at stake are not generalizable: we might call them "historic rights" rather than "human rights." Nevertheless, the view that Orthodoxy has rights in the Russian land is a key factor in the behavior of the Orthodox Church in present-day Russia and was also an important, if ambiguous, resource for the Soviet human rights movement. I return to the discussion of historic rights later.

SOVIET LAW ON RELIGION

On October 1, 1990, the Supreme Soviet of the Congress of People's Deputies of the USSR adopted a new law on religion, the Law on Freedom of Conscience and Religious Organizations. Later in the same month the Supreme Soviet of the Russian republic (RSFSR) passed a comparable piece of legislation, the Law on Freedom of Religion.[14] These two laws completely overturned previous Soviet legislation on religion. To understand the situation of Russian Orthodoxy and human rights in the Soviet period, however, one must examine the earlier legislation.

Soviet law on religion embodied two cardinal principles. First, only individual believers had rights; churches and religious associations did not. Second, the right of believers to practice their religion was limited to the area of ritual.

These principles stood out clearly in the first piece of Soviet legislation on religion, the decree of the Soviet of People's Commissars on Separation of the Church from the State and the Schools from the Church of January 1918.[15] The decree revoked all civil restrictions connected with religious affiliation and mandated that "in all official documents every mention of a citizen's religious affiliation or nonaffiliation shall be removed." It granted citizens the right to "confess any religion or profess none at all," "free performance of religious rites . . . as long as it does not disturb public order or infringe upon the rights of citizens of the Soviet Republic," and the right "to receive and give religious instruction privately."

Religious associations, however, were denied virtually all rights, not just the privileges connected with religious establishment such as administration of oaths, sanctification of public ceremonies, and registration of marriages and births. The decree barred religious associations from holding property, organizing schools, and going to law. It stated categorically that ecclesiastical and religious associations "do not have the rights of a legal entity."

The only concession concerned access to property designed for ritual use: "Buildings and objects intended especially for religious rites shall be handed over, by special decision of the local or central governmental authorities, free of charge for use to responsible religious associations." Since this provision appeared in the article nationalizing the property of religious associations (Article 13) it clearly meant to distinguish use from ownership. Moreover, as the article left the granting of use of state property to the "special decision" of the state authorities, it could scarcely be interpreted to imply a firm right to such use. Finally, the use of state property by believers was granted specifically for the performance of rituals. Social service, missionary work, political action, religious publishing, and other types of religious activity outside the ritual sphere were not mentioned at all.

It is interesting to note that the decree of the Soviet of People's Commissars made no mention of atheism. The right to profess no religion covers the case of atheism but extends also to agnosticism, free-thinking, and deism. Furthermore, the decree did not accord special privileges to nonbelievers or systems of nonbelief. Yet atheism played an integral role in the formation and evolution of the Soviet Union as an ideological state, and eventually it found a privileged place in Soviet fundamental law. The constitution of 1977, continuing in the tradition of its predecessor (1936), granted a kind of establishment to atheism in so far as it accorded the leading role in Soviet society to "the Communist Party armed with Marxist-Leninist doctrine" (Article 6).[16] It also granted an advantage to atheists in the matter of propagating their faith: "Freedom of conscience is guaranteed to citizens of the USSR, that is, the right to confess any religion or to confess none at all, to perform religious cults or to conduct atheistic propaganda" (Article 52).[17] In other words, atheists had a constitutional right to spread their word; believers did not.

The most detailed piece of legislation on religion in the Soviet period was the Law on Religious Associations of 1929.[18] The law introduced the distinctive mechanism for the regulation of religion in the Soviet Union, the *dvadtsatka*, or "group of twenty." The decree of January 1918 provided that buildings and cult objects could be handed over for use to "responsible religious associations." The problem for the state was how to implement this policy without appearing to extend recognition or privileges to actual ecclesiastical institutions, such as conciliar bodies, the patriarch, bishops, assemblies of clergy or parish councils. The Law on Religious Associations came up with a solution: the authorities at the city or district level would lend state property to groups of not fewer than twenty believers who accepted formal registration as a religious association and responsibility for the property temporarily entrusted to them. The *dvadtsatka* was an ad hoc group, not a corporate body. The rights of legal entity and the right of assembly without the permission of the local authorities were denied to it. Needless to say, the *dvadtsatka* did not correspond to the canonical institutions of any church. Strictly speaking, with the introduction of the *dvadtsatka* the Russian Orthodox parish as well as all ecclesiastical institutions beyond the parish level ceased to exist as entities enjoying recognition or protection under public law.

As long as state policy aimed at the destruction of the church the Law on Religious Associations corresponded to reality and assisted the implementation of policy. The change of direction during the war years, however, produced a contradictory situation. The Russian Orthodox Church, permitted and even encouraged to reconstitute itself, naturally followed its traditional canons. On the local level this meant the reconstitution of the parish with a clerical rector at its head. The regulations on parish life adopted by the Local (i.e., National) Council of the Russian Orthodox Church in January 1945 acknowledged the *dvadtsatka* but stipulated that the clerical rector should head it.[19] The "religious association" of 1929 became a "parish society," though not with the sanction of Soviet law.

The contradiction lasted until the Khrushchev persecution, which undid the religious settlement of the war years. In July 1961 a council of bishops of the Russian Orthodox Church approved the elimination of the clergy from chairmanship and membership of parish councils, effectively removing them from parish government.[20] The bishops claimed to be remedying abuses as well as relieving priests of burdensome secular duties to allow them more time for pastoral work. In fact the hierarchs were bowing to state pressure to restore a strict interpretation of the *dvadtsatka* of 1929. The All-Russian Council of 1971, the first national council of the church held after 1945, did not abrogate the arrangements of 1961, nor did the amendments to the Law on Religious Associations in 1975 change it in any fundamental way.[21] Not until the Gorbachev reforms of the mid-1980s was there a hint in any official source that Soviet law on religion needed to be changed.

The Orthodox Rights Movement

The Orthodox rights movement was part of the Soviet human rights movement and developed along parallel lines.[22] The Soviet human rights movement dates from the Constitution Day demonstration in Moscow's Pushkin Square on December 15, 1965, by intelligentsia protesting the arrest of the writers Andrei Sinyavsky and Yuly Daniel. The key demand was a public trial for the accused. The protesters believed that publicity would expose the gap between the letter of Soviet law and its administration by the authorities. "Respect the Soviet Constitution!" was the slogan of the day.[23]

On the same day the Orthodox rights movement surfaced in an open letter to N. V. Podgorny, chairman of the Presidium of the Supreme Soviet of the USSR, written by the Moscow priests Gleb Yakunin and Nikolai Eshliman. The priests presented a detailed brief alleging violations of Soviet law on religion by the state authorities. Two days earlier the priests had sent a letter to Patriarch Aleksii I arguing their case in theological terms. They sent copies of both letters to the entire Russian Orthodox hierarchy.[24] While there had been other protests by Orthodox clergy and laity in 1965 regarding the state of affairs produced by the Khrushchev persecution, the witness of Yakunin and Eshliman was especially important because of its connection with the wider Soviet human rights movement.

The number of clergy and laity involved in the Orthodox rights movement was small. It was a movement of heroic individuals, as was the Soviet human rights movement generally. As for the hierarchs, they made a practice of disciplining activist clergy and keeping their distance from dissident laity.[25] Yakunin and Eshliman, for example, were removed from their parishes and banned from exercising priestly office (although not defrocked) following the open letters of 1965.

There were numerous links between the Orthodox activists and the wider human rights movement. The first human rights organization in the Soviet Union, the Initiative Group for the Defense of Human Rights in the USSR, formed in 1969, counted the Orthodox lay historian Anatoly Levitin-Krasnov among its founders. The Committee for Human Rights in the USSR, formed in 1970 by Valery Chalidze and others, took a lively interest in religious rights cases.[26] Orthodox publicists contributed frequently to the *samizdat* literature in which the Soviet dissident intelligentsia conducted its debates.[27] The greatest publicist of the period, the Orthodox layman Aleksandr Solzhenitsyn, publicly embraced the Orthodox rights movement in his "Lenten Letter" to Patriarch Pimen in 1972. The letter appeared in the Western press shortly after Solzhenitsyn's first major interview with Western reporters in many years in March 1972.[28] The interview marked the beginning of the explosive period of Solzhenitsyn's activism, culminating in the publication of *The Gulag Archipelago* in December 1973 and his expulsion from the Soviet Union the following February.

The Moscow Helsinki Watch Group, which announced its program in May 1976, found its Orthodox counterpart in the Christian Committee for the Defense of the Rights of Religious Believers in the USSR, although Orthodox Christians were also to be found in the leadership of the Helsinki Group. The Christian Committee, founded in December 1976 by Father Gleb Yakunin and others, was a watch group specializing in religious cases.[29] Its interdenominational concern with the rights of all believers, not just Orthodox, reflected the extent to which the Orthodox rights movement had been shaped by the general human rights movement. The Christian Committee also followed the lead of the Helsinki Group in promoting the internationalization of the struggle for human rights on the basis of the Helsinki accords of 1975. In October of that year Father Yakunin and the lay church historian Lev Regelson addressed an open letter to the delegates of the Fifth Assembly of the World Council of Churches meeting in Nairobi in which they put forward the idea of an interchurch effort to defend religious rights, in essence the idea that the Christian Committee was formed to serve a year later.[30]

During the repressions of the late 1970s and early 1980s the Orthodox rights movement suffered the same fate as the general human rights movement. The attack on the leadership of the Helsinki Group began with the arrest of many of its founding members in February and March 1977, including Yury Orlov, Anatoly Shcharansky and the Orthodox layman Aleksandr Ginzburg. The repression of the Christian Committee began on the eve of the invasion of Afghanistan and the exile of Andrei Sakharov from Moscow (December 1979–January 1980). Father Gleb Yakunin was arrested in November 1979, and most of the other leaders were detained in the following months. In 1980 Yakunin was sentenced to five years in prison followed by five years of internal exile.

The association of the Orthodox rights activists with the general human rights movement was not just pragmatic but extended to values and methodology. The distinguishing characteristic of the Soviet human rights movement in contrast to other dissident tendencies (especially nationalism) was its paramount concern with law and the cultivation of respect for law in Soviet society. In the words of Pavel Litvinov the movement represented

> not only a rebirth of goodness and mercy, but the birth of a sense of law in Soviet society. For the first time the intelligentsia recognized that the Soviet constitution, in spite of all its imperfections, is a fundamental law which in its letter protects their dignity as citizens, on paper defends human rights. The human rights movement discovered a powerful lever of social transformation, namely law, when it turned the attention of the Soviet bureaucracy as well as of society and the rest of the world to the lack of conformity between the conduct of the regime and the constitution and Soviet legislation, and also to the many international conventions and treaties on human rights which the Soviet Union has ratified not so much with a view to their execution as to its own international reputation.[31]

The same attention to law was typical of the Orthodox rights movement. Yakunin and Eshliman's letter to Podgorny is a good example, indeed one of the earliest examples of the new legal consciousness cited by Litvinov. The letter protested the policies of the Council for Russian Orthodox Church Affairs of the Council of Ministers of the USSR, the state agency responsible for supervision of the Orthodox Church.[32] The priests charged that the council's policies violated both the principles and the particulars of Soviet law on religion. In the introduction to the letter, for example, the priests faulted the council for conducting most of its business orally. "The *very method* of using unofficial oral decrees, which the leaders and representatives of the Soviet for Russian Orthodox Church Affairs chose as a means of systematic interference in the internal life of the Orthodox Church, is a violation of the principles of the Law."[33] In the body of the letter the authors discussed eight types of violations of Soviet law on religion: registration of clergy as a means of interfering with their placement, mass closing of churches and monasteries and illegal liquidation of religious societies, registration of baptisms and other sacramental acts, restriction of ritual practices, violation of the principle of freedom of conscience with respect to children, interference in the financial life of church communities, limitation of the number of members of a religious society to the group of twenty, and limitations on the staffing of clerical positions.

The argumentation in all of these cases was deliberately legalistic. The priests took their stand on the decree on Separation of the Church from the State and the Schools from the Church, the Law on Religious Associations, and other relevant legislation. In many particulars their arguments were quite compelling. It was difficult to deny, for example, that the registration of baptisms by local governmental authorities amounted to official documentation of religious affiliation, specifically excluded by the decree on Separation of the Church from the State and the Schools from the Church. The priests also made a good case when they argued that the customary limitation of the responsible membership of religious associations to twenty individuals was not warranted by the Law on Religious Associations, which required only that associations be composed of "not fewer" than twenty citizens. The authors exposed another unwarranted inference when they argued that legal liquidation of a prayer house by local authorities should not automatically signify the dissolution of the religious association that occupied it.

From the beginning the Soviet human rights movement wrestled with the tension between respect for Soviet law and the need to change it. In the area of religious rights this tension was especially severe because of the paucity of rights accorded to religion in the first place. In their letter to Podgorny, Yakunin and Eshliman held firmly to the theme of respecting and enforcing existing Soviet law. As the rights movement gained momentum, however, its critique became more radical. The internationalization of the struggle for rights after the Helsinki accords of 1975 also tended to sharpen criticism of Soviet reality. In 1977, when a nationwide discussion of the draft of the new constitution was taking place, the Christian Committee ventured to raise the issue of the preferential treatment of atheism in the constitution in a letter to Brezhnev.[34]

To be sure, there was no contradiction between preaching respect for law and attempting to change it at the same time. The new legal consciousness embraced both causes. Almost no one in the Soviet human rights movement advocated working for change by violent, extralegal means.

The Orthodox rights activists represented a challenge to the church as well as to the state. They did not question the legitimacy of the Patriarchal church, as some Russian Orthodox splinter groups did. They did not even question the policy of peaceful accommodation with the Soviet state. They did question the church's acquiescence in policies that turned accommodation into a one-sided relationship of dependence prejudicial to the integrity of the church, and they challenged the Patriarch and the bishops to play a more aggressive role in contesting such policies.

Again, Fathers Yakunin and Eshliman stated the case best. Their letter to Patriarch Aleksii I in 1965, incorporating the legal case made in the letter to Podgorny, lent theological and ecclesiastical perspective to their critique. In spirit the letter was prophetic rather than legalistic. The priests cried out against practices in the earthly, everyday church which contradicted the transcendent reality of the church.

The letter consisted of three parts. In the first the authors pointed out that a theological as well as a legal principle was at stake in the violation of religious rights. Citing the words of Jesus, "Render unto Caesar the things that are Caesar's, and unto God the things that are God's" (Mark 12:17), the priests argued that these words "put an end to the claims of a pagan state to total dominion over man," which is why "for the first time in history Christian doctrine proclaimed the infinite value of human personality."[35] In the second part of the letter the authors discussed a matter not raised in the letter to Podgorny: the prerogatives of the parish priest. With copious citations from Orthodox canon law the authors argued that the decision of the council of bishops in 1961 to remove priests from the parish councils produced a flagrantly uncanonical state of affairs at the local level of Orthodox church life and offended the dignity of the priestly office. An epigraph to this section of the letter put it poignantly: "the hireling is not a shepherd" (John 10:12). In the last part of the letter the authors reviewed the glories and tribulations of the Orthodox Church in Russian history and concluded with an appeal to the patriarch to lead the church out of its bondage to secular authority, if necessary at the price of his own security. "The patriarch is appointed to be like John the Forerunner, the friend of the Bridegroom, who lays down his life for the purity of the bride."[36] More particularly they called on Aleksii to summon a widely representative national council of the Russian Orthodox Church which would meet to restore the canonical norms of church life.

Patriarch Aleksii I did not take up the challenge addressed to him by the dissident priests. The next national council took place after his death, in 1971, and met for the purpose of electing his successor. It did not undo the arrangements of 1961. The new patriarch, Pimen, soon faced a similar challenge, however. In his "Lenten Letter" of 1972, Aleksandr Solzhenitsyn cited the examples of Yakunin and Eshliman seven years earlier and implored Pimen to take the initiative in the struggle to free the church from bondage even at the price of personal martyrdom. "Do not let us suppose, do not make us think that for the archpastors of the Russian Church earthly power is higher than heavenly power, earthly responsibility more fearsome than responsibility before God."[37]

Not all Orthodox rights activists approved of the tactic of challenging the patriarch and bishops to confront the state authorities at any price. One of the responses elicited by Solzhenitsyn's "Lenten Letter" provided evidence of divided opinion. It came from the pen of Father Sergei Zheludkov, a priest in the city of Pskov with a long record of involvement in the struggle for Orthodox rights and close ties to the dissident intelligentsia. He took exception to Solzhenitsyn's all-or-nothing approach, arguing that it would lead to martyrdom and an underground church. He held that the legal church "cannot be an island of freedom in our strictly and homogeneously organized society run from a single Center." He approved of the hierarchy's policy "somehow to sign into the system and for the time being to make use of the opportunities permitted by it."[38] But in spite of disagreements over the hierarchy's actual or potential role in the struggle for rights, most Orthodox dissidents agreed that the patriarchal church *was* the Russian Orthodox Church on whose behalf they were fighting. This consensus in itself testified to a considerable degree of good will toward the church on the part of the activists. Their tolerance demonstrated Christian patience and love. It also reflected a recognition that the real antagonist of the human rights movement was not the Orthodox Church but the Soviet state.

1980–1988: The Millennium Arrives

In many ways the outlook for human rights in the Soviet Union seemed bleaker in 1980 than it did in 1965. The repressions of the late 1970s closed down the Soviet human rights movement and confirmed the doubts of many concerning the prospects for changing the Soviet system by legal means. Orthodox activists experienced these doubts as acutely as their secular colleagues. Legalism seemed to have led to a dead end. The way was open for reconceiving the struggle for Orthodox rights along more radical lines, such as an underground church or an alliance with right-wing Russian nationalism.

Yakunin, as ever the leading Orthodox dissident, announced his break with the legalist approach in a report on "The Present Situation of the Russian Orthodox Church and the Prospects of a Religious Renewal in Russia," dated August 15, 1979.[39] In it he advocated the creation of a "catacomb church" through secret (though canonical) ordinations of bishops and priests. The underground clergy would minister to the far-flung masses of Russian Orthodox Christians whose needs were not being met by the severely restricted Moscow Patriarchate. If the Patriarchate refused to collaborate in setting up such a network, as it almost surely would, Yakunin advocated turning to a sister Orthodox church, such as the Orthodox Church in America, for assistance.[40] The practicality of such an approach was debatable. In the context of the human rights struggle, however, the important point was that Yakunin had lost confidence in his own movement.

Yakunin's pessimism toward the Moscow Patriarchate was unrelieved. He went so far as to assert that "if the freedom to conduct religious propaganda were suddenly granted in our country, the members of the Moscow Patriarchate would be incapable of profiting from this opportunity."[41] Ironically, the one servant of the patriarchal church on whom Yakunin passed favorable judgment, Father Dmitry Dudko, scandalized the dissident community a few months later with a nationally televised recantation of his role in the human rights struggle of the 1970s.[42] It seemed as if history were playing tricks on Yakunin.

And so it was, though more benignly than he or his colleagues could have imagined in the dark days of 1979–80. For even as the dissidents walked the *via dolorosa* of prison, exile, or capitulation, changes were in the making in church-state relations and in the Soviet state itself which by the mid-1980s produced a more favorable environment for human rights in the Soviet lands than at any time since the Bolshevik revolution. On the one hand, an acceleration of the Orthodox Church's vindication of its historic rights in the Russian land enhanced the visibility of the church in Soviet society. Second, the accession to power of a group of reform Communists led by Mikhail Gorbachev in 1985 opened the way to a rapid advancement of human rights in all spheres of Soviet life.

The improvement of the church's historic rights began before Gorbachev's accession to power. In the late 1970s and early 1980s the Patriarchate's long-term strategy of loyalty to the state began to pay off more palpably than before, at least for the central church institutions. The number of theological students doubled between 1971 and 1981.[43] The Publishing Department of the Patriarchate increased its staff and managed to get a new building constructed in central Moscow to accommodate work on an expanded range of projects.[44] A large construction project was authorized in 1983 with the return of the buildings and grounds of the Danilov Monastery to the church. The Danilov, named for St. Daniil, a medieval grand prince of Moscow, was the city's oldest monastery. The restoration of the facility brought an Orthodox monastic presence to the capital for the first time in decades as well as providing a highly visible residence for the patriarch and a seat for the Holy Synod and some other units of the Patriarchate.

The church in the provinces did not benefit to the same extent as the central institutions, although there were some improvements. There was a modest increase in the building and reopening of churches in some parts of the country starting in the late 1970s.[45] At about the same time deanery and diocesan conventions of clergy, indispensable to the rebuilding of the Orthodox Church on the provincial level, began to be held again after a lapse of almost three decades.[46]

The gains for the Orthodox Church in the early 1980s, while small compared to the expansion at the end of the decade, were exceptional in two respects. First, they exceeded earlier gains by an appreciable margin. Second, they occurred during a time of unprecedented lassitude and decline in the Soviet Union as whole. Indeed, the Orthodox Church was about the only institution in the country to show any vigor in the late 1970s and early 1980s. To explain this phenomenon one should probably reckon with a number of factors ranging from the hand of Providence to the machinations of atheist bureaucrats. The timing of the concessions to the church, for example, makes it tempting to suspect that they were intended as a reward to pliant hierarchs at a time when harsh punishment was being meted out to Orthodox rights activists. But the growth in the church's strength could also be seen as an example of the countercyclical capacity of religion to show vitality when secular power structures fall into decline.

In any case, the Orthodox hierarchy won real gains, not just cosmetic improvements, during the period. The bishops showed particular skill in their manipulation of a date of great symbolic importance in Russian history: 1988, the millennial anniversary of the baptism of the people of Kiev under Prince Vladimir in 988. In the struggle for historic rights, historic occasions play a key role. By declaring their intention to celebrate the millennium in a grand way the Orthodox hierarchy was able to wage a more or less open campaign to enhance the visibility of the church in Soviet society. In this effort the church probably benefited not a little from the support it enjoyed among some of the more nationalistic members of the Soviet establishment.

But the decisive change that allowed the Moscow Spring of 1988 to happen occurred not in the church but in the ruling elite of the Soviet state. Coming to power in 1985, Mikhail Gorbachev and his associates promptly set about implementing an ambitious reform agenda: first *glasnost'*, or freedom of expression; then *perestroika*, or the restructuring of social, political, and economic institutions. In terms of rights issues the most promising aspect of the reform effort was the idea of "a state based on law" (*pravovoe gosudarstvo*) and the calls for upgrading the legal profession, making legal services more available to ordinary citizens, and establishing the independence of legal counsel.[47] That the immediate source of these ideas was the "legalist" thinking of the Soviet human rights movement was too plain to be missed. The movement had won its case, albeit posthumously.

In the spring of 1988, virtually on the eve of the church millennium, the reform process took a great leap forward when Gorbachev's government declared its intention to create a new national parliament, the Congress of People's Deputies. Elections to this body were held in March 1989; it met for the first time in June. Similar parliaments were later created on the republican level. A substantial body of human rights legislation, including the 1990 laws on freedom of religion mentioned above, was one of the most notable accomplishments of the new parliamentary institutions.

Before 1988 the Communist reformers made no public statements on religion. Their silence left the religiously oriented public in a state of uncertainty about the reform process. In May 1987 a group of nine prominent Orthodox clergy and laymen tied to the Orthodox rights movement tried to bring the matter to a head in open letters to Chairman Gorbachev and Patriarch Pimen.[48] They called on Gorbachev to extend glasnost and perestroika to the religious sphere by granting believers the right to publish scriptures and religious literature, to be heard in the mass media, to participate in the preparation of legislation affecting religious life, to engage in philanthropy and social service—in short, to participate openly and equally in Soviet society. In effect the nine called for a consistent policy: "We wish to believe in the reality of the restructuring that lies ahead. But the process of democratization going on in our country is essentially indivisible. The Russian Orthodox Church cannot be left out of it."

To the patriarch the nine declared that they did not expect the renewal of freedom to be any easier to achieve in the church than in Soviet society at large: "Immobilized, mute and timid for so many years, [the church] has to learn all over again how to walk and talk." The group implored the patriarch "not to let slip the unique historical opportunity which the Lord is sending our Homeland and our Mother Church."

Despite the lack of official statements, however, a great liberalization of the conditions of religious life was already underway by mid-1987. Religious dissidents, including Father Yakunin, were released from exile or detention. Yakunin's sacerdotal functions were restored by the Patriarchate, and he was assigned to a parish in the Moscow area.[49] A program to upgrade Jewish institutions was openly discussed by official spokesmen.[50] Adult baptisands and parents presenting children for baptism, at least in Moscow, were no longer asked to show their domestic passport before receiving the sacrament, i.e., the rite was no longer subject to civil registration.[51] As we have noted, this practice was long singled out by critics as an affront to religious conscience and a flagrant violation of Soviet law. Another sign of improvement was the series of three international scholarly conferences on Russian Orthodox history and tradition commemorating the millennium of the baptism of Russia.[52] The conferences marked the first time that the church was allowed to sponsor international meetings on a subject other than ecumenism or world peace. The second and third conferences in the series featured participation by distinguished Soviet scholars from secular institutions as well as clergy and theologians. The open collaboration between secular and ecclesiastical scholars was another "first" for the postwar period.

As for the legal status of religion, there was evidence that new legislation was being prepared at the highest levels. In the January 1986 issue of the *Journal of the Moscow Patriarchate* there appeared a mysterious last page entitled "Our Legal Advice: The Rights and Obligations of Religious Societies."[53] In actuality the page did not relay "advice" from any ecclesiastical source but presented eight draft paragraphs of a secular law code employing the terminology, but departing from the substance, of the Law on Religious Associations of 1929. The draft explicitly recognized religious associations as legal entities with the right to make contracts and act as plaintiff or defendant in a court of law. It granted religious associations the right to purchase (not merely take on loan) and hold title to various kinds of property including ritual objects, means of transport, and buildings. The right of religious organizations to employ temporary or permanent staff on contract was also recognized. In short, the "Advice" subverted the entire tradition of Soviet legislation on religion. Since such a publication could not have appeared at the time without official approval, it encouraged hopes for a breakthrough to religious liberty in the USSR. The unanswered question was whether the principles of "Our Legal Advice" would be written into state law; and if so, when?

The intentions of the Communist reformers with respect to religion were publicly clarified in April 1988 when Chairman Gorbachev held an unprecedented and highly publicized roundtable meeting with the senior hierarchs of the Russian Orthodox Church.[54] The tone and substance of his remarks were conciliatory even though he felt obliged to declare that Lenin's 1918 Decree on the Separation of the Church from the State and the School from the Church was a measure that "opened the way for the church to pursue its activities without any sort of outside interference." He conceded that "mistakes" were made with respect to the church and religious believers in the 1930s and thereafter, observed that the errors were being corrected, wished the church well on the eve of its millennium and invited the Orthodox community to collaborate in the work of perestroika on the grounds that "we have a common history, one Fatherland and one future." The last point was especially poignant in that it was a major ideological retreat for a Communist leader to envision religion as having any sort of future, never mind the same as his own. Most importantly, Gorbachev announced that "at the present time a new law on freedom of conscience is being devised in which the interests of religious organizations as well as others will be reflected." The long-rumored prospect was now official.

When the church observed its millennium in June 1988, then, it did so in a spirit of confidence and independence. The main event was a national church council composed of the hierarchy and elected clerical and lay representatives. The gathering was only the third national council of the Russian Orthodox Church in the Soviet period (the others were in 1945 and 1971). It was the first to be held for a purpose other than electing a successor to a deceased patriarch.

In the area of rights the most important action of the council was the adoption of a fundamental statute for the Russian Orthodox Church.[55] Based firmly on Orthodox canon law and the abrogated precedent of 1945, the new statute formally ended the bondage of the church to the pattern dictated by the Law on Religious Associations of 1929 and the humiliating pseudo-council of 1961. It went much further than the statute of 1945 in spelling out structures of authority and decision-making in the church. A tiered set of institutions at the diocesan, episcopal, and national level was set up to exercise the church's newly won sovereignty over its affairs. At the time of its adoption, of course, the statute contradicted existing Soviet laws on religion despite a note to the contrary placed at the head of the document. The discrepancy may explain why the church delayed formal publication of the statute.[56] Nevertheless, the text circulated freely and its provisions began to be implemented immediately following the council.

Thus the millennium passed amidst a great liberation. Seventy years after the Bolshevik revolution, the Russian Orthodox Church emerged from its Babylonian exile to claim "a future and a hope" (Jeremiah 29:10).

Russian Orthodoxy and Human Rights Since 1988

The *annus mirabilis* of 1988 marked the end of the long struggle for civil rights and the beginning of a new period in the history of the Russian Orthodox Church. The new era is without precedent. Never before, not even in prosperous periods of its life under the tsars, did the Russian Church enjoy the freedom of action that it possesses today. What the church will do with its freedom—how it will respond to the challenges of a complex modern civilization, how it will deal with the religious pluralism of post-soviet society, what positions it will take with regard to the state, the schools, private property, and the whole range of modern rights issues—all of these are open questions. The answers will come, some soon, others more slowly, as the Russian Orthodox community brings its rich tradition of piety and theology to bear on them. One safe prediction is that the new situation will stimulate a great deal of fresh theological reflection.

In terms of Russian Orthodoxy and human rights the period since 1988 has been shaped by three developments: the rebuilding of church institutions, the codification of legal rights, and the emergence of rights issues quite different from those which occupied the church in the Soviet period.

The rebuilding of the Russian Orthodox Church has proceeded with remarkable rapidity and on a larger scale than even the friends of the church expected. In the period 1985–1987 the church opened or reopened a total of 29 parishes, a respectable number by prereform standards. In 1988, however, 809 new parishes were registered; in the first nine months of the following year, 2,185. In roughly the same period a half dozen new theological schools and a dozen new monasteries were opened.[57] The repossession of historic monuments large and small—from the Kiev Caves Monastery to street corner chapels and rural pilgrimage sites—also proceeded rapidly in all areas of Orthodox settlement. The boom continued in the 1990s. By late 1993 the number of new and reopened parishes in the Moscow Patriarchate surpassed 7,000, bringing the total number of patriarchal parishes to more than 14,000. In other words, the Patriarchate doubled in size in a five-year period. In the same period the number of monasteries rose from about 20 to more than 200; the number of theological schools, from four to 38.[58] The number of historic Orthodox monuments restored during the period is incalculable.

The scale of the Orthodox renewal in Russia and the other countries of the Moscow Patriarchate would appear to make it the largest revival of historic Christianity in the twentieth century. At the very least the rebuilding of Orthodoxy has dramatically altered the Russian landscape. Russia is beginning to look like an Orthodox country again.

To be sure, one would have to examine the spiritual dimensions of the Orthodox revival in order to evaluate it adequately. But the material facts alone prove at least a couple of things. They prove that the Orthodox Church's claim to possess historic rights in the Russian land enjoys a good measure of popular support. Second, they show that the Moscow Patriarchate, whatever its failings, possesses greater reserves of energy and imagination than its Soviet-era detractors allowed. When Father Yakunin wrote in 1979 that "if the freedom to conduct religious propaganda were suddenly granted in our country, the members of the Moscow Patriarchate would be incapable of profiting from this opportunity,"[59] he scarcely imagined that the hour would come when his proposition could be verified. But the hour came, and the proposition turned out to be wrong.

The codification of the civil rights of the Russian Orthodox Church and other religious associations in the Soviet lands was achieved with the adoption of laws on religious freedom by the legislatures of the USSR and the RSFSR in October 1990.[60] The All-Union law ceased to apply after the dissolution of the USSR at the end of 1991. The 1990 RSFSR law remains in effect in the post-soviet Russian Federation.

The All-Union (USSR) law carried the principles of "Our Legal Advice" (1986) to their logical conclusion. It recognized religious organizations as legal entities (Article 13) and their right to acquire and hold various kinds of property (Articles 17–20). It recognized as "religious organizations" not just local congregations but "directorates and central institutions, monasteries, religious brotherhoods, missionary societies (missions), religious schools and also associations of religious organizations" (Article 7). It confirmed the right of religious organizations to establish ties with groups outside the territory of the USSR, the right of believers to leave the country for pilgrimages and other religious purposes (Articles 9, 22, 24), the right of parents and guardians to raise children in a religion (Article 3), and the right of all Soviet citizens to pursue religious education "in the language of their choice, individually or together with others" (Article 6). It recognized the right of religious organizations to conduct religious services and other rituals in houses of worship, religious centers, private homes, cemeteries and crematoria without conditions. Services in hospitals, prisons, and homes for the elderly and invalids were admitted "at the request of citizens" inhabiting the institutions, with religious organizations having the right to solicit such requests (Article 21).

The law granted religious organizations the right to solicit voluntary contributions of money and other property, exempting such contributions from taxation (Article 18). The right of religious organizations to form business enterprises (e.g., publishing, restoration, agricultural concerns) and social service institutions such as hospitals and shelters was also recognized. Profits from such enterprises were declared taxable (Article 19) unless applied to charitable or educational ends (Article 23). Discriminatory tax rates on clerical income were eliminated (Article 26).

The RSFSR law recognized all the aforementioned rights and then some, allowing considerably wider latitude to religious expression than the All-Union law. The law explicitly recognized the religious liberty of foreign citizens on Russian soil (Article 4). It authorized the Russian government "upon the request of mass religious organizations . . . to make decisions regarding the declaration of great religious holidays as additional nonworking holidays" (Article 14). It recognized the right of registered religious organizations to offer instruction in schools and other educational institutions "on an optional basis." As for the military, the All-Union law provided only that "the command of military units will not prevent military personnel from taking part in religious services or performing religious rituals during their free time" (Article 21). The RSFSR law put the matter in more positive terms, speaking of "the right to conduct and participate in religious rites in military units of all branches of service" and charging military administrations actively to assist citizens with arrangements for religious observance (Article 22). The RSFSR law also provided for conscientious objection to the bearing of arms by means of an alternative service option (Article 7).

Another area in which the All-Union and RSFSR laws differed was that concerning the monitoring of religious organizations. Under the All-Union law, registration with the state authorities was required of all religious organizations seeking recognition as legal entities. To supervise the process the law provided for "a state organ on religious affairs" to be formed by the Council of Ministers of the USSR (Article 29), i.e., a body much like the Soviet-era Council for Religious Affairs. The responsibilities of the "organ" included liaison with analogous bodies on the republican level, information gathering on religious activities and on implementation of the laws on religion, offering expert advice to organs of administration and the courts, assisting religious organizations in negotiations with state authorities and promoting understanding and tolerance between religious confessions in the country and abroad. Such a broad mandate clearly envisioned the continuation of an active, even interventionist, role for the state in religious affairs.

The RSFSR law broke with the Soviet tradition of monitoring religion when it declared that "executive or administrative organs of state authority and state job positions specially intended to resolve issues related to the exercise of citizens' rights to freedom of religion may not be instituted on the territory of the RSFSR" (Article 8). Implementation of the law on religion was assigned to the Ministry of Justice and local law enforcement agencies. The Council for Religious Affairs was duly abolished in the RSFSR on January 1, 1991. On the other hand, the RSFSR law preserved the same registration requirement as the All-Union law. It also followed the All-Union law in providing for an "expert" council of "representatives of religious organizations, social organizations, state organs, religious experts, legal experts, and other specialists in the sphere of freedom of conscience and religion" to conduct research and give advice on issues involving religious organizations under the auspices of the Committee on Freedom of Conscience, Religion, Charity, and Philanthropy of the Russian parliament. While a council of experts is a far cry from the Council for Religious Affairs with its plenipotentiaries, the RSFSR law still envisions a degree of collaboration between governmental and religious authorities which a more precise law might have sought to avoid.

In the past, of course, state intervention in the religious sphere was prompted mainly by ideological considerations. The aim was to promote atheism and discourage religious belief. The new laws placed atheism on an equal footing with other attitudes toward religion. Soviet citizens were always free to confess any religion or none at all, but only atheists enjoyed the right to propagate their views. The new laws granted all citizens the right to propagate their views and barred the state from financing either atheist propaganda or religious activities. In terms of the constitutional history of the USSR the disestablishment of atheism was perhaps the most significant achievement of the new legislation. A year before its demise the USSR became a secular state.

With the adoption of the 1990 laws on religion most of the issues which exercised the Russian Orthodox Church and the Soviet human rights movement during the long years of captivity passed into history. Implementation of the new rights will take time, and there will be complications along the way. But the old issues are unlikely to return to center stage. New issues are already taking their place.

One of these came into view even before the 1990 laws on religious liberty were finalized: the role to be played by the Orthodox Church in the legislative process itself. During the Soviet period, of course, there was no role for the church to play in the legislative arena. But in a democratic Russia, where the legislative process is presumably responsive to civil society, the question of the church's role, and that of other religious forces, naturally arises.

The Russian Orthodox episcopate was deeply involved in official discussions of the draft of the All-Union law of 1990. The bishops went so far as to publish critical commentaries on the draft before and after its adoption, winning a number of changes to their liking and failing to get their way on others.[61] For example, they urged deletion of a sentence in the section on separation of church and state providing that "the activities of state organs, organizations and employees may not be accompanied by divine liturgies, religious rituals and ceremonies."[62] The provision was in fact deleted, which opened the way for blessings, prayers, and other overtly religious actions to be performed on state occasions. So, for example, when Boris Yeltsin was inaugurated as the first democratically elected president of Russia in July 1991, the patriarch of Moscow took part in the ceremony, blessing the new officeholder and making a speech exhorting the president and people of Russia "to take up each other's burdens, and thus . . . fulfill the law of Jesus."[63] In the negative column, the bishops proposed wording guaranteeing that religious instruction could be given "in the [public] schools on a voluntary extra-curricular basis." Patriarch Aleksii, a member of the Soviet parliament at the time, vigorously supported the amendment; but it was rejected by a vote of 303 to 46.[64] The All-Union law did not explicitly bar religious instruction from the schools, however; and, as we have noted, the RSFSR law was hospitable to it. In fact many Russian schools currently accommodate religious instruction, usually conducted by clergy or itinerant missionaries. The decision to allow or disallow rests with local school administrations.

Another deficiency in the All-Union law from the bishops' point of view was its treatment of Orthodox parish communities as legal entities distinct from the church as a corporate body. As the bishops saw it, the legal entity of parishes should derive from that of the church as a whole because "in the [Orthodox] Church there cannot be 'religious communities' which are independent from the hierarchical center and from each other."[65] The practical issue was the degree of latitude to be enjoyed by local Orthodox churches in relation to the central church administration. The Moscow Patriarchate faced vigorous challenges from competing Orthodox jurisdictions in the late Gorbachev and early post-soviet years and feared secessionist movements in its ranks (with good reason). The bishops wanted to ensure that any Orthodox parish that abandoned the Moscow Patriarchate would lose its property and rights of legal entity.

The theoretical issue was the degree to which the "self-understanding of the Church," as the bishops called it, should be taken into account by secular lawmakers. Secular law aims to treat all religions equally, but this is easier said than done. A law that regards local religious communities as autonomous entities, for example, has a different meaning for churches with congregationalist polities (e.g., Baptist churches) than for a church with an episcopal-sacramental polity.

The prominence of the Orthodox hierarchy in the legislative debates of 1990 pointed to an even larger issue: the role to be played by the Orthodox Church in the post-soviet Russian state. Religious minorities as well as atheists and secularists worry that the church is bent on securing a privileged position for itself in the new Russia. The sheer size of the Orthodox Church and its thousand-year tradition of state establishment are certainly grounds for the minorities' fears. So is the display, episodic but frequent, of the symbols and clerical personnel of Orthodoxy on all sorts of official occasions. So are the innumerable cases of direct church-state collaboration, including pooling of funds, which can be documented throughout Russia today.

One may cite the reconstruction of the Cathedral of Christ the Savior in central Moscow as a case in point. This church, once the largest in Moscow, was built in the nineteenth century to commemorate Russia's victory over Napoleon. In 1931 it was dynamited by the Communist city government. In January 1995 the patriarch and the mayor of Moscow laid the cornerstone of a replacement structure, which is being built with heavy reliance on state funds. Naturally the finished product will not be a historical monument or military shrine or Baptist or Adventist prayer house, but an Orthodox church.[66]

Privileged treatment of the Orthodox Church was evident on the occasion of its official registration as a legal entity in the RSFSR in the spring of 1991. The formal act of registration had to be postponed because of Patriarch Aleksii II's pilgrimage to the Holy Land and other scheduling complications. Meanwhile, other religious organizations including Jehovah's Witnesses, Mormons, Baptists, Seventh-Day Adventists, and Buddhists were officially registered by the republican authorities. Nevertheless, when the patriarch returned home and went to register his church, the official document he received from the hands of the Minister of Justice bore a registration number rich in symbolism: the number 1.[67]

In short, the blurring of distinctions between church and state is pervasive in present-day Russia and will remain so until clarified by more precise laws. Clearer legislation, in turn, depends on the clarification of attitudes in Russian civil society as a whole, including the Orthodox Church. In other words, the issue of church-state relations will remain a lively one in Russia for a long time to come.

Foreign experts can play a useful role by bringing the experience of other countries to the attention of Russian legislators, church leaders and legal scholars; but in the end the issues of religion and polity facing Russia must be settled in a way that makes sense to the Russians themselves. Every legal tradition represents a synthesis of universal notions of rights with concrete historical conditions and commitments. The tendency of European and American critics of Russia has been to concentrate on the universal and ignore the particular. But in Russia as elsewhere the particular demands its due.

In the present case respect for the particular means making a sympathetic penetration of the modern history of the Russian church and resisting doctrinaire approaches. Because the mentality of Russian Orthodoxy is deeply colored by a long tradition of religious establishment, and because the idea of religious establishment is viewed with suspicion by most modern human rights theorists, the application of human rights theory to the case of Russian Orthodoxy can quickly degenerate into polemics and simplistic dichotomies. But if the job of thinking about human rights is in the first instance not to change the world but to understand it, the case of Russian Orthodoxy (and other Orthodox churches) is a rich subject for the investigator.

The study of religious establishment—particularly de facto sociocultural establishment, which is a vaster phenomenon than the juridical variety—is one of the most neglected subjects in the comparative study of religion. The special pathos of the Russian church in the twentieth century is also scantly appreciated. The Russian Orthodox Church was not disestablished by a constitutional process but by a cruel and arbitrary power determined to eradicate the church altogether. Far from living "at ease in Zion," the leaders of the church trod the path of persecution and martyrdom.[68] That the blood of the martyrs is the seed of the church is a truism of church history. What is not so widely recognized is that the principle applies just as much to priestly church establishments as to prophetic minorities. The aura of sanctity about the patriarchal church was enhanced, not diminished, by Communist persecution.

The mentality of establishment is not confined to church circles. The Russian state is as interested in promoting close church-state relations as the episcopate, and with good reason. Present-day Russia is not a peaceful, prosperous, or productive country. Devastated by decades of oppression, Russian civil society must be rebuilt from the ground up. In these circumstances no Russian government, particularly not a democratic one, can afford to draw a *cordon sanitaire* between itself and the largest and best organized institution of Russian civil society.[69]

Interreligious, intercommunal, and international relations are other arenas in which complex rights issues are emerging for Russian Orthodoxy. Most of the faith communities of post-soviet Eurasia are experiencing genuine religious liberty for the first time, and there is confusion about what it means. There is a real danger that the free market in religion will spawn violent ethnic and religious conflicts. In Ukraine, for example, no fewer than three separate Eastern church jurisdictions—Ukrainian Orthodox (Moscow Patriarchate), Ukrainian Autocephalous, and Ukrainian Catholic—vie for a share of the rich ecclesiastical patrimony of the region. Competing Orthodox jurisdictions also disturb the peace of the church in the Russian Federation.

The growth of nontraditional Christian sects and exotic non-Christian or pseudo-Christian cults in Russia represents an even more baffling challenge to Orthodoxy. The Russian Orthodox community has long been used to dealing with Muslim Tatars, Buddhist Mongols, and other peoples of the Russian Federation whose religious orientation is a matter of historic tradition. It has a harder time coming to terms with Russians who embrace nontraditional religious options. Orthodox sensitivities in this regard have been greatly exacerbated by the tidal wave of foreign missionaries that has washed over Russia since 1988. The church views most of the newcomers as interlopers whose vocation is to rustle the Russian people away from its true shepherds. The irony is that the foreign missionaries operate under the warrant of the 1990 law on religious liberty which the Orthodox Church helped set in place.

Refusal to accept this irony for what it is led the senior hierarchy of the Russian Orthodox Church to launch what can be termed its most controversial initiative of the 1990s relative to human rights: agitation to amend the 1990 legislation on religion in such a way as to bar or otherwise limit the religious activities of foreigners on the territory of the Russian Federation. An amended law was in fact adopted by the Russian parliament in the summer of 1993, only to be vetoed by President Yeltsin. A revised version of the amendment also turned out to be a dead letter following Yeltsin's forcible dispersal of the parliament in the bitter conflict of September–October 1993. Still, the issue has not been laid to rest. Another revision of the 1990 law has been under discussion in the Duma since 1994. At hearings on the matter in early 1995 the Patriarchate let it be known that it still favors limitations on the religious activities of foreigners in Russia.[70]

The Patriarchate's campaign drew a good deal of international attention and prompted the intervention of Western-based human rights activists. International conferences on the issue were held in 1994 and 1995 at which the proposed limitations on religious activity in Russia were roundly criticized as violating the international human rights norms stated in the Universal Declaration, the Helsinki Final Act, the Vienna Concluding Document (1989), and other instruments to which Russia is a party.[71] There is no reason to suppose that the monitoring of religious conditions in Russia and other post-Communist states will cease any time soon. Western missionary and human rights groups are well organized, well financed, and well connected politically. Russian church leaders will not be able to ignore them. Even less will a democratically oriented Russian government find it easy to countenance violations of treaties to which it is a signatory. In effect, the environment in which the Russian Orthodox Church carries out its ministry has been internationalized.

The outlook for relations between the Russian Orthodox Church and Western religious and rights organizations should not be painted too darkly. Strong internationalist currents have long existed in the church, especially among the hierarchy. An interesting feature of the Russian bishops' commentary on the All-Union law of 1990, for example, was their commendation of international human rights instruments. The bishops hailed the All-Union law as the first piece of Soviet legislation that "answers to the fundamental principles of the Universal Declaration of Human Rights, the Final Act of the Conference on Security and Cooperation in Europe and the other agreements reached by participating governments in the course of implementing the Helsinki process."[72]

Even more important as a stimulus to internationalism is the composition of the patriarchal church itself. Always more cosmopolitan than its reputation, the Moscow Patriarchate became a truly international community of churches following the breakup of the USSR in 1991. Preeminent not just in Russia, the patriarchal church is the largest church in Ukraine and Belarus, one of the largest in the Baltic countries, and a significant presence on the religious scene in all fifteen post-soviet states. The church also has close, if no longer juridical, ties to a daughter-church in North America, the Orthodox Church in America. The leadership of the Patriarchate is deeply committed to holding this diverse community of churches together to the extent possible in the face of ethnic, political, and ecclesiastical pressures to the contrary. Many churchmen surely recognize that the interests of the Patriarchate and its huge flock in the Near Abroad and elsewhere will be better protected in the long run through reliance on international human rights norms than by religious protectionism, ad hoc political pressures, or other artificial arrangements.

Critics of the Moscow Patriarchate view its efforts to preserve its organization in the Near Abroad as a dangerous manifestation of neo-soviet "empire-saving."[73] The accusation should not be dismissed lightly, since the alienation of some twenty-five million Russians from the Russian state is certainly a political earthquake that will send aftershocks through the region for years to come. But it is equally important to recognize that there is an ecclesiastical principle at stake in the ambitions of the Moscow Patriarchate. Sectarianism, splintering and the proliferation of jurisdictions are not the final word in church polity from an Orthodox point of view. Nor is there any theological reason for the church to mirror the political divisions of the age. It may be a good thing for post-soviet Eurasia to divide into ethnically based democratic republics. But the Russian church is not a republican entity any more than it was a tsarist or Soviet entity. Its citizenship is in heaven. Like the cross of Christ in which it glories, the Orthodox Church stands "towering o'er the wrecks of time."

Notes

1. For statistics on prerevolutionary church institutions, see Igor Smolitsch, *Geschichte der russischen Kirche, 1700–1917*, vol. 1 (Leiden: E. J. Brill, 1964): pp. 705–13.

2. There were approximately 15,000 functioning Orthodox churches in the Soviet Union by the end of World War II, many of them in the newly incorporated territories. After the Khrushchev persecution there were about 6,000 or 7,000. The best recent sources of information on the Russian Orthodox Church prior to the expansion of the late 1980s are Nathaniel Davis, *A Long Walk to Church: A Contemporary History of Russian Orthodoxy* (Boulder: Westview Press, 1995); Jane Ellis, *The Russian Orthodox Church: A Contemporary History* (Bloomington and Indianapolis: Indiana University Press, 1986); Dimitry Pospielovsky, *The Russian Church Under the Soviet Regime 1917–1982*, 2 vols. (Crestwood, N.Y.: St. Vladimir's Seminary Press, 1984); and William C. Fletcher, *Soviet Believers: The Religious Sector of the Population* (Lawrence: The Regents Press of Kansas, 1981).

3. The primacy of grace was the theme of one of the earliest and most celebrated Russian sermons, Metropolitan Hilarion's "Sermon on Law and Grace." Hilarion became the first Russian (non-Greek) metropolitan of Kiev in 1051. For a partial English translation see Serge A. Zenkovsky, *Medieval Russia's Epics, Chronicles, and Tales*, rev. ed. (New York: Dutton, 1974), pp. 85–90.

4. Evgeny Barabanov sums up the view of many modern Russian Orthodox thinkers when he writes: "The Church is not defined just by her sanctuary and liturgy, her theology and tradition. In essence and idea she is that Absolute Reality whose being is not and cannot be divided. Over against the Church stand evil and death, the falsehood and darkness of the world, but in all being there does not exist a positive reality or grace which on its deepest level, if not in our ideologized consciousness, could be opposed to the Church. The Church is the emerging solidarity of all things, and her essence lies in joining together everything divided and broken. All of us are called to build the Church out of everything which has not yet become part of her, everything which has not visibly and perceptibly entered into her. For we know that nowhere, not on any paths, will man reach the fullness of what God has revealed in His Body—the Holy Church." "Pravda gumanizma," *Samosozanie: sbornik statei*, ed. P. Litvinov, M. Meerson-Aksenov; and B. Shragin (New York: Khronika Press, 1976), p. 26.

5. The uniqueness of persons is connoted by the root word of *lichnost'*: *lik*, "face." *Lik* (sing.) is also used as a collective noun referring to the company of saints, angels, or choristers, as in the expression *prichislit' k liku sviatykh*, "to reckon among the face[s] of the saints," i.e., to canonize.

6. For a somewhat different interpretation see the discussion of "individualism without freedom" in Byzantine society in Alexander Kazhdan and Giles Constable, *People and Power in Byzantium: An Introduction to Modern Byzantine Studies* (Washington, D.C.: Dumbarton Oaks Center for Byzantine Studies, 1982).

7. One should not forget that "the rights of man and citizen" came to Russia on the points of Napoleon's bayonets.

8. See Andrzej Walicki, *Legal Philosophies of Russian Liberalism* (Oxford: Clarendon Press, 1987), ch. 1: "The Tradition of the Censure of Law." A notable exception to antilegalism among Russian Orthodox thinkers was Vladimir Sergeevich Soloviev (1853–1900), whose contribution to legal consciousness and the theory of human rights in Russia is analyzed by Walicki in ch. 3: "Vladimir Soloviev: Religious Philosophy and the Emergence of the 'New Liberalism.' "

9. Vladimir Zelinsky, *Prikhodiashchie v tserkov'* (Paris: La Press Libre, 1982), pp. 47, 54.

10. See the penetrating discussion of this problem in Zelinsky, *Prikhodiashchie v tserkov'*, pp. 46–47.

11. In the fall of 1990 a journalist asked new Patriarch Aleksii II whether he believed the Russian Orthodox Church needed to repent for any of its actions during the Soviet period. His answer illustrates the organic, establishmentarian view we are discussing. "Has the Russian Church sinned against the Russian people?" he asked. "But what is the Russian Church if not this same Russian people viewed in terms of their spiritual aspirations? In the Russian Church as a whole there is no sin which is separate from the sin of the Russian people." The patriarch went on to defend Metropolitan Sergii's controversial declaration of loyalty to the Soviet state in 1927 which I discuss below. *Literaturnaia gazeta*, November 28, 1990, p. 9.

12. John Meyendorff, "The Russian Church After Patriarch Tikhon," *St. Vladimir's Theological Quarterly* 19, no. 1 (1975): 40.

13. Quoted by Meyendorff, "The Russian Church After Patriarch Tikhon," pp. 39–40, from *Patriarkh Sergii i ego dukhovnoe nasledstvo* (Moscow, 1947), p. 62. The text of Metropolitan Sergii's 1927 encyclical is included in the latter source.

14. The All-Union law, "O svobode sovesti i religioznykh organizatsiiakh," was published in *Pravda*, October 9, 1990, p. 4. The RSFSR law, "O svobode veroispovedanii," was published in *Sovetskaia Rossiia*, November 10, 1990, p. 5, and in *Vedomosti s"ezda narodnykh deputatov i Verkhovnogo Soveta RSFSR*, no. 21 (1990), Stat'ia 240. For further comment, see note 60.

15. English translations of the decree on Separation of the Church from the State and the Schools from the Church may be found in William B. Stroyen, *Communist Russia and the Russian Orthodox Church 1943–1962* (Washington, D.C.: The Catholic University of America Press, Inc., 1967), pp. 117–18; and in Richard H. Marshall, Jr. et al., eds., *Aspects of Religion in the Soviet Union 1917–1967* (Chicago and London: University of Chicago Press, 1971), pp. 437–38. I quote from Stroyen's translation, except that I have changed the word "government" to "state" in the title of the decree.

16. Konstitutsiia (Osnovnoi zakon) Soiuza Sovetskikh Sotsialisticheskikh Respublik (Moscow, 1977), Stat'ia 6. The corresponding article of the constitution of 1936 is Article 126. The language of 1977 is more doctrinaire. For an English translation of the constitution of 1977, see *The Soviet Union Through Its Laws*, ed., trans. and with an intro. by Leo Hecht (New York: Praeger, 1983), pp. 17–60. For a translation of the constitution of 1936, see *Basic Laws on the Structure of the Soviet State*, trans. and ed. by Harold J. Berman and John B. Quigley, Jr. (Cambridge: Harvard University Press, 1969), pp. 3–28. A translation of the two constitutions may also be found in David Lane, *Politics and Society in the USSR* (New York: New York University Press, 1978), Appendix C/1–2.

17. Konstitutsiia SSSR, Stat'ia 52. The corresponding article of the constitution of 1936 is Article 124.

18. English translations of the Law on Religious Associations may be found in Stroyen, *Communist Russia and the Russian Orthodox Church*, pp. 121–27; and in Marshall et al., eds., *Aspects of Religion in the Soviet Union*, pp. 438–45.

19. Polozhenie ob upravlenii russkoi pravoslavnoi tserkvi, *Pravoslavnyi tserkovnyi kalendar' na 1946 god* (Moscow, 1946), pp. 58–60. An English translation may be found in Stroyen, *Communist Russia and the Russian Orthodox Church*, pp. 136–40. Articles 39 and 40 pertain to the *dvadtsatka*.

20. The text of the measures approved by the council of bishops in 1961 was published in *Zhurnal moskovskoi patriarkhii*, no. 8 (1961): 15–17. See also the summary of the conciliar discussions on pp. 9–15.

21. An English translation of the 1975 amendments to the Law on Religious Associations along with the articles which they replaced may be found in Pospielovsky, *The Russian Church Under the Soviet Regime*, 2: 493–500.

22. The best general account of the Soviet human rights movement is Ludmilla Alexeyeva, *Soviet Dissent: Contemporary Movements for National, Religious, and Human Rights* (Middletown, Conn.: Wesleyan University Press, 1985). Detailed discussions of Orthodox rights activism may also be found in the works by Jane Ellis and Dimitry Pospielovsky already cited.

23. Alexeyeva, *Soviet Dissent*, p. 275.

24. For a complete English translation of the two letters along with the cover letter to the hierarchy see "Documents: Appeals for Religious Freedom in Russia," *St. Vladimir's Seminary Quarterly* 10, nos. 1–2 (1966): 67–111. Large excerpts appear in Michael Bourdeaux, *Patriarch and Prophets: Persecution of the Russian Orthodox Church Today* (New York and Washington: Praeger, 1970), pp. 189–223. A fine edition of Yakunin's writings in the Soviet period including the letters coauthored with Eshliman has appeared in French: Gleb Yakounine, *Un prêtre seul au pays des soviets*, presented by François Rouleau with a preface by Olivier Clément (Limoges: Editions Criterion, 1984).

25. There were a few bishops, however, who resisted the antireligious campaign, criticized the council of 1961 and supported Orthodox dissidents. The most vocal episcopal dissidents, Ermogen (Golubev) of Kaluga (earlier, of Tashkent and Central Asia) and Pavel (Golyshev) of Novosibirsk, were eventually forced out of service. Their activities and fates are described by Ellis, *The Russian Orthodox Church*, pp. 17, 68, 235–44; and by Pospielovsky, *The Russian Church Under the Soviet Regime*, pp. 327, 393–94, 421–22. See also the materials on the case of Archbishop Ermogen in Bourdeaux, *Patriarch and Prophets*, pp. 238–54.

26. For example, the case of the believers of Naro-Fominsk. See Valery Chalidze, *To Defend These Rights: Human Rights and the Soviet Union*, trans. by Guy Daniels (New York: Random House, 1974), pp. 199–208. Updated information appears in Ellis, *The Russian Orthodox Church*, p. 295.

27. For a fairly representative sample of dissident *samizdat* from the period of the human rights movement, see Michael Meerson-Aksenov and Boris Shragin, eds., *The Political, Social, and Religious Thought of Russian "Samizdat": An Anthology*, trans. by Nickolas Lupinin (Belmont, Mass.: Nordland, 1977).

28. For an account of the interview, with excerpts, see *New York Times*, April 3, 1972. "A Lenten Letter," translated by Ludmilla Thorne, appeared in *New York Times*, April 9, 1972, sec. 4: 18. A translation by Alexis Klimoff may be found in John B. Dunlop, Richard Haugh, and Alexis Klimoff, eds., *Alexander Solzhenitsyn: Critical Essays and Documentary Materials* (Belmont, Mass.: Nordland, 1973), pp. 472–77.

29. See Alexeyeva, *Soviet Dissent*, pp. 255–59; Ellis, *The Russian Orthodox Church*, pp. 373–81.

30. English translations of Yakunin and Regelson's letter may be found in Meerson-Aksenov and Shragin, eds., *Political, Social and Religious Thought of Russian "Samizdat"*; Father Gleb Yakunin and Lev Regelson, *Letters from Moscow: Religion and Human Rights in the USSR*, ed. by Jane Ellis (Keston: Keston College Centre for the Study of Religion and Communism; San Francisco: H. S. Dakin, 1978).

31. Pavel Litvinov, "O dvizhenii za prava cheloveka v SSSR," *Samosozanie: sbornik statei* (New York: Khronika Press, 1976), p. 86.

32. The Council for Russian Orthodox Church Affairs was later replaced by the Council for Religious Affairs.

33. "To the Chairman of the Presidium of the Supreme Soviet of the Union of Soviet Socialist Republics," *St. Vladimir's Seminary Quarterly* 10, nos. 1–2 (1966): 68.

34. See Ellis, *The Russian Orthodox Church*, pp. 255–56.

35. "To His Holiness, the Most Holy Patriarch of Moscow and of All Russia," *St. Vladimir's Seminary Quarterly* 10, nos. 1–2 (1966): 79.

36. Ibid., p. 104.

37. "Vserossiiskomu Patriarkhu Pimenu: velikopostnoe pis'mo," *Vestnik russkogo studencheskogo khristianskogo dvizheniia* 103 (1972): 148–49.

38. "Pis'mo A. Solzhenitsynu," *Vestnik russkogo studencheskogo khristianskogo dvizheniia* 103 (1972): 157.

39. The original Russian text is in *Arkhiv samizdata*, no. 3751 (October 26, 1979). In the preparation of this essay I have used the French translation, "La situation actuelle de l'Eglise orthodoxe russe et les perspectives d'un renouveau religieux en Russie," in Gleb Yakounine, *Un prêtre seul au pays des soviets*, pp. 137–74.

40. "La situation actuelle de l'Eglise orthodoxe russe," pp. 166–74.

41. Ibid., p. 151.

42. For Yakunin's praise of Dudko, see "La situation actuelle de l'Eglise orthodoxe russe," p. 148. A detailed discussion of Dudko's recantation appears in Ellis, *The Russian Orthodox Church*, pp. 430–39.

43. Ellis, *The Russian Orthodox Church*, pp. 120–21.

44. Pospielovsky, *The Russian Church Under the Soviet Regime*, 2: 427–31.

45. Pospielovsky, *The Russian Church Under the Soviet Regime*, 2: 404–6.

46. Ellis, *The Russian Orthodox Church*, pp. 93–94.

47. See, for example, the article by V. Savitsky, "Prestizh advokatury," *Pravda*, March 22, 1987, p. 3.

48. The nine were Father Gleb Yakunin, Father Nikolai Gainov, Andrei Bessmertnyi, Valery Borshchov, Viktor Burdiug, Vladimir Zelinsky, Evgeny Pazukhin, Viktor Popkov, and Vladimir Poresh. The letters were released at a news conference in Moscow in May 1987. The letter to Gorbachev was published in the Paris newspaper *Russkaia mysl'*, no. 3676 (June 5, 1987), p. 6. The letter to Patriarch Pimen was published in no. 3682 (July 17, 1987), pp. 6–7.

49. *New York Times*, June 8, 1987 and August 23, 1987, sec. 4:1. Yakunin was subsequently elected to the parliament of the Russian republic. In 1993, however, the Patriarchate banned its clergy from standing for public office. Running for a seat in the post-soviet Duma at the time, Yakunin refused to comply and was defrocked.

50. See the account of Konstantin M. Kharchev's visit to New York, *New York Times*, October 30, 1986. Kharchev was chairman of the Council for Religious Affairs at the time.

51. This is one of the changes noted by the group of nine in their open letters to Gorbachev and Patriarch Pimen (see above, note 48).

52. The conferences were held in Kiev, July 1986; Moscow, May 1987; and Leningrad, February 1988.

53. *The Journal of the Moscow Patriarchate*, 1986, no. 1: 80 [English edition]. The title in the Russian edition is "Nashi iuridicheskie konsul'tatsii: Prava i obiazannosti religioznogo obshchestva." The reference is the same.

54. See the report in *Pravda*, April 30, 1988.

55. "Ustav ob upravlenii Russkoi Pravoslavnoi Tserkvi," *Pomestnyi sobor Russkoi Pravoslavnoi Tserkvi. Troitse-Sergieva Lavra. 6–9 iiunia 1988 goda. Materialy*, Kniga pervaia (Moscow: Izdanie Moskovskoi Patriarkhii, 1990), pp. 24–49. The Ustav was adopted on June 8, 1988.

56. Prior to formal publication in 1990 (see note 55) the statute was published in typescript format in the newsletter of the Patriarchate's Department of External Church

Relations: "Informatsionnyi biulleten' otdela vneshnikh tserkovnykh snoshenii Moskovskogo Patriarkhata," 1988, no. 7–9 (October 4, 1988). A gloss on the title of the statute reads: "This Statute has been composed in harmony with existing legislation on religious cults and may be changed or supplemented in the event of new legislation." I thank Mr. Alexis Liberovsky, archivist of the Orthodox Church in America, for supplying me with a copy of the "Informatsionnyi biulleten' " edition of the statute.

57. Metropolitan Vladimir of Rostov, "The Current State of the Russian Orthodox Church After the Adoption of the New Statute," *St. Vladimir's Theological Quarterly* 34, nos. 2–3 (1990) :117–39. See also Kyrill, archbishop of Smolensk and Kaliningrad, "The Church in Relation to Society Under 'Perestroika,' " ibid., pp. 141–60. Both documents originally appeared in *Zhurnal moskovskoi patriarkhii*, 1990, no. 2.

58. The data are given in "Ko dniu tezoimenitstva Predstoiatelia Russkoi Pravoslavnoi Tserkvi," *Zhurnal moskovskoi patriarkhii*, no. 2 (1994): 9. For a scrupulously careful presentation of the data on the size and material condition of the Russian Orthodox Church since World War II, see Nathaniel Davis, *A Long Walk to Church: A Contemporary History of Russian Orthodoxy* (Boulder: Westview Press, 1995).

59. "La situation actuelle de l'Eglise orthodoxe russe," p. 151.

60. See above, note 14. All-Union law, "O svobode sovesti i religioznykh organizatsiiakh"; RSFSR law, "O svobode veroispovedanii." Quotations from the All-Union law are my own translations. Quotations from the RSFSR law are taken from the English translation prepared by the Foreign Broadcast Information Service: "RSFSR Law on Freedom of Religion," JPRS-UPA-90–071, December 19, 1990 (reproduced by U.S. Dept. of Commerce, National Technical Information Service, Springfield, Va.). I thank Ms. Deborah Jones, Librarian of the Hudson Institute, for retrieving the last-named source.

61. "Zaiavlenie Pomestnogo Sobora Russkoi Pravoslavnoi Tserkvi v sviazi s publikatsiei proekta Zakona SSSR 'O svobode sovesti i religioznykh organizatsiiakh,' " *Zhurnal moskovskoi patriarkhii*, no. 9, (1990): 9–11; and "Opredelenie o priniatom Zakone SSSR o svobode sovesti," ibid., no. 2 (1991): 2–5.

62. "Zaiavlenie Pomestnogo Sobora Russkoi Pravoslavnoi Tserkvi," p. 10.

63. Quoted by Dimitry V. Pospielovsky, "The Russian Orthodox Church in the Postcommunist CIS," *The Politics of Religion in Russia and the New States of Eurasia*, ed. Michael Bourdeaux, International Politics of Eurasia series, ed. Karen Dawisha and Bruce Parrott, vol. 3 (Armonk, N.Y. and London: M.E. Sharpe, 1995), p. 49. See also "Yeltsin Sworn in as Russia's Leader," *New York Times*, July 11, 1991.

64. "Zaiavlenie Pomestnogo Sobora Russkoi Pravoslavnoi Tserkvi," pp. 10–11; "Verkhovnyi sovet SSSR odobril zakonoproekt o svobode sovesti," *Russkaia mysl'*, October 5, 1990, p. 20.

65. "Zaiavlenie Pomestnogo Sobora Russkoi Pravoslavnoi Tserkvi," p. 10; cf. "Opredelenie o priniatom Zakone SSSR o svobode sovesti," p. 4.

66. The cost of the project is estimated at $200 million; see "A Rebirth in Russia," *New York Times*, April 24, 1995, p. A4. The project is not popular with the intelligentsia, including Orthodox intelligentsia who see it as misdirecting resources that would better be applied to rebuilding the church at the parish level. See "Pokaianie tozhe mozhet byt' vygodnym," *Nezavisimaia gazeta*, April 7, 1994, p. 6; and "Lichnyi narodnyi khram: khram Khrista Spasitelia prevrashchaetsia v banal'nuiu udarnuiu stroiku," ibid., January 10, 1995, p. 2. The host of a television show on Orthodoxy and Russian culture recently said of the

challenges facing contemporary Russia: "the main thing is to build the spiritual cathedral of St. Sophia, not the crude material cathedral of Christ the Savior; the main thing is to create the spiritual foundations of democracy." "Imperiia kul'tury, ili o pravoslavnykh storonnikakh demokraticheskoi Rossii," *Literaturnaia gazeta*, April 26, 1995, p. 15.

67. *Nezavisimaia gazeta*, June 1, 1991.

68. Writing of the early Soviet decades, Vladimir Zelinsky rightly observed: "The future historian will by no means judge those times to be the worst in the life of the Russian episcopate. One cannot deny it: individuals to whom fate seemed to have guaranteed a peaceful existence under the wing of tsarist Orthodox Russia did not go to pieces when faced with arrest, prison, and concentration camps. Some were even able to die in joy with a prayer for their executioners on their lips, as in apostolic times. Should the age of persecution return again, the majority of our bishops would find the strength to walk the same path as their predecessors." *Prikhodiashchie v tserkov'*, p. 104.

69. No less an authority than James H. Billington offered the following assessment in mid-1994: "With the collapse of the world's first atheist state, the historic religion of Russia has emerged as the central cultural force in the country's new national self-consciousness. As a cohering ideology, Orthodoxy has replaced communism as the lodestar of Russian society. Along with the army, the Church is one of the few national institutions that is still respected." "The Case for Orthodoxy," *The New Republic*, May 30, 1994, pp. 24–25.

70. Coverage of the issue in the mainline Russian press has generally been unsympathetic to the protectionist cause. See Aleksandr Nezhnyi, "Kto boitsia cheloveka s evangeliem," *Izvestiia*, July 15, 1993, p. 5; and "Vse religii ravny . . . No est' bolee ravnye?" *Literaturnaia gazeta*, February 22, 1995, p. 2. Debates on the issue have appeared in "thick" journals, e.g., "Spor o svobode sovesti," *Novyi mir*, no. 9 (1993): 156–71; and "Svoboda sovesti, religiia, pravo (materialy 'kruglogo stola')," *Voprosy filosofii*, no. 12 (1994): 3–18. For an overview of the issue since 1988, see Michael Bourdeaux, "Glasnost and the Gospel: The Emergence of Religious Pluralism," *The Politics of Religion in Russia and the New States of Eurasia*, pp. 113–27. For the course of events in 1994 and early 1995, see Lauren B. Homer, "Latest Legal Developments Affecting Religion in Russia," *East-West Church & Ministry Report* 3, no. 1 (Winter 1995): 1–4.

71. For an excellent exposition of the criticisms see W. Cole Durham, Jr., Lauren B. Homer, Pieter van Dijk, and John Witte, Jr., "The Future of Religious Liberty in Russia: Report of the De Burght Conference on Pending Russian Legislation Restricting Religious Liberty," *Emory International Law Review* 8, no. 1 (Spring, 1994): 1–66. The essay includes an English translation of the proposed amendment of August 27, 1993 (Appendix A). I thank Ms. Lauren B. Homer, President, Law and Liberty Trust, and Mr. Scott M. Ellsworth of the J. Reuben Clark Law School, Brigham Young University, for directing me to this and related sources.

72. "Opredelenie o priniatom Zakone SSSR o svobode sovesti," *Zhurnal moskovskoi patriarkhii*, no. 2 (1991): 2. See also the precise citation of the Vienna Concluding Document in argumentation for changes in the draft of the 1990 law in "Zaiavlenie Pomestnogo Sobora Russkoi Pravoslavnoi Tserkvi v sviazi s publikatsiei proekta Zakona SSSR 'O svobode sovesti i religioznykh organizatsiiakh,' " ibid., no. 9 (1990): 10.

73. See John B. Dunlop, "The Russian Orthodox Church as an 'Empire-Saving' Institution," *The Politics of Religion in Russia and the New States of Eurasia*, ed. Michael Bourdeaux, pp. 15–40.

12

Muslim Women Between Human Rights and Islamic Norms

MIRIAM COOKE AND BRUCE B. LAWRENCE

None of the three major topics to be addressed in this essay is self-evident, and while we hope to open up new perspectives on Muslim women as a group, illumining both differences and convergences on universal norms, we must begin with the knotty but pivotal topic of this volume as a whole: human rights.

Can human rights be universalized beyond specific historical and cultural contexts? Or have they come into prominence in the late twentieth century precisely because they do mark a specific if elusive context, namely, the transition within the world system from generalized warfare in the two world wars to bipolar conflict in the cold war, and now with the West vs. the non-West? In the context of Western global hegemony under siege, can human rights ever find expression except as a reflex of power so pervasive that it feels no need to account for its own interests, but only for the deviance of noncompliant others?

These are the questions that elites throughout the world debate today. Yet, they remain unanswerable as long as the prism of inquiry reflects only irreconcilable opposites. Instead of talking about We vs. They, we need to identify who is concerned about human rights. Many are people like us, two professors in a major American university, who recognize the limits as well as the benefits of concern for human rights. The limits are internal and evident: despite good intentions, we recognize that at best we reflect the views of other elites, and not the views of all strata of American or European society. The benefits are diffuse and conjectural: as elites advocating change, we hope that our vision is broad enough, our arguments persuasive enough to be relevant to others engaged in the quest for social justice.

The current concern for human rights emerged in the aftermath of World War II. It is framed by the United Nations and its 1945 Charter. But it is also framed by the anticolonial struggles in the middle decades of this century. From a European or American perspective, the Charter is taken for granted as an advance in pursuing and maintaining human life and dignity, but from an Asian or African perspective, the Charter becomes problematic precisely because its emergence coincided with the end of European colonialism in the East, and the beginning of the postcolonial era.

The fact of postcolonialism complicates all attempts to talk globally as Euro-Americans *and* address responsibly those who are Asian or African. How can former colonizers and colonized dialogue without replicating familiar structures of domination and silencing? When we invoke human rights as universal, we must remember the historical context and the class relatedness of their exposition in the West. Human rights should not be used as a flag flown over one group, exempting that group from criticism while rigorously monitoring others. An alternative has been suggested by Irene Bloom in her introduction: the current human rights debate should represent the halting but persistent search for global justice. If so, then the related purpose of this essay on Islamic complexities and contributions is to prevent post-cold war warriors from hijacking human rights to their own narrowly self-serving interests.

We all suspect that we share values and rights, and yet we have difficulty agreeing what they might be. Why? Is it because we have different worldviews? Or, is it because we suspect the others' motives behind claims of universality? Though both fault lines are possible, they are not identical, and it becomes more difficult to distinguish between them when the debate is framed as a clash between individual rights on the one hand and collective duties and responsibilities on the other. Each presupposes the other, and yet, like all seeming incommensurates, the one is always assumed to prevail over the other. Part of the friction is metaphysical: Mark Juergensmeyer is certainly right to underscore the fact that many cultures do not accept the notion, often advocated by human rights libertarians, "that individuals possess on their own rights that do *not* come from the community or from God."[1]

Yet even accounting for rights under a collective or transcendent rubric leaves the thorny problem of motives. For instance, in 1989 was the Ayatollah Khomeini right to proclaim himself the defender of Islam and then to issue a *fatwa* condemning to death his co-religionist Salman Rushdie for publishing *Satanic Verses*, a novel written in England and in English, which the Ayatollah declared to be so deeply offensive to all Muslims that its author was a heretic? Or were Western governments, their spokespersons, and myriads of concerned citizens right to protest that Muslim sensibilities aside, Rushdie, a Pakistani expatriate residing in England, was entitled to freedom of expression? Or was Rushdie defended only because he lived in England? For if the *fatwa* against Rushdie was wrong, then why just over three years later, in 1992, was there not an international outcry when Egyptian fundamentalists killed their co-religionist and compatriot, the journalist Farag Foda, for writing in Egypt and in Arabic what they had condemned as heresy?

The Rushdie affair highlights a problem of motivational ambivalence that can be recast in general terms. When non-Western governments and organizations trace their sovereignty to a "universal" conception of religious and communal duties that supersedes individual rights, their stated intent may be to defend their community, but they may also be struggling to define their own space in a postcolonial world dominated by Western powers. When Western governments and their human rights organizations respond by urging individual rights as universal virtues that override specific cultural norms, their stated intent may be to uphold the integrity of individual persons, but they may also be claiming to represent a superior cultural as well as political order.

In the late twentieth century, it is not enough to claim universals, one must also examine who is making these claims, and why. In a recent talk at Oxford University, the Egyptian activist and writer Nawal El Saadawi listed the universal virtues—touted by Western governments as also by Western intellectuals—whose meaning is pressed into the service of political and economic ends when applied to countries they wish to dominate. These exportable goods include "security, stability, protection, peace, democracy, development, structural adjustment, family planning, and human rights."[2] Such honeyed platitudes, she warned, may turn into weapons harming those on whose behalf they are invoked. In the light of the Gulf War, of Somalia and Bosnia, we would be naive to deny that such verbal manipulation takes place. Some have even gone so far as to claim that "the UN is neither willing nor capable of protecting human rights *qua* human rights . . . (that the UN) is nothing more than an instrument of the U.S. and other Western powers, (with the result that) national sovereignty is the only way of safeguarding the human rights of the masses which are now threatened by a powerful state (the U.S.) in a unipolar world."[3]

Such caveats notwithstanding, we contest the reductionist claim that human rights discourse is *always* manipulated in the interests of power. Because we do believe that universal human rights is a pivotal notion, we advocate the need to contextualize its discourse, to approach rights from many angles, with many voices. We must acknowledge the differences between elites and nonelites, between generic human rights—life, freedom, and property— and women's rights as human rights, but also between rights and duties.

In order to bridge the seeming chasm between individual rights and collective duties, we will examine the emerging debate about women's rights as human rights not as an abstract issue but as a crucial test case for the future of one group, Muslim women in the postcolonial era. Since our focus is religious rather than political, we will limit ourselves to scriptural and juridical prescriptions and their numerous contemporary interpretations: voting rights and driving licenses certainly matter, but our concerns are with the contemporary religious justifications for expanding or denying educational and professional opportunities to Muslim women.

During the first three decades following the 1948 UN Universal Declaration of Human Rights, women's rights were at best a side issue. While there was a convention on the political rights of women in 1952, and on marriage provisions in 1962, it was not until 1979 that the UN General Assembly adopted the Convention on the Elimination of all Forms of Discrimination Against Women (CEDAW). Three years later, in 1982, a committee was formed to implement this convention. However, ten more years elapsed before the UN adopted a general recommendation on the need to monitor and stop violence against women in 1992.

Instead of devising concrete steps to protect the human rights of women, nearly fifty years of human rights debates have presumed to account for women, but only under a ubiquitous, often monolithic plea for all human rights. Few are willing to account for multiple perspectives or to grant to their opponents the modicum of good will without which civil discourse and collective advocacy cannot succeed. Rather than focusing on the plight of women, most human rights advocates and opponents have framed their arguments within abstract religiocultural referents. Religion, unqualified except as a universal human reflex, is a special favorite for metatheoretical obfuscations around human rights. Some claim that religion is the clinching cultural marker, as do Francis Fukuyama and Samuel Huntington. Others assert that religion has value mainly as a political resource, as do the editors of *Religion, the Missing Dimension of Statecraft*.[4]

It is a long journey from generalizations about religious values and public policy to the actual situation of Asian and African Muslim women. We must listen to what is being said and written within the societies themselves, if we are to understand the genuine opposition to European and American notions of human rights. We propose to examine the debate surrounding human rights and women's rights in the Islamic world beginning with the writings of one of the most frequently cited advocates of Islamic exceptionality, the Pakistani journalist-cum-activist, Mawlana Abu'l A'la Mawdūdī. We shall place Mawdūdī into a larger Muslim context so as to frame his voice in a debate internal to Islam. Finally, we shall allude to the role played by contemporary interpreters of Islamic legal texts in highlighting the dissonance between traditional juridical norms and the situation of Muslim women in the late twentieth century.

There is a sense in which the issue of women's rights as human rights has become the litmus test for all religious traditions or civic orders that uphold human rights as the key to global justice. Yet emic and etic perspectives do not easily mesh. From a Muslim perspective, it is difficult to apply the litmus test because men have cast women as the bearers of cultural norms and values.[5] To demand an accounting of their status according to universal criteria is already to undercut the integrity of Islamic culture, and make it seem vulnerable to outside influences. On the other hand, many outside observers looking at Muslim societies see the issue in terms of women as secluded, veiled, oppressed. In other words, these Muslim women should be liberated from Islamic tradition; they cannot be revalued in terms of Islam. In both cases, Muslim women cease to be individuals; they function as symbols of a collectivity.[6]

We are interested in the individuals and their struggle for women's rights as part of a broader search for social justice for all. In her *Women and Human Rights* (1993), the Croatian lawyer Katarina Tomasevski insists on the interdependence and mutual reinforcement of the women's agenda and the human rights agenda.[7] If their connection is overlooked, then "the human rights of women fall through the cracks. They are deleted from the human rights agenda because they pertain to women and from the women's agenda because human rights are seen to belong elsewhere. . . . Silence, as we have learned too well, is the best friend of human rights violations. . . . Women's rights have retained, and thereby strengthened, the conceptual universality of human rights" (ibid. xi, xiv). Those who fight for women's rights are in fact struggling for the rule of justice. They are not, as patriarchal advocates maintain, trying to claim for themselves rights and privileges at the expense of the general welfare. For a woman to be educated and to have equal access to work opportunities does not mean the end of the family and the unweaving of the social fabric. Rather, the education of future mothers means, as women's rights activists assert, the strengthening of the next generation; the addition of women to the workforce improves its productivity. The elimination of discrimination against women is the indispensable step that must be taken if a just society is to be created.

Muslim women constitute a special group of women, if only because Islam as an ancient, multivalent, religious culture is replete with sacred texts locating them and their men in social collectivities from family to state. Many have emphasized the communal aspect of Islamicate societies, which they have credited with the persistence of indigenous values and the empowerment of protest to colonial rule. One way to understand the recent assertion of the Islamic "difference" is to trace the emergence of attention to what has been called the "woman question." As Deniz Kandiyoti explains, discussion of women's rights began in the nineteenth century under the leadership of an educated, nationalist, male elite (whose) concern with women's rights, centering around the issues of education, seclusion, veiling and polygyny, coincided with a broader agenda about "progress" and the compatibility between Islam and modernity. . . . The "woman question" emerged as a hotly contested ideological terrain where women were used to symbolize the progressive aspirations of a secularist elite, or a hankering for cultural authenticity expressed in Islamic terms.[8]

It is this century-old Muslim-versus-modernist approach to the "woman question" that has then been contrasted with the post-World War II accent on individualism in the West. While individualism had philosophical antecedents going back to the Enlightenment, in the view of Muslim authors, it did not become essentialized as a global standard till the appearance of the UN Declaration of Universal Human Rights. Numerous books address this topic, but few go beyond a reiteration of the Declaration and a contrast of its pronouncements with Islamic law and practices, as also with the colonial legacy of Muslim countries.[9]

An opposite approach has recently emerged. It is epitomized in this volume by Richard Bulliet's essay. Islam, in Bulliet's view, is not primarily a communitarian religiopolitical system but one that has historically allowed for a radical sense of personal freedom and individualism, not yet acknowledged in Western media or even in the academy. The Islamic worldview is predicated, in Bulliet's words, on the individual "intrinsically enjoy[ing] the freedom to choose his or her authoritative definition of Islam, whether it be grounded in the law, or in the practice of a pious or political leader, or in the traditional usages of his or her community."[10] In this sense, Bulliet is asserting, as do Little, Kelsay, and Sachedina, that Islamic societies have practiced "a kind of pluralism under the umbrella of a state religion," even though it remains "far from the religious liberty advocated in contemporary human rights formulations."[11]

Still another approach is to articulate a clash between individual rights and collective duties, between Western and Islamic values, *not* on the basis of essential differences between cultures but due to contrasting strategies often predicated on the self-interest of the same parties within one culture. This is the approach made by the Moroccan sociologist Fatima Mernissi. In her 1992 *Islam and Democracy: Fear of the Modern World*,[12] she shows how Muslim Arab leaders have elaborated the dichotomy between the UN Charter and Islamic law so that "one law gives citizens freedom of thought, while the *shari'a*, in its official interpretation based on *ta'a* (obedience), condemns it." She explains that these leaders suffer from "a grave malady . . . which they hush up as shameful: their visceral rejection of the principle of equality." Yet, they wish to be members of the United Nations. Therefore, they must practice hypocrisy so as to "present a modern face at the UN in New York, and the face of an Abbasid caliph to terrorize us at home" (ibid. 60, 67).

Why are these leaders so duplicitous? Fear, replies Mernissi. And her chapter titles list the bugaboos: the Foreign West; the Imam; Democracy; Freedom of Thought; Individualism; the Past; the Present. Mernissi is consistent in her emphasis on leaders, on interpreters, on individuals who would manipulate texts and people so as to hold on to their own positions of power. For in Mernissi's view, there is an intrinsic compatibility between Islam, particularly the Qur'ān, and the UN Charter. The Qur'ān "gives a strong sense of self and of one's rights, however much they are flaunted, and the energy to get angry and to imagine the world otherwise." It is the Qur'an, properly understood and interpreted, that teaches Muslims the importance of the term *ḥaqq*, or right (ibid. 81). Mernissi neither claims the precedence of Islam in the human rights debates, nor does she argue for its essential individualism. Rather, she is trying to understand how it is that two laws that share so much in their spirit differ so greatly in their application.

Rather than argue over whether Islam is individualistic or collective in its normative prescriptions, or examine individual distortions of Western or Islamic norms, we suggest the need to probe more deeply into what is meant by the notions of "the individual" and 'the collective.' Each is a dynamic, dialectical construct. They function in constant tension one to the other, but they are not mutually exclusive. Rather, in Roy Mottahedeh's inimitable formulation, they are contraries rather than contradictories that continue to be shaped and reshaped in various contexts.[13] And it is only in the present context of Islamic revivalism that individual rights have come to be seen negatively because they are framed as unrelated to, or even in competition with, collective duties.

To clarify how these two contraries may seem to be contradictories, we need to go more deeply into the context of Islamic revivalism. We begin with Mawlana Abu'l A'la Mawdūdī, a South Asian Muslim who has spearheaded, even as he has symbolized, the latest phase of Islamic revivalism.[14] It is with reference to his arguments that other Muslims have entered the human rights debate.

Mawdūdī's thoughts on Islam and human rights were first published in English by the Islamic Foundation of Europe in 1976. The pamphlet, totaling 39 pages, was titled *Human Rights in Islam*. The initial chapter had been originally presented as a radio talk in Urdu in January 1948, one year before the United Nations resolution on human rights had been adopted. Subsequent chapters were added as late as 1975, and the entire pamphlet was reprinted in 1980.

Mawdūdī approaches the subject of human rights within a framework that stresses Islamic origins, integrity and superiority in the entire development of human rights. The initial and overriding consideration is set forth in the first chapter: the collective idiom of Islamic identity. The Islamic state is the inescapable point of orientation; it places obligations on the ruler and the ruled alike, and such obligations assume a metaphysical and juridical priority in Muslim governance. It is only with reference to these obligations and as confirmation of them that "Islam has also laid down universal fundamental rights for humanity," rights which are to be honored in all circumstances by non-Muslims as well as by Muslims.

Mawdūdī contrasts the centuries-old Islamic posture with the concept of human rights in the West. For Europeans, the notion of universal human rights is of comparatively recent origin, dating only from the seventeenth to eighteenth centuries, and it is randomly observed. Despite numerous professions of allegiance to human rights, including the UN Declaration, human rights, he declares, "continue to be violated and trampled upon" by Western nations.

Mawdūdī then proceeds to elaborate the complementarity but also the distinction between what he calls "basic human rights" and "the rights of citizens in an Islamic state." The logic of his argument is that Muslim citizens have all basic human rights, but that these rights fall short of the rights enjoyed by the citizen in the Islamic state. What are basic human rights? They are eight: life; safety; chastity of women (which is also said to have as its parallel, noted but unelaborated, the chastity of men); a basic standard of life; freedom (with a lengthy excursus on the superior record of Muslim nations in abolishing slavery compared to the record of the modern West); justice; equality; the right to cooperate and not to cooperate. All these "basic human rights" are guaranteed to citizens in the Islamic state, but they are supplemented by the following fifteen provisions that are guaranteed only to the citizens of the Islamic state:

1. the security of life and property
2. the protection of honor
3. the sanctity and security of private life
4. the security of personal freedom
5. the right to protest against tyranny
6. freedom of expression
7. freedom of association
8. freedom of conscience and conviction
9. protection of religious sentiments

10. protection from arbitrary imprisonment
11. the right to the basic necessities of life
12. equality before the law
13. rulers are not above the law
14. the right to avoid sin, and
15. the right to participate in the affairs of state, with special emphasis on the *shura* or legislative assembly as an instrument of popular representation.

After further enumerating the rights of enemies in war, Mawdūdī concludes with a double message of triumph and warning. He sounds a triumphant tone because "the world has not been able to produce more just and equitable laws than those given 1400 years ago" (by God to Muslims through the Holy Qur'ān). At the same time, he is warning Muslims against looking "for guidance to the West" and also against "rulers who claim to be Muslims (but) have made disobedience to their God and the Prophet the basis and foundation of their government."[15]

In other words, Islam both in theory and practice has anticipated and thus rendered redundant the post-1948 UN initiative on global human rights. To the extent that those rights exist everywhere, they are correctly framed in an Islamic idiom. To the extent that the West claims leadership in their advocacy, they are diminishing, not enhancing, their applicability to Muslims and others.

The influence of Mawdūdī's pamphlet has been as determinative as its contents are brief. In a sense, the theoretical discussion of Islam and human rights has not advanced beyond Mawdūdī, though its scope has been amplified. There are two major channels through which Mawdūdī's approach to human rights and Islam has been disseminated:

1. Newspapers and periodicals of the Muslim world, like the Kuwaiti weekly *al-Mujtama'* and the Yemeni monthly *al-Irshad*, repeat his attack on the hypocrisy of Western advocates of human rights. They challenge the Western monopoly of human rights as a narrowly defined form of ideological imperialism foisted on the rest of the world. In particular, they fault Western human rights advocates for their failure to deal with the right to life issue in their own societies. Abortion, by denying life to unborn children, makes a mockery of human rights at the most fundamental level. If the unborn cannot be protected and vouchsafed their rights, then who can? The argument may sound familiar. Though it has been often observed that the Moral Majority and its successor, Operation Rescue, are only concerned with human rights from conception to birth, it is nonetheless true that many traditional Muslims, who have little else in common with Christian antiabortionists, also accent violations of unborn children's rights as a glaring instance of Western hypocrisy on the human rights issue.

2. Through its extensive publishing network the Islamic Council of Europe (ICE) promotes Mawdūdī's stance on human rights, as well as on a host of other topics. Neither popular nor academic, but rather semipopular with a quasi-academic format, the ICE publications appear mostly in English. They are aimed at a double audience: Muslim readers with a knowledge of English and contacts in the Western world; non-Muslim readers with an awareness of Islam and interests in the Arab/Muslim world.

Extending Mawdūdī's accent on human rights as an Islamic initiative, belatedly and perversely imitated by the United Nations, there has emerged the Universal *Islamic* Declaration on Human Rights. Proclaimed in April 1980, it was published in September 1981, under the direction of Salem Azzam, secretary general to the Islamic Council of Europe. It reiterates Mawdūdī's 23 rights (8 + 15) in a declaration applicable only to Muslims, with Qur'ānic and *ḥadīth* references set forth as an appendix.[16] It confirms the Islamic contention that the UN Declaration of Human Rights is limited because it is more recent than the Qur'ān and it is also *only* human; the sacred context provided by the Qur'ān must be restored for human rights to become viable.

Others echo the Universal Islamic Declaration on Human Rights, when they postulate an unbridgeable chasm between Islamic and Western approaches to human rights. In the words of two Muslim apologists, the "West places more emphasis on rights while Islam values obligations. . . . Western liberalism emphasizes self-interest, while Islam values collective good. The former posits a competitive social order, while the latter prescribes a cooperative one."[17] Common to all Muslim participants in the human rights debate is their consensus denial that any contradiction could exist between divine revelation and human rights. In an Islamic context, they are interlocking, the latter deriving from the former. Both are described and implemented under the umbrella concept of social justice which entails not only justice within, but also for, society conceived as part of the *umma*, or community, consecrated to God's will.

From this basic premise, the Islamic difference on the topic of human rights can expand to encompass a wide range of issues. Of the many Muslim publications in English since the appearance of Mawdūdī's 1976 tract, few detail the issues as fully as the International Commission of Jurists report issuing from the December 1980 Kuwait seminar on Islam and human rights. Attended by 65 experts and scholars from various disciplines, nearly all of them Muslim, the seminar was divided into six committees, dealing with six discrete topics: economic, cultural, and social rights in Islam; education; the right to work and social and legal problems of Muslim minorities in secular states; the treatment of non-Muslim minorities; freedom of opinion and expression; individual security rights in Islam and safeguards of human rights in judicial proceedings; the legal status of women in Islam.[18]

It is worth noting that the Kuwait Seminar took place in December 1980, within a year after the passage of the CEDAW. While Mawdūdī had mentioned women's rights in the above pamphlet, it was only in an elusive reference to the protection of chastity.[19] The Kuwait seminar, by contrast, appointed an entire committee to discuss women in Islam. It consisted of three papers, all of which limited themselves to theoretical concerns. One paper repeated the Islamic claim for precedence over the West in advocating equal rights for men and women, while quoting passages from the Qur'ān which disprove claims (made by Westerners) that Islamic law advocates sex discrimination, condones polygamy, and assures easy divorce for men. Another paper stressed the compatibility of Islamic and modern views of the role of women. The third paper focused on the family as the institution ensuring the good of society itself. Muslim women, the author argued, are entitled to all the rights accorded men in matters such as education, contracts, obligations, the right to ownership, trade, and civil law in general. However, although women can assume some public functions, they may not be heads of state nor may they vote.

The key to this last argument was women's primary role: to maintain and nurture the family. Here is the loophole that allows the interpreter to move from the goal of equality to the advocacy of "complementarity" as the optimal Islamic norm. This, too, is the position of the late Iranian Shi'i scholar, Murtada Mutahhari, the foremost expositor of an accommodationist worldview, one that is Islamically grounded yet attuned to the range of modern philosophical and scientific thought. In a Persian work written before the Islamic revolution in Iran (1394 A.H./1975 C.E.) and translated into English under the title *The Rights of Women in Islam* (Teheran, 1401/1981), he sets forth an approach to the redefinition of Muslim rights as human rights that includes women's rights. Using Qur'ānic evidence, Mutahhari suggests that there ought to be equivalence—certainly not uniformity or identity—of rights in Islam for men and women.[20]

All of these interpreters underscore the repeated assertion that Islam was the pioneer of human rights, that the divine law (*sharī'a*) offers a comprehensive code of life protecting the collective good as well as individual rights, and that the guidelines of the Qur'ān, the *sunna*, and juridical methods (consensus, analogy, and independent reasoning) ensure the sanctity of the Islamic way of life.

The Kuwait seminar's goal was modest: to prescribe the *ideal* Islamic view on human rights, including women's rights, not to describe the operative norm in present-day Muslim countries. The conclusion, echoing Mawdūdī, acknowledges that "contemporary Islamic practise cannot be said to conform in many aspects with the true principles of Islam." And with reference to the situation of women, in particular, the shortfall between Islamic (read: Qurʾānic) guidelines and current observances is stressed:

> Islam has numerous provisions for eliminating various discriminatory practices against women, basing these provisions on principles that only recently have been recognized within the framework of human rights. If a large gap remains today between these principles and actual practice in the majority of Islamic states, it is because these states have not truly abided by Islam's instructions about the status of women. Other factors that help create this gap include the spread of illiteracy, women's ignorance of their legal rights in Islam, and economic, social and cultural factors making it difficult for women to exercise these rights.[21]

What could have been helpfully stressed in the Kuwait gathering, and also in much other Muslim writing on the subject of human rights generally, and women's rights in particular, is the cultural context within which Islamic precepts are practiced or abused. It is impossible to consider women's rights in Islam today apart from the contemporary context. That context is shaped, above all, by religious revivalism.

It is usually assumed that fundamentalist movements are bent on curtailing women's rights, and that therefore revivalist religion and universal human rights for women are incompatible concepts. However, some feminist activists in the Muslim world like Nawal El Saadawi and Fatima Mernissi, and in the West, like Rebecca Cook, are beginning to suggest that it is important for women to work precisely there, "within the religious paradigm to develop female [sic] interpretations to free women from religious subordination."[22] This is already happening in some Muslim countries. As a result of the recent emergence of Islamic fundamentalist movements, some women—particularly lawyers and theologians—have attempted to counteract growing pressure to reduce women's visibility and efficacy in the public realm through what might be called Islamic feminist legal interpretations of scripture. The initiative began in the 1970s and in isolated pockets throughout the Islamic world. By the mid-1980s some groups were already exchanging information and coordinating activity, e.g., Women Living Under Muslim Laws. The network, which is based in France, has two projects that its international coordinator Marie-Aimée Hélie-Lucas defines as "(1) to identify and challenge different interpretations of religious texts and to promote women's interpretations; and (2) to compile and compare laws drawn from these interpretations, which primarily affect women."[23] Recently, a women's *Sharīʿa* college was founded in Qum, the most holy city in Iran. Shiʿi women are being trained to become official interpreters of Islamic juridical texts.

These revisionist interpreters, who include men as well as women, challenge antiwomen legislation. They argue for the need to change such laws in light of social circumstances that have altered since the revelation of the Qur'ān in the seventh century. For example, the vexed problem of the Qur'ānic verse that claims that one woman's witness is equal to half of a man's witness (which has led to the claim by some that one woman is therefore worth half a man) may be resolved by an examination of the social conditions of women in seventh-century Arabia. One modern-day interpreter, the juridical scholar and historian of religions Abdulaziz Sachedina has argued that the stipulation does not refer to the act of witnessing but to the recording of the witnessing, not to the seeing but to the writing. Women were not generally as literate as men. If they could not read, the witnesses could not write down what they had witnessed and then return to the text later. They would have to remember what they had said. Since memory is not as reliable as writing, such witnesses would need to have another person who had been present at the incident to confirm and to support the remembered evidence. Interpreted in this way, the verse does not refer to the sex of the witness but to his or her literateness.[24] Once this verse is thus reinterpreted, the assumption that Muslims consider one woman to be equivalent to half a man must be rethought. Such a rethinking would force contemplation of another scriptural-juridical change: women's inheritance. The fourth chapter in the Qur'ān entitled "Women" allocates to women half of the inheritance given to equivalent men in the family. With this new interpretation, such a division of inheritance might no longer be valid.

Pro-women interpreters of Islamic law begin from the premise that women, like men, share human rights to life, property, and freedom, these rights having been provided by the Qur'ān.

Life: the Qur'ān expressly forbids the practice of female infanticide—a practice that exists until today and all over the world, not just in China, India, or Africa, as is commonly supposed.

Property: the "Women" chapter carefully prescribes women's independent legal status, entailing ownership and disposition of property. In the seventh century already, valuables which women were given as dowry or which they earned or which they inherited were theirs alone (compare this with the situation of women in Europe as late as the nineteenth century). Property provisions are important in themselves but they also entail more than material wealth; they are connected to the right to life. To be able to *own* is at least a first step toward being able to resist *being owned*, and then disposed of! As the Indian economist Amartya Sen argues, research into the startling disparity between the expected ratio of women to men in the total world population and actual demographic figures "suggests a link between employment and survival prospects."[25] Hence, these first two rights—to life and to property—must be linked to each other and also to the third right.

Freedom: Women—*al-mu'minat*—like men—*al-mu'minun*—must be given freedom, which includes access to education, and also to employment should they so desire. This extrapolation is evident in view of the rights to property provisions in the Qur'ān. It is the women themselves—not men, not society, not culture—who are then responsible for deciding to what extent their participation in what some consider to be men's activities jeopardizes the integrity of the family and therefore, perhaps, of the community also.

These pro-women interpreters can point to another crucial area of control to which Muslim women have rights: the body. It is the women—not men, not society, not culture—who should decide what should happen to their bodies. For women to make informed choices about their bodies—whether they wish to have part or all or *none* of their sexual organs excised, whether they wish to spend their life with a man or a woman—they must be educated to know what these choices might be.[26] This holds true also for decisions about marriage. These interpreters are explaining that it is not enough to know that the Qur'ān allows men to marry up to four women—"Marry women of your choice, two, three, or four." It is essential to be able to read the last part of the verse also to understand that multiple wives are permissible only in a situation where a man is certain that he can treat each one of the four as he treats the other three—"But if ye fear that ye shall not be able to deal justly with them then only one" (4:3). Some have interpreted this verse and a later one in the same "Women" chapter—"Ye are never able to be fair and just as between women, even if it is your ardent desire" (4:129)—to mean that this proviso is in itself a prohibition. However, interpretations are myriad and some will insist that such equal treatment is not only possible but that the Prophet, who was not divine but the Perfect Person (*al-insan al-kamil*), set the model by treating equally his more than four wives. The woman made dizzy by the polemics surrounding this verse needs to know that she has the right to participate in the writing and the signing of the marriage contract—Muslim marriages entail not only a social contract but a written contract also. In other words, if she does not like the idea of sharing her husband with one other woman, let alone three, she has the right to express her desire in such a way that it becomes law. The Muslim woman who loves her husband so much that she wants him to herself forever need do one thing only: write into her marriage contract a clause stipulating monogamy. She might add sexual satisfaction. In case of violation of either clause, she has the right to divorce.

Another critical legislation connected with women that is currently under revision is rape, a term that has only recently attracted interpreters' attention.

Originally called "forced adultery" (*zina' bil-jabr*), it was not treated as a category separate from adultery; both were crimes which demanded four male witnesses.[27] Yet, adultery is radically different from rape in that it assumes at least some level of reciprocity.

Does the fact that the Qur'ān does not have a term for rape mean that this crime did not exist in seventh-century Arabia? Or, does it mean that contemporary Arabians had a different notion of the individual's, particularly the female's, relationship to and ownership of body? Was violation and penetration of a woman's body considered to be a communal affair? Hina Azam has traced the first use of the terms *ightasaba* (or, sexual usurpation) and *istakraha* (sexual coercion) to Malik b. 'Anas's eighth-century *Muwatta'*. In it, he assigns the punishment for rape differently according to whether the woman is free or a slave. The freewoman receives the equivalent of a dowry from the rapist. The slave girl receives nothing beyond reprieve from stoning; it is her master who is recompensed and this amount is calculated according to the decrease in her value. Azam concludes that women in early Islam had degrees of control over their bodies that varied in accordance with their legal status, i.e., free or bound. With the abolition of slavery, one might expect such a distinction no longer to pertain.[28] However, there does seem to be a deeper problem. In both cases, the rape was monetarily evaluated: a woman as a commodity had been damaged; either the commodity itself or the owner had to be materially restored. New thinking is required that will give women agency when such crimes are perpetrated against them.

Muslim women have advocates for their rights. Of course, they also have their detractors. In Pakistan, the country of origin for Mawdūdī, the current conflict goes beyond his formulations. On the one side are religious scholars belonging to Mawlana Mawdūdī's Jama'at-i Islami movement as well as pious laymen (such as Israr Aḥmad and Muḥammad Salah ad-din of Lahore). On the other side are educated upper-class women in decision-making positions who are members of the thirty-year-old All-Pakistani Women's Association, known as APWA, or of the more recent Women's Action Forum.[29] On occasion, they have formed strategic alliances, for instance in defending a young Pakistani woman who in 1982 was sentenced to death for adultery.[30]

The struggle in Pakistan is emblematic. There are as yet no mechanisms for allowing a direct dialogue between opposing sides on the issue of Islam and human rights/women's rights. At the macro-level, in international symposia, English-language books and periodicals, the Western and Muslim elites most concerned with human rights do not even talk the same language. At the micro-level, within the context of particular Muslim countries, there are no rules by which a fair airing of opposing views can be articulated. Both sides have become mired in their own particularities. Western observers generally overlook the theoretical, collective dimension of human rights concerns of Muslim advocates. Muslim parties in the debate rarely move beyond the two-tiered listing of rights proposed by Mawlana Abu'l A'la Mawdūdī; they scarcely ever question how shared Islamic ideals are applied to the actual situation of given Asian, African, and Middle Eastern countries.

Dialogue is essential. Silence is not an option. We have to find ways to communicate with respect. Rhetorical exchanges between cosmopolitan elites will always leave out the unemployed, illiterate men and women, those whose rights are the most consistently violated.[31] Nor can we resort to cultural relativism. It is not acceptable for men of one newly imagined community to target women's bodies as a major component of a policy of genocide. We must speak out, but we must also listen. Recognition of the other's right to speak as well as respect for her difference are *sine qua non* for the beginning of meaningful dialogue.

Only now can we begin to speculate about universals and to ask whether the lives of women are shaped more by their unique cultures, or by universal issues related to gender? Can women understand each other—and help each other—across cultural divides? What can or should we in America and Europe do? Can we allow ourselves to be silenced because we are told that whatever we say is necessarily imperialist and then end up watching Muslim women and children in Bosnia being expropriated, tortured, raped, and killed? How can the world community guarantee women's rights to freedom of expression and organization and to life? Or, are these rights merely illusions?

All these questions underscore the importance of specifying women's rights so that human rights may cease to be rights for men alone. The Slovenian sociologist Renata Saleci puts it aptly when she notes that the post-Enlightenment subject of human rights debates has largely been "an abstract entity, separated from other individuals . . . this position of a fixed self-identical subject is clearly a male position."[32] This is beginning to change, if slowly. Human rights have to become more than just another honeyed platitude so that they may function as a genuine tool of social justice. But they will never satisfy merely as *human* rights. They are rights specific to particular humans, and they must specify women as well as men if they are to be rights that include all humankind. The extent to which Muslim women have rights that distinguish them from other women as well as from Muslim men needs to be considered again in the circumstances of present-day polities, that is, the postcolonial, economically disadvantaged, and socially unsettled nations of Africa and Asia with large Muslim populations. Human rights are about the just accommodation of ideals to men's and women's practices of everyday life always in full awareness of historical contingencies.

NOTES

1. See Mark Juergensmeyer, "Hindu Nationalism and Human Rights," essay 9 in this volume; italics added by us.

2. See Nawal El Saadawi, "Dissidence and Creativity in the Arab World," Amnesty International talk at Oxford University on February 12, 1995.

3. Chandra Muzaffar, *Human Rights and the New World Order* (Penang: Just World Trust, 1993), pp. 160–61; see review by Peter van Ness, *Journal of Asian Studies* 53, no. 2 (May 1994): 514–16.

4. Douglas Johnston and Cynthia Sampson, eds. *Religion, the Missing Dimension of Statecraft* (New York: Oxford University Press, 1994).

5. It is precisely for this reason that the Serbs have targeted Muslim women and their bodies in their genocidal policies to take over Bosnia. To organize mass rapes of women of one culture and to impregnate them with babies of another culture is to shame and emasculate the first culture and to make it incapable of surviving.

6. On this same question, see Bruce B. Lawrence, "Woman as Subject/Woman as Symbol: Lessons from the Shah Bano Case About the Status of Muslim Women in the Age of Islamic Fundamentalism," *Journal of Religious Ethics* 22, no. 1 (Spring 1994): 163–85.

7. Katarina Tomasevski. *Women and Human Rights* (London: Zed Books, 1993).

8. Deniz Kandiyoti, ed. *Women, Islam, and the State* (Philadelphia: Temple University Press, 1991), pp. 3–7.

9. Among those that have appeared in Arabic are the following: by Lebanese legist Sobhi Mahmassani, *Arkan huquq al-insan:bahthun muqarinun fi'l-shari'ah al-islamiya wa'l-qawanin al-haditha* (Basic Concepts of Human Rights: A Comparative Study of Islamic and Modern Laws) (Beirut: Dar al-'ilm lil-malayin, 1979); by Egyptian sociologist 'Ali 'Abd al-Wahid Wafi, *Huquq al-insan fi'l-islam* (The Rights of Man in Islam) (Cairo: Dar al-nahdah, 1979); by Egyptian revivalist Muhammad al-Ghazzali. *Huquq al-insan bayna ta'alim al-islam wa i'lan al-umam al-muttahidah* (The Rights of Man Between the Teachings of Islam and the Declarations of the United Nations) (Cairo: Dar al-kutub al-haditha, 1965)

10. See Richard Bulliet, "The Individual in Islamic Society," in this volume.

11. See David Little, John Kelsay, and Abdulaziz A. Sachedina, *Human Rights and the Conflict of Cultures: Western and Islamic Perspectives on Religious Liberty* (Columbia: University of South Carolina Press, 1988), pp. 94–95.

12. Fatima Mernissi. *Islam and Democracy: Fear of the Modern World* (Reading, Mass.: Addison-Wesley, 1992).

13. Roy Mottahedeh, *The Mantle of the Prophet: Religion and Politics in Iran* (New York: Simon & Schuster, 1985), pp. 107–8. The distinction is also elaborated in Bruce B. Lawrence, *Defenders of God* (San Francisco: Harper & Row, 1989), pp. 16–17.

14. The articles and books on Mawdūdī are legion, but among the most accessible and helpful are: Charles J. Adams, "The Ideology of Mawlana Mawdudi," in *South Asian Politics and Religions*, ed. Donald E. Smith (Princeton: Princeton University Press, 1966), pp. 371–97; Khurshid Ahmad and Zafar Ishaq Ansari, eds., *Islamic Perspectives: Studies in Honour of Mawlana Sayyid Abul A'la Mawdudi* (Jeddah: Saudi Publishing House, 1979), and Sheila McDonough, *Muslim Ethics and Modernity: A Comparative Study of the Ethical Thought of Sayyid Ahmad Khan and Mawlana Mawdudi* (Waterloo, Ont.: Wilfred Laurier University Press, 1984). Concerning the group which Mawdūdī founded, Jama'at-i Islami, there is now

a full and provocative study by Seyyed Vali Reza Nasr. *The Vanguard of the Islamic Revolution: The Jama'at-i Islami of Pakistan* (Berkeley: University of California Press, 1994).

15. For this and all prior quotations, see Abul A'la Mawdudi, *Human Rights in Islam* (Leicester: Islamic Foundation, 1976/1980).

16. Other books from the Council, such as *The Challenge of Islam* (ed. Altaf Gauhar, 1979) and *Islam and Contemporary Society* (ed. Salem Azzam, 1982) also contain articles on Islam and human rights, chiefly by the distinguished Pakistani lawyers, A. K. Brohi and K. M. Ishaque. Another article, as yet unpublished, by the Pakistani jurist, Dr. Javid Iqbal of the Lahore High Court, also addresses the issue of human rights and Islam, with single-minded conformity to the model of Mawdūdī's seminal pamphlet. He contributed "Human Rights in Islam" to the Third Pakistan-French Colloquium held at Islamabad on April 5, 1982, but it proves to be a recitation of lists, one the 14 canonically required human rights, the other the 23 rights announced by the Islamic Council of Europe in September 1981.

17. See Abdul Aziz Said and Jamil Nasser, "The Use and Abuse of Democracy in Islam," in *International Human Rights: Contemporary Issues*, ed. J. L. Nelson and V. M. Green (Standardville, N.Y.: H R Publishing Group, 1980), p. 62.

18. Niall MacDermot, ed., *Human Rights in Islam: Report of a seminar held in Kuwait, December 1980* (Geneva: International Commission of Jurists, 1982).

19. Mawdūdī did write a separate essay on the seclusion of women in Islam, but in it he stressed the duties and values of Muslim women rather than their human rights. See Mawlana Abul A'la Mawdudi. *Purdah and the Status of Women in Islam* (Lahore: Islamic Publications, 1987).

20. To escape domestic duties as the inevitable outcome of an argument for complementarity between women and men in Islamic societies, Zaynab al-Ghazali, the Egyptian leader of the Muslim Ladies' Association, provides a unique scenario that few other women could pursue: confirming that while Muslim women's primary role should be domestic, she also argues that they may engage in the public domain if they have time. In *Days from my Life* (1966), she describes her own participation in the *jihad* to establish an Islamic state in Egypt as fully lawful. How was that possible? Both because she could not have children and because her (second) husband had agreed not to interfere in her mission when they signed the marriage contract. See Cooke, "Zaynab al-Ghazali: Saint or Subversive?" *Die Welt des Islams* 34, no. 1 (1994): 1–20.

21. MacDermot, ed., *Human Rights in Islam*, p. 8.

22. Rebecca Cook, "Gaining Redress Within a Human Rights Framework" in Joanna Kerr, ed., *Ours by Right: Women's Rights as Human Rights* (London and Atlantic Highlands, N.J.: Zed Books, 1993), p. 14. See also Rebecca Cook, *Human Rights of Women* (Philadelphia: University of Pennsylvania Press, 1994).

23. Marie-Aimée Hélie-Lucas, "Women Living Under Muslim Laws" in Kerr, ed., *Ours by Right*, p. 57.

24. Abdulaziz Sachedina, "Is Woman Half of Man? How Male/Female Testimonies are Evaluated in Muslim Law," lecture given at Duke University on March 30, 1995.

25. Amartya Sen, "More than 100 Million Women are Missing," *New York Review of Books* 37/20, December 20, 1990, p. 64.

26. Education is a key theme and one that Fatima Mernissi accents whenever she gives speeches, e.g., meeting at an Agdal (Rabat) primary school, March 8, 1985, and then at the

Middle East Studies Association Plenary Session on "Women and Human Rights in the Middle East," Research Triangle Park, November 1993.

27. This was also true in the 1983 Safia Bibi Case. A Pakistani peasant girl who had been raped by her landlord and his son was sentenced to fifteen lashes and a fine. Many women's rights advocates protested, and the case became a pretext for revising the reactionary Hudood Ordinance that Zia ul-Haq had passed in 1979, thus clarifying the distinction between rape and adultery. See Lawrence, "Women as Subject/Women as Symbol," p. 178.

28. Hina Azam, "Rape and Islamic Law," unpublished paper.

29. For a fuller account of Women's Action Forum and its opposition to the patriarchal norms of present-day Pakistani politics, see Khawar Mumtaz and Farida Shaheed, *Women of Pakistan: Two Steps Forward, One Step Backward* (London: Zed Press, 1987). The dilemma of informed women participants in Pakistani public life is highlighted by Ayesha Jalal in her essay "The Convenience of Subservience: Women and the State of Pakistan," in Deniz Kandiyoti, ed., *Women, State, and Islam* (Philadelphia: Temple University Press, 1991), pp. 77–114.

30. The story appeared in several Pakistani dailies on June 1, 1982. To understand the complicated historical context in which human rights as an issue has been viewed within modern-day Pakistan, see John Kelsay, "Saudi Arabia, Pakistan, and the Universal Declaration of Human Rights," in Little, Kelsay, and Sachedina, pp. 33–52. Kelsay makes the valuable point that shifting ideological forces within Pakistan moved that country from seeming to be in accordance with the Universal Declaration of Human Rights in the 1950s to opposing it, especially on the principle of religious liberty (Article 18). By contrast, the Saudis have been uniform in their opposition to Article 18 because of the exclusivist Wahhabi ideology that informs their official pronouncements.

31. A thoughtful essay on how the traditional view of women continues to be perpetuated by Mawdūdī followers in contemporary Pakistan, partially due to female illiteracy, is Barbara D. Metcalf, "Islamic Arguments in Contemporary Pakistan," in *Islam and the Political Economy of Meaning: Comparative Studies of Muslim Discourse*, ed. William R. Roff (Berkeley and Los Angeles: Social Science Research Council, New York and University of California Press, 1987), pp. 132–59. The special pamphlet that she examines was published in Lahore in 1982. Many of its views are paralleled in the special monthly issue of Dr. Israr Ahmad's periodical *Mithaq*, also published in Lahore in 1982 (May) and dedicated to "The Place of Women in Islam."

32. Renata Saleci, *The Spoils of Freedom. Psychoanalysis, and Feminism After the Fall of Socialism* (London/New York: Routledge, 1994), pp. 113–15.

CONTRIBUTORS

Richard Ashcraft is Professor of Political Science at the University of California at Los Angeles. He is the author of *Revolutionary Politics and Locke's Two Treatises of Government* (Princeton: Princeton University Press, 1986); *John Locke's Two Treatises of Government* (London: Allen and Unwin, 1987), and numerous articles on political theory. He has also edited *John Locke: Critical Assessments* (London: Routledge, 1991).

Irene Bloom is the Wm. Theodore and Fanny Brett de Bary and Class of 1941 Collegiate Associate Professor of Asian Humanities at Columbia University and Chair of the Department of Asian and Middle Eastern Cultures at Barnard College. She is editor, with Wm. Theodore de Bary, of *Principle and Practicality* (New York: Columbia University Press, 1987) and, also with Wm. Theodore de Bary, of *Approaches to the Asian Classics* (Columbia University Press, 1990; 1995 rev. ed. entitled *Eastern Canons: Approaches to the Asian Classics*). She is the editor and translator of *Knowledge Painfully Acquired: The K'un-chih chi of Lo Ch'in-shun* (Columbia University Press, 1989; rev. ed., 1995). With Joshua A. Fogel, she is editor of *Meeting of Minds: Intellectual and Religious Interaction in East Asian Traditions of Thought* (forthcoming, Columbia University Press, 1996).

Richard Bulliet is Professor of History at Columbia University and Director of its Middle East Institute. His main publications include *The Patricians of Nishapur* (Cambridge: Harvard University Press, 1972); *The Camel and the Wheel* (Harvard University Press, 1975; reprinted by Columbia University Press, Morningside Books, 1990); *Conversion to Islam in the Medieval Period* (Harvard University Press, 1979); and *Islam: The View from the Edge* (Columbia University Press, 1994).

Miriam Cooke, Professor of Arabic Literature at Duke University, specializes in war and gender studies in the modern Middle East. In addition to her monograph on women's literature from the Lebanese civil war, *War's Other Voices* (Cambridge: Harvard University Press, 1988), she has coedited three anthologies: with Margot Badran, *Opening the Gates: A Century of Arab Feminist Writing* (London: Virago, 1990); with Angela Woollacott, *Gendering War Talk* (Princeton: Princeton University Press, 1993); and, with Roshni Rustomji-Kerns, *Blood Into Ink: Women Write War in the Middle East and South Asia* (Boulder: Westview Press, 1994).

Margaret E. Crahan is the Dorothy Epstein Professor of History at Hunter College of the City University of New York. From 1982 to 1994 she was the Henry R. Luce Professor of Religion, Power, and Political Process at Occidental College. Dr. Crahan has done fieldwork in Argentina, Brazil, Chile, Colombia, Costa Rica, Cuba, El Salvador, Guatemala. Honduras, Mexico, Nicaragua, Panama, Paraguay, Peru, Spain, Switzerland, and Uruguay. She has published over sixty articles and books, including *Africa and the Caribbean: Legacies of a Link* (Baltimore: Johns Hopkins University Press, 1979) and *Human Rights and Basic Needs in the Americas* (Washington, D.C.: Georgetown University Press, 1982).

Joseph W. Elder is Professor of Sociology and South Asian Studies at the University of Wisconsin, Madison. He is author and editor of numerous publications on India, including *Chapters in Indian Civilization: A Handbook of Readings to Accompany the Civilization of India Syllabus* (Department of Indian Studies, University of Wisconsin, 1967) and *Lectures in Indian Civilization*. In cooperation with the Center for South Asian Studies and the Video Resource Center at the University of Wisconsin, he has also produced many video recordings on India society and culture, among them "Sitala in Spring: Festival of the Bengali Goddess of Health and Illness" (1960); "An Indian Pilgrimage—Kashi" (1969); "An Indian Pilgrimage—Ramdevra" (1974); "Four Holy Men: Renunciation in Hindu Society" (1976); "Village Man, City Man" (1975); and "The Wages of Action: Religion in a Hindu

Village" (1979). For many years he was director of the National Resource Center for South Asian Studies at the University of Wisconsin and president of the American Association of Indian Studies. In 1995 he was awarded the Special Service Award of the Association for Asian Studies.

Lenn E. Goodman is Professor of Philosophy at Vanderbilt University. His contributions to Jewish philosophy include *On Justice* (New Haven: Yale University Press, 1988) and *God of Abraham* (New York: Oxford University Press, 1996). He has translated and commented on a number of classics from Jewish and Arabic philosophy, including Saadiah Gaon's *Commentary on the Book of Job* (Yale University Press, 1988), Ibn Tufayl's *Hayy Ibn Yaqzan* and *The Case of the Animals vs. Man Before the King of the Jinn*, by the Sincere Brethren of Basra (New York: Twayne, 1978). His studies of the Jewish and Islamic philosophical traditions include *Ramban* (New York: Viking Press, 1976) and *Avicenna* (London: Routledge, 1992), along with other books and articles.

Mark Juergensmeyer is Professor of Sociology and Chair of Global and International Studies at the University of California, Santa Barbara. His most recent book, *The New Cold War? Religious Nationalism Confronts the Secular State* (Los Angeles: University of California Press, 1993) was listed by the *New York Times* as one of the notable books of 1993.

John Kelsay is Associate Professor of Religion at the Florida State University. He is coauthor (with David Little and Abdulaziz Sachedina) of *Human Rights and the Conflict of Cultures: Western and Islamic Perspectives on Religious Liberty* (Columbia: University of South Carolina Press, 1988). He is the author of *Cross, Crescent, and Sword: The Justification and Limitation of War in Western and Islamic Traditions* (Westport, Conn.: Greenwood Press, 1990), *Just War and Jihad: Historical and Theological Perspectives on War and Peace in Western and Islamic Traditions* (Greenwood Press, 1991); and *Islam and War: A Study in Comparative Ethics* (Louisville, Ky.: Westminster/John Knox Press, 1993); and coeditor of several works in comparative religious ethics, including most recently, *Religion and Human Rights* (The Project on Religion and Human Rights, 1994).

John Langan, S.J., is the Rose Kennedy Professor of Christian Ethics in the Kennedy Institute of Ethics at Georgetown University. He has been Visiting Professor of social ethics at the Yale Divinity School and Visiting Fellow at the Jesuit Institute at Boston College. Among the books he has edited are *Human Rights in the Americas* (Washington, D.C.: Georgetown University Press, 1982), *The Nuclear Dilemma and the Just War Tradition* (New York: Lexington

Books, 1986), *Catholic Perspectives on Medical Morals: Foundational Issues* (Dordrecht, Neth.: Kluwer Academic Publishers, 1989), *The American Search for Peace: Moral Reasoning, Religious Hope, and National Security* (Georgetown University Press, 1991), and *Catholic Universities in Church and Society* (1993). He is currently working on books on capitalism and the moral life and on the ethics of humanitarian intervention.

Bruce B. Lawrence, Professor of History of Religions and Islamic Studies at Duke University, is the author of six books and numerous articles on Islam and Islam-related topics. His most recent book, *Defenders of God: The Fundamentalist Revolt Against the Modern Age* (San Francisco: Harper, 1989), was awarded the 1990 prize of the American Academy of Religion for excellence in religious studies (historical). He is currently preparing a monograph on the interaction of religion and ideology in the twentieth century.

David Little is Senior Scholar at the United States Institute of Peace in Washington, D.C., where he directs the project on Religion, Nationalism, and Intolerance. He is the author of several reports on that project's work, including, most recently, *Ukraine: The Legacy of Intolerance* (1991), *Sri Lanka: The Invention of Enmity* (Washington, D.C.: U.S. Institute of Peace Press, 1994), and (with Scott Hibbard) *Sino-Tibetan Coexistence: Creating Space for Tibetan Self-Direction* (U.S. Institute of Peace Press, 1994). He is coauthor (with John Kelsay and Abdulaziz Sachedina) of *Human Rights and the Conflict of Cultures: Western and Islamic Perspectives on Religious Liberty* (Columbia: University of South Carolina Press, 1988).

J. Paul Martin, Executive Director of the Center for the Study of Human Rights at Columbia University since its founding in 1978, teaches human rights at Columbia's School of International and Public Affairs and human rights education at Teachers College. He is the author of a number of articles on human rights education; two of the most recent will appear in a forthcoming University of Pennsylvania Press volume on *Human Rights Education.* Besides directing the Center's new program in Religion, Human Rights, and Religious Freedom, funded by the Pew Charitable Trust, he is a member of the core team of the Emory University Law School project on religious proselytization in Africa and Eastern Europe and will contribute essays to the project.

Wayne L. Proudfoot is Professor and Chair of the Department of Religion at Columbia University. He is the author of *Religious Experience* (Los Angeles: University of California Press, 1985), which won the 1986 American Academy of Religion Award and is currently working on a book on pragmatism and American religious thought.

Abdulaziz Sachedina is Professor of Religious Studies at the University of Virginia. He is the author of *Islamic Messianism: The Idea of the Mahdi in Twelver Shi'ism* (New York: State University of New York Press, 1981) and *The Just Ruler in Shi'ite Islam: The Comprehensive Authority of the Jurist in Imamite Jurisprudence* (New York: Oxford University Press, 1988). He is coauthor (with David Little and John Kelsay) of *Human Rights and the Conflict of Cultures: Western and Islamic Perspectives on Religious Liberty* (Columbia: University of South Carolina Press, 1988). He is currently working on a study of Islamic approaches to medical ethics.

Robert A. F. Thurman is the Jey Tsong Khapa Professor of Indo-Tibetan Buddhist Studies at Columbia University. He is the translator of *The Holy Teaching of Vimalakirti—a Mahayana Scripture* (University Park: Pennsylvania State University Press, 1976) and author of *Tsong Khapa's Speech of Gold in the "Essence of True Eloquence"* (Princeton: Princeton University Press, 1984; reprinted in 1991 under the title *The Central Philosophy of Tibet: A Study and Translation of Jey Tsong Khapa's Essence of True Eloquence*). Recent publications include *The Tibetan Book of the Dead: The Great Book of Natural Liberation through Understanding in the Between* (New York: Bantam Books, 1994) and *Essential Tibetan Buddhism* (San Francisco: Harper, 1995).

Paul Valliere is the McGregor Professor in the Humanities at Butler University and Head of Butler's Department of Philosophy and Religion. His publications include *Holy War and Pentecostal Peace* (New York: Seabury Press, 1983); and *Change and Tradition in Russian Civilization*, 2d ed. (Hayden McNeill, 1995); an entry on "Tradition" in *The Encyclopedia of Religion,* ed. Mircea Eliade (New York: Macmillan, 1987), and numerous articles and book chapters on Russian Orthodoxy.

INDEX

~

Note: With the exception of proper names, all Arabic terms that carry the prefix "al" are indexed below under "a."